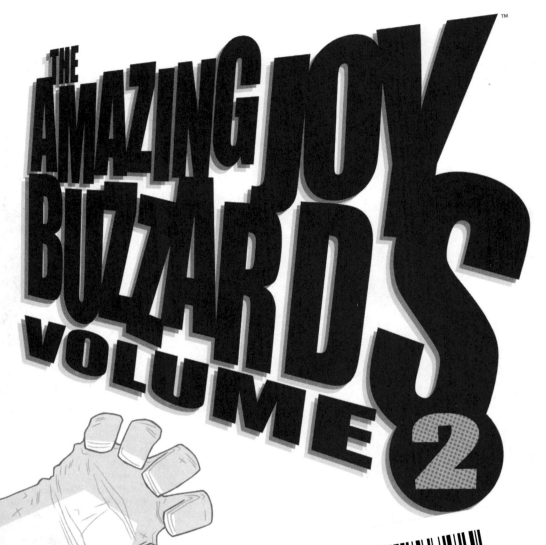

THE AMAZING JOY BUZZARDS VOLUME 2 ™

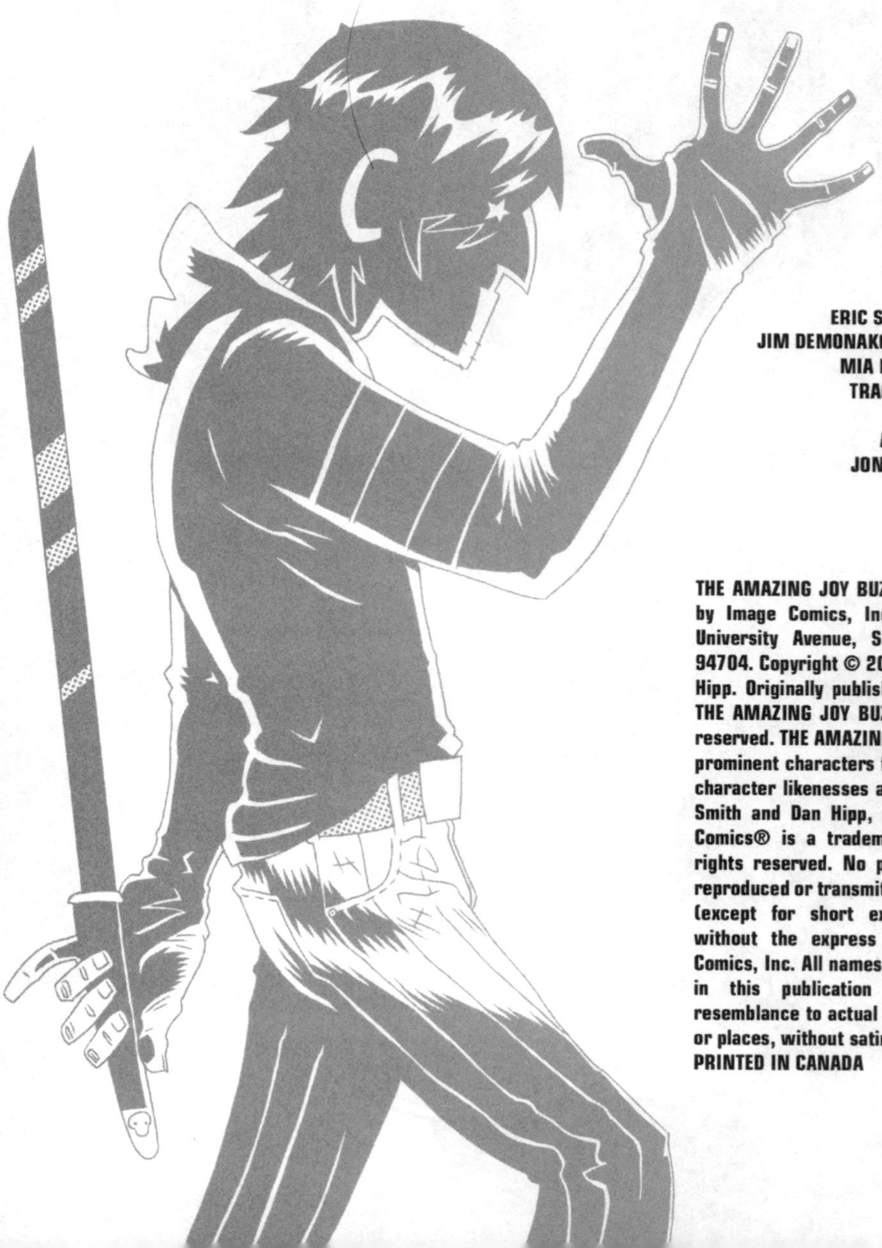

IMAGE COMICS, INC.

ERIK LARSEN - *Publisher*
TODD McFARLANE - *President*
MARC SILVESTRI - *CEO*
JIM VALENTINO - *Vice-President*

ERIC STEPHENSON - *Executive Director*
JIM DEMONAKOS - *PR & Marketing Coordinator*
MIA MacHATTON - *Accounts Manager*
TRACI HUI - *Administrative Assistant*
JOE KEATINGE - *Traffic Manager*
ALLEN HUI - *Production Manager*
JONATHAN CHAN - *Production Artist*
DREW GILL - *Production Artist*

www.imagecomics.com

THE AMAZING JOY BUZZARDS, VOL 2. 2006. Published by Image Comics, Inc., Office of publication: 1942 University Avenue, Suite 305, Berkeley, California 94704.
PRINTED IN CANADA

THE AMAZING JOY BUZZARDS™

CREATED AND PRODUCED BY

MARK ANDREW SMITH

AND

DAN HIPP

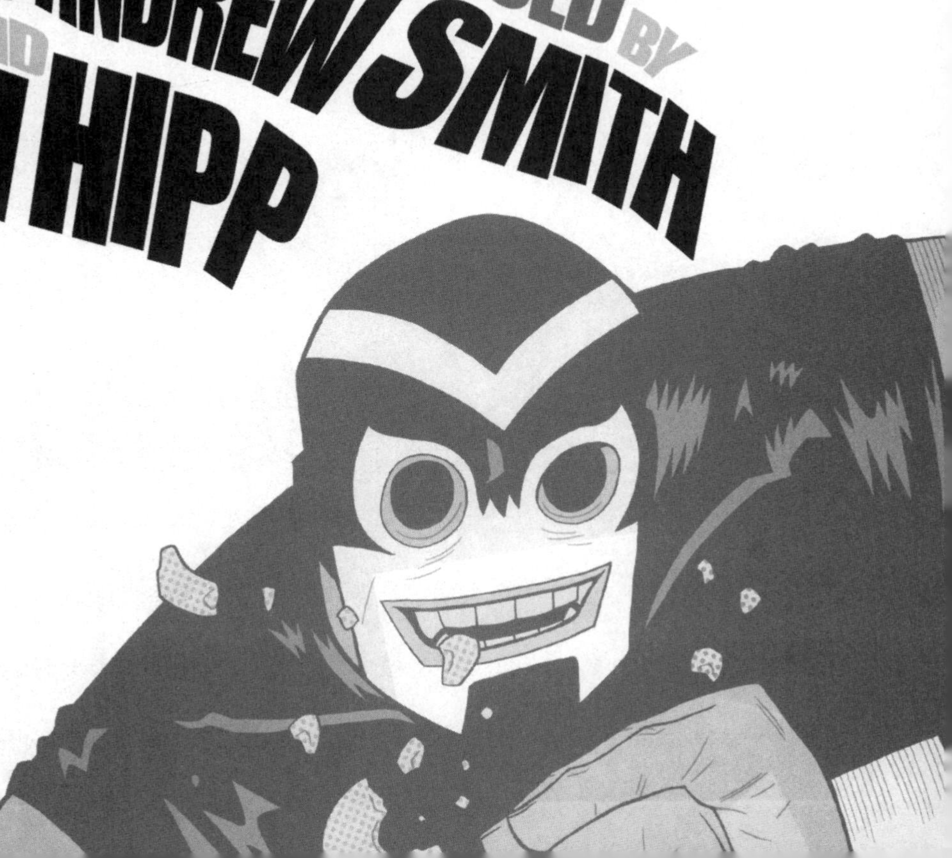

SMITH HIPP

ART STORY

SMITH

HIPP

Book Design by Hipp

Messrs. Smith and Hipp gratefully acknowledge the following contributions of illustrious illustration to Vol. 2 of The Amazing Joy Buzzards...

MARK ENGLERT

THE AMAZING
JOY BUZZARDS
IN
LONDON
CALLING!

ORIGINALLY
APPEARING
IN THE AMAZING
JOY BUZZARDS
VOLUME TWO:
ISSUE 3

KHARY RANDOLPH

EL CAMPEON
VERSUS
EL CHICOS
MUERTES!

ORIGINALLY
APPEARING
IN THE AMAZING
JOY BUZZARDS
VOLUME TWO:
ISSUE 3

SEAN GALLOWAY

EL CAMPEON
IN
LOST
IN THE
SUPER-
MARKET!

ORIGINALLY
APPEARING
IN THE AMAZING
JOY BUZZARDS
VOLUME TWO:
ISSUE 3

JIM MAHFOOD

STEVO AND
SMOKEDOG
TEAM-UP!

ORIGINALLY
APPEARING
IN THE AMAZING
JOY BUZZARDS
VOLUME TWO:
ISSUE 4

DAVE CROSLAND

THE AMAZING
JOY BUZZARDS
IN MARS
NEEDS
KITTENS!

ORIGINALLY
APPEARING
IN THE AMAZING
JOY BUZZARDS
VOLUME TWO:
ISSUE 4

JIM PEZZETTI

THE AMAZING
JOY BUZZARDS
AND
THE
DEVIL'S
ZAPATOS!

ORIGINALLY
APPEARING
HERE FOR
THE FIRST
TIME!

OH,
IT'S
TRUE!

...good on ya, lads.

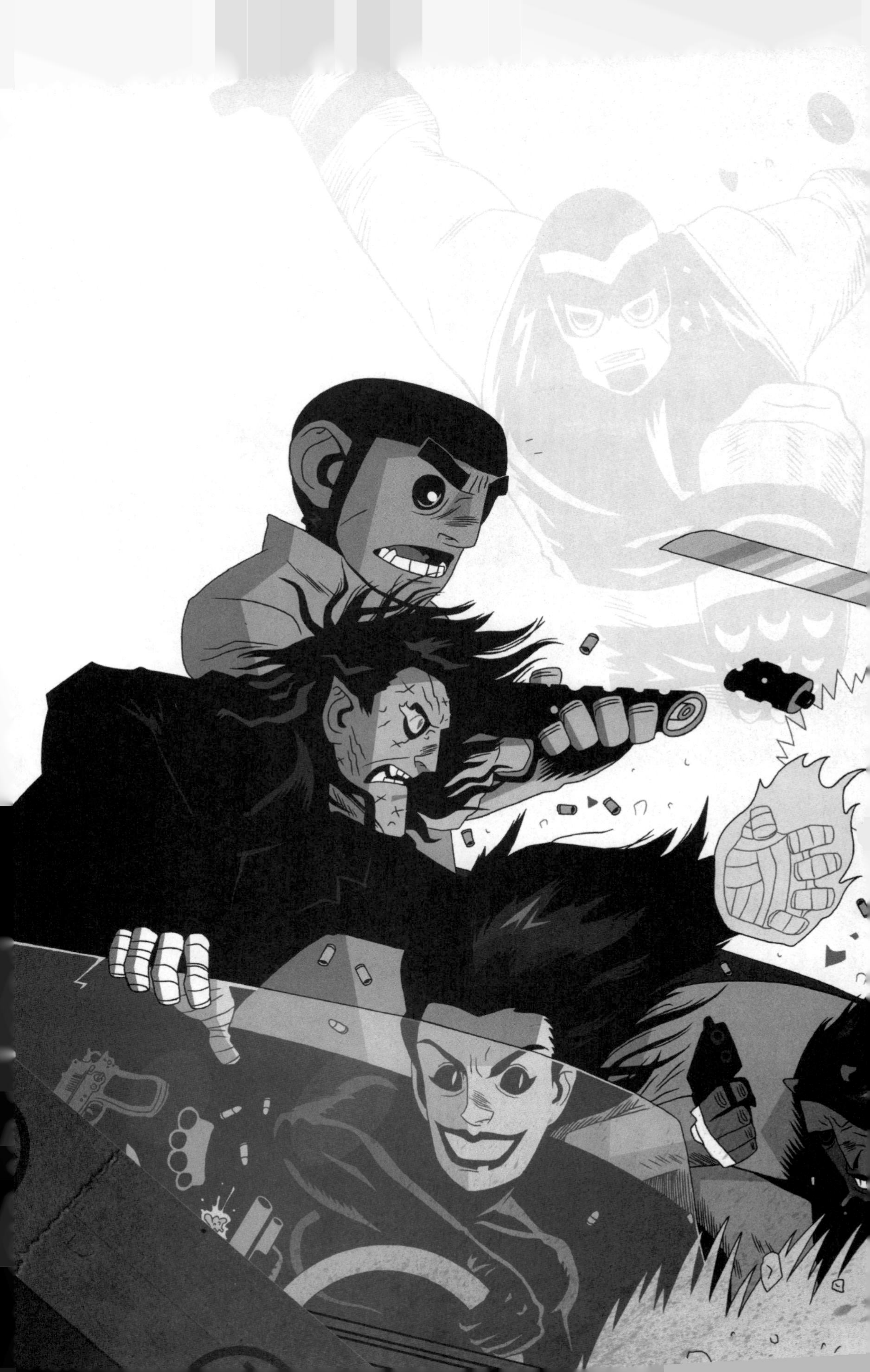

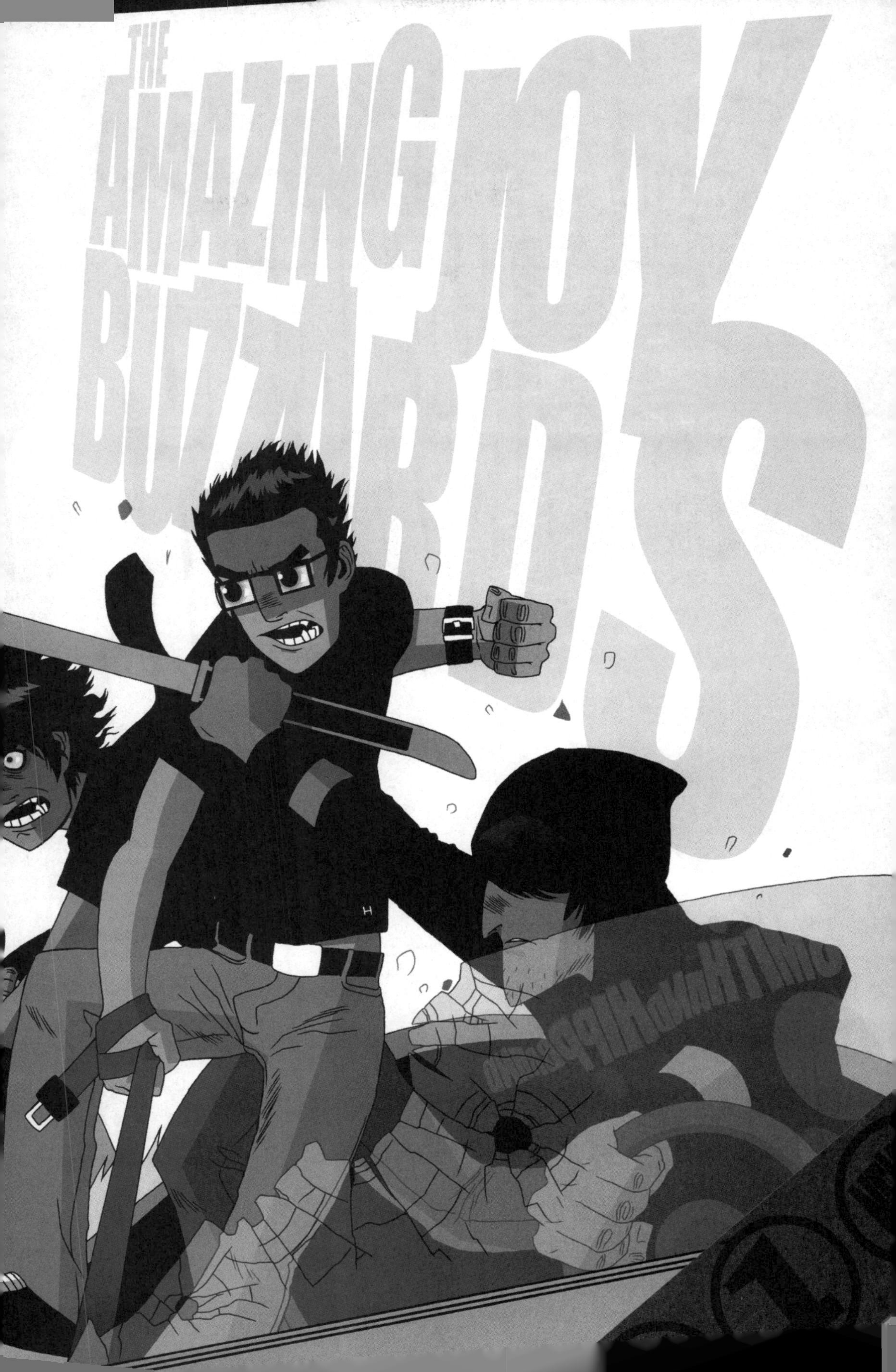
THE AMAZING JOY BUZZARDS

READ THIS FIRST!
PREVIOUSLY

THE AMAZING JOY BUZZARDS ARE AN EPIC ROCK GROUP THAT FIGHTS EVIL IN ALL IT'S FORMS.

THE BAND MEMBERS ARE **BIFF ASHBY**, **GABE CARLYLE** AND **STEVO VARGAS**. GABE CARRIES AN AMULET WHICH CAN SUMMON THE MYTHICAL MEXICAN WRESTLER **EL CAMPEON**.

THE BAND IS MANAGED BY **DALTON WARNER** OF THE **CREATIVE INTERNATIONAL ARTISTS AGENCY**.

THE **CREATIVE INTERNATIONAL ARTISTS AGENCY** IS REALLY THE **CENTRAL INTELLIGENCE AGENCY**, UNBEKNOWNST TO THE BAND.

DALTON USES THE BAND AS A COVER TO GET INTO PLACES HE MIGHT OTHERWISE BE UNABLE TO. HE ALSO USES THE BAND'S KNACK FOR DEFEATING SUPERNATURAL EVILS TO HIS ADVANTAGE.

FRIENDS TO THE BAND, **PROFESSOR YU** AND HIS DAUGHTER **BETTY** (GIRLFRIEND OF GABE), WERE RECENTLY IN SOUTH AMERICA TO VISIT A COLLEAGUE; **PROFESSOR BAFANOPOLIS**. THEY FOUND HIS LAB IN RUINS. THERE WAS A MYSTERIOUS CALLING CARD LEFT IN THE RUBBLE...

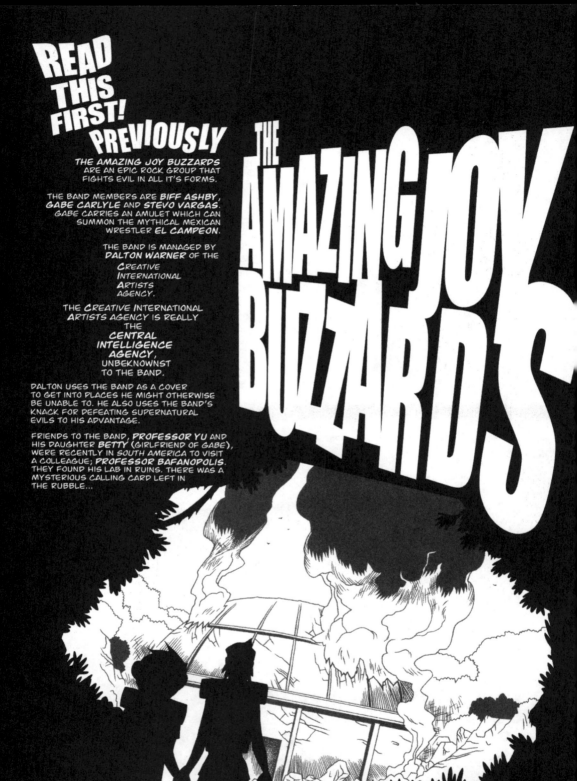

THE AMAZING JOY BUZZARDS

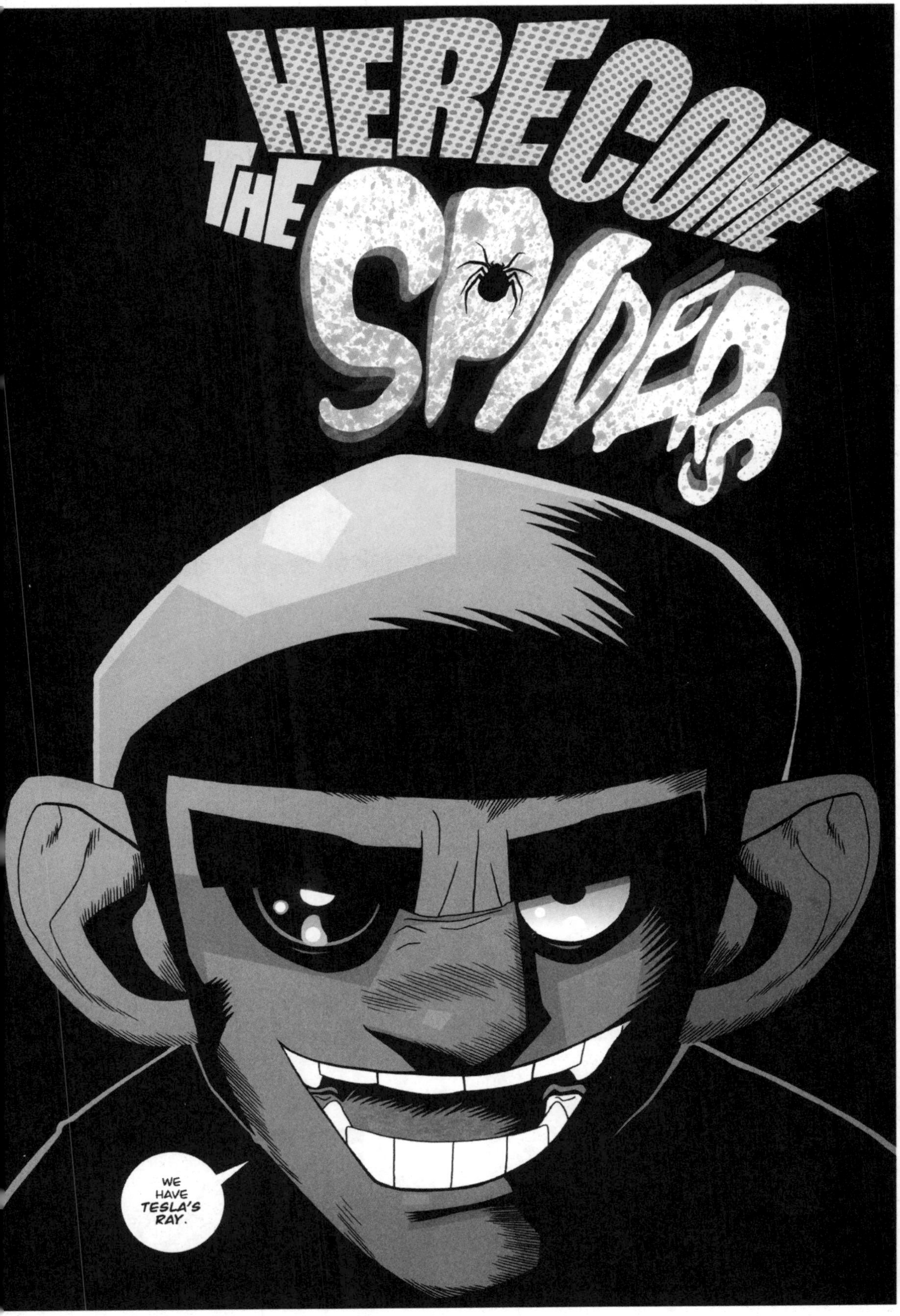
HERE COME THE SPIDERS
WE HAVE TESLA'S RAY.

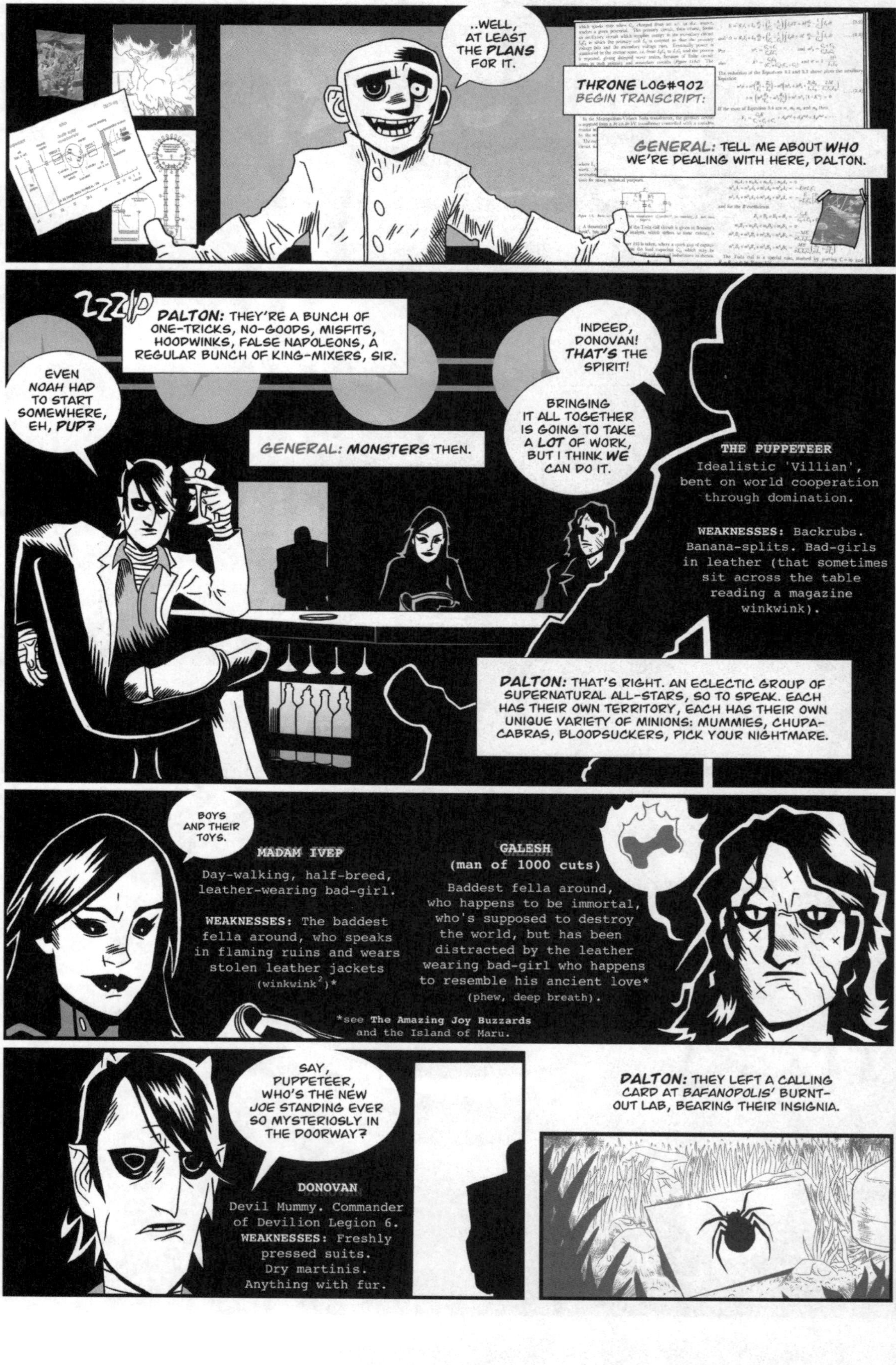
..WELL, AT LEAST THE PLANS FOR IT.
THRONE LOG#902 BEGIN TRANSCRIPT:
GENERAL: TELL ME ABOUT WHO WE'RE DEALING WITH HERE, DALTON.
ZZZIP
DALTON: THEY'RE A BUNCH OF ONE-TRICKS, NO-GOODS, MISFITS, HOODWINKS, FALSE NAPOLEONS, A REGULAR BUNCH OF KING-MIXERS, SIR.
EVEN NOAH HAD TO START SOMEWHERE, EH, PUP?
INDEED, DONOVAN! THAT'S THE SPIRIT!
BRINGING IT ALL TOGETHER IS GOING TO TAKE A LOT OF WORK, BUT I THINK WE CAN DO IT.
GENERAL: MONSTERS THEN.
THE PUPPETEER
Idealistic 'Villian', bent on world cooperation through domination.
WEAKNESSES: Backrubs. Banana-splits. Bad-girls in leather (that sometimes sit across the table reading a magazine winkwink).
DALTON: THAT'S RIGHT. AN ECLECTIC GROUP OF SUPERNATURAL ALL-STARS, SO TO SPEAK. EACH HAS THEIR OWN TERRITORY, EACH HAS THEIR OWN UNIQUE VARIETY OF MINIONS: MUMMIES, CHUPACABRAS, BLOODSUCKERS, PICK YOUR NIGHTMARE.
BOYS AND THEIR TOYS.
MADAM IVEP
Day-walking, half-breed, leather-wearing bad-girl.
WEAKNESSES: The baddest fella around, who speaks in flaming ruins and wears stolen leather jackets (winkwink²)*
GALESH (man of 1000 cuts)
Baddest fella around, who happens to be immortal, who's supposed to destroy the world, but has been distracted by the leather wearing bad-girl who happens to resemble his ancient love* (phew, deep breath).
*see The Amazing Joy Buzzards and the Island of Maru.
SAY, PUPPETEER, WHO'S THE NEW JOE STANDING EVER SO MYSTERIOSLY IN THE DOORWAY?
DONOVAN
Devil Mummy. Commander of Devilion Legion 6.
WEAKNESSES: Freshly pressed suits. Dry martinis. Anything with fur.
DALTON: THEY LEFT A CALLING CARD AT BAFANOPOLIS' BURNT-OUT LAB, BEARING THEIR INSIGNIA.

GENTLE-MEN...

(AHEM).

LADIES AND GENTLEMEN. ALLOW ME TO INTRODUCE YOU TO OUR NEWEST ASSOCIATE, EL CHUPA.

EL CHUPA
Sworn enemy of El Campeon.

HOMETOWN:
Isla Mujeres, Mexico.
AFFILIATIONS:
Chupacabra's Local 148 Union,
Carpe Noctrum.

OH, YOU'RE EL CHUPA! YOU DID THAT JOB A COUPLE YEARS BACK. THE DEVIL'S ZAPATOS ORDEAL, YEAH?

GOOD TO FINALLY MEET YOU, OLD BOY. I'M A BIG FAN OF YOUR WORK.

WHO'S YOUR TAILOR? CAN I GET HIS CARD?

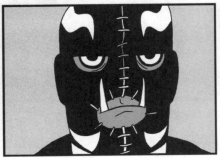

RIGHT. STRONG, SILENT, AND RIDICULOUS. I GET IT.

DALTON: THEY STARTED OUT SMALL-TIME IN ASIA AND ROSE THROUGH THE RANKS OF THE CRIMINAL ELITE. SOON ENOUGH, THEY BEGAN DABBLING IN THE OCCULT AND THINGS TOOK A TURN. THEIR SYNDICATE MERGED WITH *THE SOCIETY OF GREEN MEN,* WHO FORMERLY WORKED ALONGSIDE *THE ANNENBRE.* THE SOCIETY FURNISHED THEM WITH THE *BIBLIO NOCTRUMONIKER,* GIVING THEM KEYS TO THE UNKNOWN.

DALTON: THEY BEGAN TO SCOUR THE GLOBE IN SEARCH OF THE SUPERNATURAL.

DALTON: THEY FOUND WHAT THEY WERE LOOKING FOR.

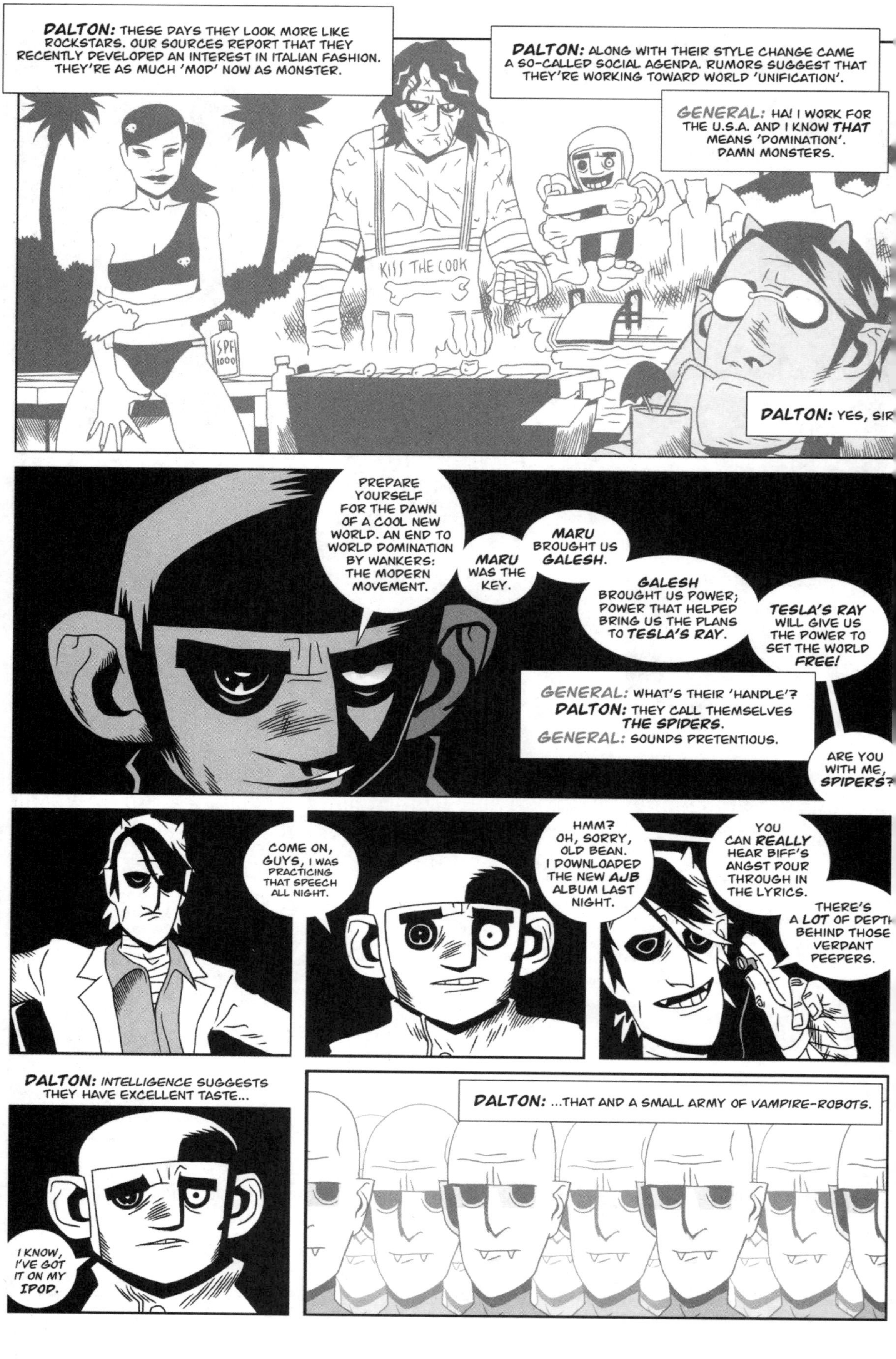
DALTON: THESE DAYS THEY LOOK MORE LIKE ROCKSTARS. OUR SOURCES REPORT THAT THEY RECENTLY DEVELOPED AN INTEREST IN ITALIAN FASHION. THEY'RE AS MUCH 'MOD' NOW AS MONSTER.
DALTON: ALONG WITH THEIR STYLE CHANGE CAME A SO-CALLED SOCIAL AGENDA. RUMORS SUGGEST THAT THEY'RE WORKING TOWARD WORLD 'UNIFICATION'.
GENERAL: HA! I WORK FOR THE U.S.A. AND I KNOW THAT MEANS 'DOMINATION'. DAMN MONSTERS.
KISS THE COOK
SPF 1000
DALTON: YES, SIR
PREPARE YOURSELF FOR THE DAWN OF A COOL NEW WORLD. AN END TO WORLD DOMINATION BY WANKERS: THE MODERN MOVEMENT.
MARU WAS THE KEY.
MARU BROUGHT US GALESH.
GALESH BROUGHT US POWER; POWER THAT HELPED BRING US THE PLANS TO TESLA'S RAY.
TESLA'S RAY WILL GIVE US THE POWER TO SET THE WORLD FREE!
GENERAL: WHAT'S THEIR 'HANDLE'?
DALTON: THEY CALL THEMSELVES THE SPIDERS.
GENERAL: SOUNDS PRETENTIOUS.
ARE YOU WITH ME, SPIDERS?
COME ON, GUYS, I WAS PRACTICING THAT SPEECH ALL NIGHT.
HMM? OH, SORRY, OLD BEAN. I DOWNLOADED THE NEW AJB ALBUM LAST NIGHT.
YOU CAN REALLY HEAR BIFF'S ANGST POUR THROUGH IN THE LYRICS.
THERE'S A LOT OF DEPTH BEHIND THOSE VERDANT PEEPERS.
DALTON: INTELLIGENCE SUGGESTS THEY HAVE EXCELLENT TASTE...
I KNOW, I'VE GOT IT ON MY IPOD.
DALTON: ...THAT AND A SMALL ARMY OF VAMPIRE-ROBOTS.

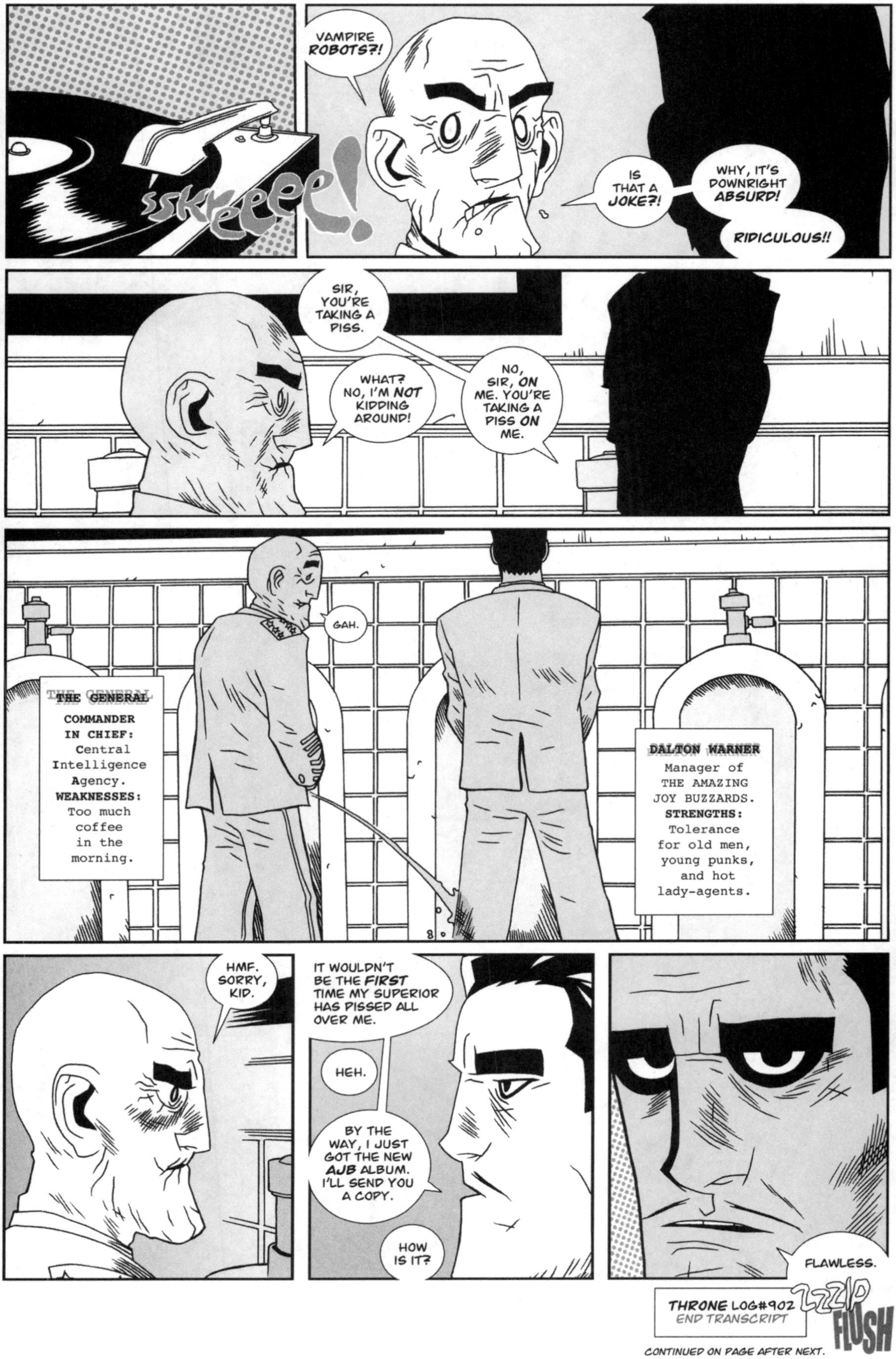
SSKREEEE!
VAMPIRE ROBOTS?!
IS THAT A JOKE?!
WHY, IT'S DOWNRIGHT ABSURD!
RIDICULOUS!!
SIR, YOU'RE TAKING A PISS.
WHAT? NO, I'M NOT KIDDING AROUND!
NO, SIR, ON ME. YOU'RE TAKING A PISS ON ME.
GAH.
THE GENERAL
COMMANDER IN CHIEF: Central Intelligence Agency.
WEAKNESSES: Too much coffee in the morning.
DALTON WARNER
Manager of THE AMAZING JOY BUZZARDS.
STRENGTHS: Tolerance for old men, young punks, and hot lady-agents.
HMF. SORRY, KID.
IT WOULDN'T BE THE FIRST TIME MY SUPERIOR HAS PISSED ALL OVER ME.
HEH.
BY THE WAY, I JUST GOT THE NEW AJB ALBUM. I'LL SEND YOU A COPY.
HOW IS IT?
FLAWLESS.
THRONE LOG#902
END TRANSCRIPT
ZZZIP
FLUSH

CONTINUED ON PAGE AFTER NEXT.

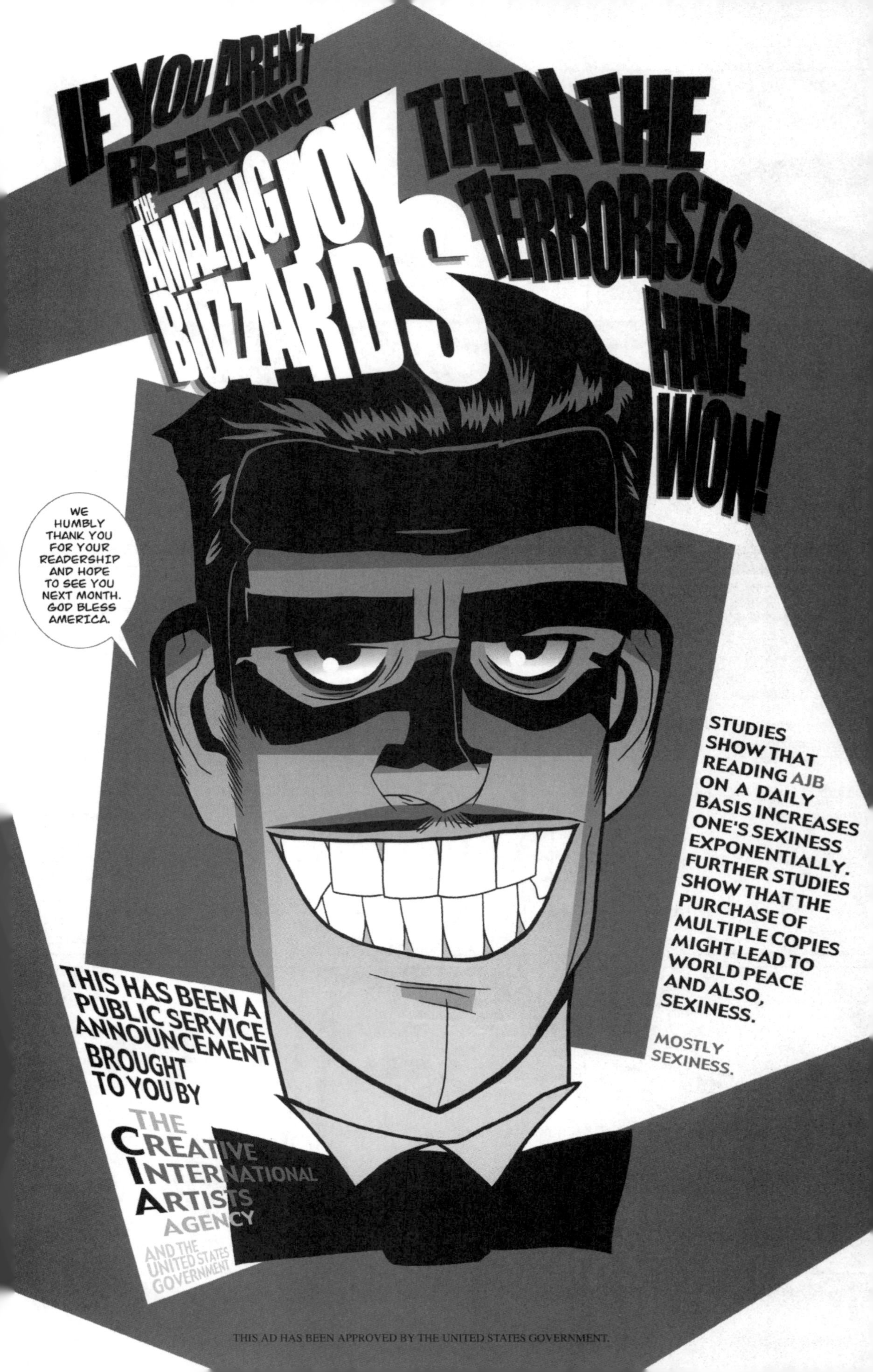
IF YOU AREN'T READING THE AMAZING JOY BUZZARDS THEN THE TERRORISTS HAVE WON!
WE HUMBLY THANK YOU FOR YOUR READERSHIP AND HOPE TO SEE YOU NEXT MONTH. GOD BLESS AMERICA.
STUDIES SHOW THAT READING AJB ON A DAILY BASIS INCREASES ONE'S SEXINESS EXPONENTIALLY. FURTHER STUDIES SHOW THAT THE PURCHASE OF MULTIPLE COPIES MIGHT LEAD TO WORLD PEACE AND ALSO, SEXINESS.
MOSTLY SEXINESS.
THIS HAS BEEN A PUBLIC SERVICE ANNOUNCEMENT BROUGHT TO YOU BY
THE CREATIVE INTERNATIONAL ARTISTS AGENCY
AND THE UNITED STATES GOVERNMENT
THIS AD HAS BEEN APPROVED BY THE UNITED STATES GOVERNMENT.

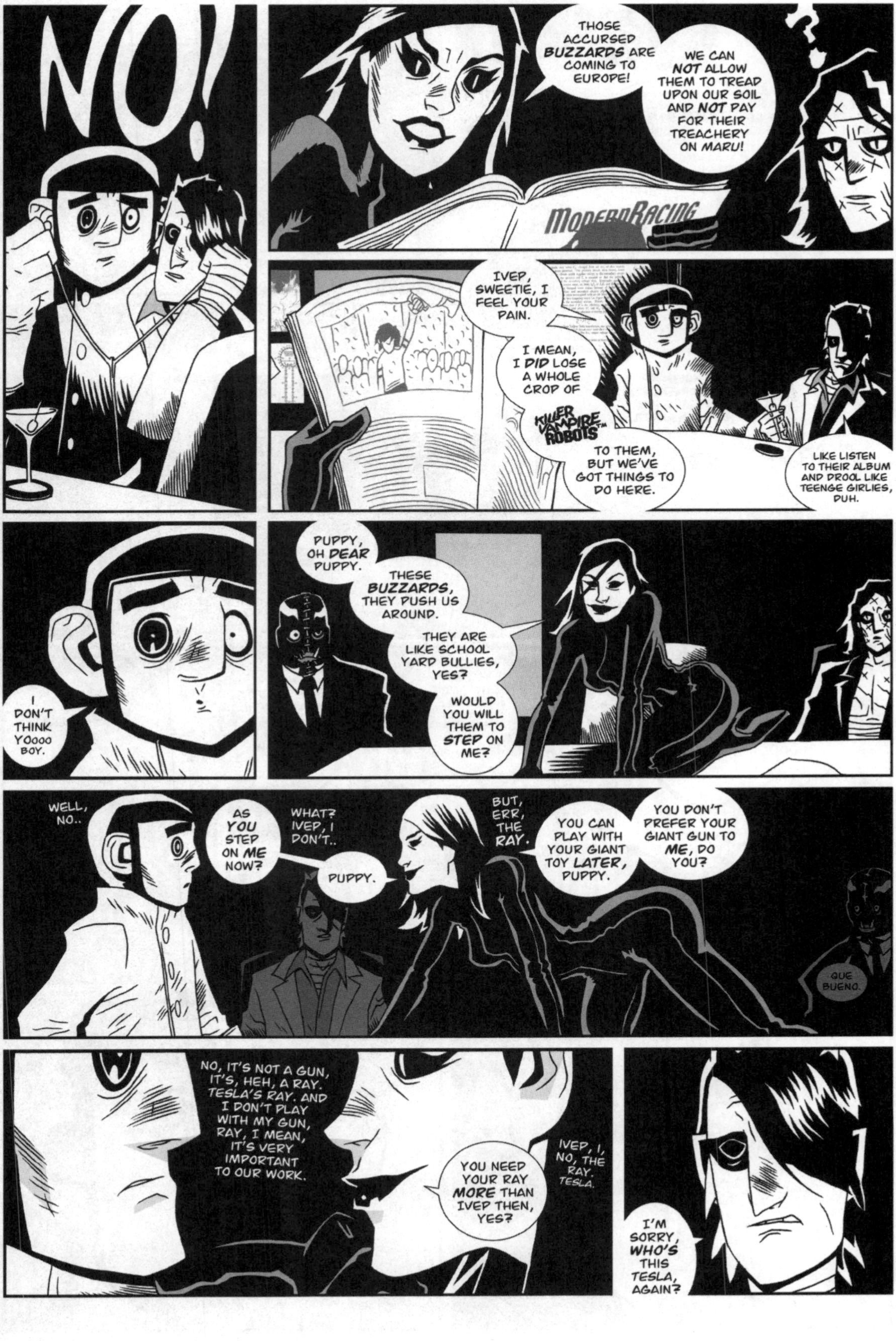
NO!
THOSE ACCURSED BUZZARDS ARE COMING TO EUROPE!
WE CAN NOT ALLOW THEM TO TREAD UPON OUR SOIL AND NOT PAY FOR THEIR TREACHERY ON MARU!
MODERN RACING
IVEP, SWEETIE, I FEEL YOUR PAIN.
I MEAN, I DID LOSE A WHOLE CROP OF
KILLER VAMPIRE ROBOTS™
TO THEM, BUT WE'VE GOT THINGS TO DO HERE.
LIKE LISTEN TO THEIR ALBUM AND DROOL LIKE TEENGE GIRLIES, DUH.
I DON'T THINK YOooo BOY.
PUPPY, OH DEAR PUPPY.
THESE BUZZARDS, THEY PUSH US AROUND.
THEY ARE LIKE SCHOOL YARD BULLIES, YES?
WOULD YOU WILL THEM TO STEP ON ME?
WELL, NO..
AS YOU STEP ON ME NOW?
WHAT? IVEP, I DON'T..
PUPPY.
BUT, ERR, THE RAY.
YOU CAN PLAY WITH YOUR GIANT TOY LATER, PUPPY.
YOU DON'T PREFER YOUR GIANT GUN TO ME, DO YOU?
QUE BUENO.
NO, IT'S NOT A GUN, IT'S, HEH, A RAY. TESLA'S RAY. AND I DON'T PLAY WITH MY GUN, RAY, I MEAN, IT'S VERY IMPORTANT TO OUR WORK.
YOU NEED YOUR RAY MORE THAN IVEP THEN, YES?
IVEP, I, NO, THE RAY. TESLA.
I'M SORRY, WHO'S THIS TESLA, AGAIN?

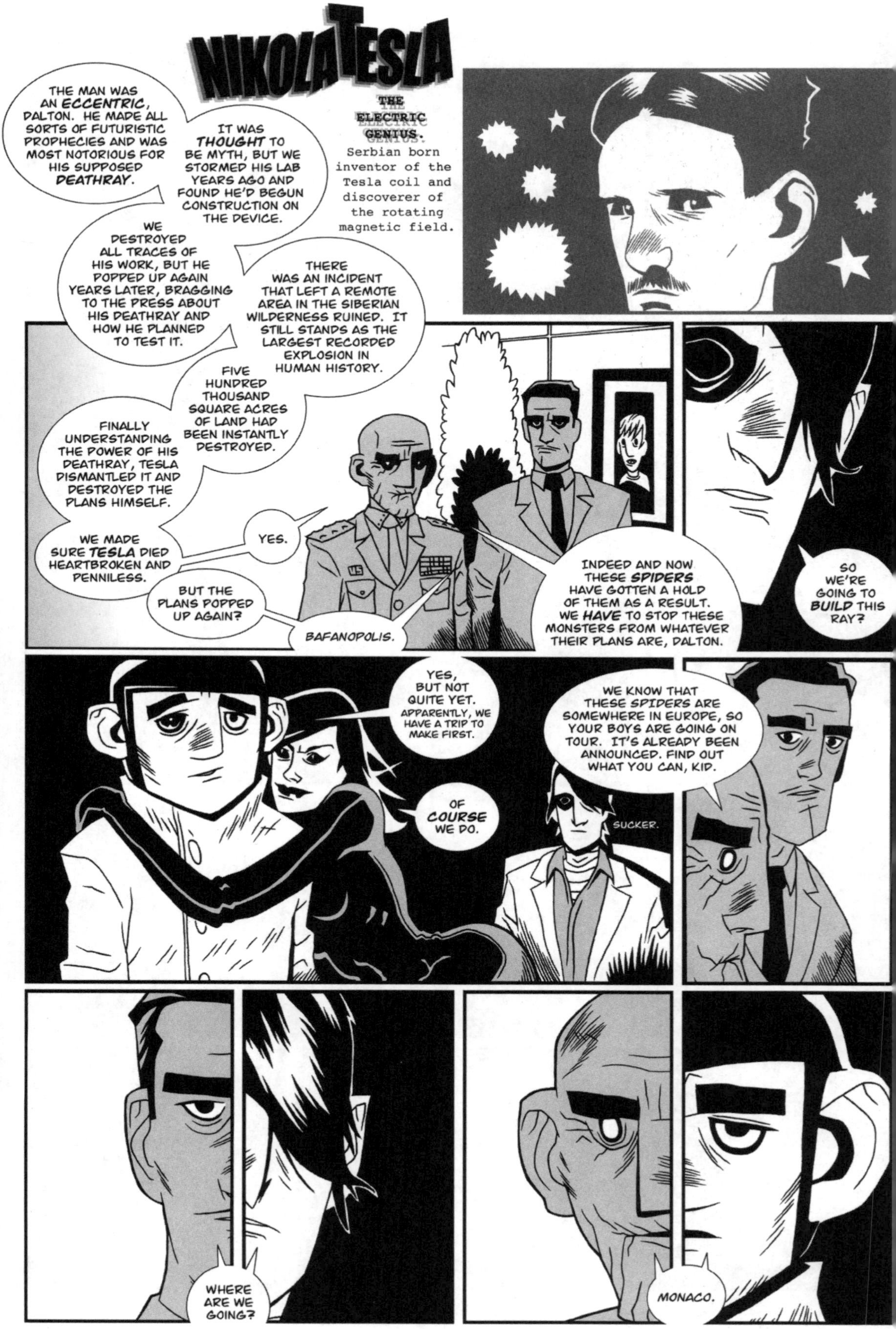

NIKOLA TESLA
THE ELECTRIC GENIUS.
Serbian born inventor of the Tesla coil and discoverer of the rotating magnetic field.
THE MAN WAS AN ECCENTRIC, DALTON. HE MADE ALL SORTS OF FUTURISTIC PROPHECIES AND WAS MOST NOTORIOUS FOR HIS SUPPOSED DEATHRAY.
IT WAS THOUGHT TO BE MYTH, BUT WE STORMED HIS LAB YEARS AGO AND FOUND HE'D BEGUN CONSTRUCTION ON THE DEVICE.
WE DESTROYED ALL TRACES OF HIS WORK, BUT HE POPPED UP AGAIN YEARS LATER, BRAGGING TO THE PRESS ABOUT HIS DEATHRAY AND HOW HE PLANNED TO TEST IT.
THERE WAS AN INCIDENT THAT LEFT A REMOTE AREA IN THE SIBERIAN WILDERNESS RUINED. IT STILL STANDS AS THE LARGEST RECORDED EXPLOSION IN HUMAN HISTORY.
FIVE HUNDRED THOUSAND SQUARE ACRES OF LAND HAD BEEN INSTANTLY DESTROYED.
FINALLY UNDERSTANDING THE POWER OF HIS DEATHRAY, TESLA DISMANTLED IT AND DESTROYED THE PLANS HIMSELF.
WE MADE SURE TESLA DIED HEARTBROKEN AND PENNILESS.
YES.
BUT THE PLANS POPPED UP AGAIN?
BAFANOPOLIS.
INDEED AND NOW THESE SPIDERS HAVE GOTTEN A HOLD OF THEM AS A RESULT. WE HAVE TO STOP THESE MONSTERS FROM WHATEVER THEIR PLANS ARE, DALTON.
SO WE'RE GOING TO BUILD THIS RAY?
YES, BUT NOT QUITE YET. APPARENTLY, WE HAVE A TRIP TO MAKE FIRST.
OF COURSE WE DO.
SUCKER.
WE KNOW THAT THESE SPIDERS ARE SOMEWHERE IN EUROPE, SO YOUR BOYS ARE GOING ON TOUR. IT'S ALREADY BEEN ANNOUNCED. FIND OUT WHAT YOU CAN, KID.
WHERE ARE WE GOING?
MONACO.

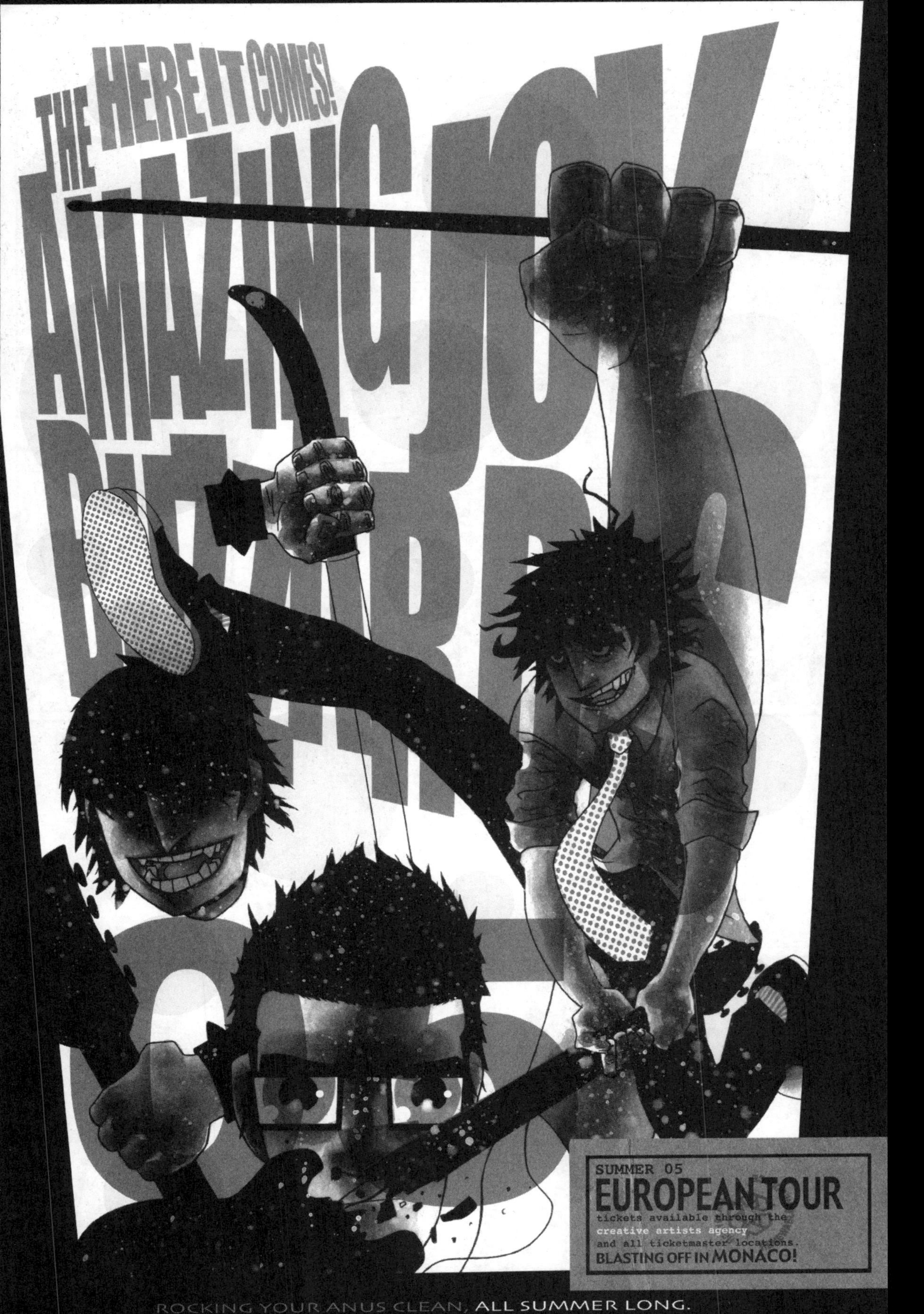
THE
HERE IT COMES!
AMAZING JOY
SUMMER 05
EUROPEAN TOUR
tickets available through the
creative artists agency
and all ticketmaster locations.
BLASTING OFF IN MONACO!
ROCKING YOUR ANUS CLEAN, ALL SUMMER LONG.

THE AMAZING JOY BUZZARDS

Rock-band of legendary proportion. Often involved in matters of supernatural interest. Unwitting pawn of the **CIA**.

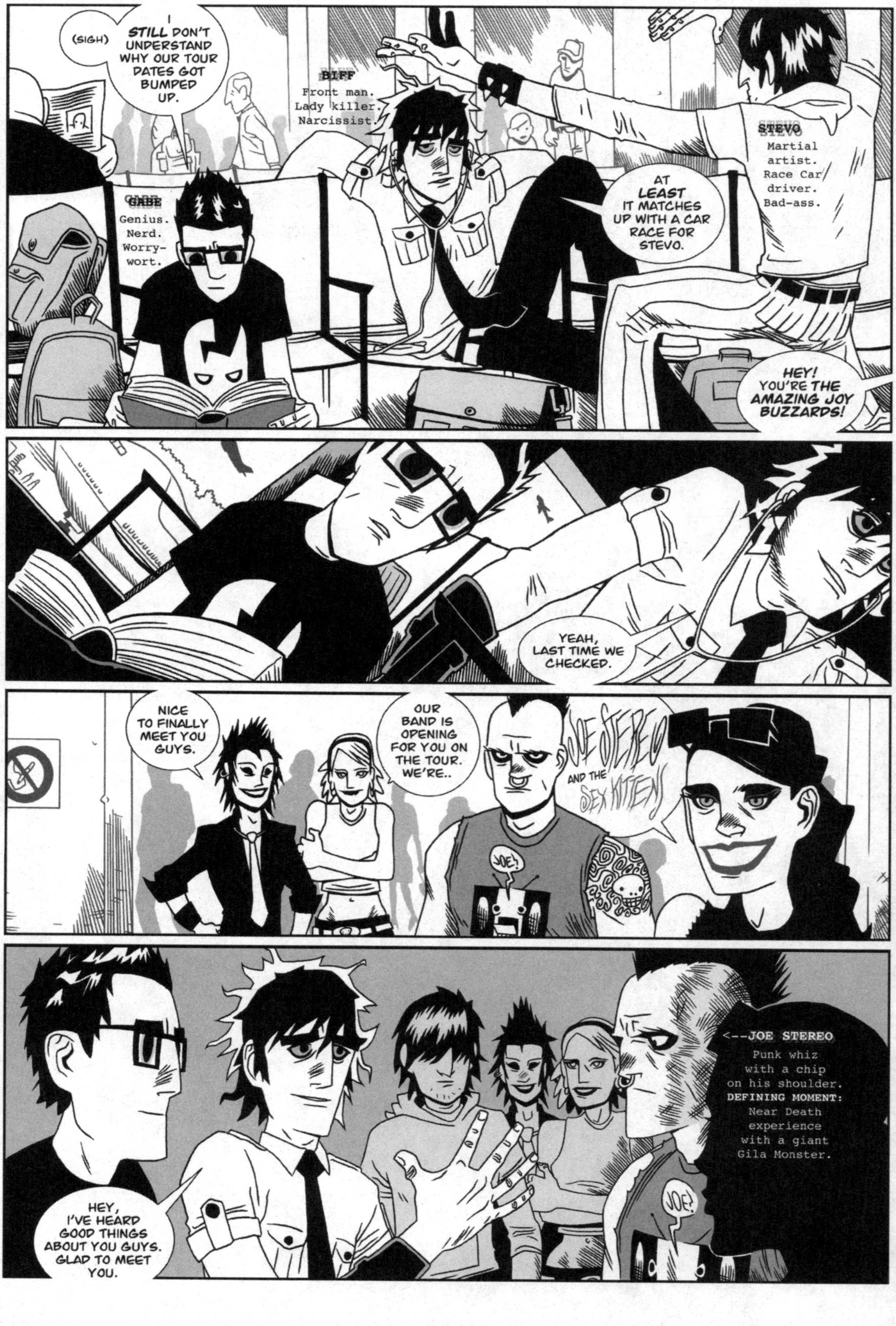
(SIGH)
I STILL DON'T UNDERSTAND WHY OUR TOUR DATES GOT BUMPED UP.
BIFF
Front man. Lady killer. Narcissist.
STEVO
Martial artist. Race Car driver. Bad-ass.
GABE
Genius. Nerd. Worry-wort.
AT LEAST IT MATCHES UP WITH A CAR RACE FOR STEVO.
HEY! YOU'RE THE AMAZING JOY BUZZARDS!
YEAH, LAST TIME WE CHECKED.
NICE TO FINALLY MEET YOU GUYS.
OUR BAND IS OPENING FOR YOU ON THE TOUR. WE'RE..
JOE STEREO AND THE SEX KITTENS
JOE!
<--JOE STEREO
Punk whiz with a chip on his shoulder.
DEFINING MOMENT:
Near Death experience with a giant Gila Monster.
HEY, I'VE HEARD GOOD THINGS ABOUT YOU GUYS. GLAD TO MEET YOU.
JOE!

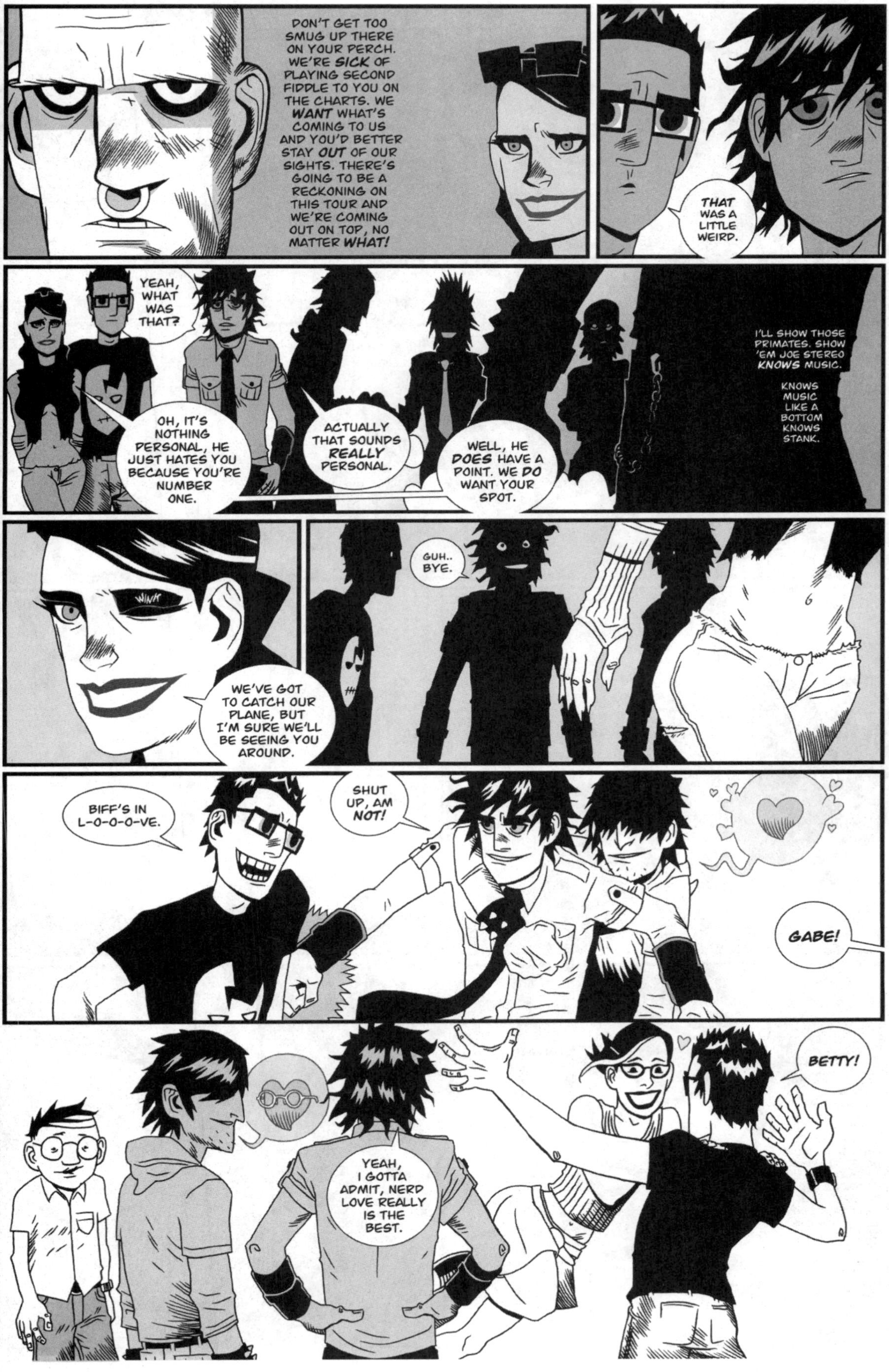
DON'T GET TOO SMUG UP THERE ON YOUR PERCH. WE'RE SICK OF PLAYING SECOND FIDDLE TO YOU ON THE CHARTS. WE WANT WHAT'S COMING TO US AND YOU'D BETTER STAY OUT OF OUR SIGHTS. THERE'S GOING TO BE A RECKONING ON THIS TOUR AND WE'RE COMING OUT ON TOP, NO MATTER WHAT!
THAT WAS A LITTLE WEIRD.
YEAH, WHAT WAS THAT?
OH, IT'S NOTHING PERSONAL, HE JUST HATES YOU BECAUSE YOU'RE NUMBER ONE.
ACTUALLY THAT SOUNDS REALLY PERSONAL.
WELL, HE DOES HAVE A POINT. WE DO WANT YOUR SPOT.
I'LL SHOW THOSE PRIMATES. SHOW 'EM JOE STEREO KNOWS MUSIC.
KNOWS MUSIC LIKE A BOTTOM KNOWS STANK.
WINK
WE'VE GOT TO CATCH OUR PLANE, BUT I'M SURE WE'LL BE SEEING YOU AROUND.
GUH.. BYE.
BIFF'S IN L-O-O-O-VE.
SHUT UP, AM NOT!
GABE!
YEAH, I GOTTA ADMIT, NERD LOVE REALLY IS THE BEST.
BETTY!

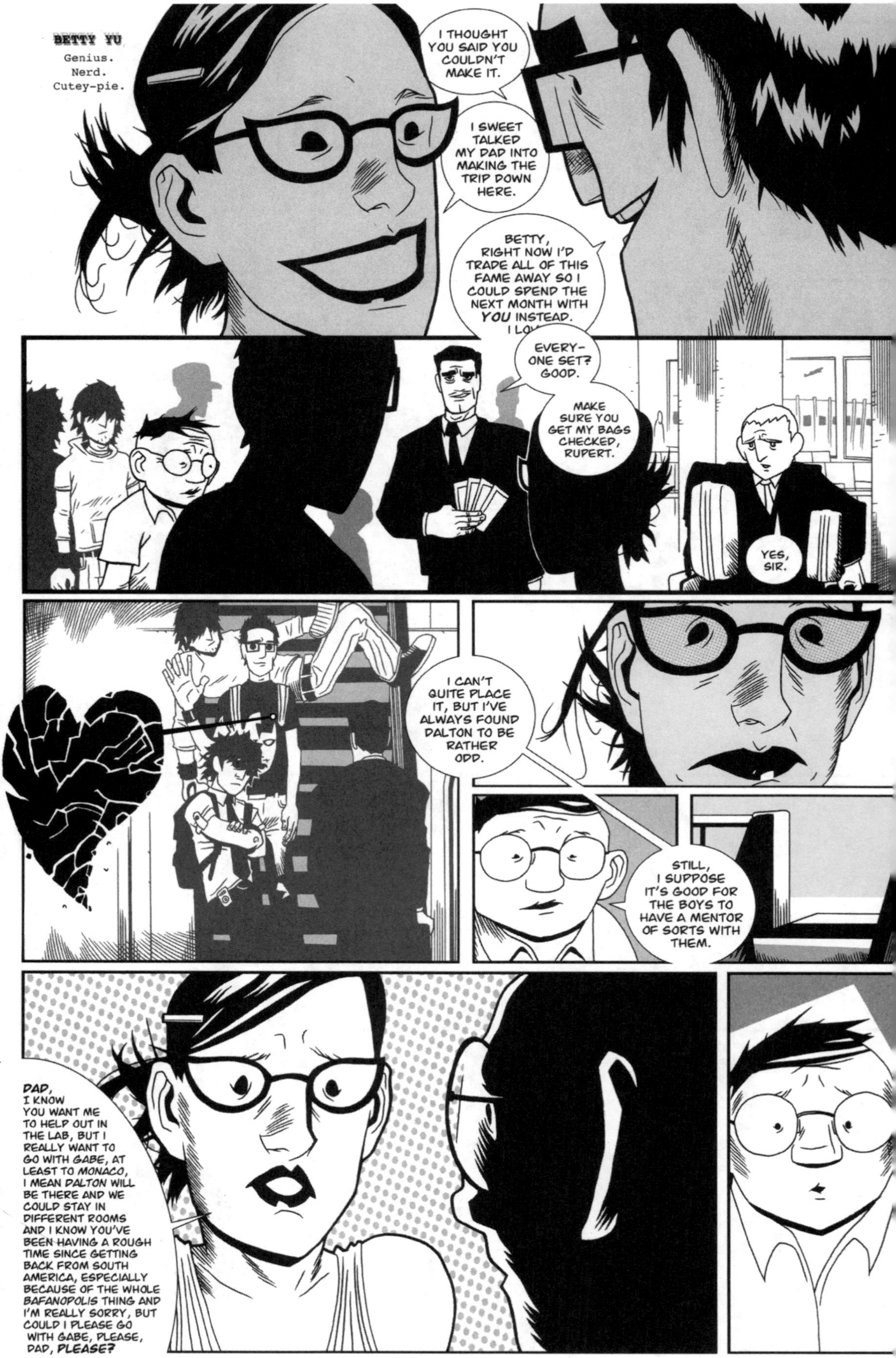
BETTY YU
Genius.
Nerd.
Cutey-pie.
I THOUGHT YOU SAID YOU COULDN'T MAKE IT.
I SWEET TALKED MY DAD INTO MAKING THE TRIP DOWN HERE.
BETTY, RIGHT NOW I'D TRADE ALL OF THIS FAME AWAY SO I COULD SPEND THE NEXT MONTH WITH YOU INSTEAD. I LOV
EVERY-ONE SET? GOOD.
MAKE SURE YOU GET MY BAGS CHECKED, RUPERT.
YES, SIR.
I CAN'T QUITE PLACE IT, BUT I'VE ALWAYS FOUND DALTON TO BE RATHER ODD.
STILL, I SUPPOSE IT'S GOOD FOR THE BOYS TO HAVE A MENTOR OF SORTS WITH THEM.
DAD, I KNOW YOU WANT ME TO HELP OUT IN THE LAB, BUT I REALLY WANT TO GO WITH GABE, AT LEAST TO MONACO, I MEAN DALTON WILL BE THERE AND WE COULD STAY IN DIFFERENT ROOMS AND I KNOW YOU'VE BEEN HAVING A ROUGH TIME SINCE GETTING BACK FROM SOUTH AMERICA, ESPECIALLY BECAUSE OF THE WHOLE BAFANOPOLIS THING AND I'M REALLY SORRY, BUT COULD I PLEASE GO WITH GABE, PLEASE, DAD, PLEASE?

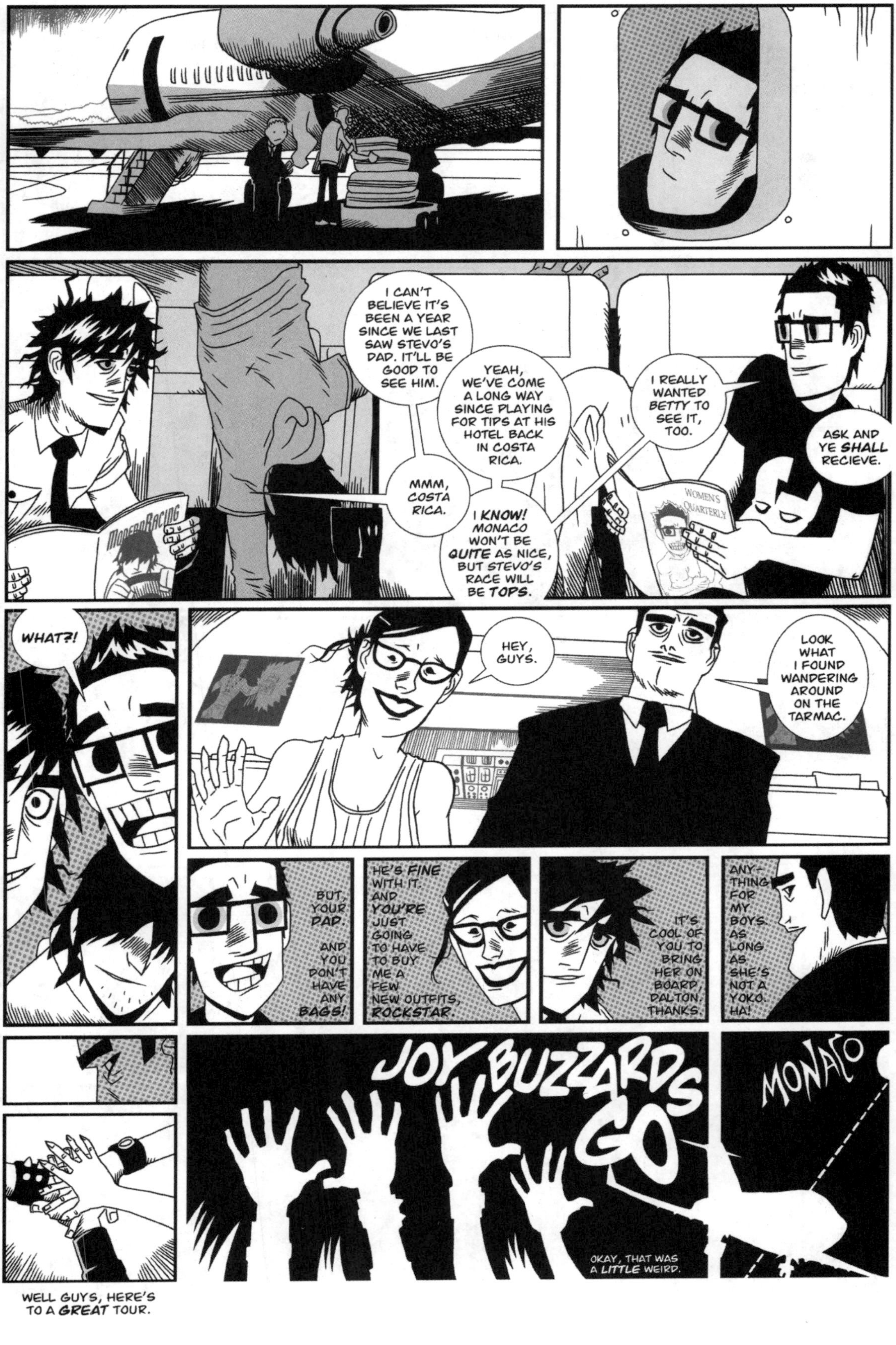

I CAN'T BELIEVE IT'S BEEN A YEAR SINCE WE LAST SAW STEVO'S DAD. IT'LL BE GOOD TO SEE HIM.
YEAH, WE'VE COME A LONG WAY SINCE PLAYING FOR TIPS AT HIS HOTEL BACK IN COSTA RICA.
MMM, COSTA RICA.
I KNOW! MONACO WON'T BE QUITE AS NICE, BUT STEVO'S RACE WILL BE TOPS.
I REALLY WANTED BETTY TO SEE IT, TOO.
ASK AND YE SHALL RECIEVE.
MODERN RACING
WOMEN'S QUARTERLY
WHAT?!
HEY, GUYS.
LOOK WHAT I FOUND WANDERING AROUND ON THE TARMAC.
BUT, YOUR DAD. AND YOU DON'T HAVE ANY BAGS!
HE'S FINE WITH IT. AND YOU'RE JUST GOING TO HAVE TO BUY ME A FEW NEW OUTFITS, ROCKSTAR.
IT'S COOL OF YOU TO BRING HER ON BOARD, DALTON. THANKS.
ANYTHING FOR MY BOYS. AS LONG AS SHE'S NOT A YOKO. HA!
WELL GUYS, HERE'S TO A GREAT TOUR.
JOY BUZZARDS GO
OKAY, THAT WAS A LITTLE WEIRD.
MONACO

ABRAHAM VARGAS
Rich, lazy man of leisure. Father to a bad-ass bass player.

EXCUSE OF CHOICE: "But I'm delicate, baby."

BOYS!

HEY, POPPA VARGAS.

STEVO, MY BOY! I'M SO PROUD OF YOU! COME HERE.

GOOD TO SEE YOU, VARGAS.

I'VE TOLD YOU, DALTON, CALL ME ABE.

BOYS, LOOK AT YOU!

ONE YEAR AND YOU'RE PRACTICALLY MEN.

AND YOU'VE BROUGHT A PRINCESS!

HA. HELLO, SIR.

NOW, BOYS, LISTEN TO ME. WE'VE GOT TO GET YOU OUT OF HERE. IT'S A MAD HOUSE OUT THERE.

OH, COME ON, IT CAN'T B ANY WORS THAN OUR ARRIVAL IN HOLLYWOO

ACTUALLY, THAT WAS LOS ANGELES, BIFF.

WHATEVER

YOU SEE? MONACO LOVES YOU BOYS! THE SURROUNDING TOWNS HAVE ALL SHUT DOWN.

I..IT.. THERE.. UH..PAGO BAH..

YOU BOYS MAY AS WELL GIVE THEM WHAT THEY WANT.

THE PLANE CREW IS UNLOADING YOUR GEAR. I'LL HAVE THEM SET IT UP.

SOMEON BETTER CAL AIR TRAFFI CONTROL

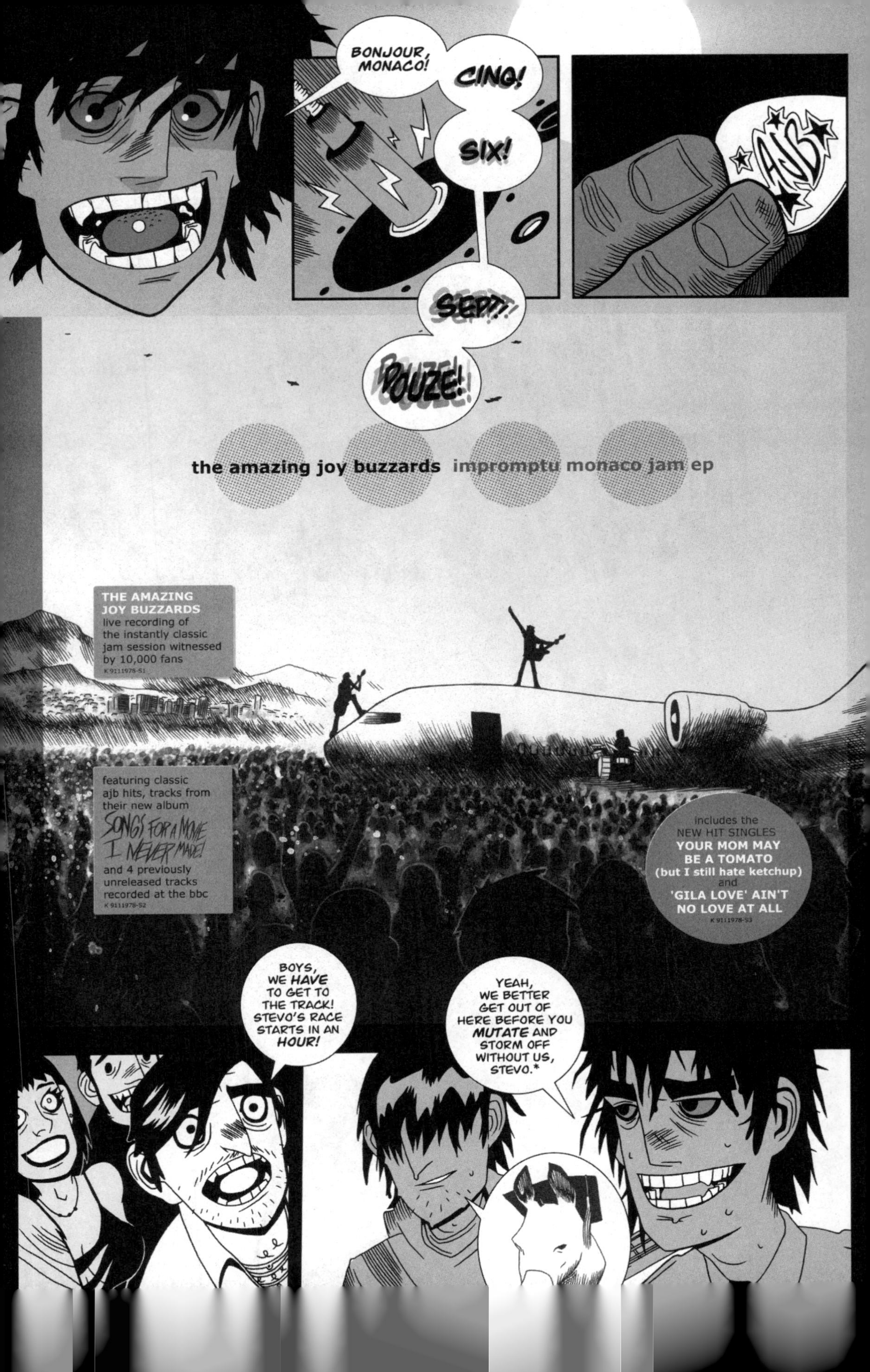
BONJOUR, MONACO!
CINQ!
SIX!
SEP?!
DOUZE!
the amazing joy buzzards impromptu monaco jam ep
THE AMAZING JOY BUZZARDS live recording of the instantly classic jam session witnessed by 10,000 fans
K 9111978-S1
featuring classic ajb hits, tracks from their new album SONGS FOR A MOVIE I NEVER MADE! and 4 previously unreleased tracks recorded at the bbc
K 9111978-S2
includes the NEW HIT SINGLES YOUR MOM MAY BE A TOMATO (but I still hate ketchup) and 'GILA LOVE' AIN'T NO LOVE AT ALL
K 9111978-S3
BOYS, WE HAVE TO GET TO THE TRACK! STEVO'S RACE STARTS IN AN HOUR!
YEAH, WE BETTER GET OUT OF HERE BEFORE YOU MUTATE AND STORM OFF WITHOUT US, STEVO.*

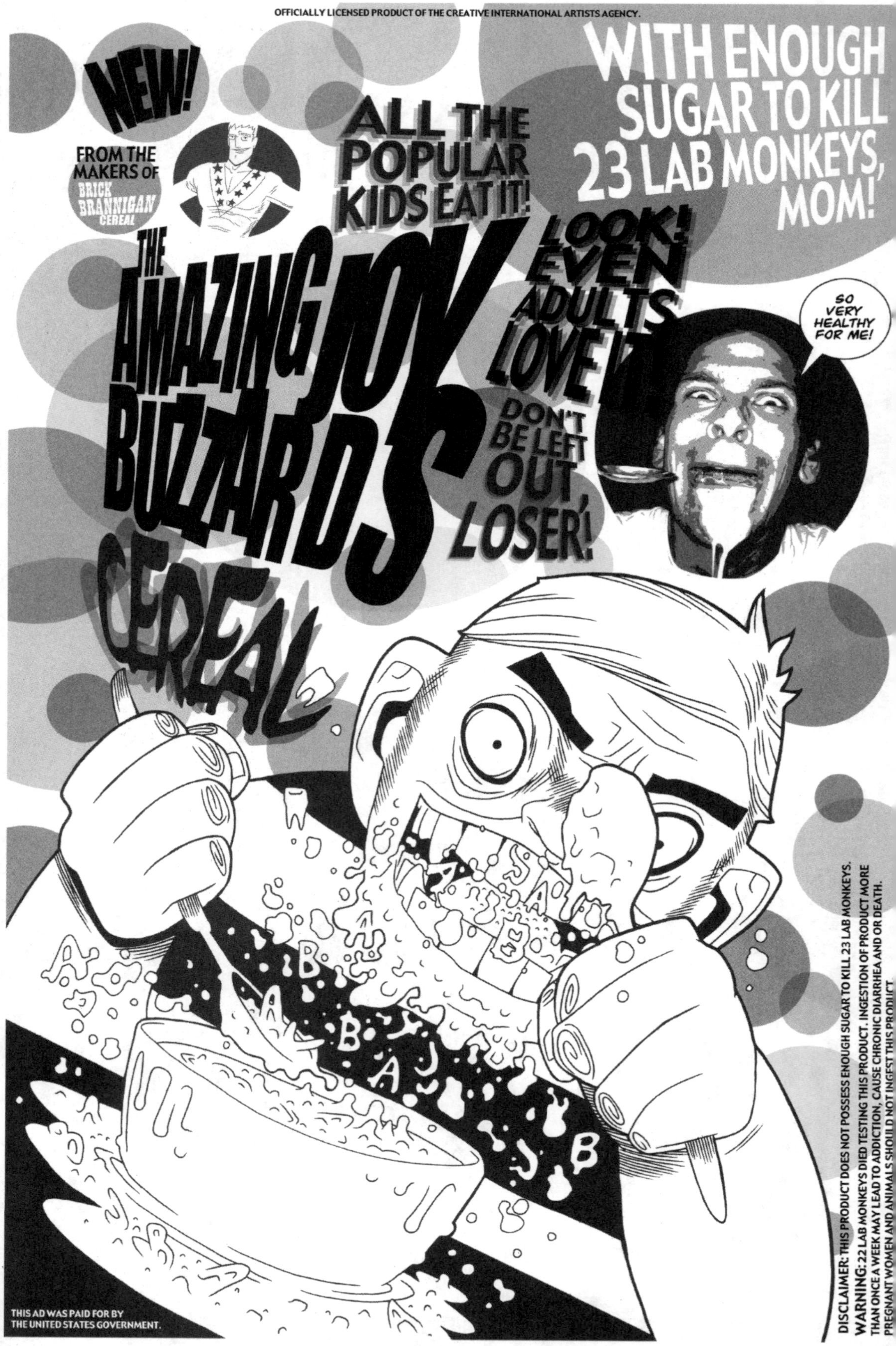

OFFICIALLY LICENSED PRODUCT OF THE CREATIVE INTERNATIONAL ARTISTS AGENCY.
NEW!
FROM THE MAKERS OF BRICK BRANNIGAN CEREAL
ALL THE POPULAR KIDS EAT IT!
WITH ENOUGH SUGAR TO KILL 23 LAB MONKEYS, MOM!
THE AMAZING JOY BUZZARDS CEREAL
LOOK! EVEN ADULTS LOVE IT!
SO VERY HEALTHY FOR ME!
DON'T BE LEFT OUT, LOSER!
THIS AD WAS PAID FOR BY THE UNITED STATES GOVERNMENT.
DISCLAIMER: THIS PRODUCT DOES NOT POSSESS ENOUGH SUGAR TO KILL 23 LAB MONKEYS.
WARNING: 22 LAB MONKEYS DIED TESTING THIS PRODUCT. INGESTION OF PRODUCT MORE THAN ONCE A WEEK MAY LEAD TO ADDICTION, CAUSE CHRONIC DIARRHEA AND OR DEATH. PREGNANT WOMEN AND ANIMALS SHOULD NOT INGEST THIS PRODUCT.

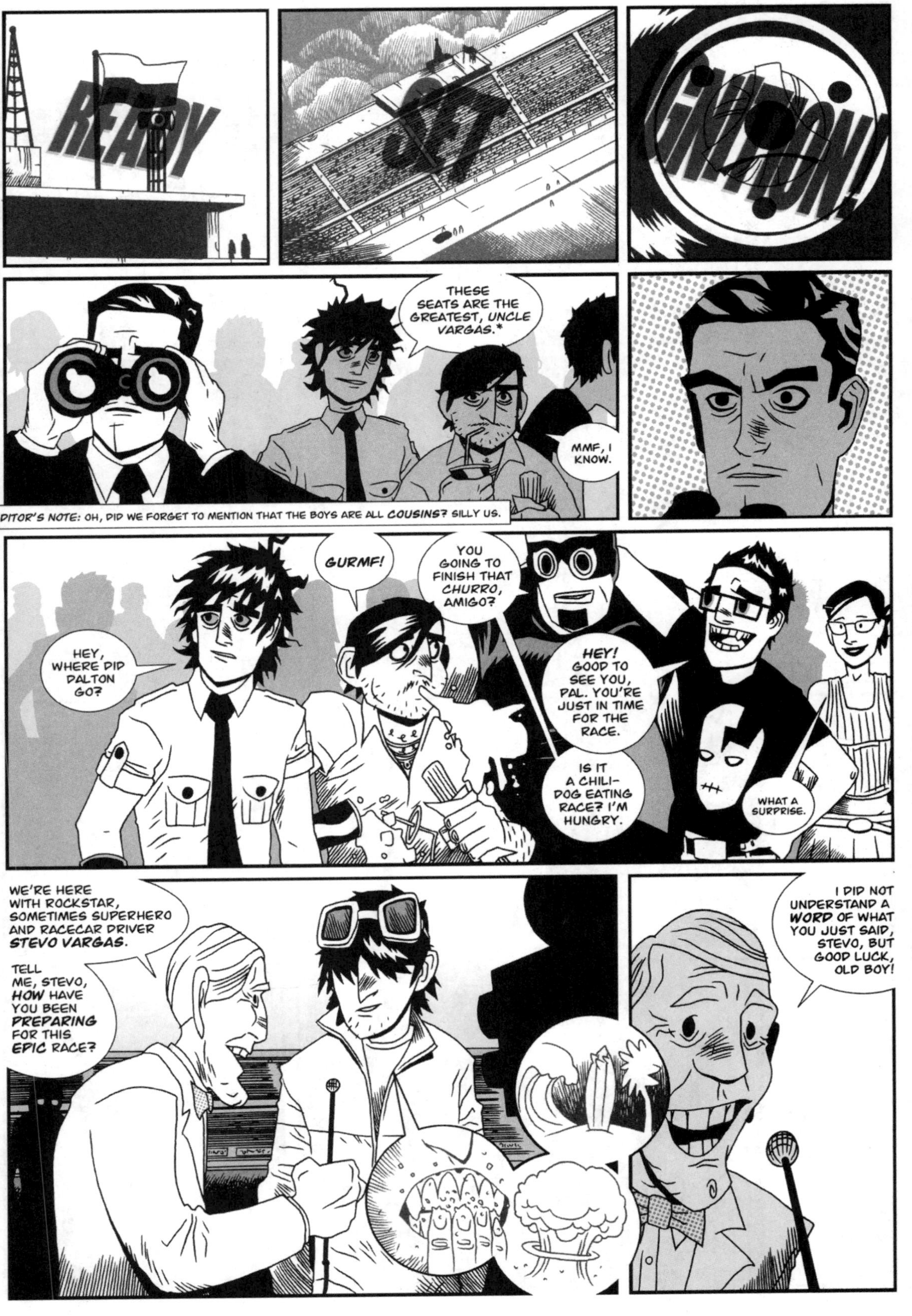
READY
SET
IGNITION!
THESE SEATS ARE THE GREATEST, UNCLE VARGAS.*
MMF, I KNOW.
*EDITOR'S NOTE: OH, DID WE FORGET TO MENTION THAT THE BOYS ARE ALL COUSINS? SILLY US.
HEY, WHERE DID DALTON GO?
GURMF!
YOU GOING TO FINISH THAT CHURRO, AMIGO?
HEY! GOOD TO SEE YOU, PAL. YOU'RE JUST IN TIME FOR THE RACE.
IS IT A CHILI-DOG EATING RACE? I'M HUNGRY.
WHAT A SURPRISE.
WE'RE HERE WITH ROCKSTAR, SOMETIMES SUPERHERO AND RACECAR DRIVER STEVO VARGAS.
TELL ME, STEVO, HOW HAVE YOU BEEN PREPARING FOR THIS EPIC RACE?
I DID NOT UNDERSTAND A WORD OF WHAT YOU JUST SAID, STEVO, BUT GOOD LUCK, OLD BOY!

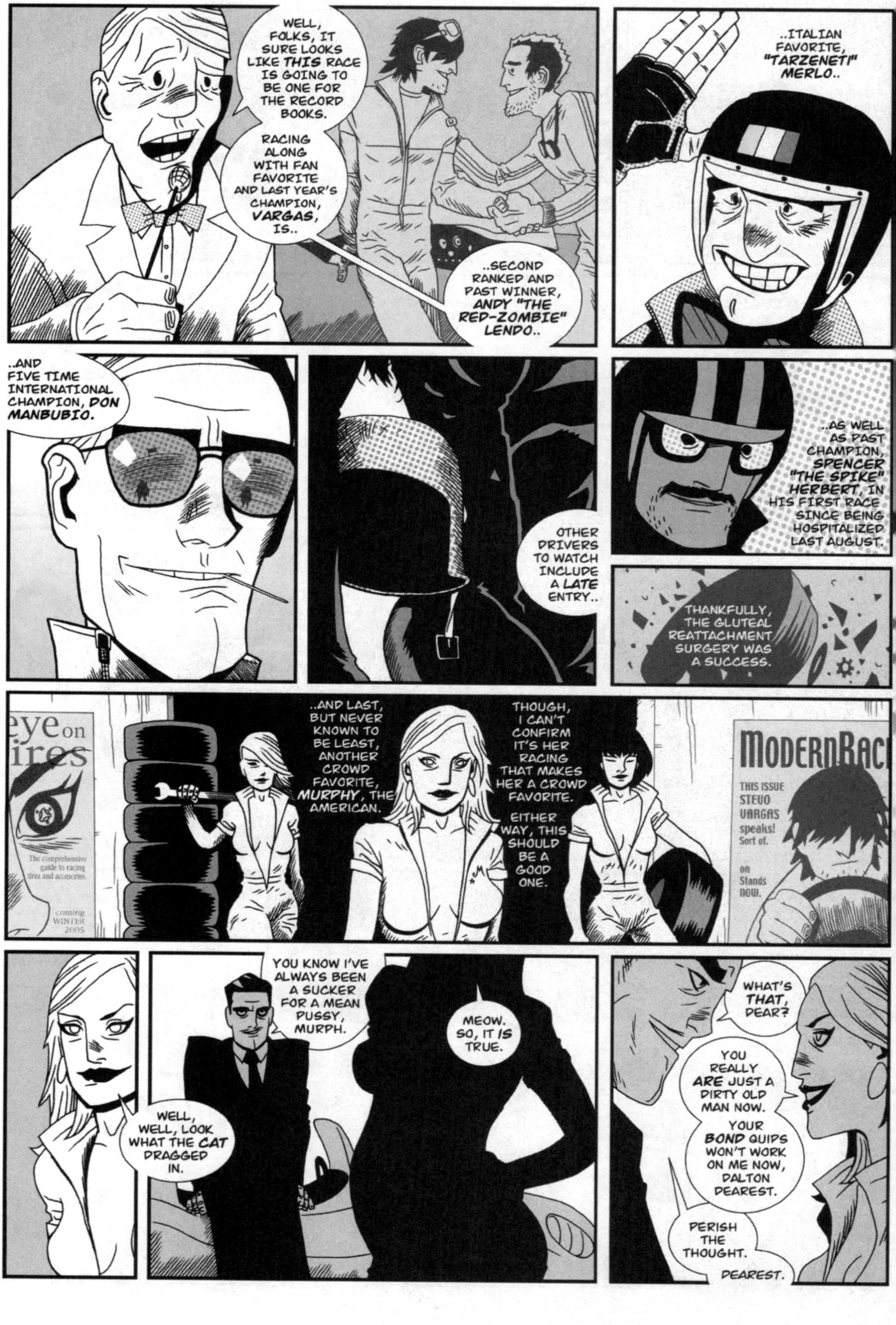
WELL, FOLKS, IT SURE LOOKS LIKE THIS RACE IS GOING TO BE ONE FOR THE RECORD BOOKS.
RACING ALONG WITH FAN FAVORITE AND LAST YEAR'S CHAMPION, VARGAS, IS..
..SECOND RANKED AND PAST WINNER, ANDY "THE RED-ZOMBIE" LENDO..
..ITALIAN FAVORITE, "TARZENETI" MERLO..
..AND FIVE TIME INTERNATIONAL CHAMPION, DON MANBUBIO.
OTHER DRIVERS TO WATCH INCLUDE A LATE ENTRY..
..AS WELL AS PAST CHAMPION, SPENCER "THE SPIKE" HERBERT, IN HIS FIRST RACE SINCE BEING HOSPITALIZED LAST AUGUST.
THANKFULLY, THE GLUTEAL REATTACHMENT SURGERY WAS A SUCCESS.
eye on tires
The comprehensive guide to racing tires and accesories.
coming WINTER 2005
..AND LAST, BUT NEVER KNOWN TO BE LEAST, ANOTHER CROWD FAVORITE, MURPHY, THE AMERICAN.
THOUGH, I CAN'T CONFIRM IT'S HER RACING THAT MAKES HER A CROWD FAVORITE.
EITHER WAY, THIS SHOULD BE A GOOD ONE.
MODERNRAC
THIS ISSUE STEVO VARGAS speaks! Sort of.
on Stands now.
WELL, WELL, LOOK WHAT THE CAT DRAGGED IN.
YOU KNOW I'VE ALWAYS BEEN A SUCKER FOR A MEAN PUSSY, MURPH.
MEOW. SO, IT IS TRUE.
WHAT'S THAT, DEAR?
YOU REALLY ARE JUST A DIRTY OLD MAN NOW.
YOUR BOND QUIPS WON'T WORK ON ME NOW, DALTON DEAREST.
PERISH THE THOUGHT.
DEAREST.

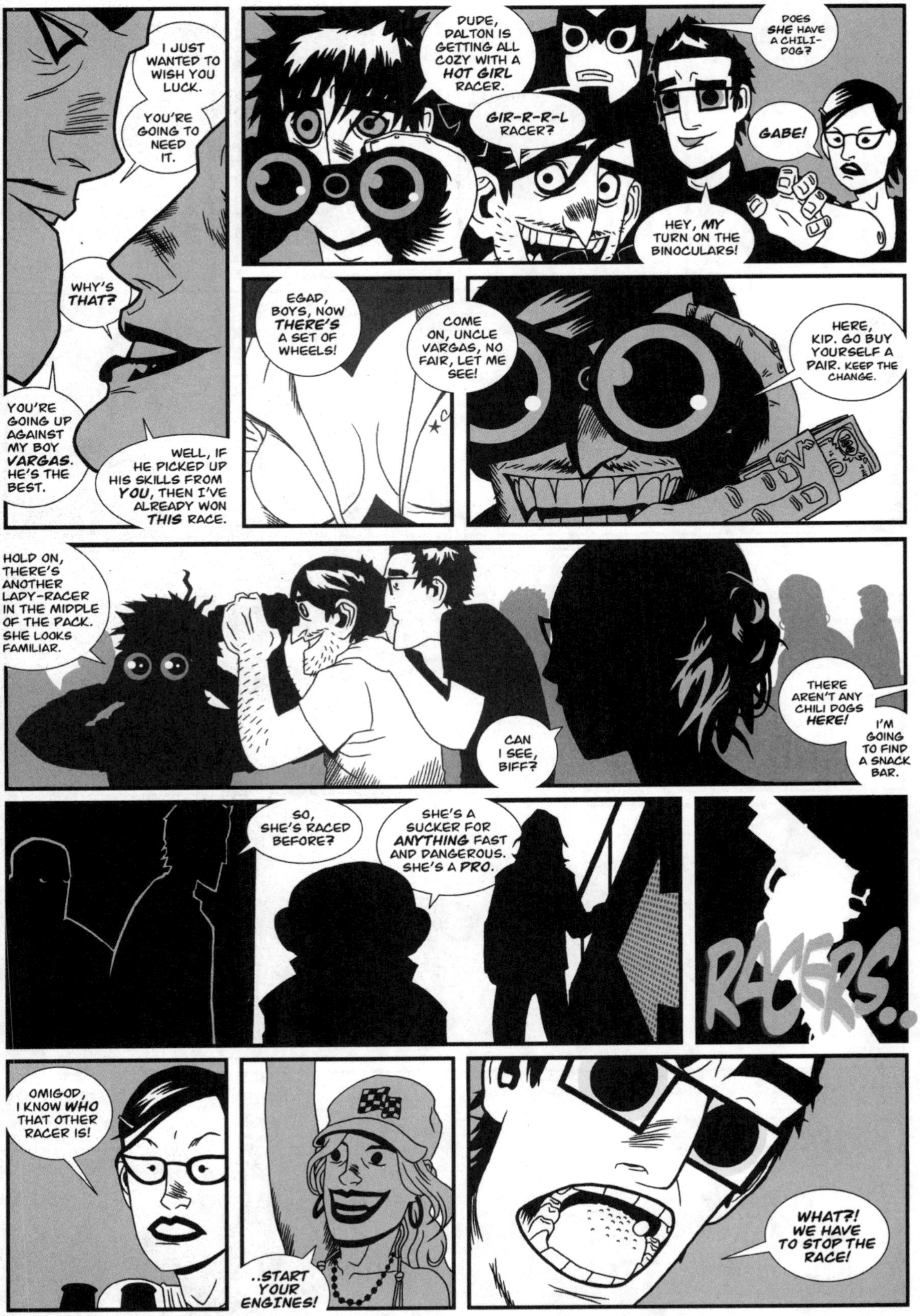
I JUST WANTED TO WISH YOU LUCK.
YOU'RE GOING TO NEED IT.
WHY'S THAT?
YOU'RE GOING UP AGAINST MY BOY VARGAS. HE'S THE BEST.
WELL, IF HE PICKED UP HIS SKILLS FROM YOU, THEN I'VE ALREADY WON THIS RACE.
DUDE, DALTON IS GETTING ALL COZY WITH A HOT GIRL RACER.
GIR-R-R-L RACER?
DOES SHE HAVE A CHILI-DOG?
GABE!
HEY, MY TURN ON THE BINOCULARS!
EGAD, BOYS, NOW THERE'S A SET OF WHEELS!
COME ON, UNCLE VARGAS, NO FAIR, LET ME SEE!
HERE, KID. GO BUY YOURSELF A PAIR. KEEP THE CHANGE.
HOLD ON, THERE'S ANOTHER LADY-RACER IN THE MIDDLE OF THE PACK. SHE LOOKS FAMILIAR.
CAN I SEE, BIFF?
THERE AREN'T ANY CHILI DOGS HERE!
I'M GOING TO FIND A SNACK BAR.
SO, SHE'S RACED BEFORE?
SHE'S A SUCKER FOR ANYTHING FAST AND DANGEROUS. SHE'S A PRO.
RACERS..
OMIGOD, I KNOW WHO THAT OTHER RACER IS!
..START YOUR ENGINES!
WHAT?! WE HAVE TO STOP THE RACE!

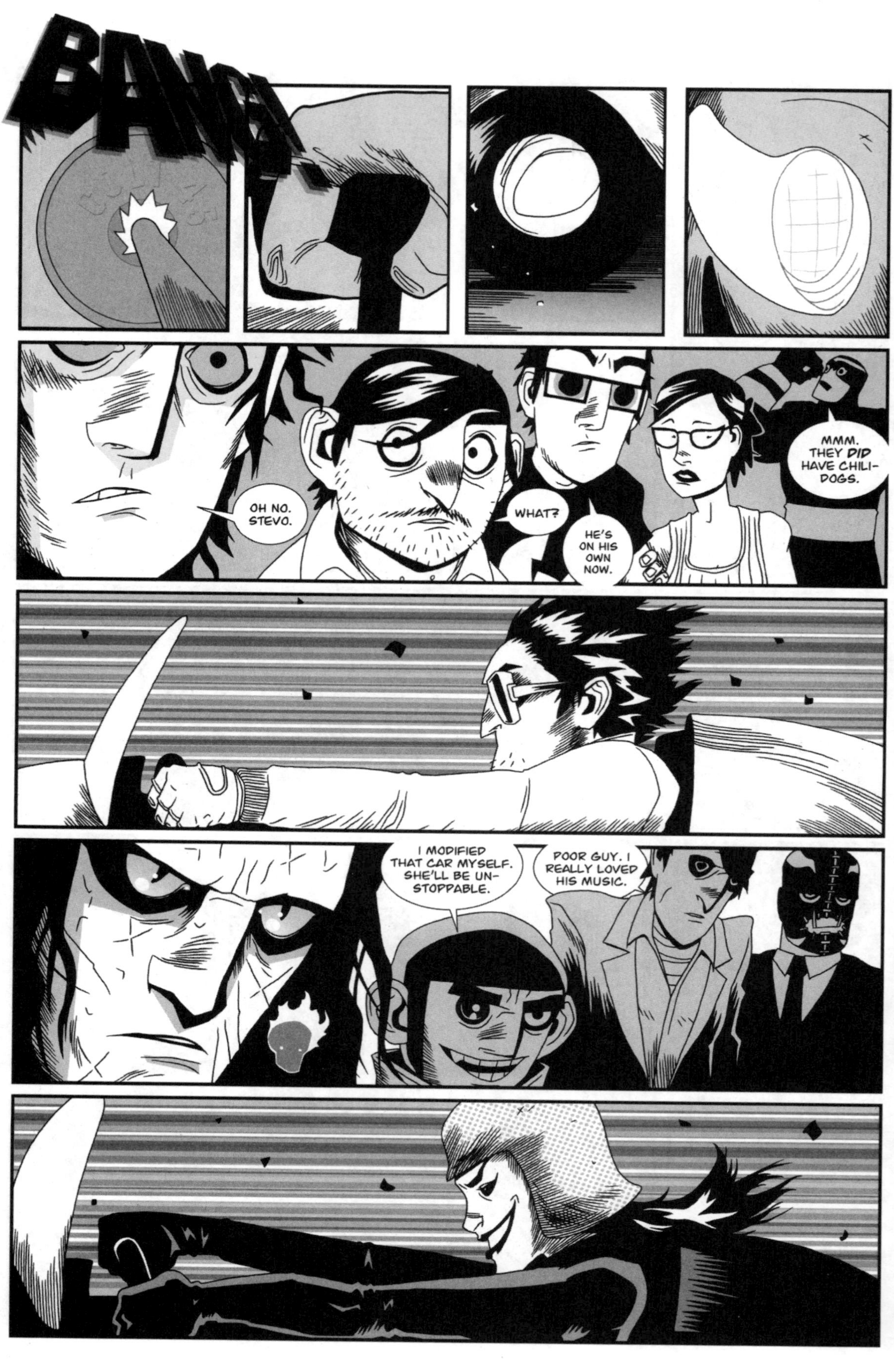
BANG!
OH NO. STEVO.
WHAT?
HE'S ON HIS OWN NOW.
MMM. THEY DID HAVE CHILI-DOGS.
I MODIFIED THAT CAR MYSELF. SHE'LL BE UN-STOPPABLE.
POOR GUY. I REALLY LOVED HIS MUSIC.

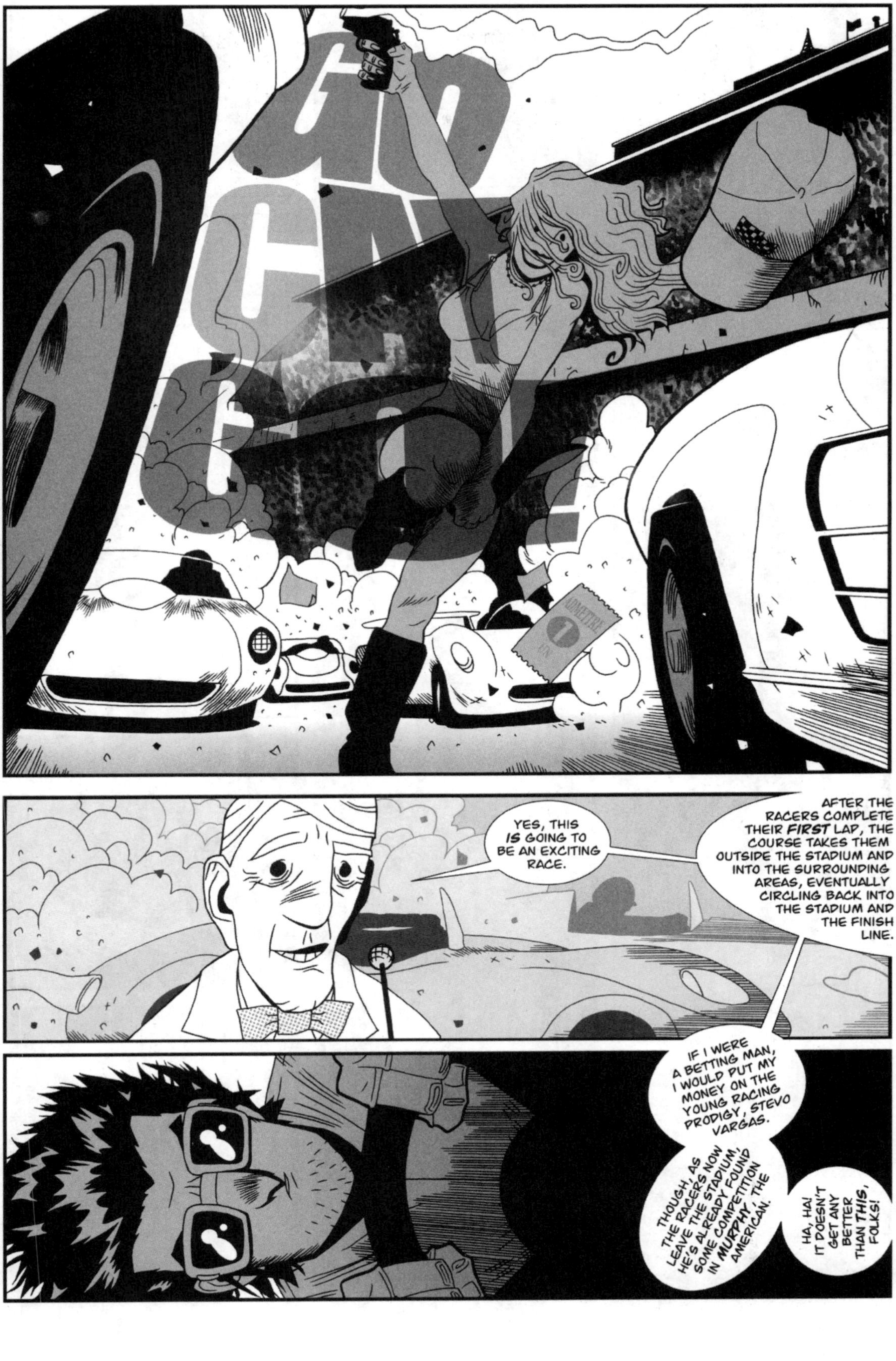

YES, THIS IS GOING TO BE AN EXCITING RACE.
AFTER THE RACERS COMPLETE THEIR FIRST LAP, THE COURSE TAKES THEM OUTSIDE THE STADIUM AND INTO THE SURROUNDING AREAS, EVENTUALLY CIRCLING BACK INTO THE STADIUM AND THE FINISH LINE.
IF I WERE A BETTING MAN, I WOULD PUT MY MONEY ON THE YOUNG RACING PRODIGY, STEVO VARGAS.
THOUGH, AS THE RACERS NOW LEAVE THE STADIUM, HE'S ALREADY FOUND SOME COMPETITION IN MURPHY, THE AMERICAN.
HA, HA! IT DOESN'T GET ANY BETTER THAN THIS, FOLKS!

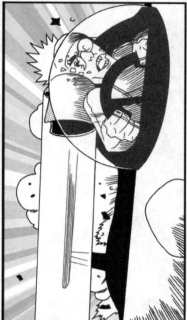

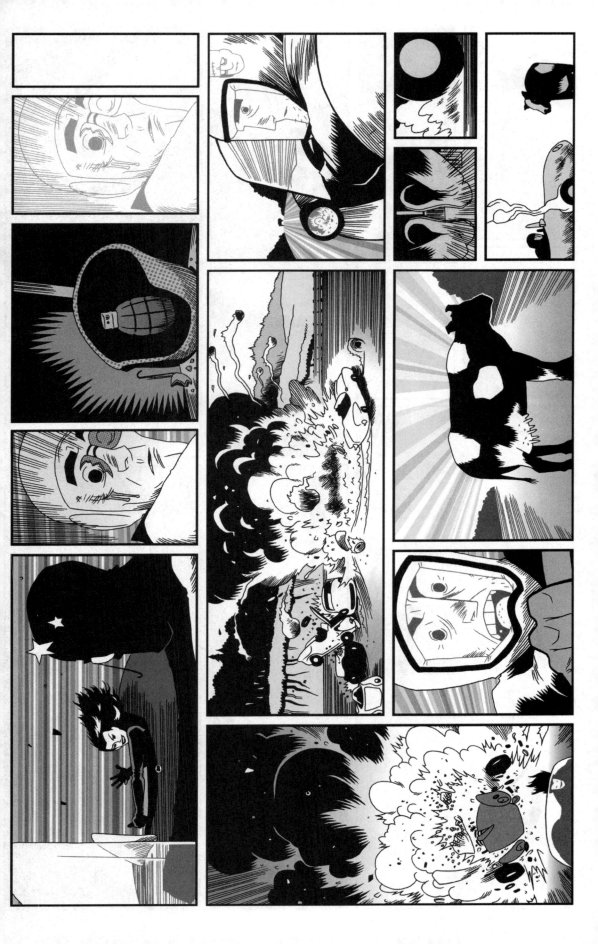

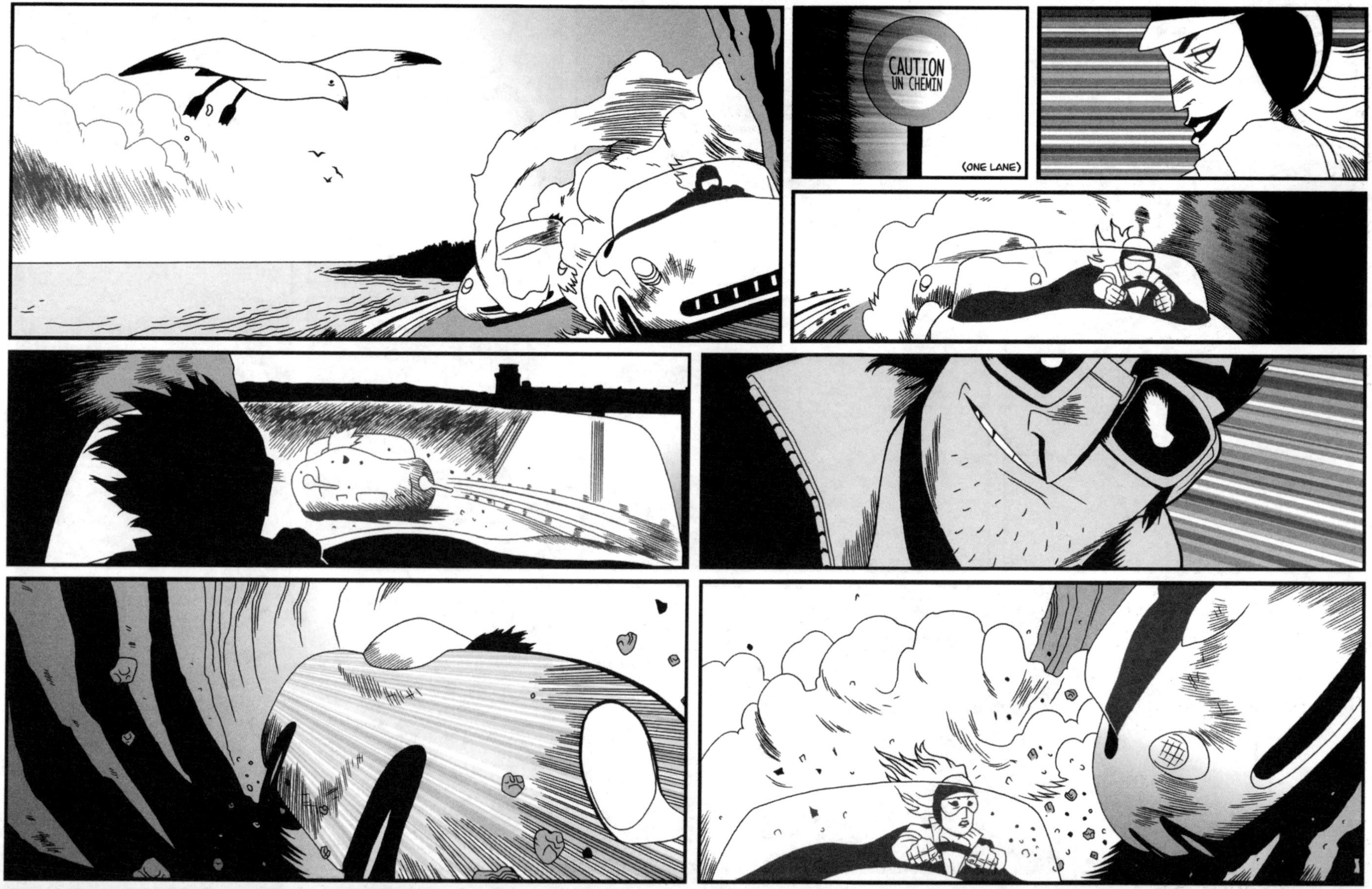
CAUTION
UN CHEMIN
(ONE LANE)

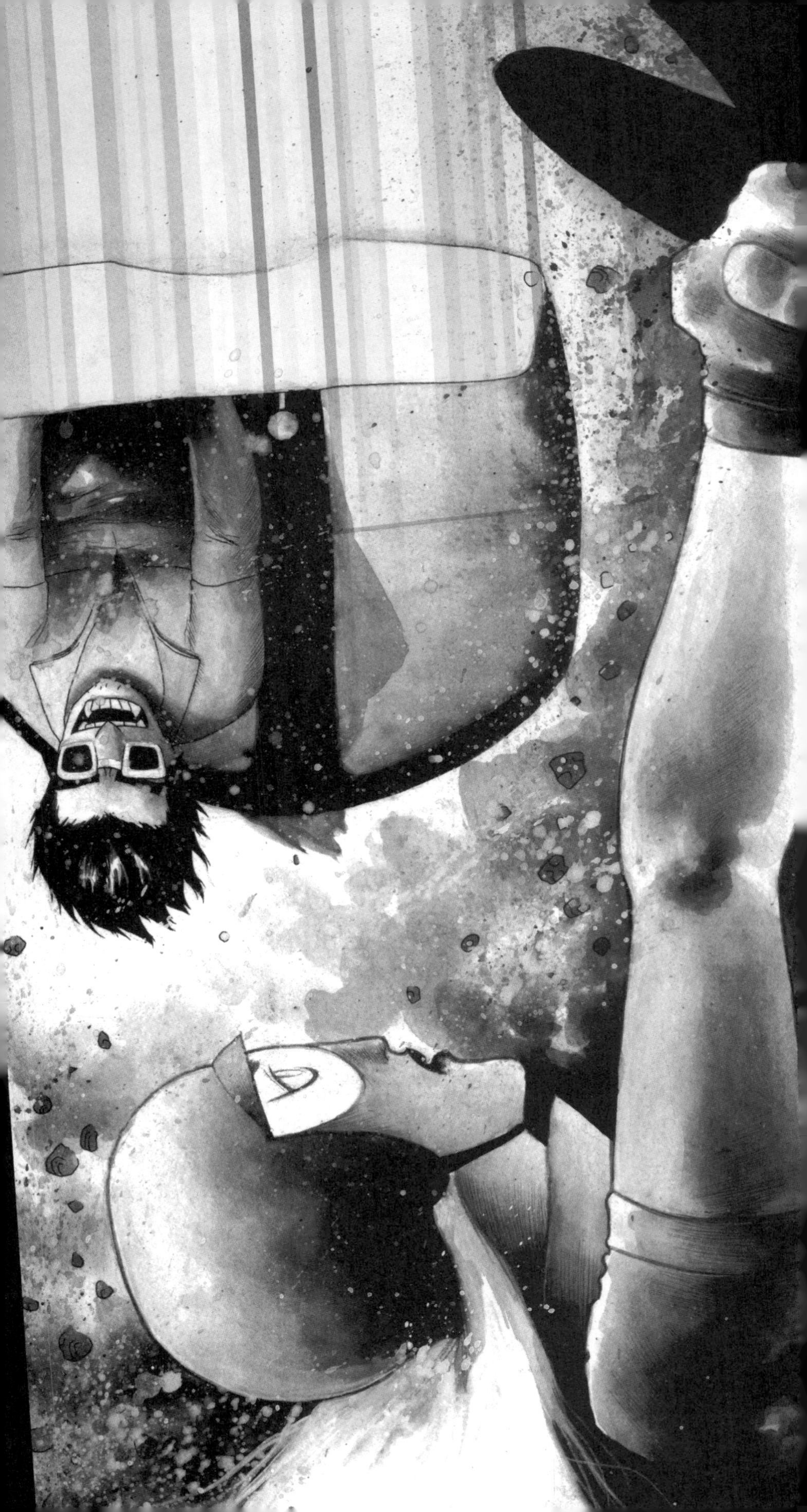

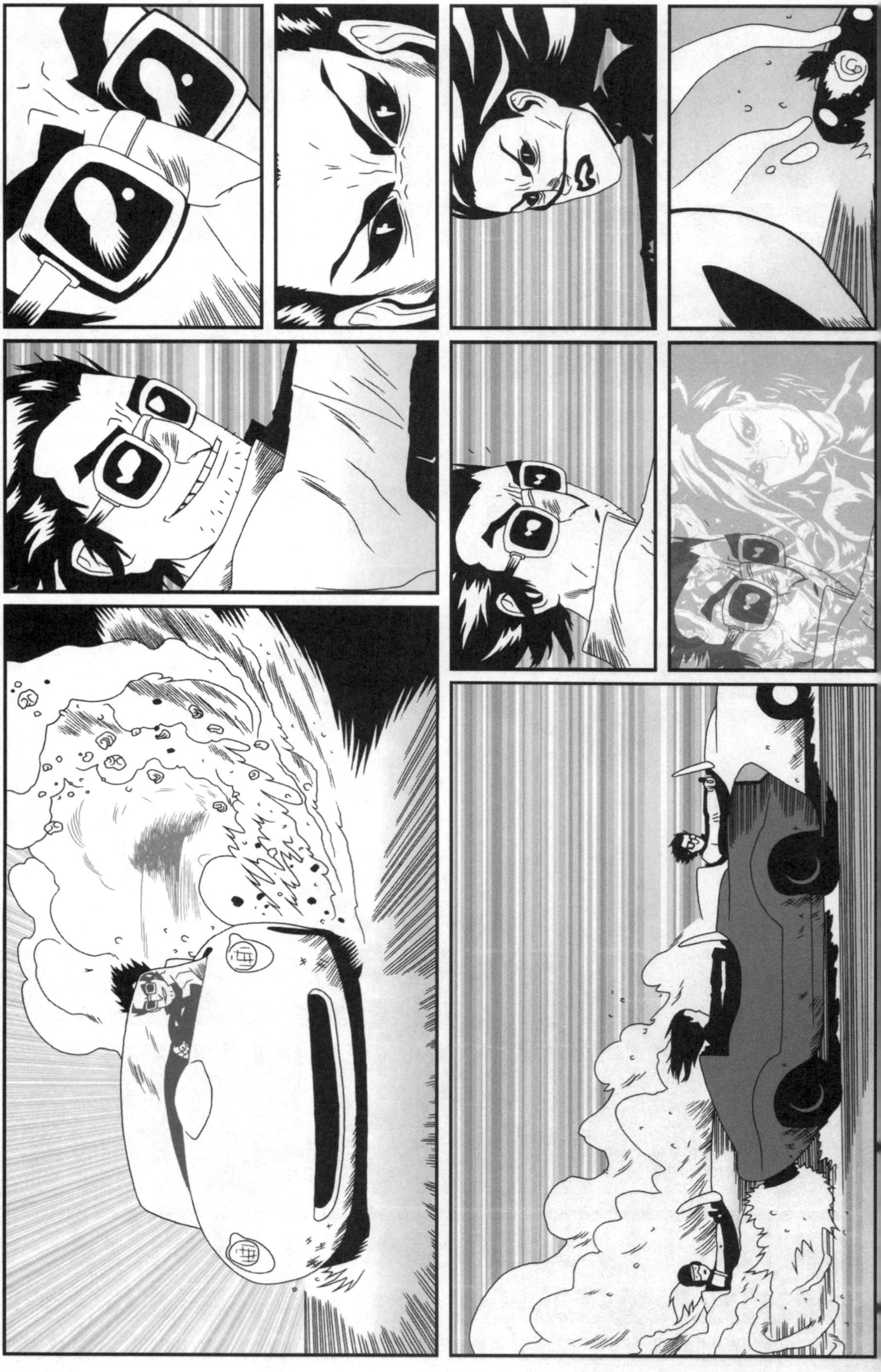

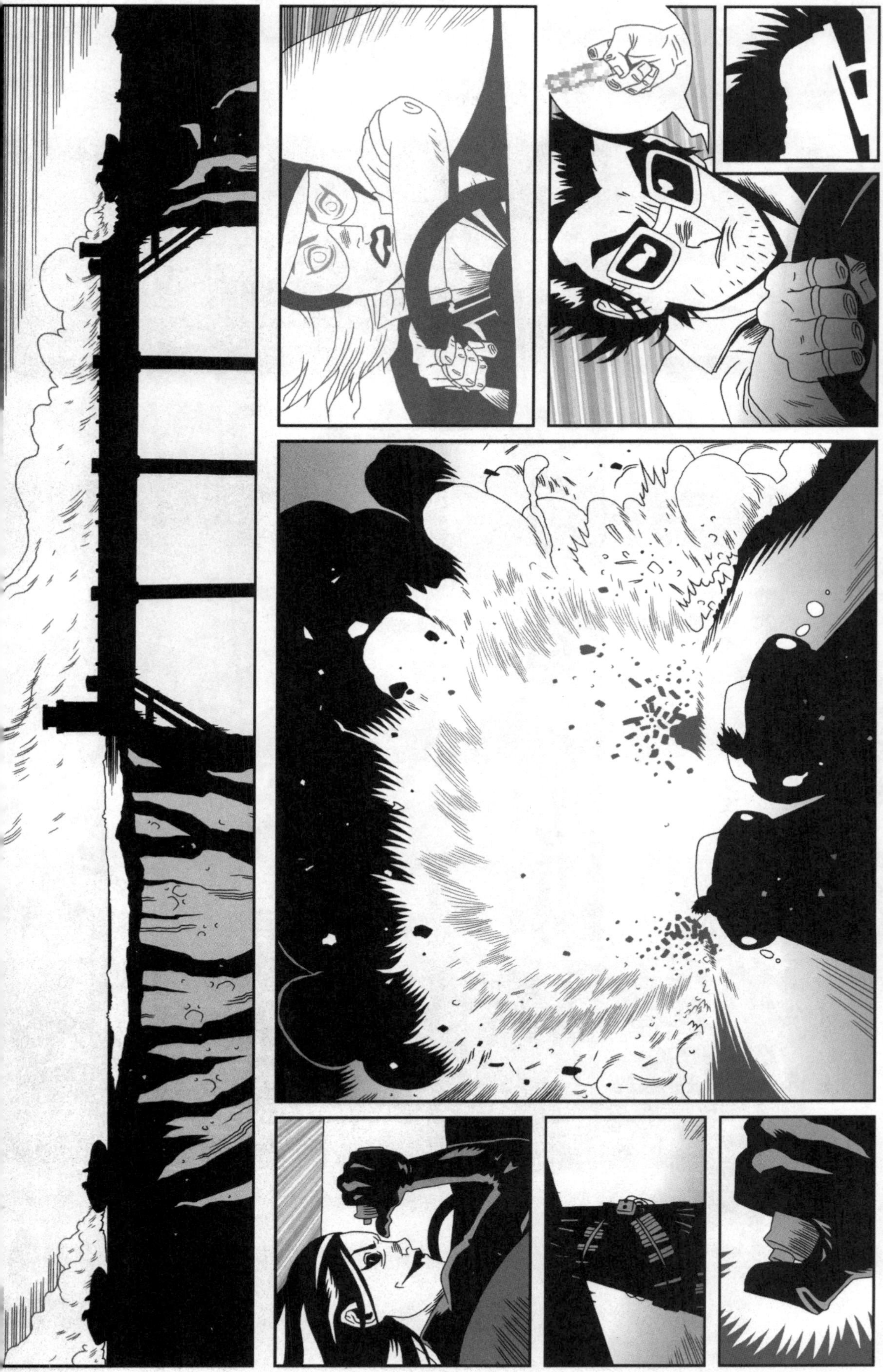

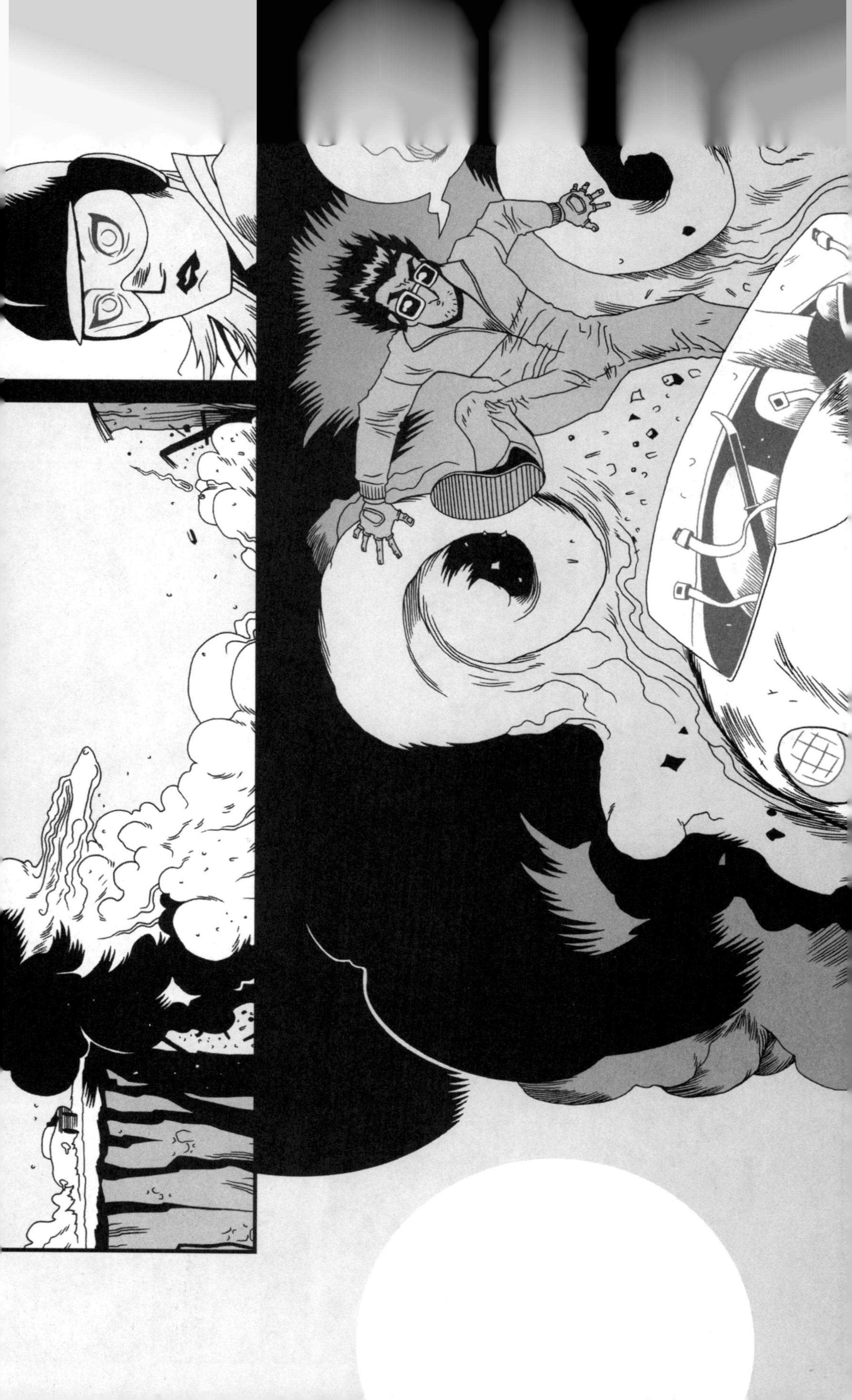

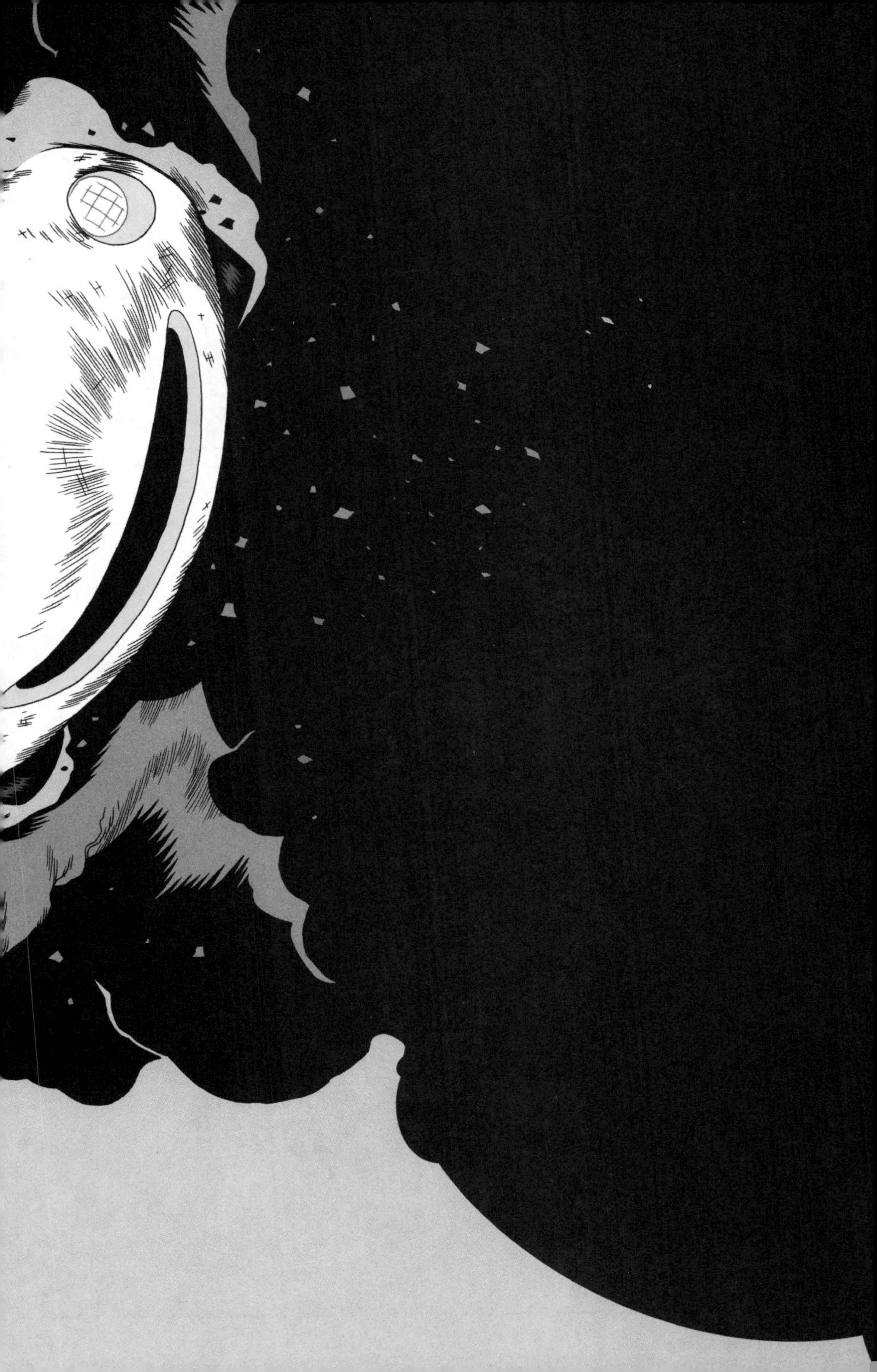

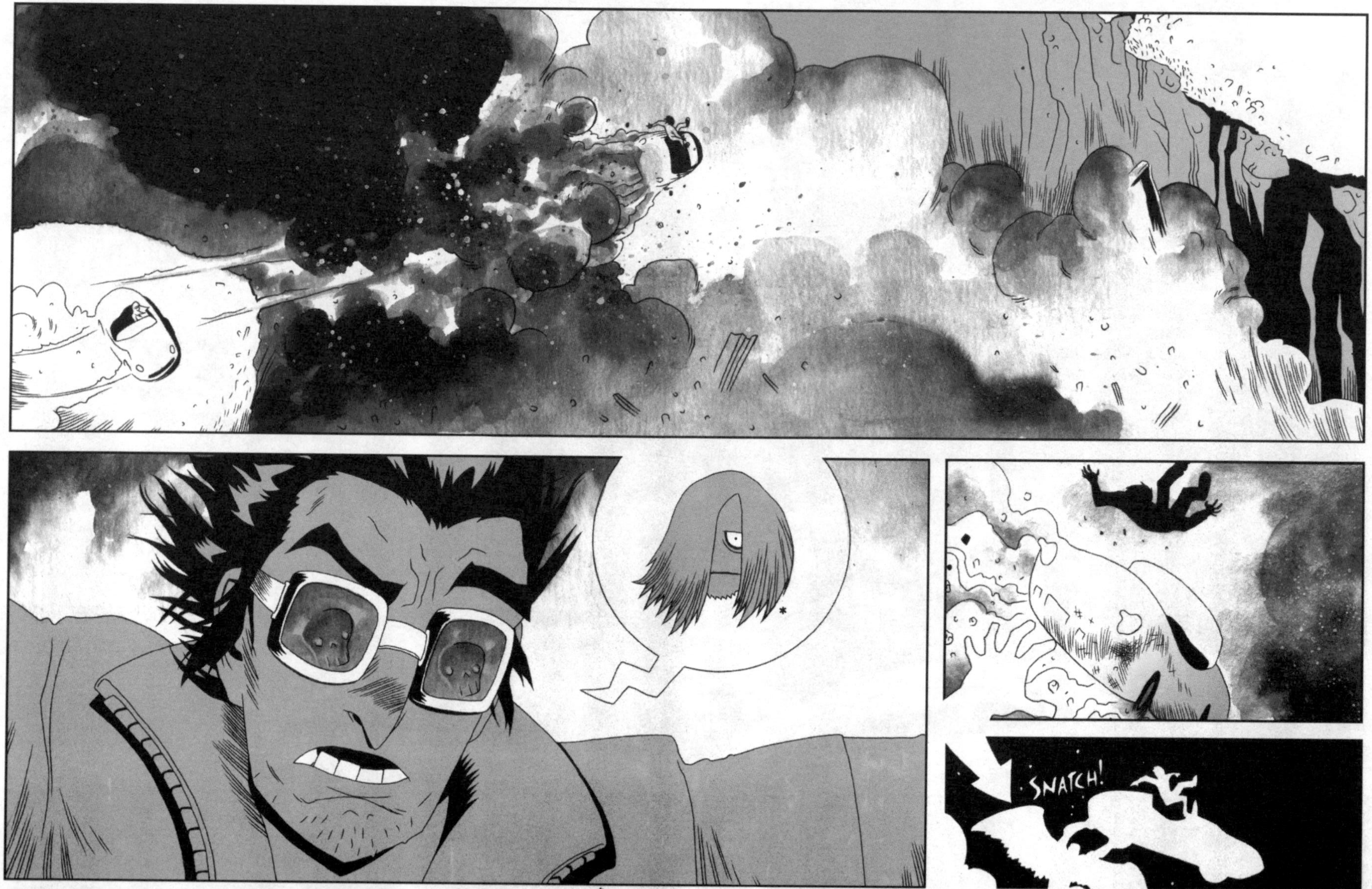
*
SNATCH!

*EDITOR: DON'T ASK US WHAT IT MEANS. WE JUST WORK HERE

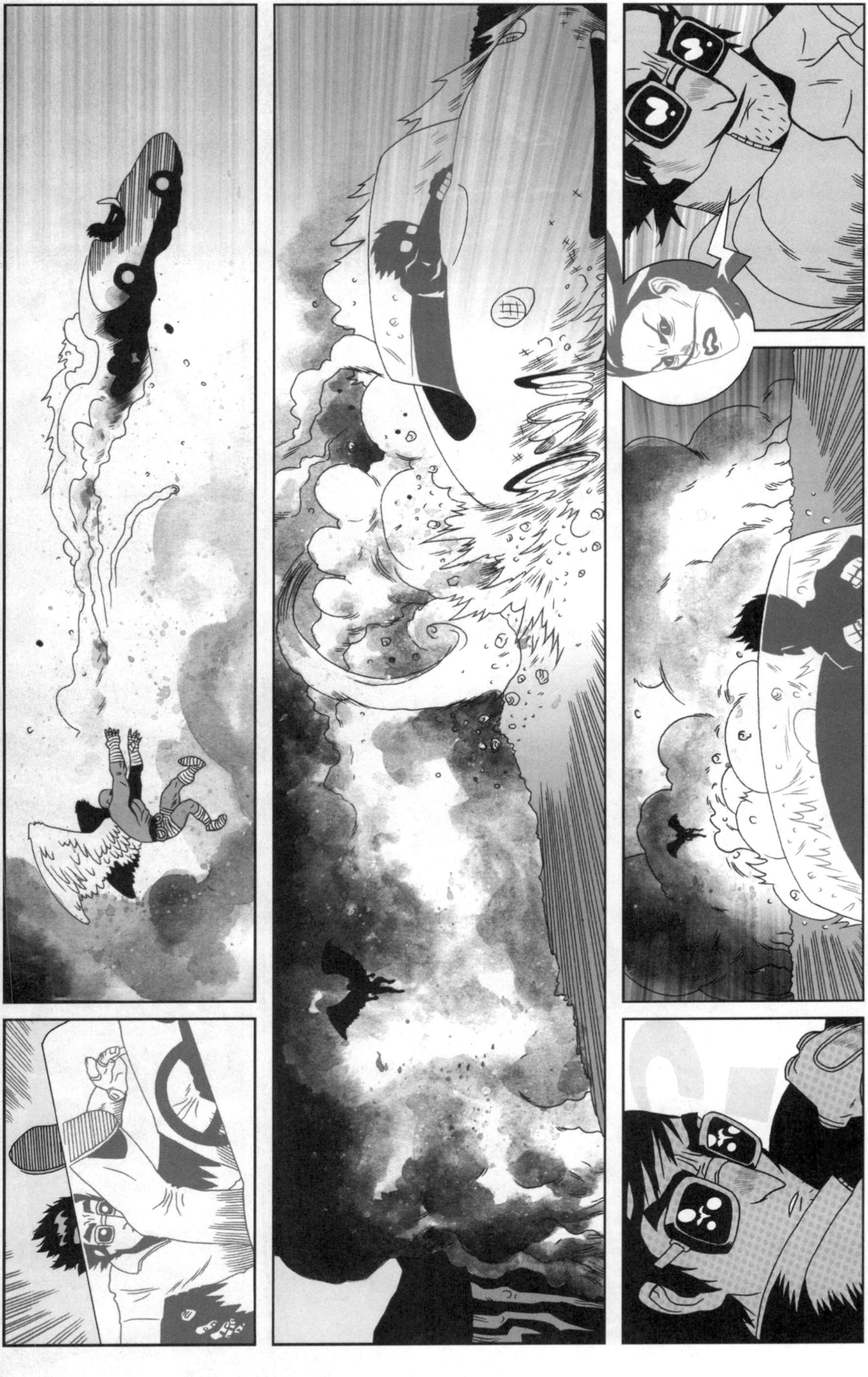

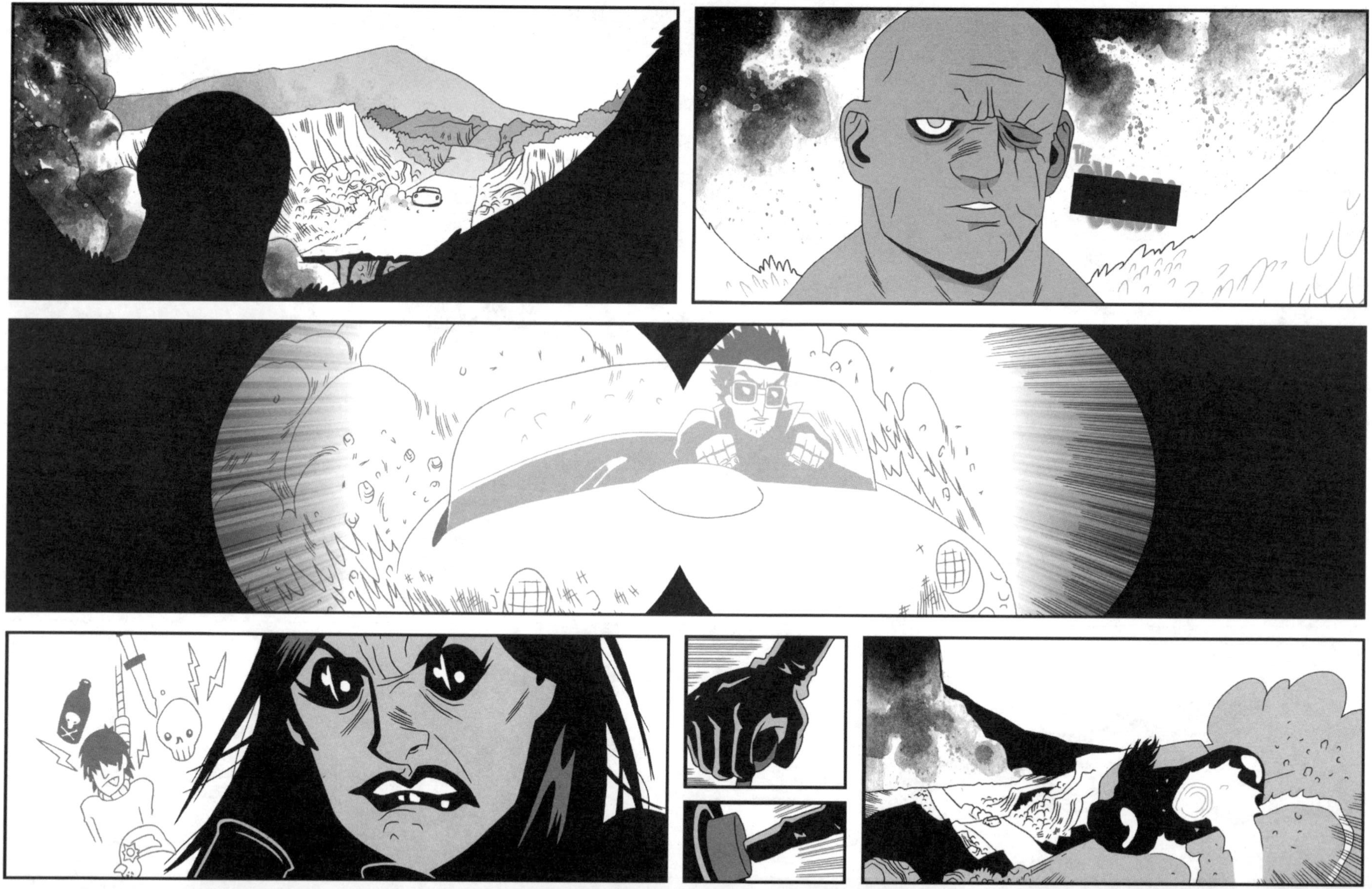
THE [redacted]

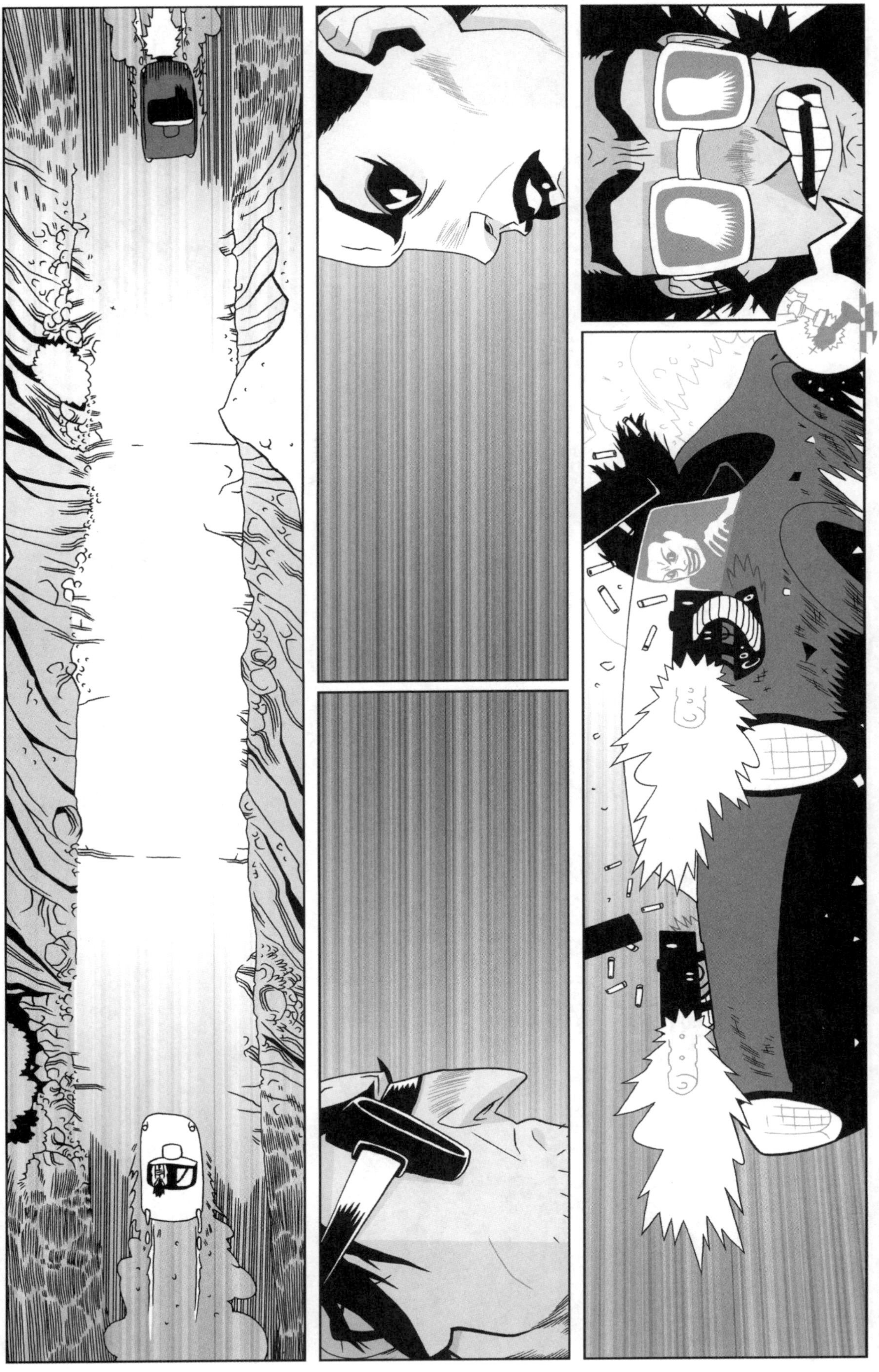

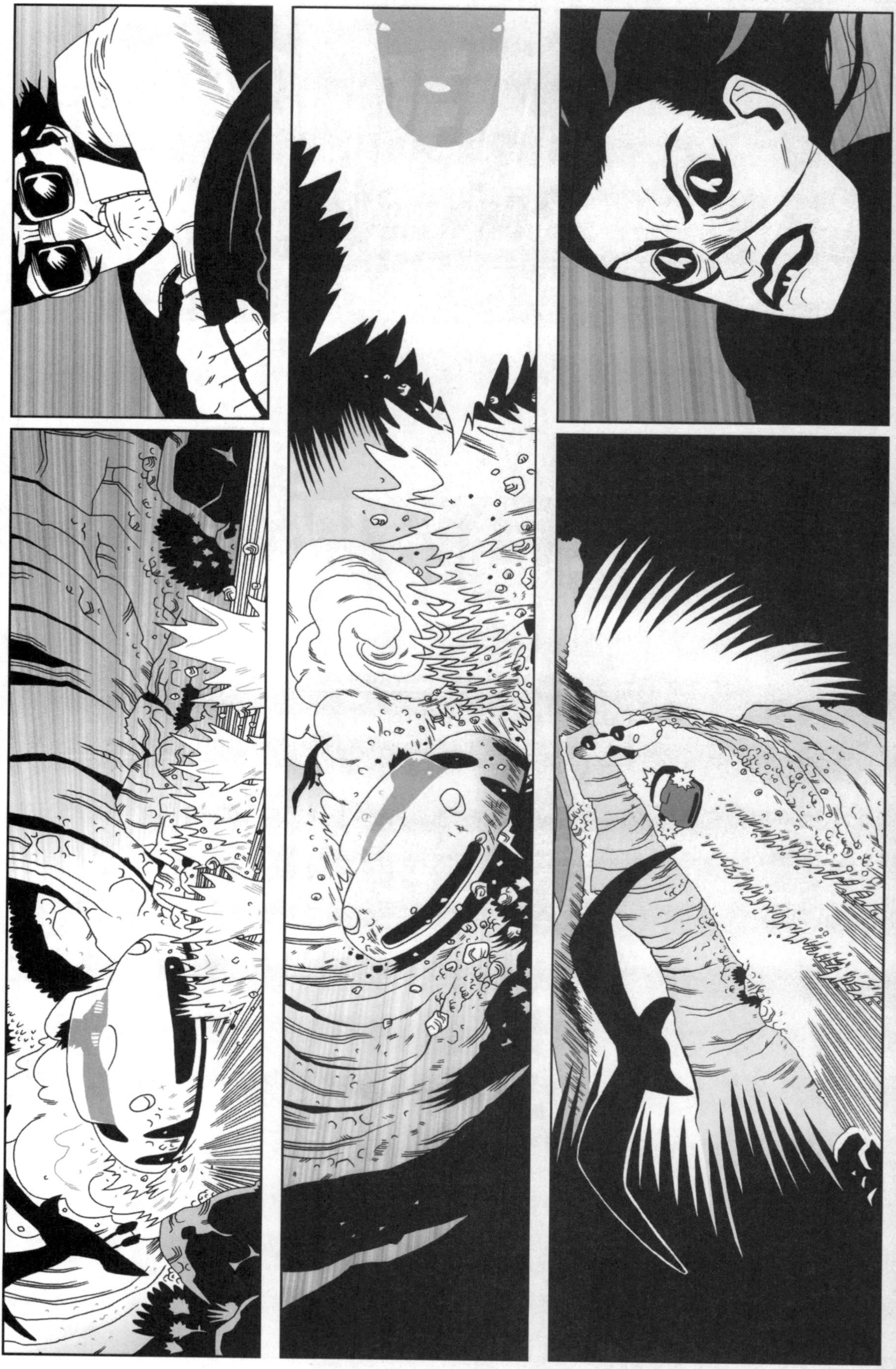

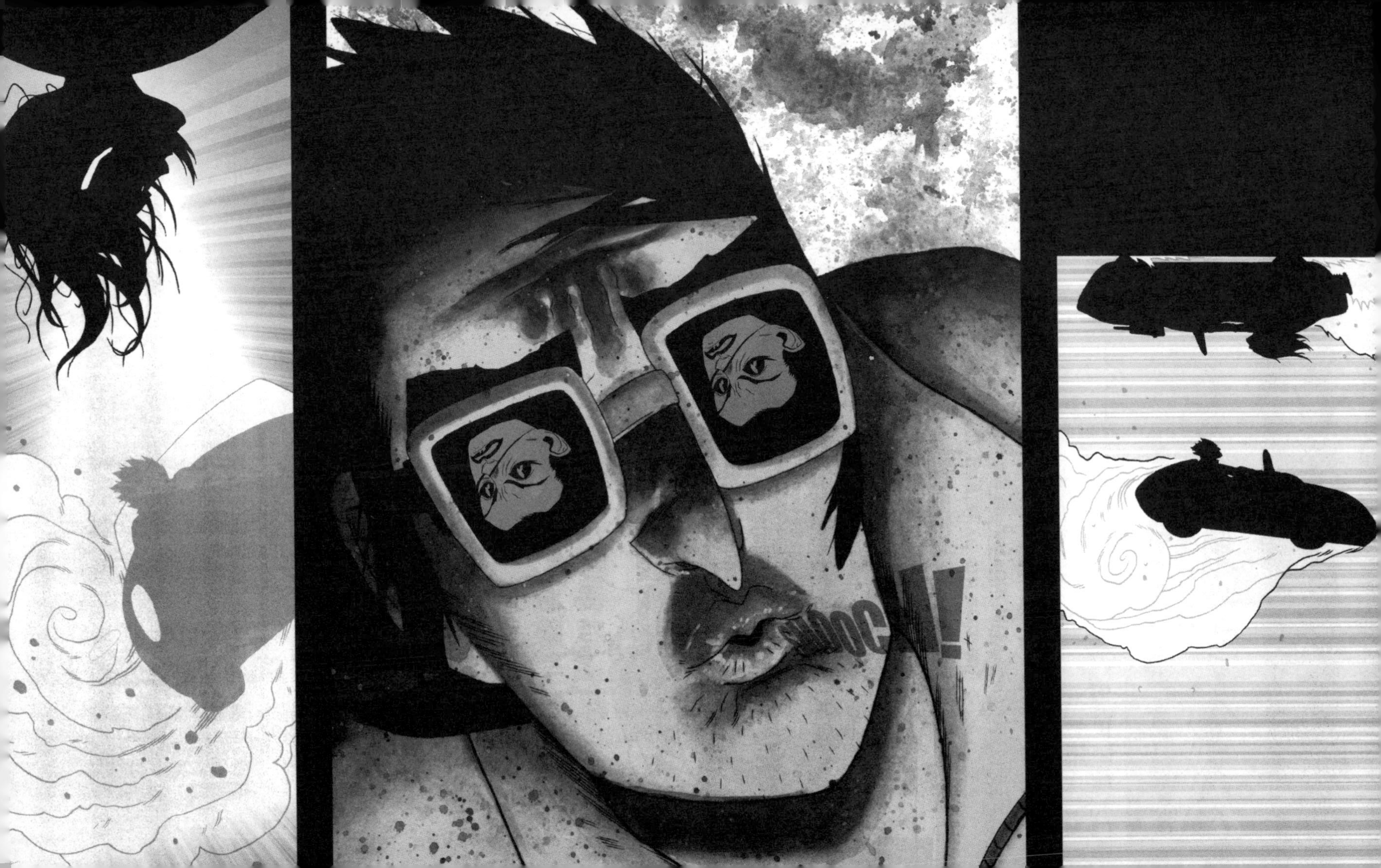

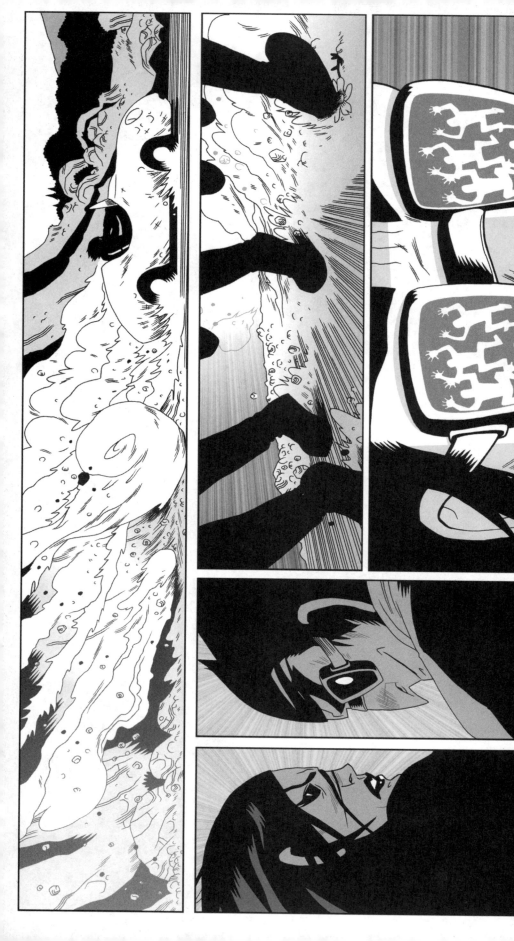

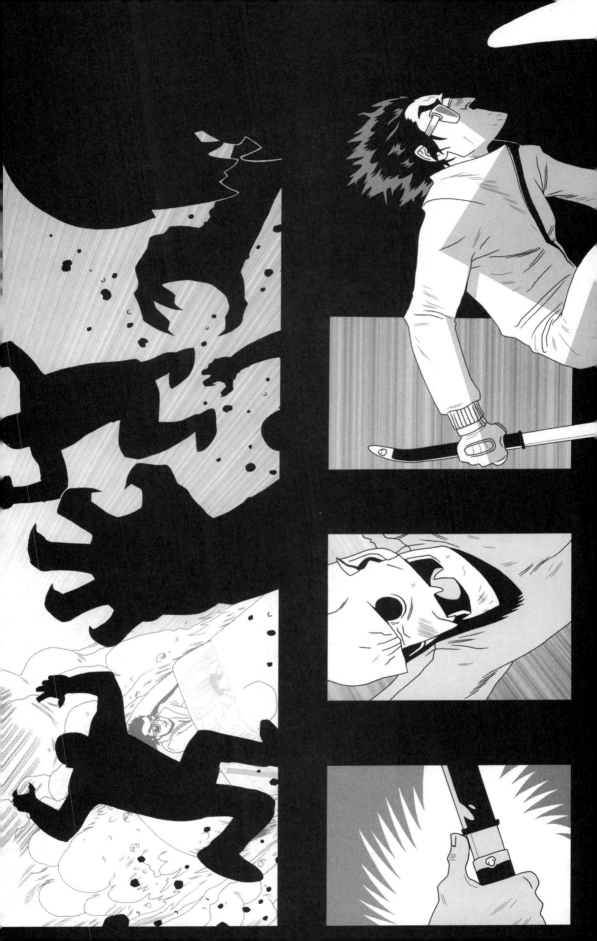

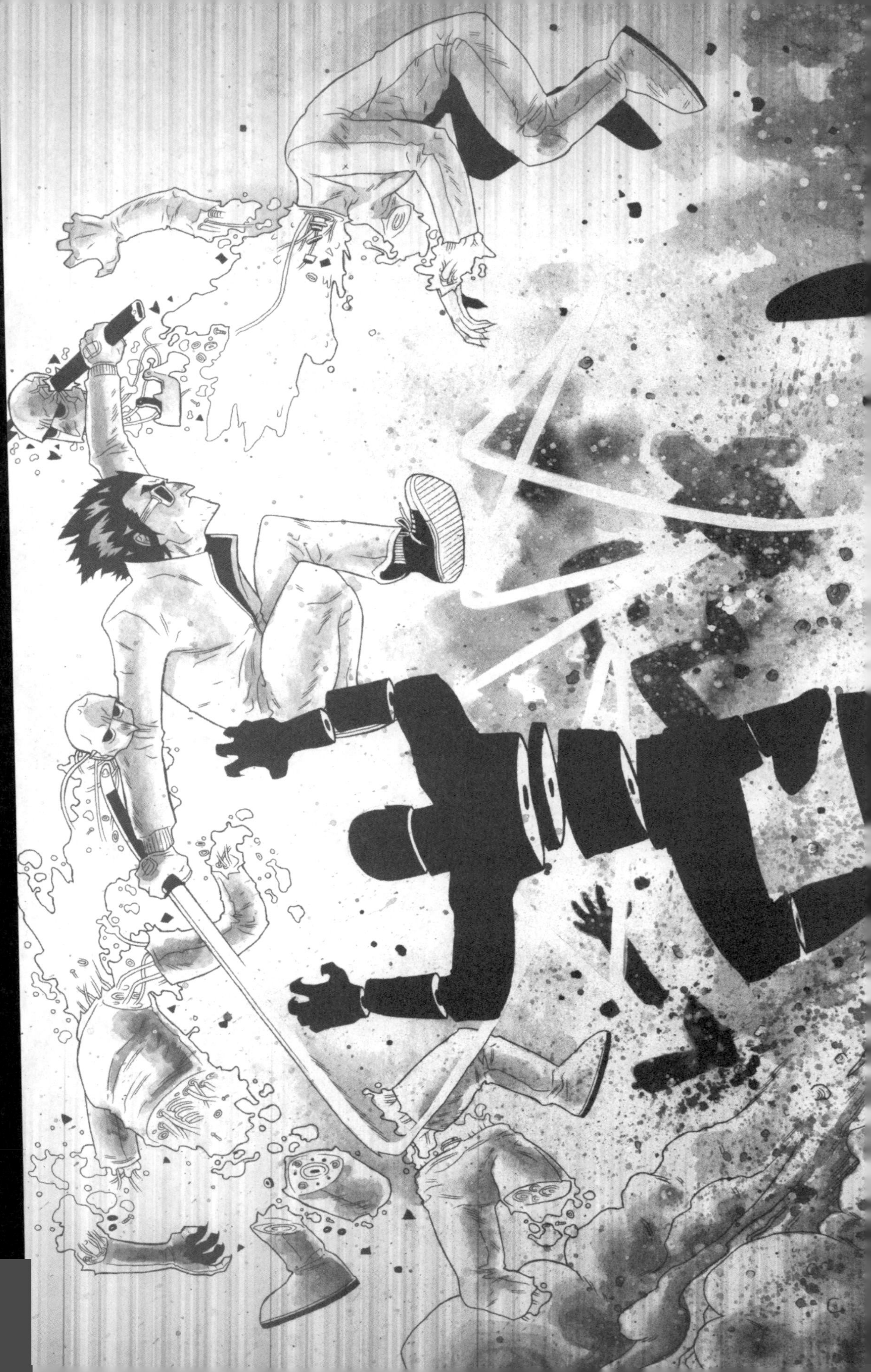

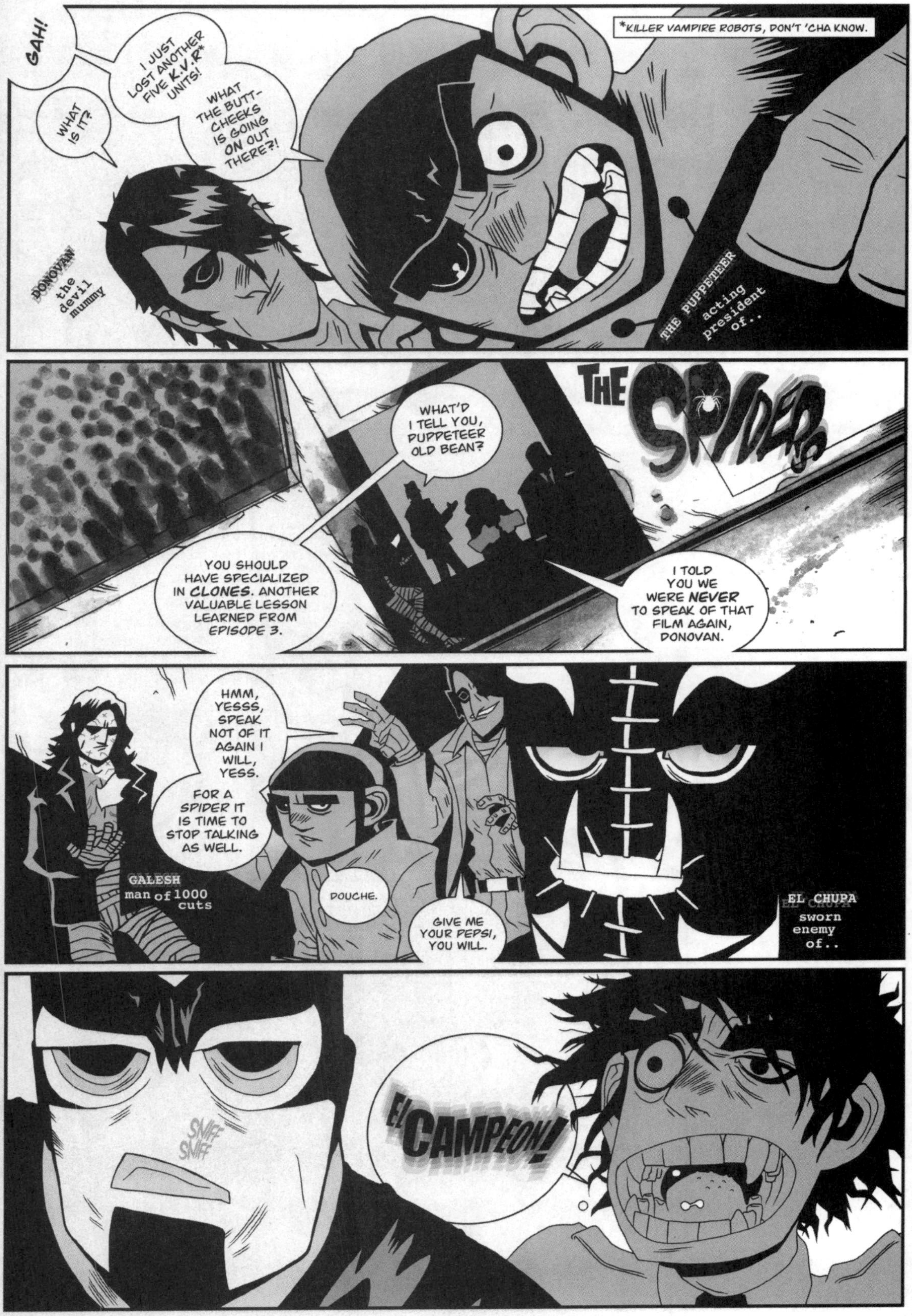
*KILLER VAMPIRE ROBOTS, DON'T 'CHA KNOW.
GAH!
I JUST LOST ANOTHER FIVE K.V.R* UNITS!
WHAT IS IT?
WHAT THE BUTT-CHEEKS IS GOING ON OUT THERE?!
DONOVAN the devil mummy
THE PUPPETEER acting president of..
THE SPIDERS
WHAT'D I TELL YOU, PUPPETEER OLD BEAN?
YOU SHOULD HAVE SPECIALIZED IN CLONES. ANOTHER VALUABLE LESSON LEARNED FROM EPISODE 3.
I TOLD YOU WE WERE NEVER TO SPEAK OF THAT FILM AGAIN, DONOVAN.
HMM, YESSS, SPEAK NOT OF IT AGAIN I WILL, YESS.
FOR A SPIDER IT IS TIME TO STOP TALKING AS WELL.
DOUCHE.
GIVE ME YOUR PEPSI, YOU WILL.
GALESH man of 1000 cuts
EL CHUPA sworn enemy of..
SNIFF SNIFF
El CAMPEON!

SO, YOU GOING TO FINISH THAT CHILI DOG?

HERE.

HMMF. I DON'T KNOW WHY EVERYONE IS SO WORRIED. I MEAN SURE, I LET A LITTLE DOODIE SLIP *TOO* WHEN I REALIZED STEVO WAS IN DANGER, BUT THEN I REALIZED SOMETHING.

WHAT?

IT'S *STEVO* WE'RE TALKING ABOUT! IN A *RACECAR* NO LESS, AND YOU *KNOW* HE TAKES HIS SWORD WITH HIM EVERY-WHERE SINCE *MARU*.

SO TURN THOSE FROWNS UPSIDE DOWN.

SOME-THING GOT MY BOYS DOWN?

WHO IS IT? I'LL KILL 'EM. HA, HA.

GEEZ!

DON'T *DO* THAT!

DO WHAT? I WAS KIDDING.

HE'LL BE FINE. MY BOY WILL BE FINE.

OF *COURSE* HE WILL, MR. VARGAS.

STEVO'S GOTTEN THROUGH WORSE THAN THIS, SIR.

HE'S PULLED OUR FAT OUT OF THE FIRE SO MANY TIMES IT'S NOT WORTH COUNTING.*

* BUT WE DID ANYWAY: 902

STILL, WHY DO YOU THINK THAT *MARU* LADY TURNED UP *HERE*, AND WHY *NOW?*

NOT TO MENTION, HOW COME THE WORLD HASN'T BEEN DESTROYED YET?

DO YOU THINK GALESH AND THAT LITTLE GUY ARE HERE TOO?

WHAT'RE YOU TWO LOVE BIRDS ON ABOUT?

DON'T CALL US THAT.

DID I MISS OUT ON SOME-THING?

HMM. IT'S LIKE I WAS TELLING THEM, IT'S NOTHING TO SWEAT.

YOU GUYS'LL SEE. STEVO WILL BE BACK ANYTIME NOW TO WIN THE TROPHY. I'LL BET MY LEFT..

BOOM

...NUH.

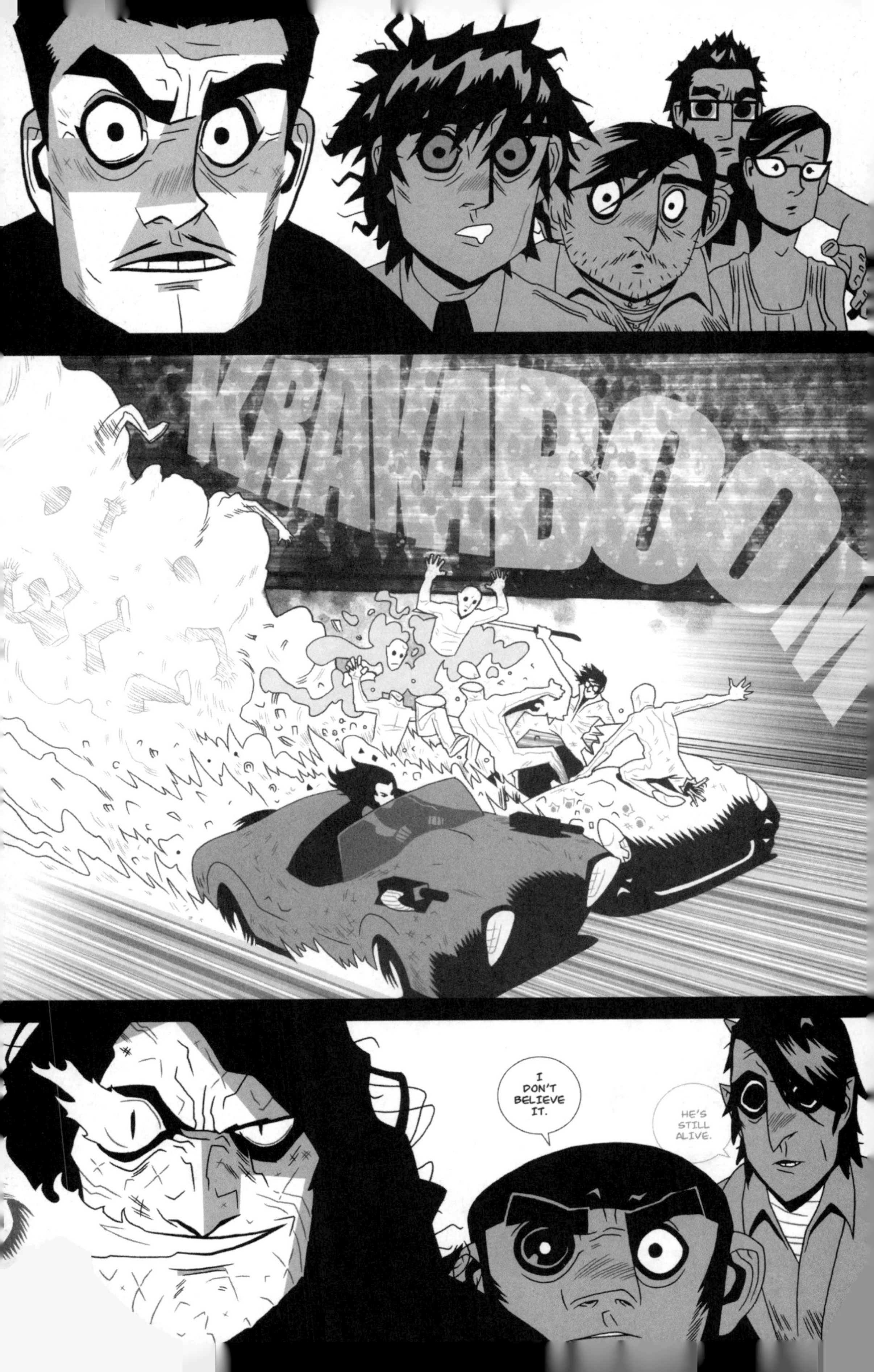

KRAKABOOM
I DON'T BELIEVE IT.
HE'S STILL ALIVE.

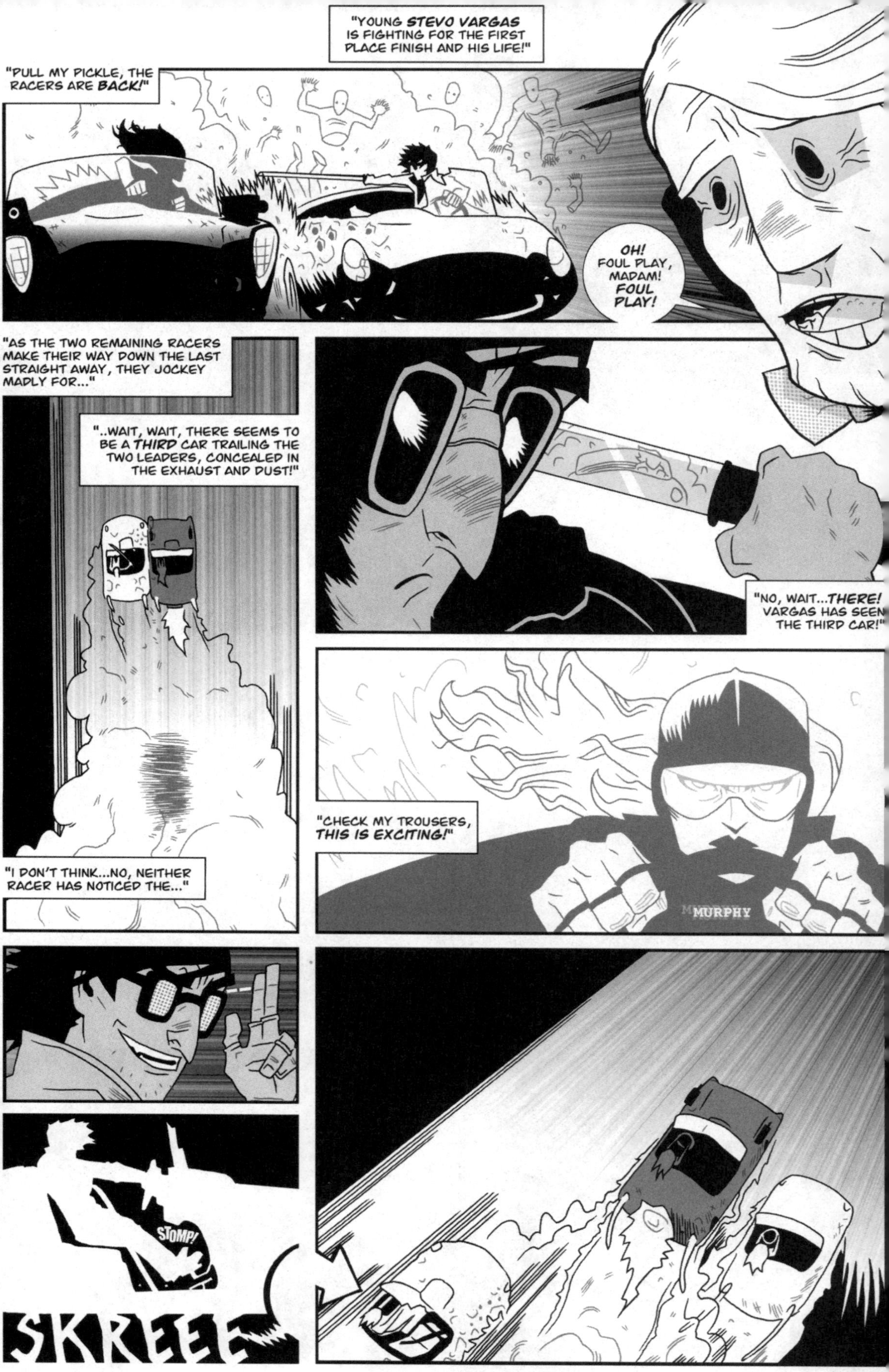
"YOUNG STEVO VARGAS IS FIGHTING FOR THE FIRST PLACE FINISH AND HIS LIFE!"
"PULL MY PICKLE, THE RACERS ARE BACK!"
OH! FOUL PLAY, MADAM! FOUL PLAY!
"AS THE TWO REMAINING RACERS MAKE THEIR WAY DOWN THE LAST STRAIGHT AWAY, THEY JOCKEY MADLY FOR..."
"..WAIT, WAIT, THERE SEEMS TO BE A THIRD CAR TRAILING THE TWO LEADERS, CONCEALED IN THE EXHAUST AND DUST!"
"I DON'T THINK...NO, NEITHER RACER HAS NOTICED THE..."
"NO, WAIT...THERE! VARGAS HAS SEEN THE THIRD CAR!"
"CHECK MY TROUSERS, THIS IS EXCITING!"
MURPHY
STOMP!
SKREEE

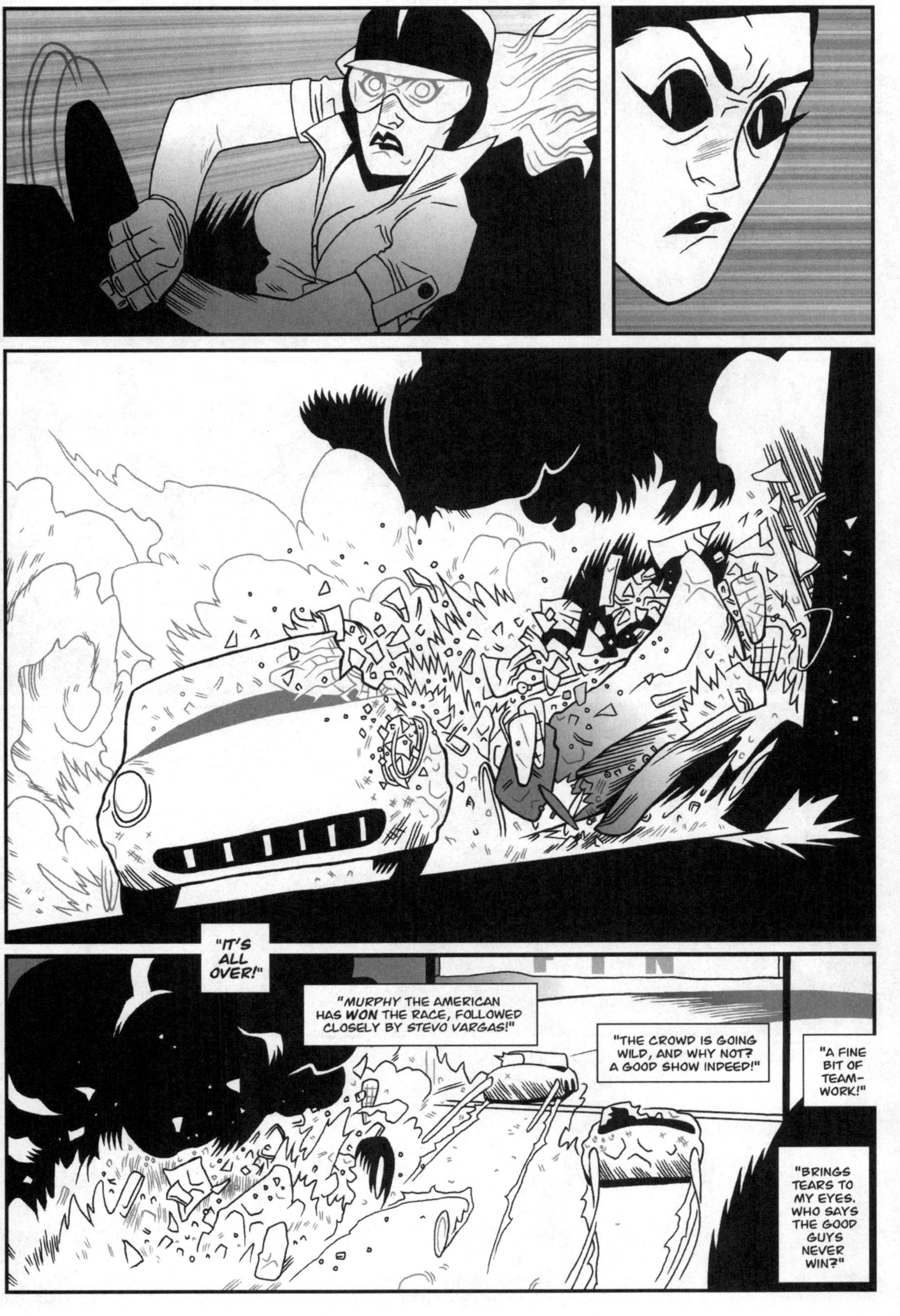
"IT'S ALL OVER!"
"MURPHY THE AMERICAN HAS WON THE RACE, FOLLOWED CLOSELY BY STEVO VARGAS!"
"THE CROWD IS GOING WILD, AND WHY NOT? A GOOD SHOW INDEED!"
"A FINE BIT OF TEAM-WORK!"
"BRINGS TEARS TO MY EYES. WHO SAYS THE GOOD GUYS NEVER WIN?"

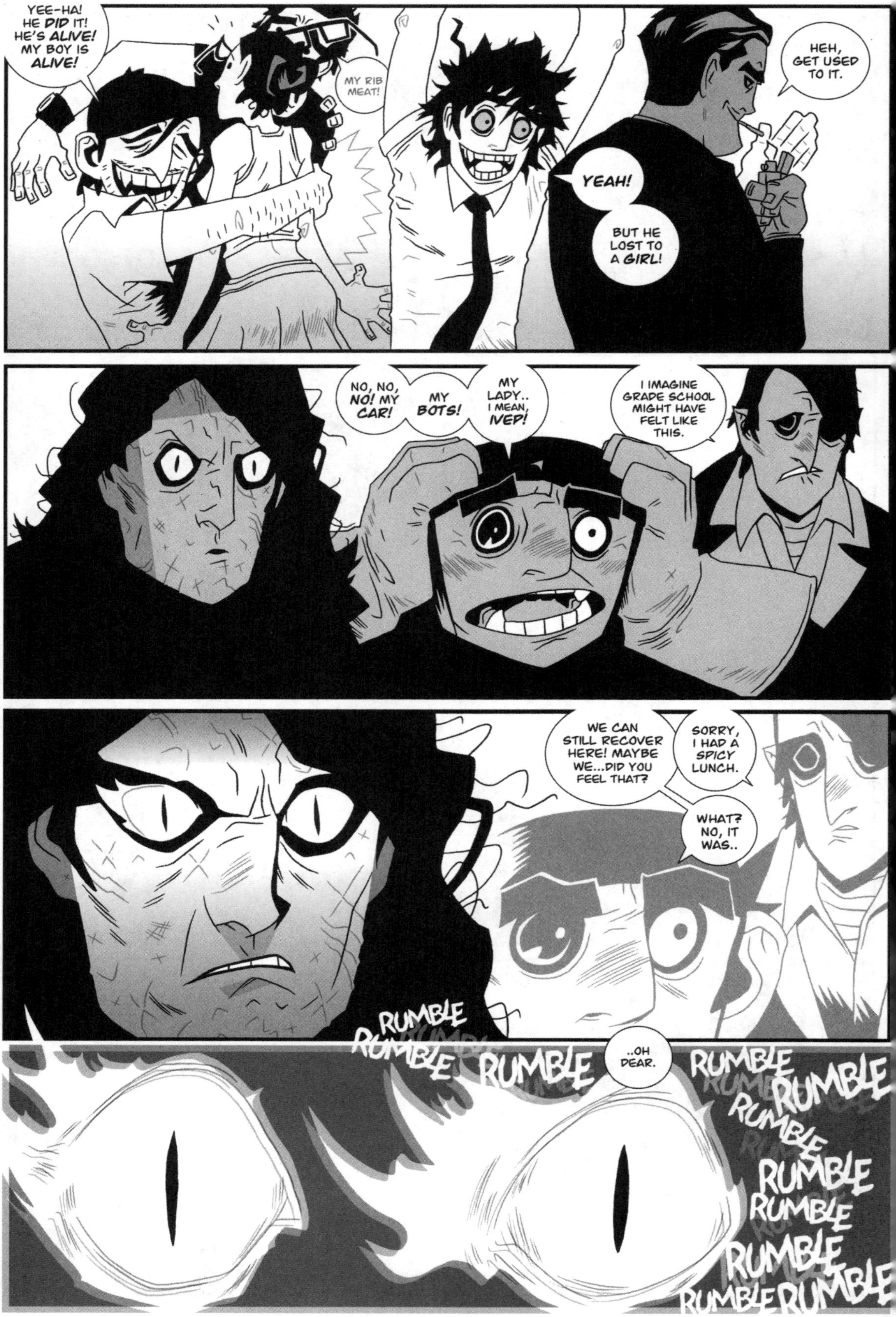
YEE-HA! HE DID IT! HE'S ALIVE! MY BOY IS ALIVE!
MY RIB MEAT!
YEAH!
BUT HE LOST TO A GIRL!
HEH, GET USED TO IT.
NO, NO, NO! MY CAR!
MY BOTS!
MY LADY.. I MEAN, IVEP!
I IMAGINE GRADE SCHOOL MIGHT HAVE FELT LIKE THIS.
WE CAN STILL RECOVER HERE! MAYBE WE...DID YOU FEEL THAT?
SORRY, I HAD A SPICY LUNCH.
WHAT? NO, IT WAS..
RUMBLE RUMBLE
RUMBLE
..OH DEAR.
RUMBLE RUMBLE RUMBLE RUMBLE RUMBLE RUMBLE RUMBLE RUMBLE

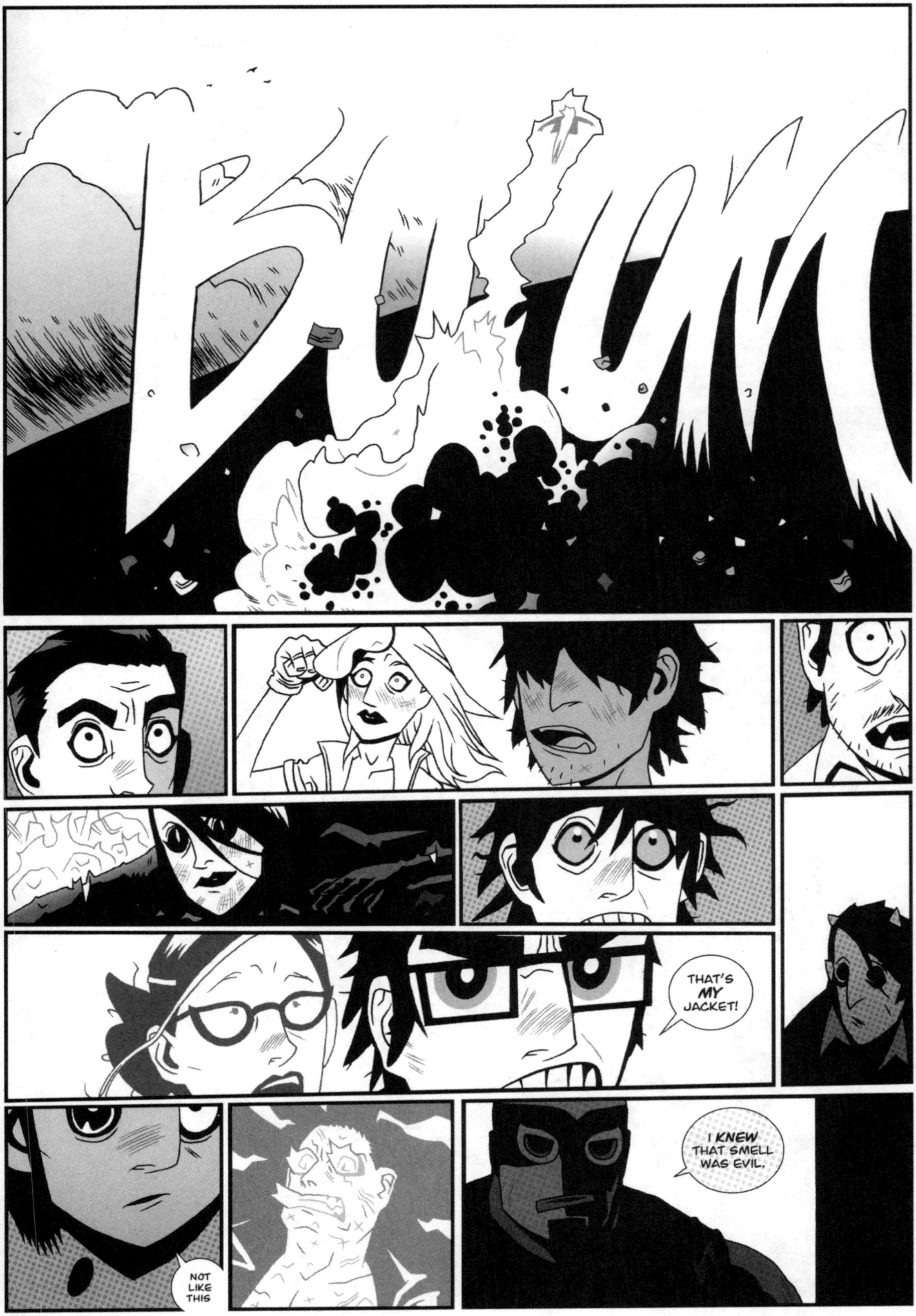
BOOM
THAT'S **MY** JACKET!
NOT LIKE THIS
I **KNEW** THAT SMELL WAS EVIL.

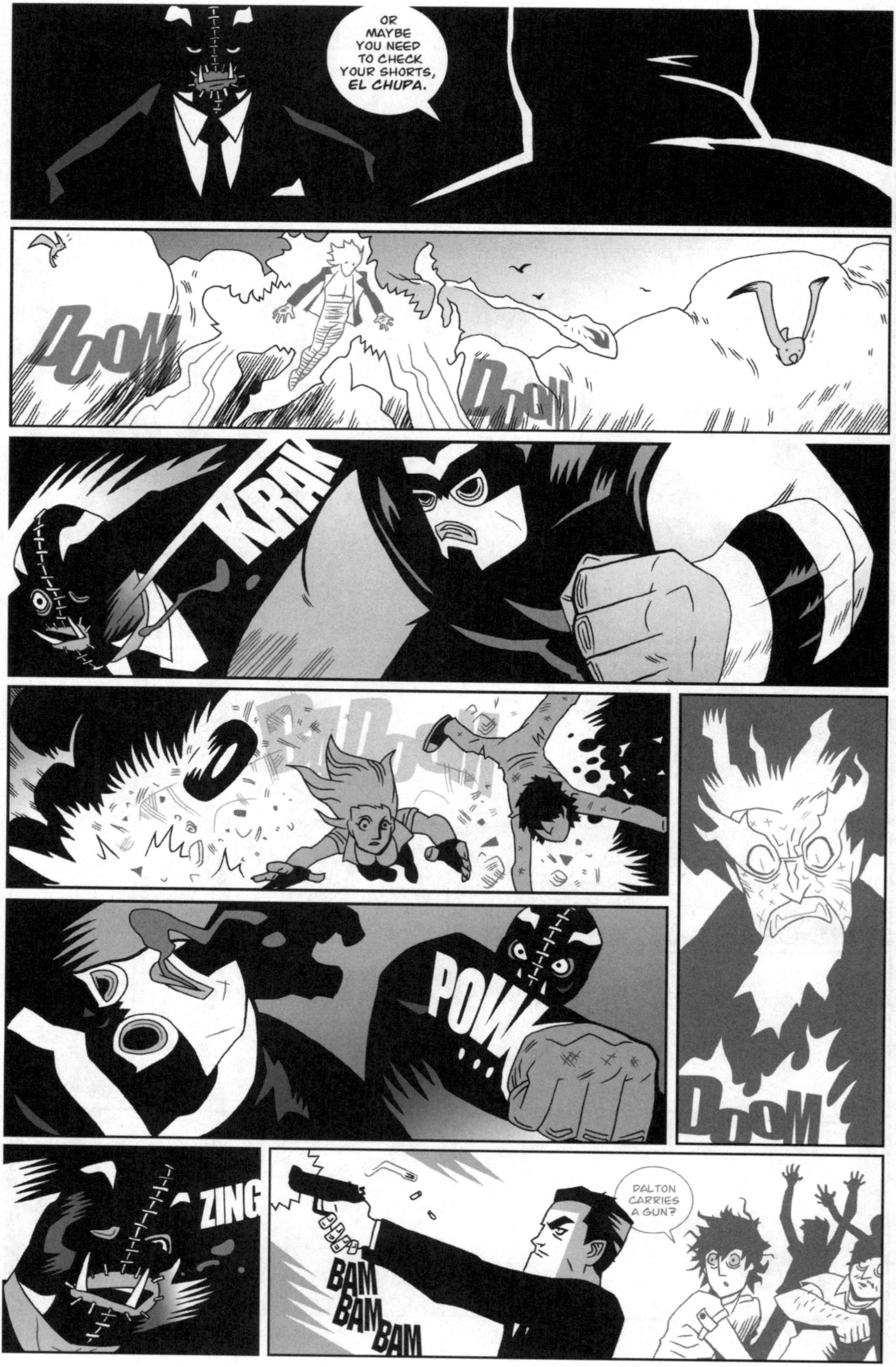
OR MAYBE YOU NEED TO CHECK YOUR SHORTS, EL CHUPA.
DOOM
DOOM
KRAK
POW
DOOM
ZING
BAM BAM BAM
DALTON CARRIES A GUN?

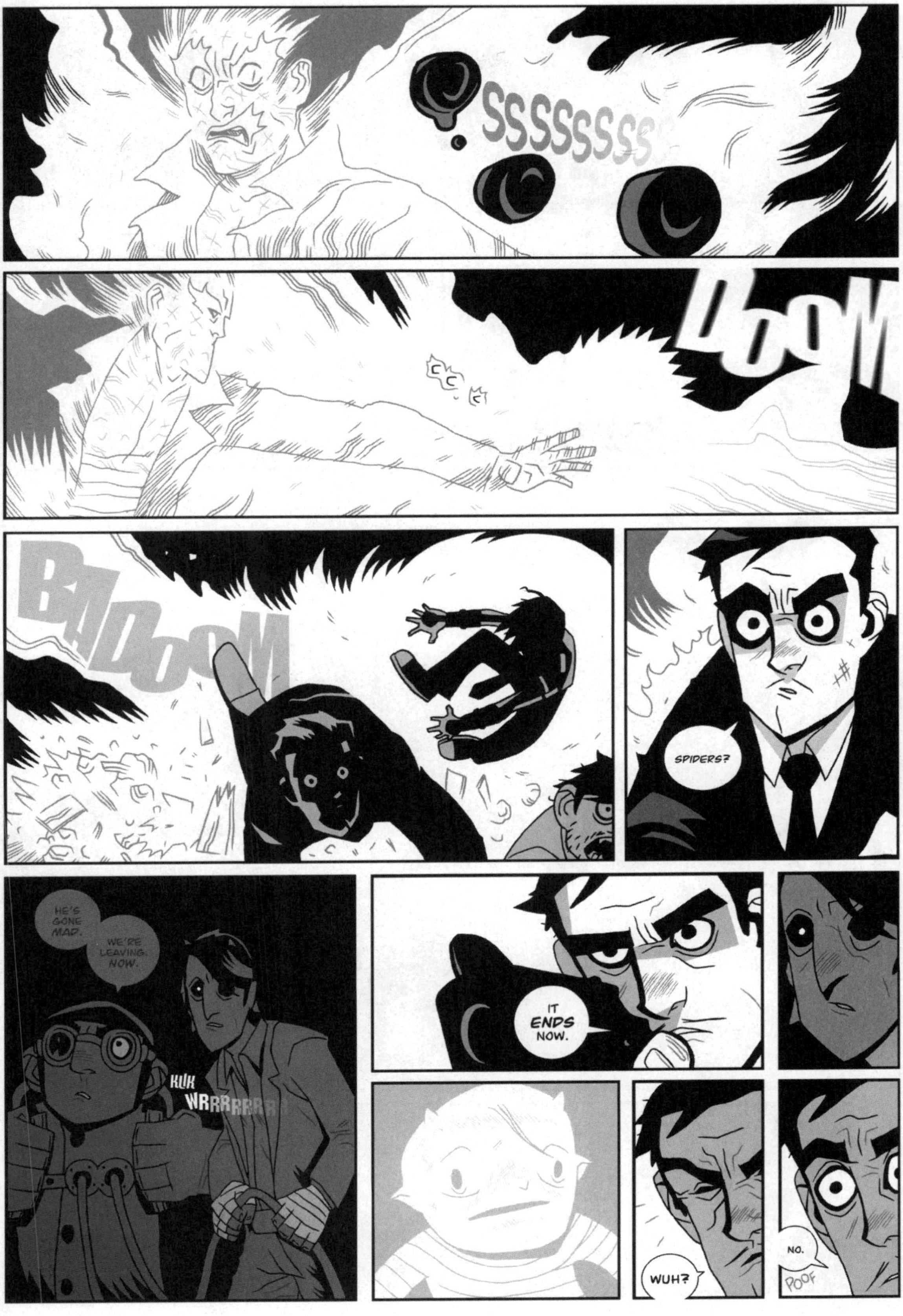
SSSSSSSSS
DOOM
BADOOM
SPIDERS?
HE'S GONE MAD.
WE'RE LEAVING. NOW.
KLIK
WRRRRRRRR
IT ENDS NOW.
WUH?
NO.
POOF

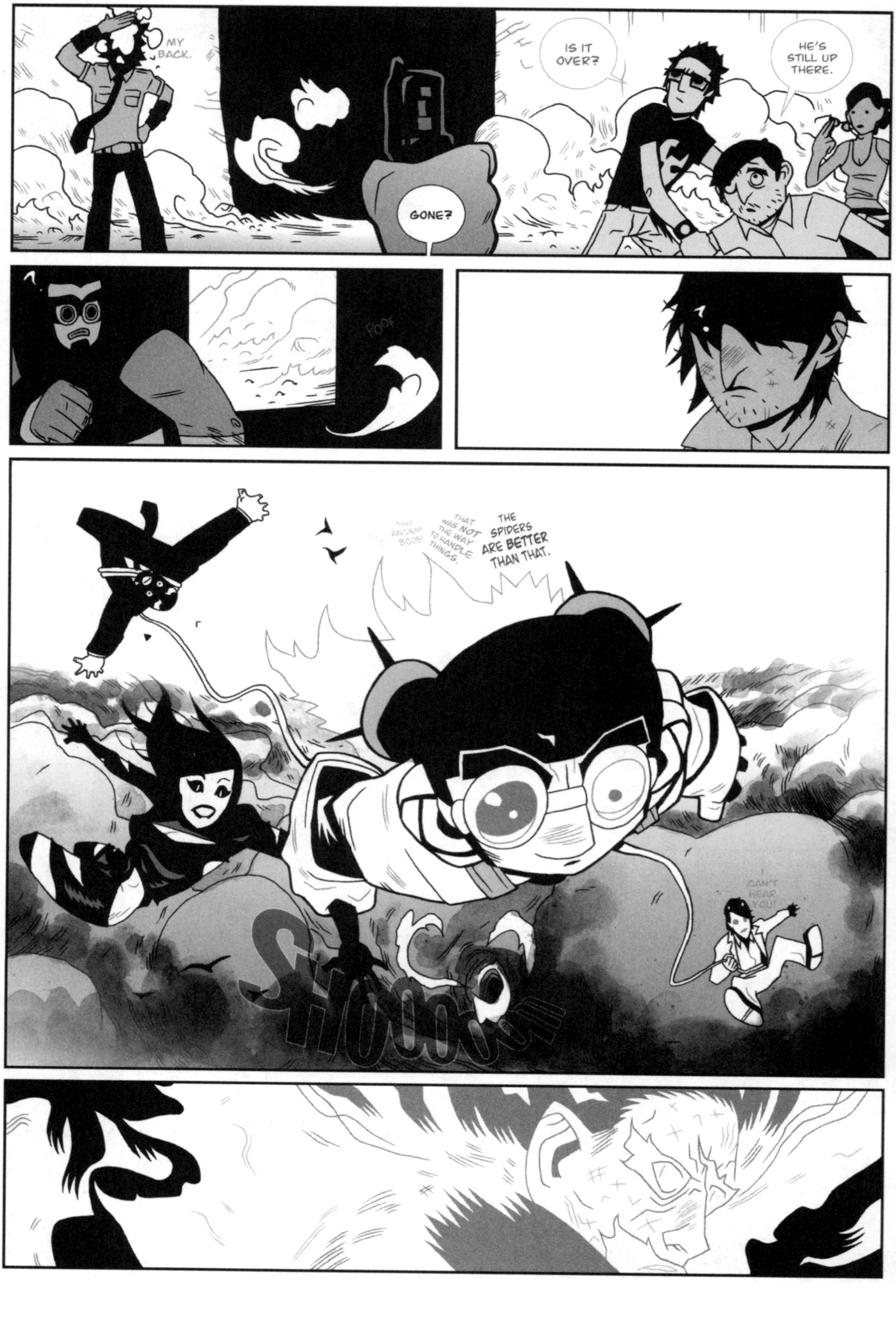
MY BACK.
IS IT OVER?
HE'S STILL UP THERE.
GONE?
POOF
THE SPIDERS ARE BETTER THAN THAT.
THAT WAS NOT THE WAY TO HANDLE THINGS.
THAT ANCIENT BOOB!
I CAN'T HEAR YOU!

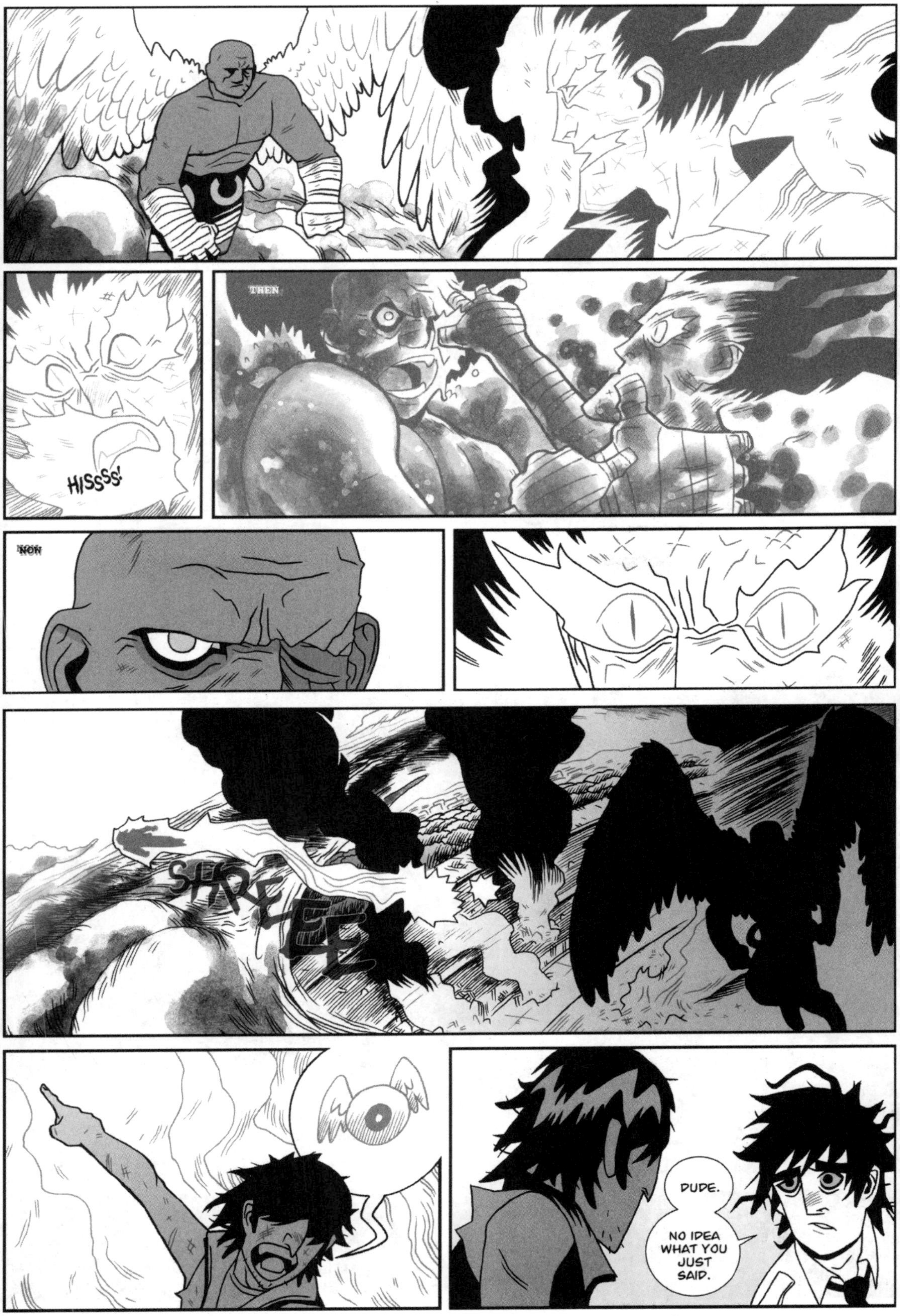
HISSSS!
THEN
NOW
SHREEEE
DUDE.
NO IDEA WHAT YOU JUST SAID.

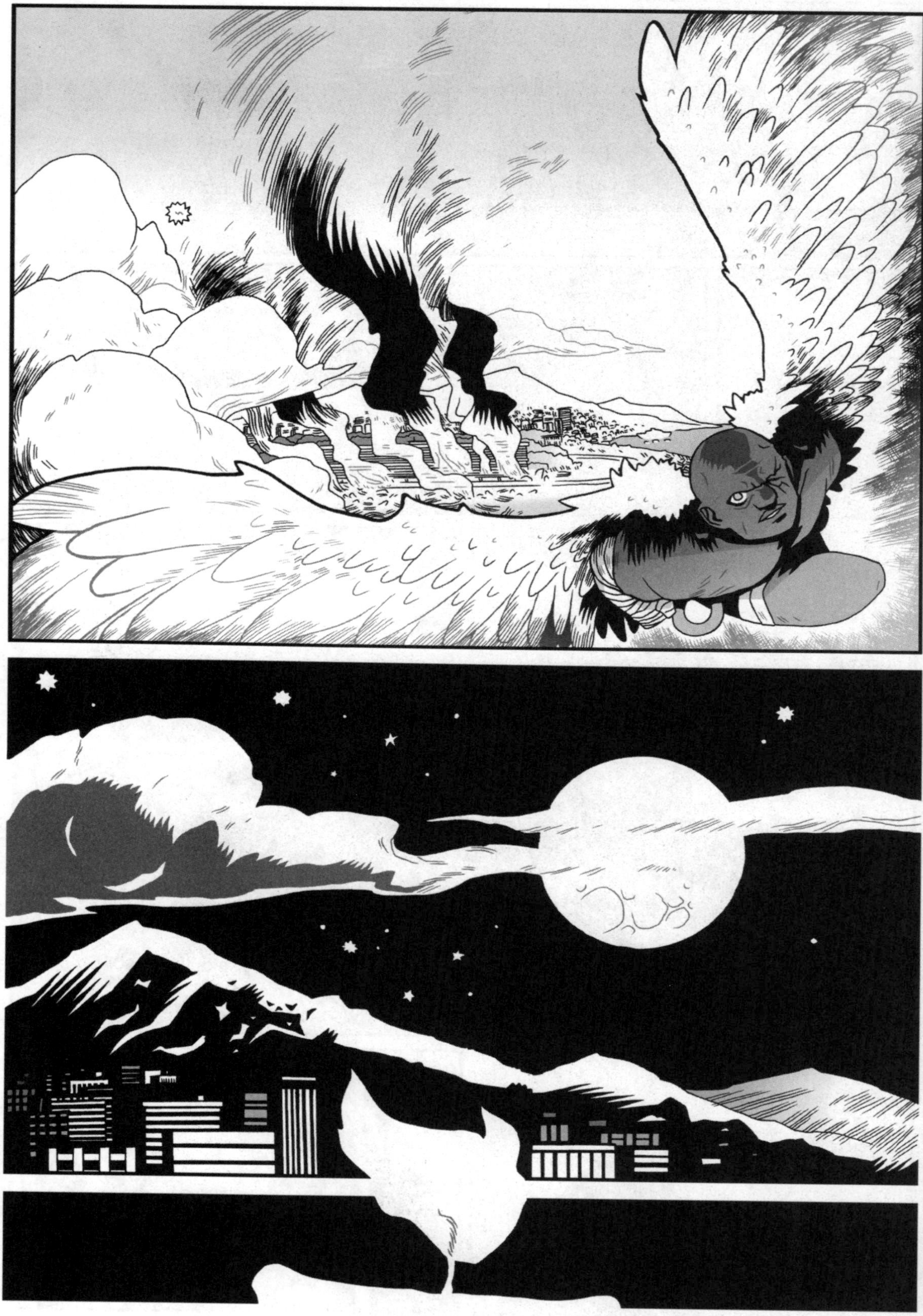

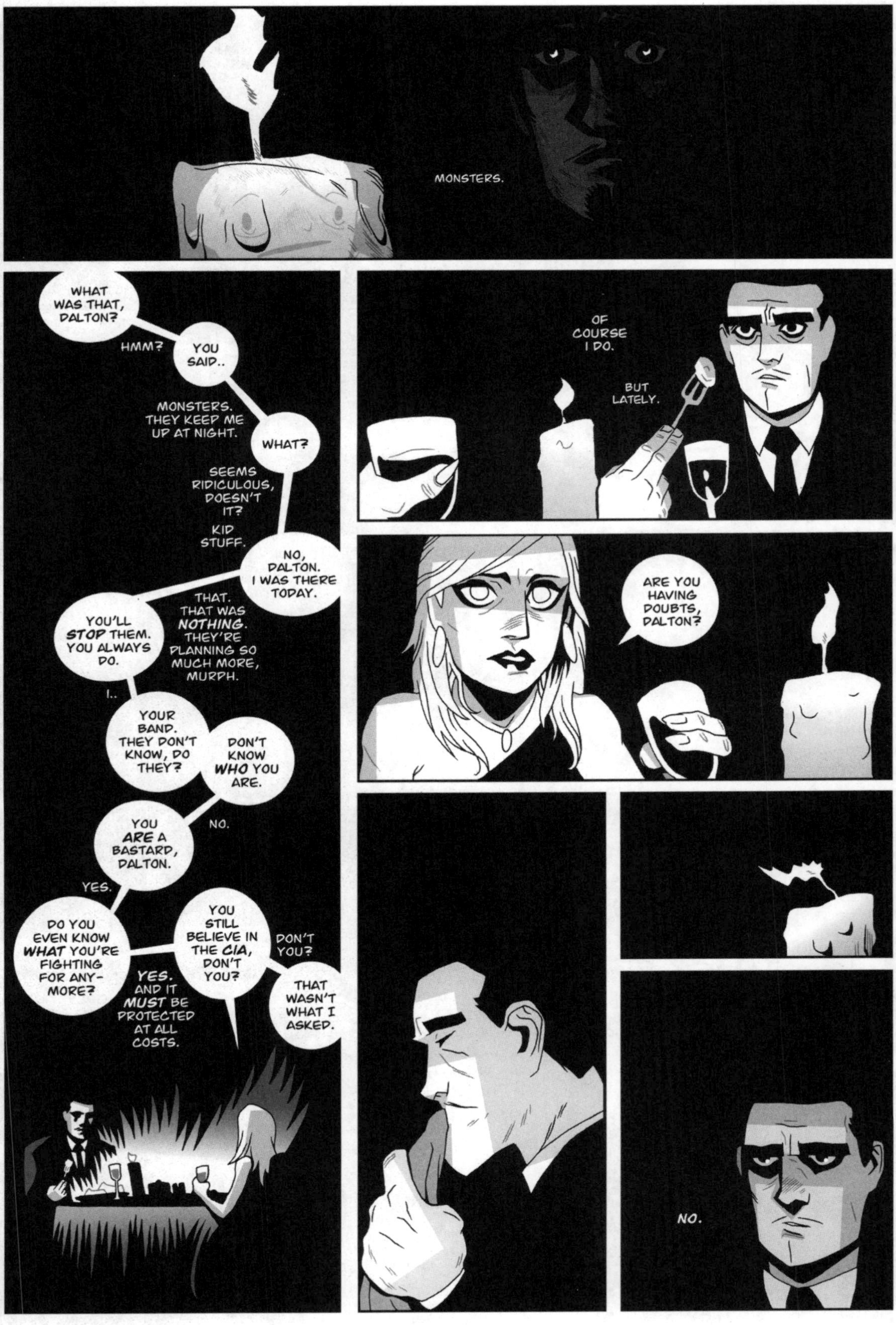
MONSTERS.
WHAT WAS THAT, DALTON?
HMM?
YOU SAID..
MONSTERS. THEY KEEP ME UP AT NIGHT.
WHAT?
SEEMS RIDICULOUS, DOESN'T IT?
KID STUFF.
NO, DALTON. I WAS THERE TODAY.
THAT. THAT WAS NOTHING. THEY'RE PLANNING SO MUCH MORE, MURPH.
YOU'LL STOP THEM. YOU ALWAYS DO.
I..
YOUR BAND. THEY DON'T KNOW, DO THEY?
DON'T KNOW WHO YOU ARE.
NO.
YOU ARE A BASTARD, DALTON.
YES.
DO YOU EVEN KNOW WHAT YOU'RE FIGHTING FOR ANY-MORE?
YOU STILL BELIEVE IN THE CIA, DON'T YOU?
DON'T YOU?
YES. AND IT MUST BE PROTECTED AT ALL COSTS.
THAT WASN'T WHAT I ASKED.
OF COURSE I DO.
BUT LATELY.
ARE YOU HAVING DOUBTS, DALTON?
NO.

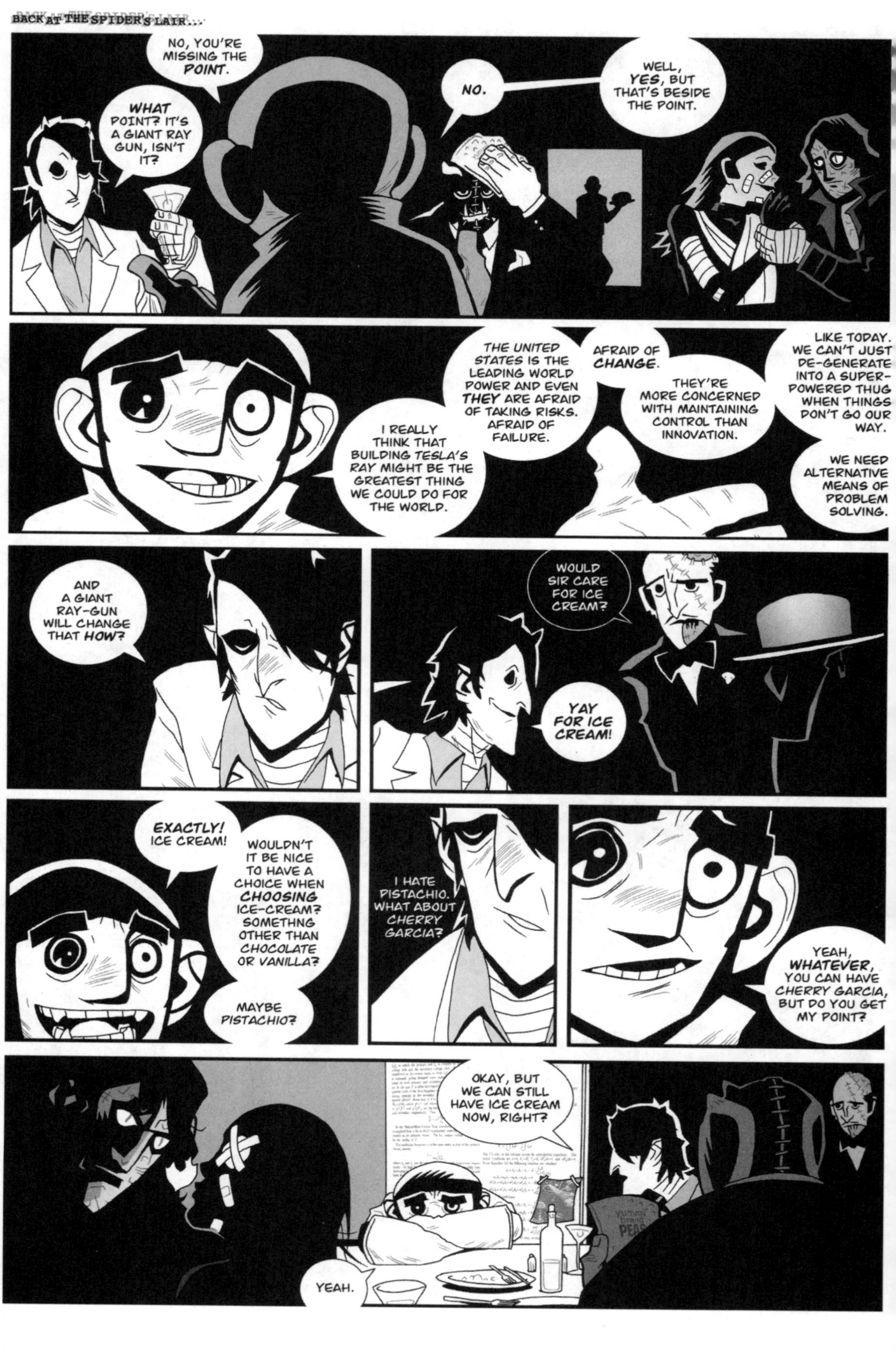
BACK AT THE SPIDER'S LAIR...
NO, YOU'RE MISSING THE POINT.
WHAT POINT? IT'S A GIANT RAY GUN, ISN'T IT?
NO.
WELL, YES, BUT THAT'S BESIDE THE POINT.
I REALLY THINK THAT BUILDING TESLA'S RAY MIGHT BE THE GREATEST THING WE COULD DO FOR THE WORLD.
THE UNITED STATES IS THE LEADING WORLD POWER AND EVEN THEY ARE AFRAID OF TAKING RISKS. AFRAID OF FAILURE.
AFRAID OF CHANGE.
THEY'RE MORE CONCERNED WITH MAINTAINING CONTROL THAN INNOVATION.
LIKE TODAY. WE CAN'T JUST DE-GENERATE INTO A SUPER-POWERED THUG WHEN THINGS DON'T GO OUR WAY.
WE NEED ALTERNATIVE MEANS OF PROBLEM SOLVING.
AND A GIANT RAY-GUN WILL CHANGE THAT HOW?
WOULD SIR CARE FOR ICE CREAM?
YAY FOR ICE CREAM!
EXACTLY! ICE CREAM!
WOULDN'T IT BE NICE TO HAVE A CHOICE WHEN CHOOSING ICE-CREAM? SOMETHING OTHER THAN CHOCOLATE OR VANILLA?
MAYBE PISTACHIO?
I HATE PISTACHIO. WHAT ABOUT CHERRY GARCIA?
YEAH, WHATEVER, YOU CAN HAVE CHERRY GARCIA, BUT DO YOU GET MY POINT?
OKAY, BUT WE CAN STILL HAVE ICE CREAM NOW, RIGHT?
YEAH.

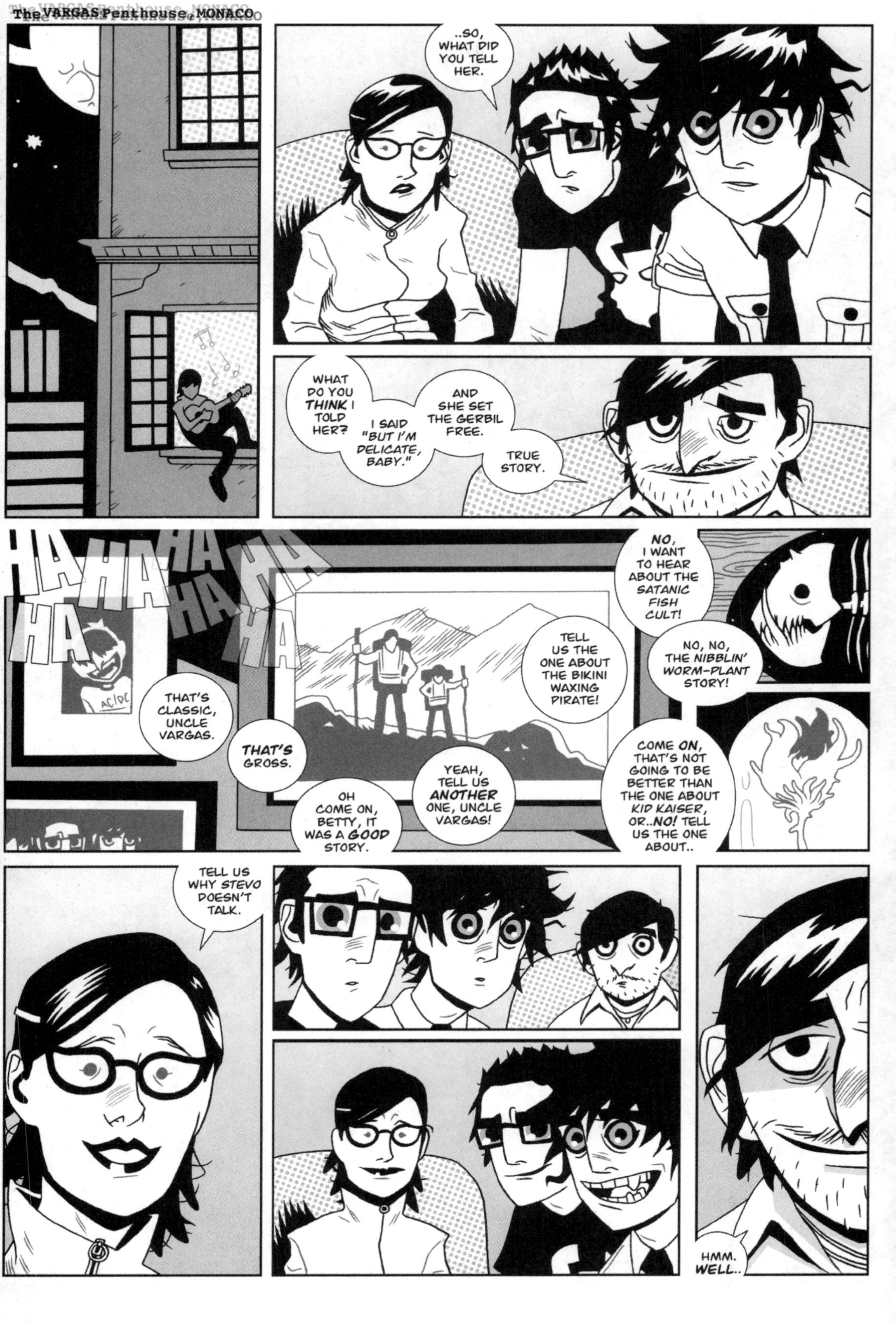

The VARGAS Penthouse, MONACO
..SO, WHAT DID YOU TELL HER.
WHAT DO YOU THINK I TOLD HER?
I SAID "BUT I'M DELICATE, BABY."
AND SHE SET THE GERBIL FREE.
TRUE STORY.
HA HA HA HA HA HA HA HA HA
AC/DC
THAT'S CLASSIC, UNCLE VARGAS.
THAT'S GROSS.
OH COME ON, BETTY, IT WAS A GOOD STORY.
YEAH, TELL US ANOTHER ONE, UNCLE VARGAS!
TELL US THE ONE ABOUT THE BIKINI WAXING PIRATE!
NO, I WANT TO HEAR ABOUT THE SATANIC FISH CULT!
NO, NO, THE NIBBLIN' WORM-PLANT STORY!
COME ON, THAT'S NOT GOING TO BE BETTER THAN THE ONE ABOUT KID KAISER, OR..NO! TELL US THE ONE ABOUT..
TELL US WHY STEVO DOESN'T TALK.
HMM. WELL..

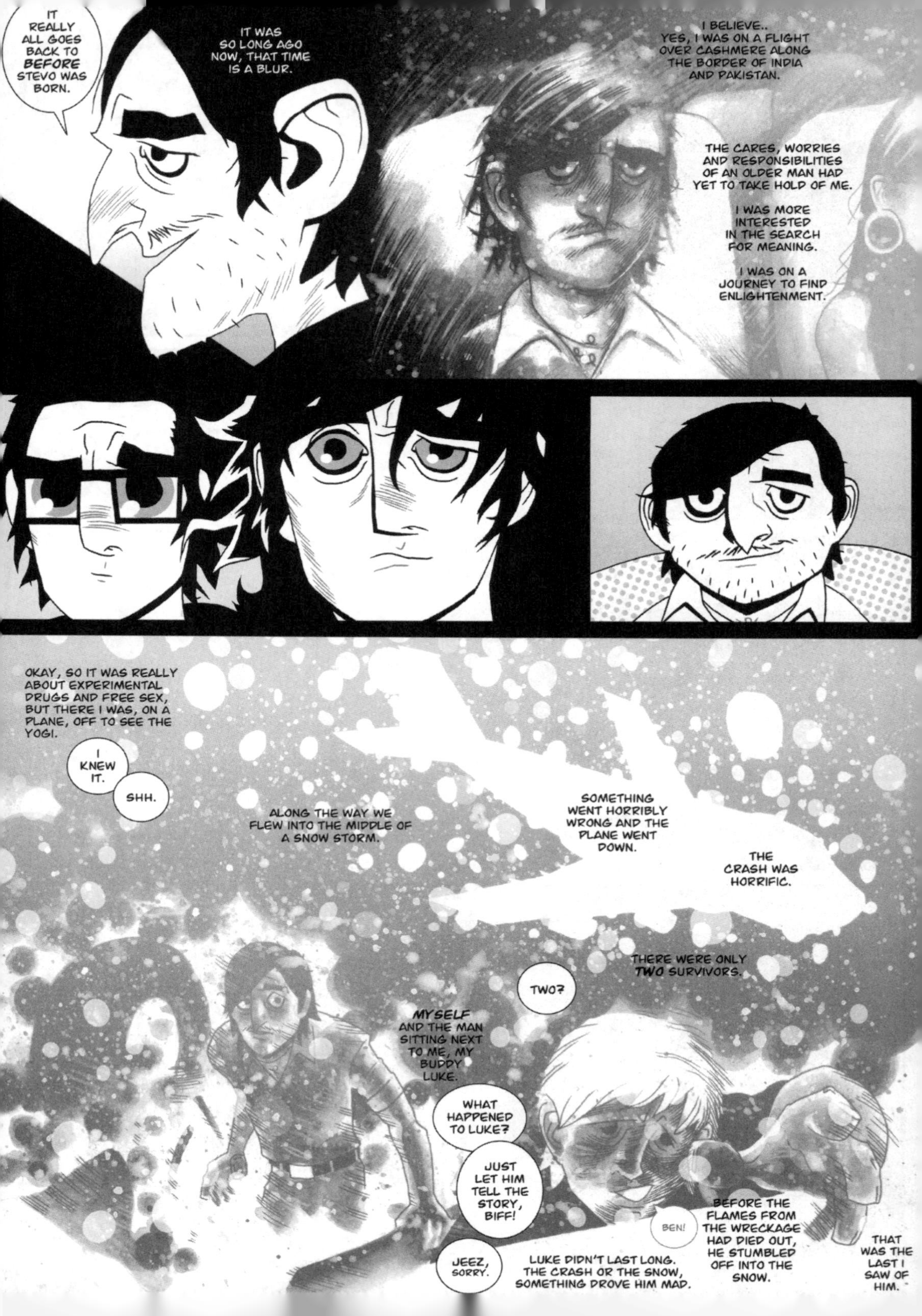
IT REALLY ALL GOES BACK TO BEFORE STEVO WAS BORN.
IT WAS SO LONG AGO NOW, THAT TIME IS A BLUR.
I BELIEVE.. YES, I WAS ON A FLIGHT OVER CASHMERE ALONG THE BORDER OF INDIA AND PAKISTAN.
THE CARES, WORRIES AND RESPONSIBILITIES OF AN OLDER MAN HAD YET TO TAKE HOLD OF ME.
I WAS MORE INTERESTED IN THE SEARCH FOR MEANING.
I WAS ON A JOURNEY TO FIND ENLIGHTENMENT.
OKAY, SO IT WAS REALLY ABOUT EXPERIMENTAL DRUGS AND FREE SEX, BUT THERE I WAS, ON A PLANE, OFF TO SEE THE YOGI.
I KNEW IT.
SHH.
ALONG THE WAY WE FLEW INTO THE MIDDLE OF A SNOW STORM.
SOMETHING WENT HORRIBLY WRONG AND THE PLANE WENT DOWN.
THE CRASH WAS HORRIFIC.
THERE WERE ONLY TWO SURVIVORS.
TWO?
MYSELF AND THE MAN SITTING NEXT TO ME, MY BUDDY LUKE.
WHAT HAPPENED TO LUKE?
JUST LET HIM TELL THE STORY, BIFF!
JEEZ, SORRY.
LUKE DIDN'T LAST LONG. THE CRASH OR THE SNOW, SOMETHING DROVE HIM MAD.
BEN!
BEFORE THE FLAMES FROM THE WRECKAGE HAD DIED OUT, HE STUMBLED OFF INTO THE SNOW.
THAT WAS THE LAST I SAW OF HIM.

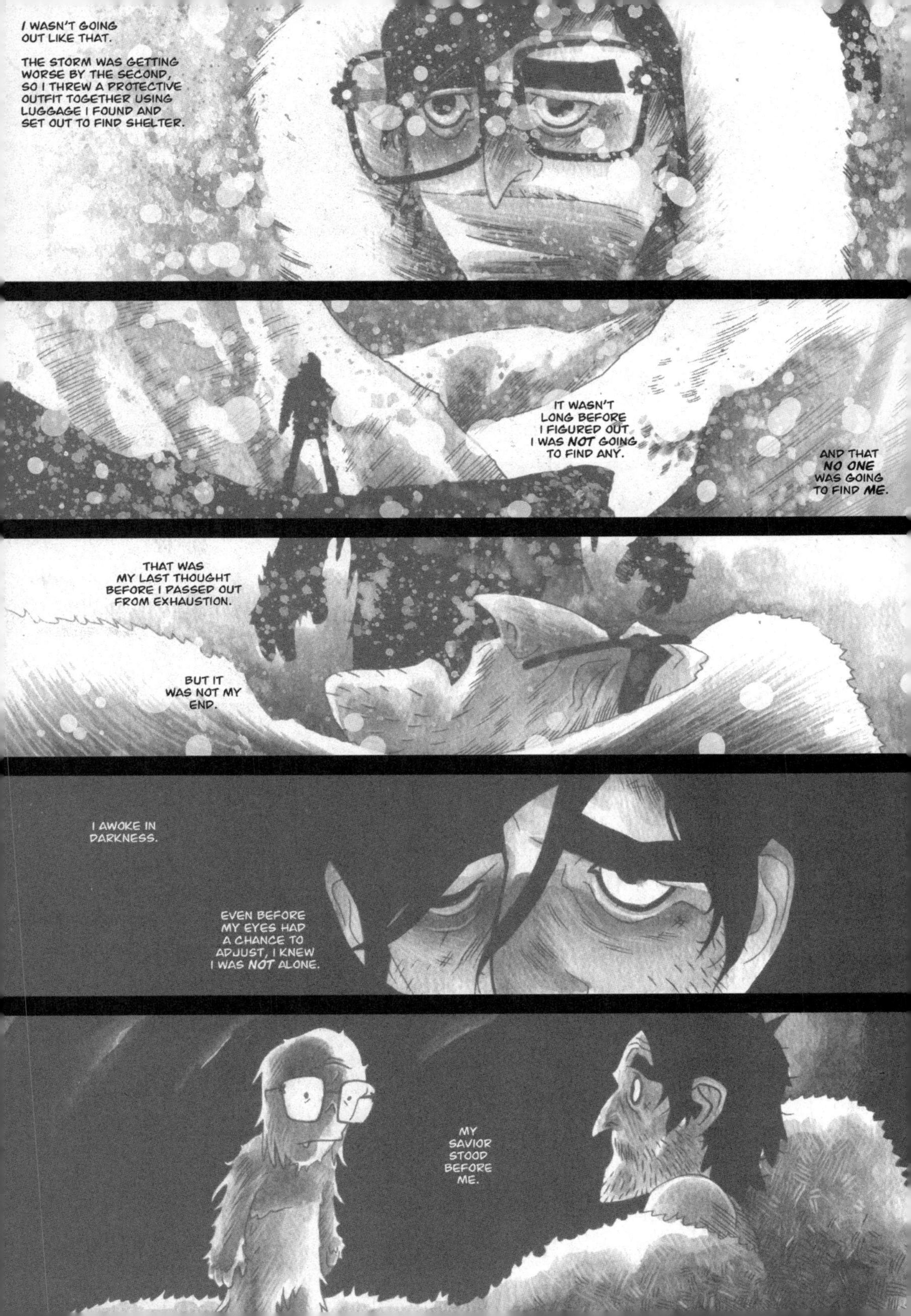
I WASN'T GOING OUT LIKE THAT.
THE STORM WAS GETTING WORSE BY THE SECOND, SO I THREW A PROTECTIVE OUTFIT TOGETHER USING LUGGAGE I FOUND AND SET OUT TO FIND SHELTER.
IT WASN'T LONG BEFORE I FIGURED OUT I WAS NOT GOING TO FIND ANY.
AND THAT NO ONE WAS GOING TO FIND ME.
THAT WAS MY LAST THOUGHT BEFORE I PASSED OUT FROM EXHAUSTION.
BUT IT WAS NOT MY END.
I AWOKE IN DARKNESS.
EVEN BEFORE MY EYES HAD A CHANCE TO ADJUST, I KNEW I WAS NOT ALONE.
MY SAVIOR STOOD BEFORE ME.

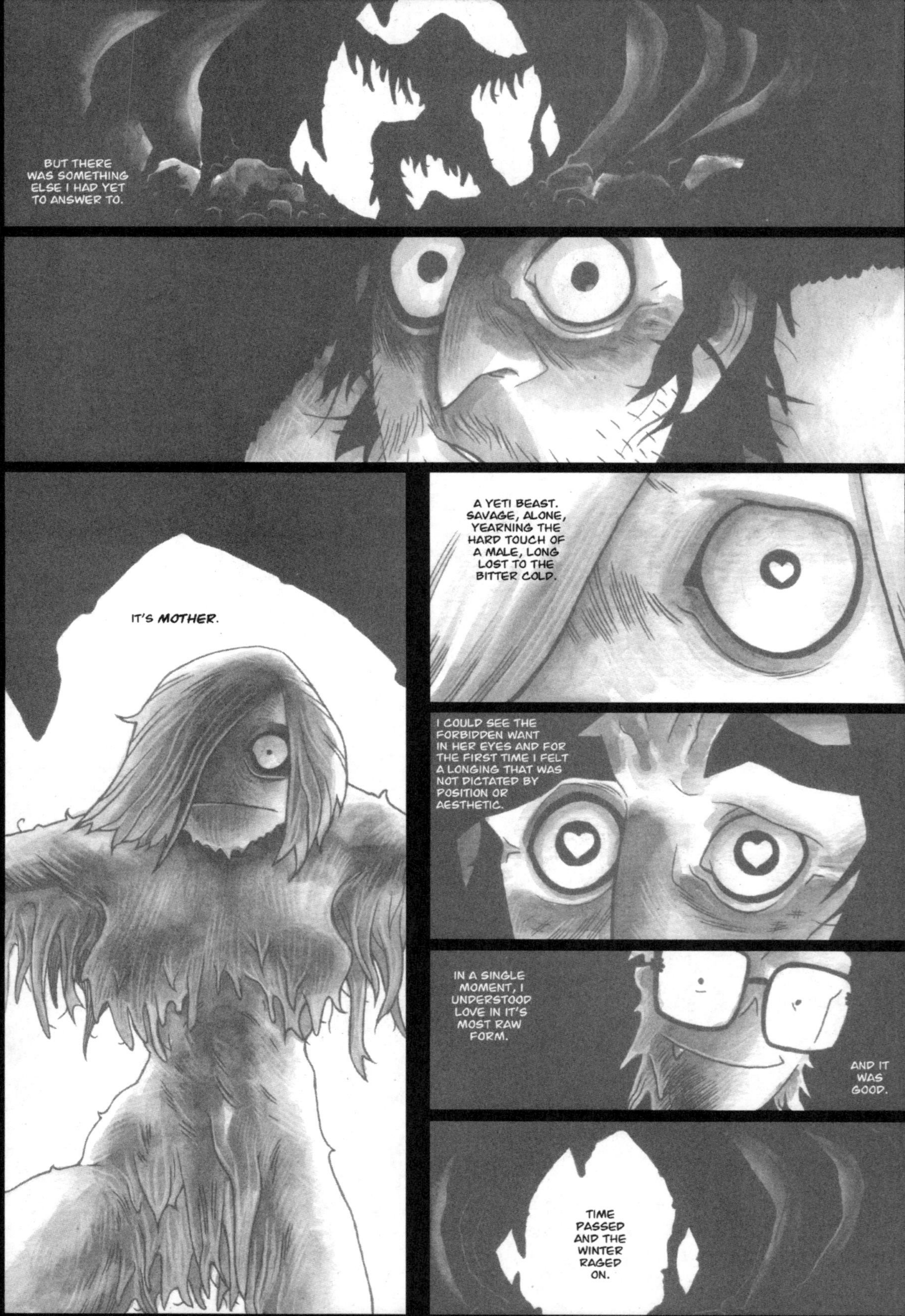
BUT THERE WAS SOMETHING ELSE I HAD YET TO ANSWER TO.
IT'S *MOTHER*.
A YETI BEAST. SAVAGE, ALONE, YEARNING THE HARD TOUCH OF A MALE, LONG LOST TO THE BITTER COLD.
I COULD SEE THE FORBIDDEN WANT IN HER EYES AND FOR THE FIRST TIME I FELT A LONGING THAT WAS NOT DICTATED BY POSITION OR AESTHETIC.
IN A SINGLE MOMENT, I UNDERSTOOD LOVE IN IT'S MOST RAW FORM.
AND IT WAS GOOD.
TIME PASSED AND THE WINTER RAGED ON.

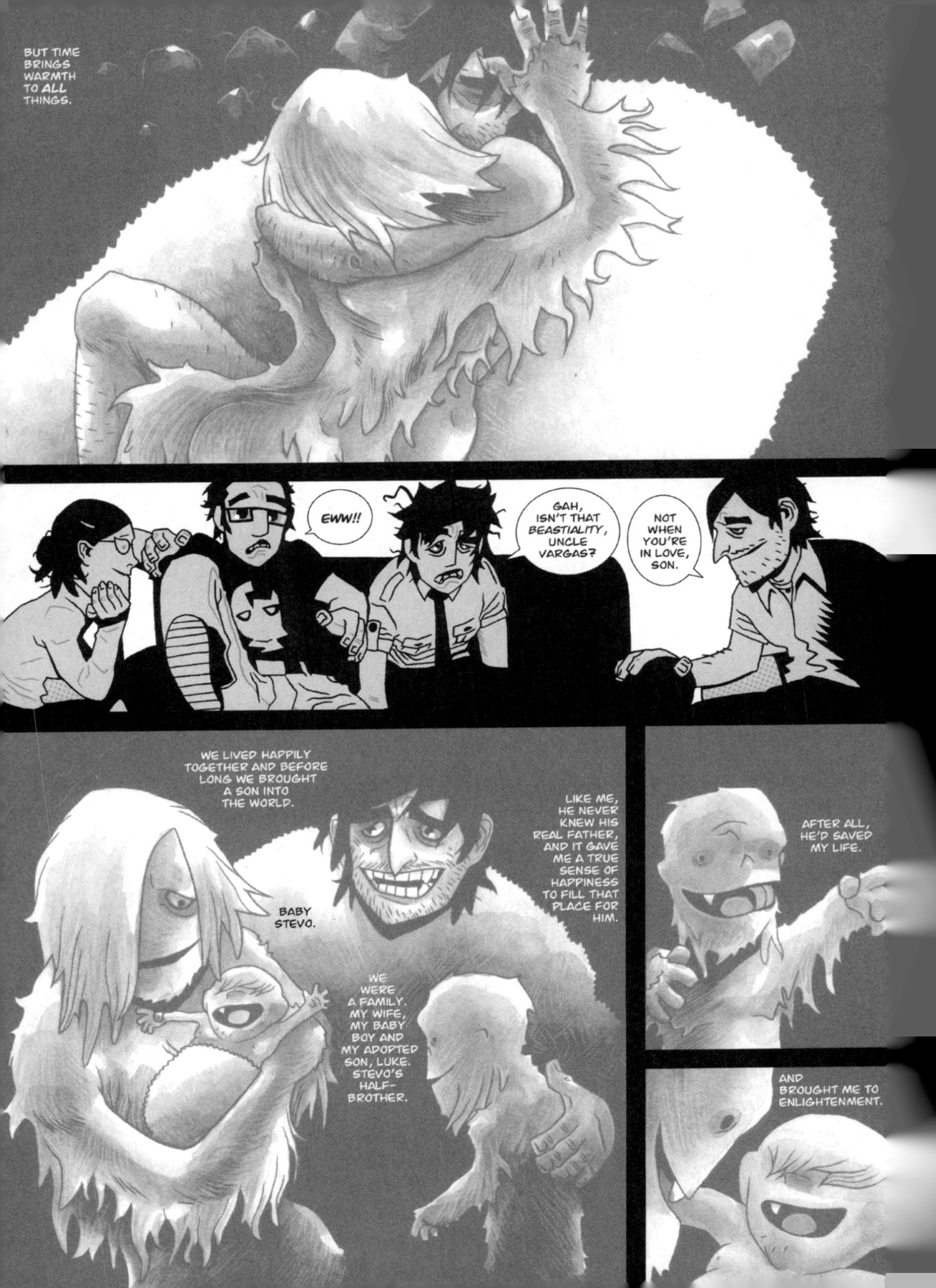
BUT TIME BRINGS WARMTH TO ALL THINGS.
EWW!!
GAH, ISN'T THAT BEASTIALITY, UNCLE VARGAS?
NOT WHEN YOU'RE IN LOVE, SON.
WE LIVED HAPPILY TOGETHER AND BEFORE LONG WE BROUGHT A SON INTO THE WORLD.
LIKE ME, HE NEVER KNEW HIS REAL FATHER, AND IT GAVE ME A TRUE SENSE OF HAPPINESS TO FILL THAT PLACE FOR HIM.
BABY STEVO.
WE WERE A FAMILY. MY WIFE, MY BABY BOY AND MY ADOPTED SON, LUKE. STEVO'S HALF-BROTHER.
AFTER ALL, HE'D SAVED MY LIFE.
AND BROUGHT ME TO ENLIGHTENMENT.

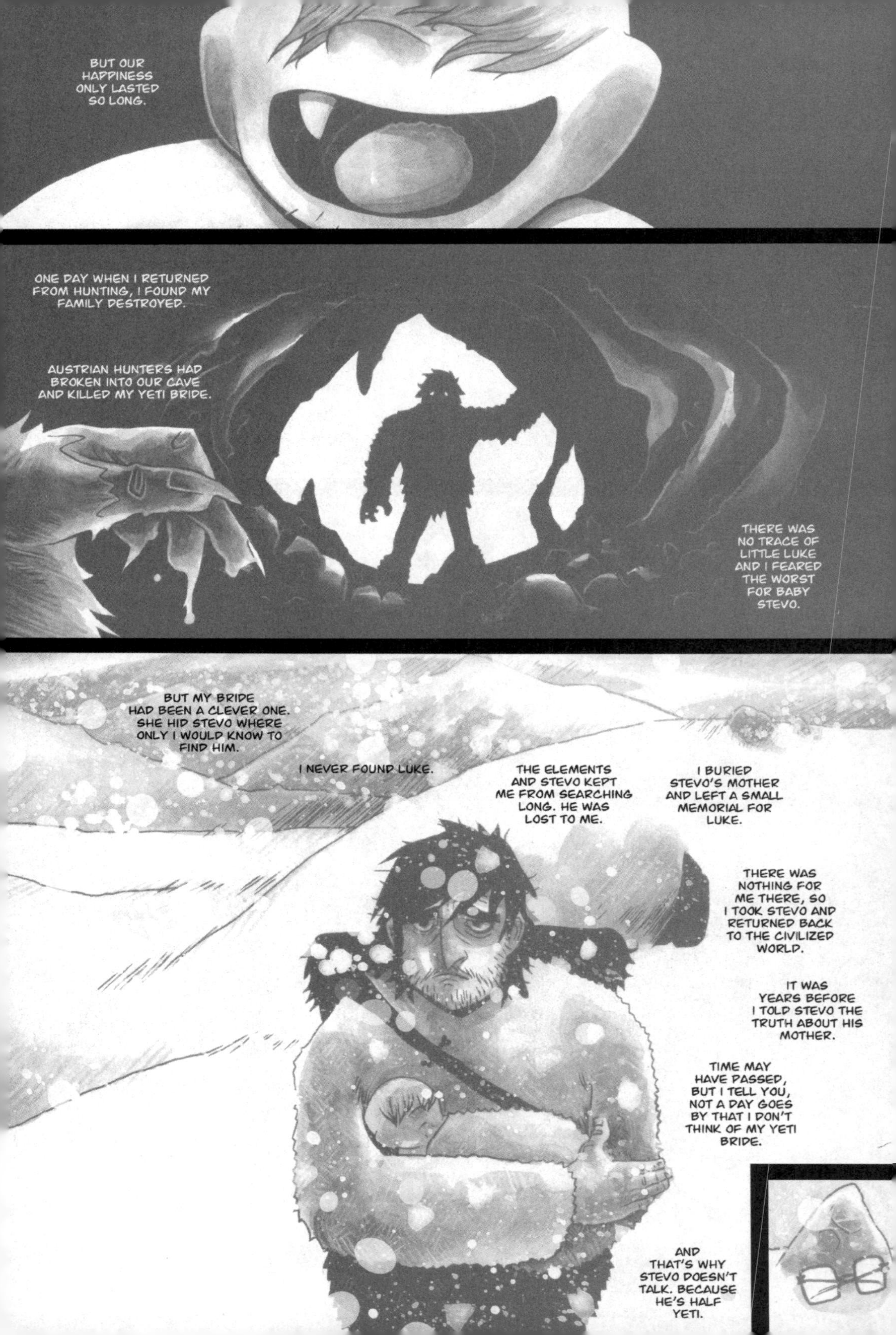
BUT OUR HAPPINESS ONLY LASTED SO LONG.
ONE DAY WHEN I RETURNED FROM HUNTING, I FOUND MY FAMILY DESTROYED.
AUSTRIAN HUNTERS HAD BROKEN INTO OUR CAVE AND KILLED MY YETI BRIDE.
THERE WAS NO TRACE OF LITTLE LUKE AND I FEARED THE WORST FOR BABY STEVO.
BUT MY BRIDE HAD BEEN A CLEVER ONE. SHE HID STEVO WHERE ONLY I WOULD KNOW TO FIND HIM.
I NEVER FOUND LUKE.
THE ELEMENTS AND STEVO KEPT ME FROM SEARCHING LONG. HE WAS LOST TO ME.
I BURIED STEVO'S MOTHER AND LEFT A SMALL MEMORIAL FOR LUKE.
THERE WAS NOTHING FOR ME THERE, SO I TOOK STEVO AND RETURNED BACK TO THE CIVILIZED WORLD.
IT WAS YEARS BEFORE I TOLD STEVO THE TRUTH ABOUT HIS MOTHER.
TIME MAY HAVE PASSED, BUT I TELL YOU, NOT A DAY GOES BY THAT I DON'T THINK OF MY YETI BRIDE.
AND THAT'S WHY STEVO DOESN'T TALK. BECAUSE HE'S HALF YETI.

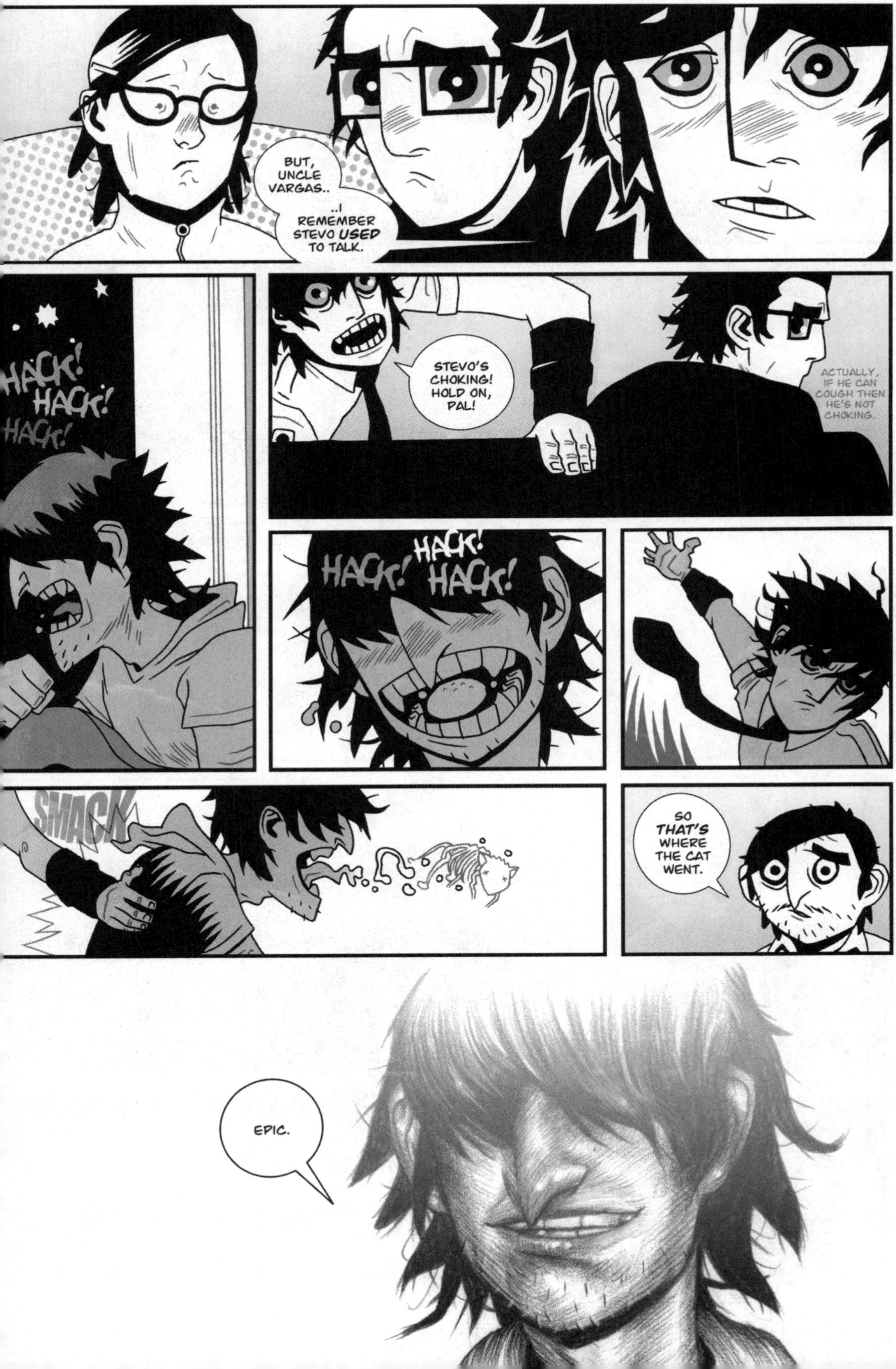
BUT, UNCLE VARGAS..
..I REMEMBER STEVO USED TO TALK.
HACK! HACK! HACK!
STEVO'S CHOKING! HOLD ON, PAL!
ACTUALLY, IF HE CAN COUGH THEN HE'S NOT CHOKING.
HACK! HACK! HACK!
SMACK
SO THAT'S WHERE THE CAT WENT.
EPIC.

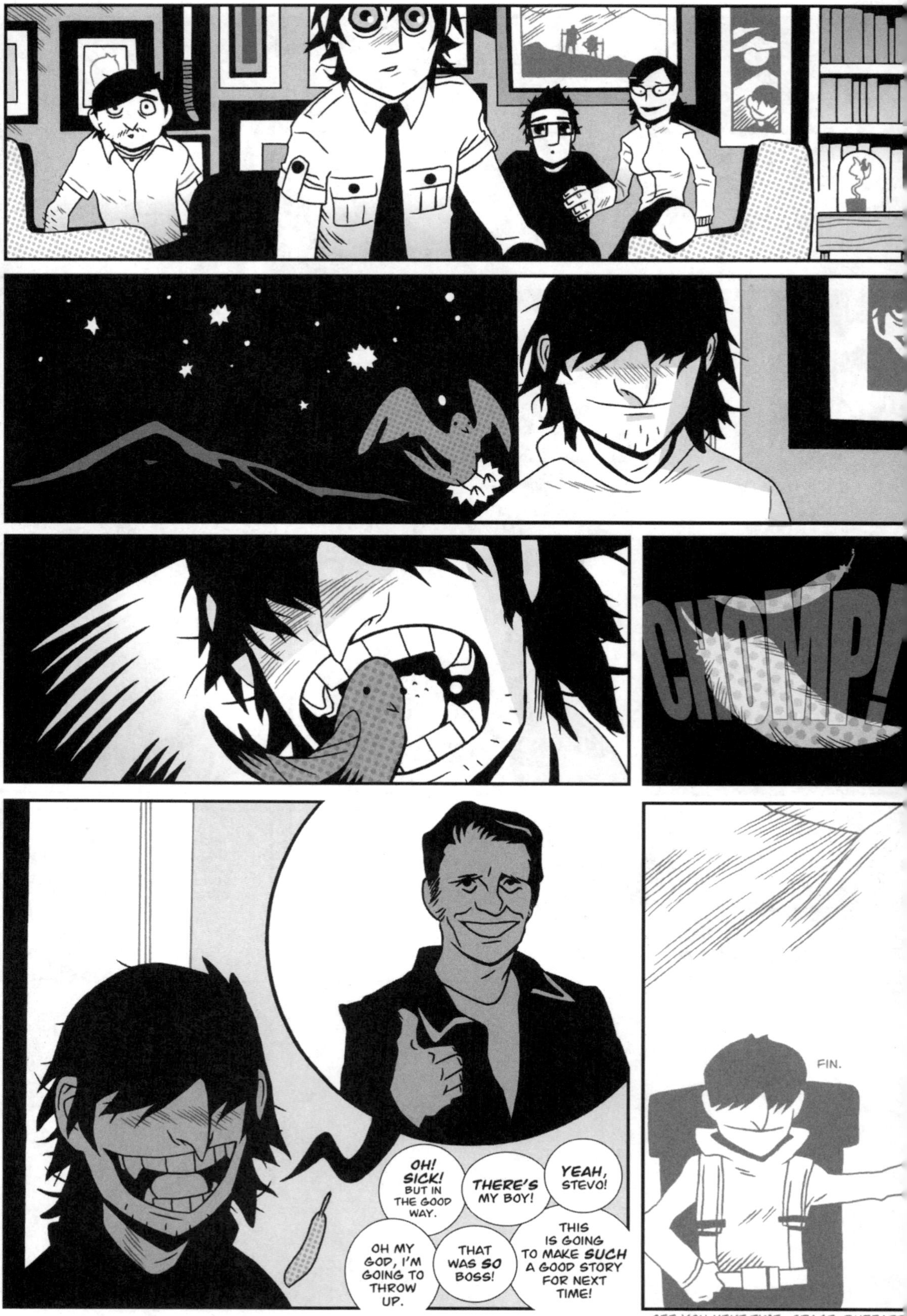
CHOMP!
OH! SICK! BUT IN THE GOOD WAY.
THERE'S MY BOY!
YEAH, STEVO!
OH MY GOD, I'M GOING TO THROW UP.
THAT WAS SO BOSS!
THIS IS GOING TO MAKE SUCH A GOOD STORY FOR NEXT TIME!
FIN.

SEE YOU NEXT TIME, SPACE-BUZZARD

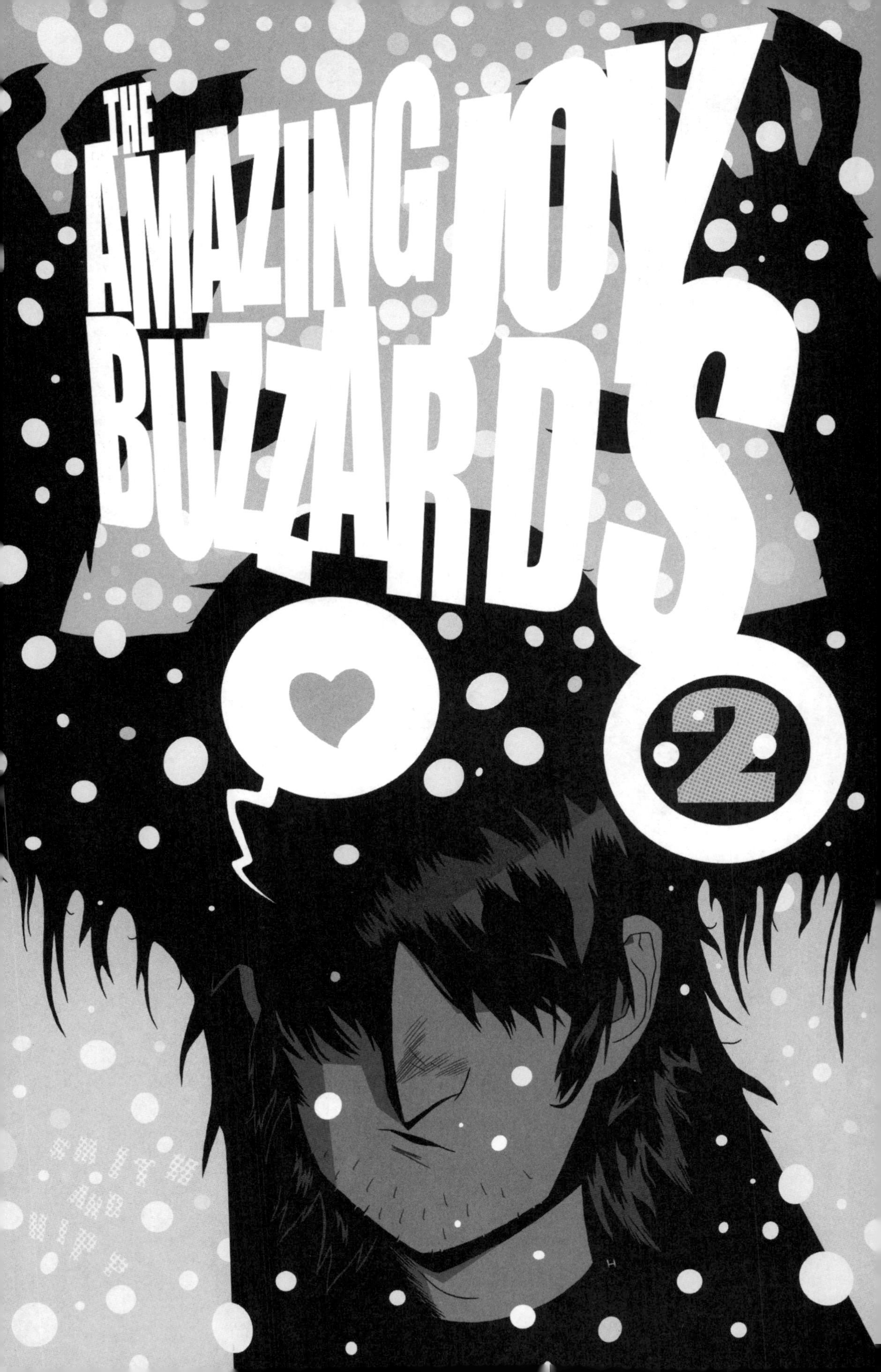
THE AMAZING JOY BUZZARDS
2

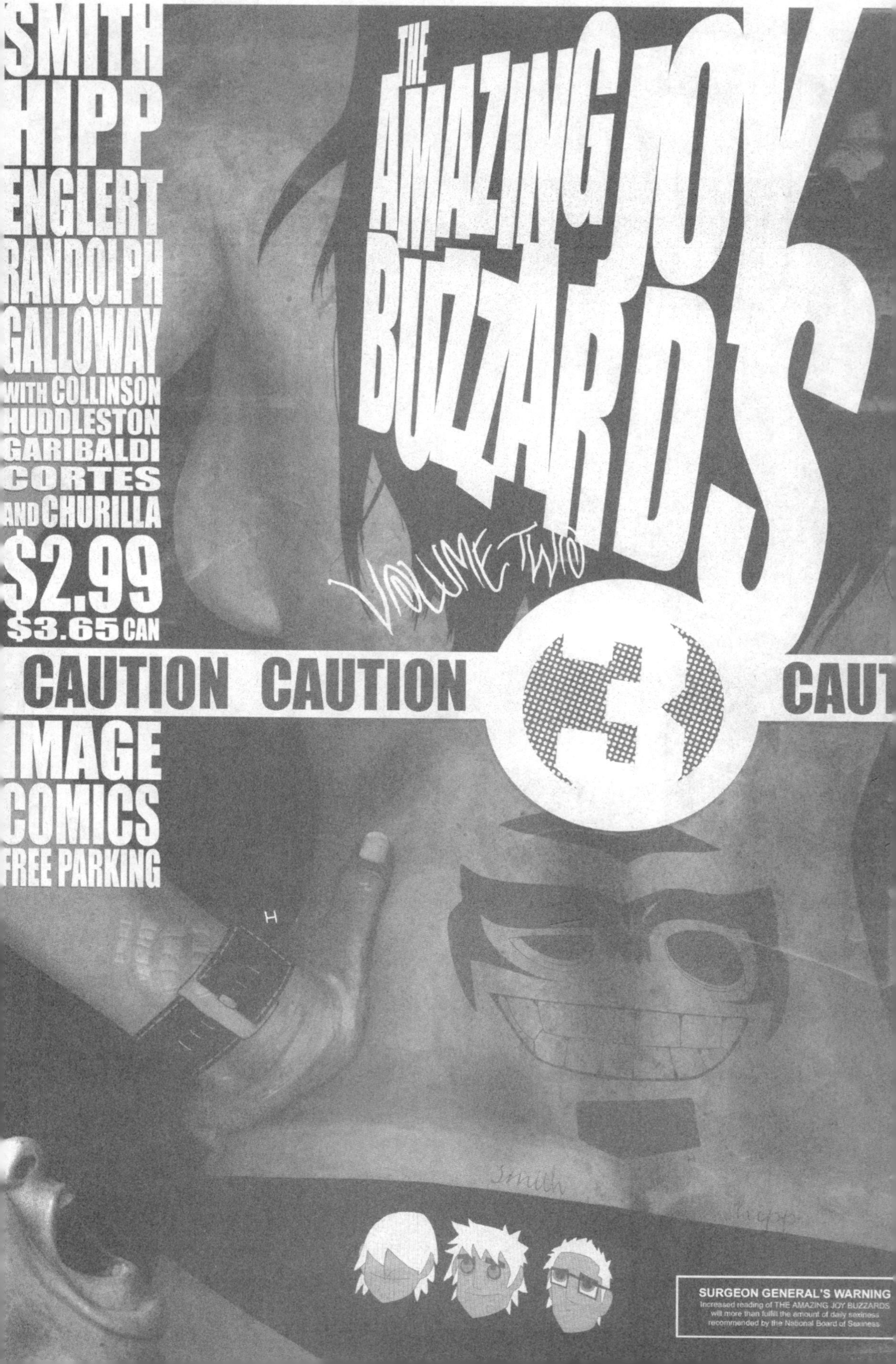
SMITH
HIPP
ENGLERT
RANDOLPH
GALLOWAY
WITH COLLINSON
HUDDLESTON
GARIBALDI
CORTES
AND CHURILLA
$2.99
$3.65 CAN
THE AMAZING JOY BUZZARDS
VOLUME TWO
3
CAUTION CAUTION CAUT
IMAGE
COMICS
FREE PARKING
SURGEON GENERAL'S WARNING
Increased reading of THE AMAZING JOY BUZZARDS will more than fulfill the amount of daily sexiness recommended by the National Board of Sexiness

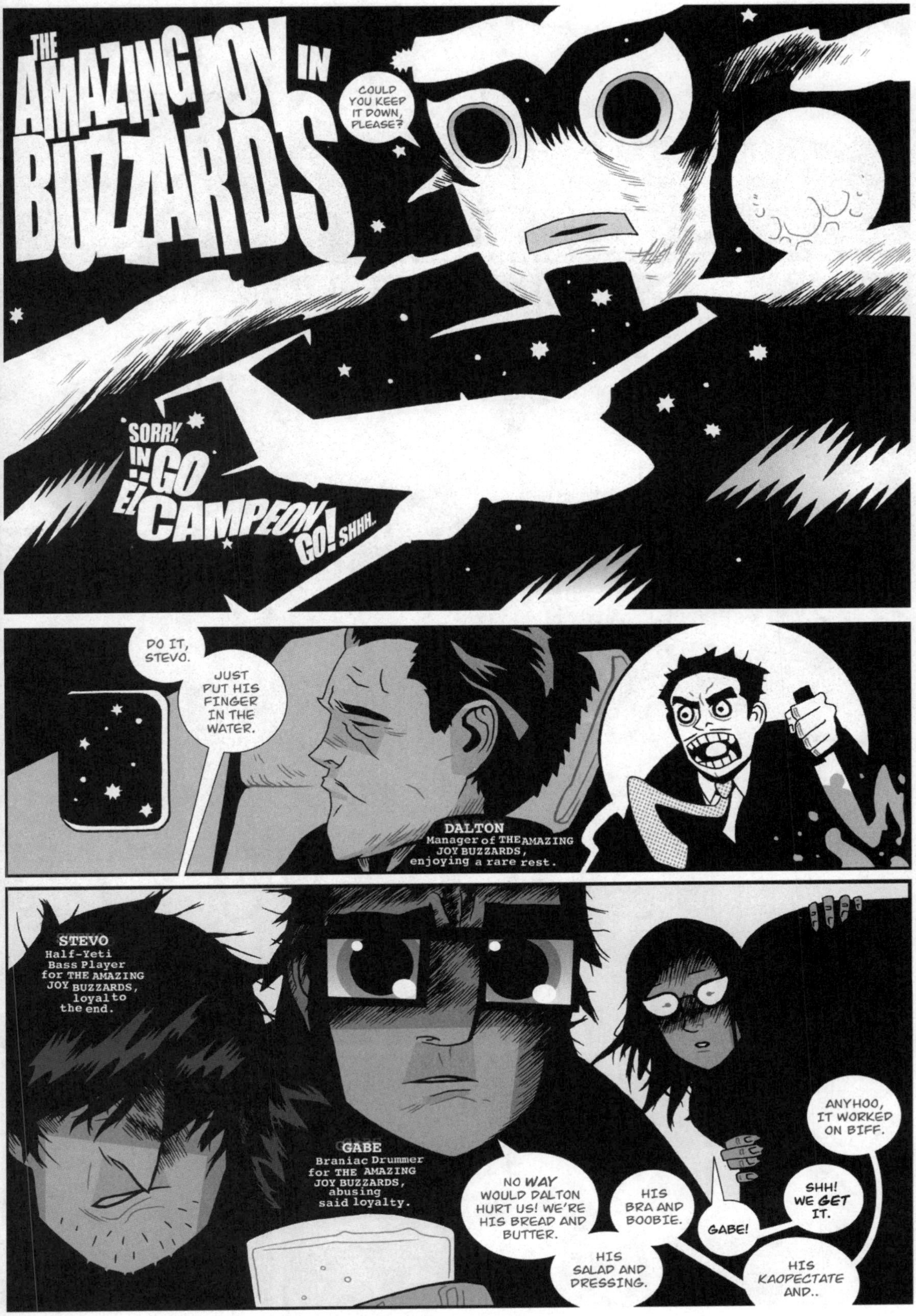
THE AMAZING JOY BUZZARDS IN
COULD YOU KEEP IT DOWN, PLEASE?
SORRY.
GO
GO EL CAMPEON GO!
SHHH..
DO IT, STEVO.
JUST PUT HIS FINGER IN THE WATER.
DALTON
Manager of THE AMAZING JOY BUZZARDS, enjoying a rare rest.
STEVO
Half-Yeti Bass Player for THE AMAZING JOY BUZZARDS, loyal to the end.
GABE
Braniac Drummer for THE AMAZING JOY BUZZARDS, abusing said loyalty.
NO WAY WOULD DALTON HURT US! WE'RE HIS BREAD AND BUTTER.
HIS BRA AND BOOBIE.
HIS SALAD AND DRESSING.
GABE!
HIS KAOPECTATE AND..
SHH! WE GET IT.
ANYHOO, IT WORKED ON BIFF.

YEAH, BUT I DON'T THINK *ANYTHING* IS GOING TO WAKE HIM AFTER THE WAY HE CHARGED THAT SHOW.

BIFF LeadSinger of THE AMAZING JOY BUZZARDS, still dreamy with pee stains.

HE WAS INCREDIBLE. POOR GUY.

YEAH, YOU GUYS WERE *TOPS!*

YOU'VE REALLY GOT THE BEST SHOW AROUND. IT'S NO WONDER YOU'RE NUMBER ONE.

BIFF IS THE NUMBER ONE EXPERT. (SNICKER)

WELL, WE *DID* HAVE A GREAT OPENING BAND.

YVONNE Guitarist of JOE STEREO and the SEX KITTENS fame.

SHIRLEY BassPlayer of aforementioned JOE STEREO and the SEX KITTENS fame.

JOE STEREO LeadSinger of.. well, you get the idea.

REALLY? THANKS, GABE.

PATTY Smitten Drummer for JOE BLABBIDY and the BLAHBLAH

BETTY Having none of that.

SO YOU GOING TO DO IT OR NOT, STEVO?!

POOF

DO *WHAT* NOW?

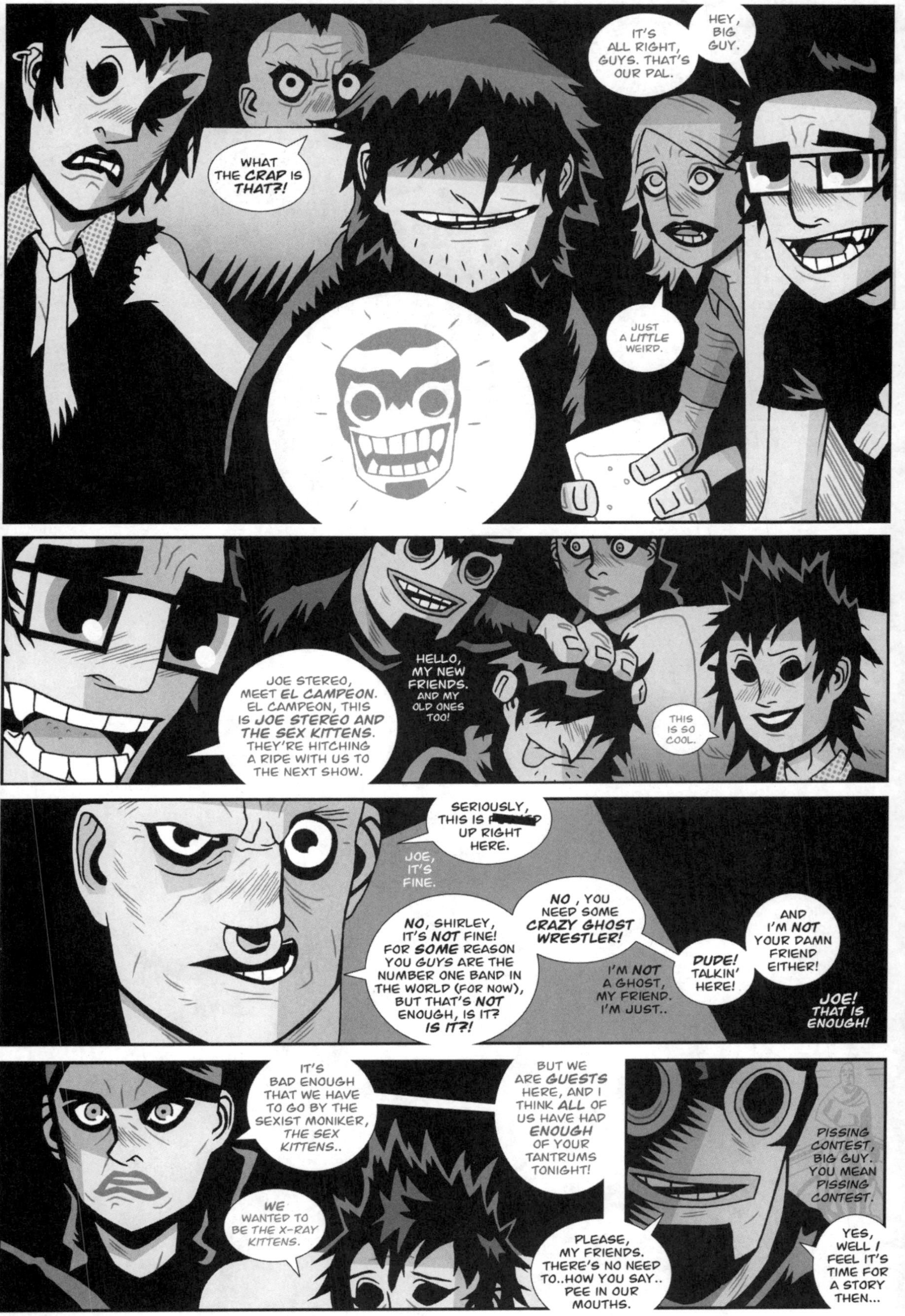

WHAT THE CRAP IS THAT?!
IT'S ALL RIGHT, GUYS. THAT'S OUR PAL.
HEY, BIG GUY.
JUST A LITTLE WEIRD.
JOE STEREO, MEET EL CAMPEON. EL CAMPEON, THIS IS JOE STEREO AND THE SEX KITTENS. THEY'RE HITCHING A RIDE WITH US TO THE NEXT SHOW.
HELLO, MY NEW FRIENDS. AND MY OLD ONES TOO!
THIS IS SO COOL.
SERIOUSLY, THIS IS [redacted] UP RIGHT HERE.
JOE, IT'S FINE.
NO, SHIRLEY, IT'S NOT FINE! FOR SOME REASON YOU GUYS ARE THE NUMBER ONE BAND IN THE WORLD (FOR NOW), BUT THAT'S NOT ENOUGH, IS IT? IS IT?!
NO , YOU NEED SOME CRAZY GHOST WRESTLER!
I'M NOT A GHOST, MY FRIEND. I'M JUST..
DUDE! TALKIN' HERE!
AND I'M NOT YOUR DAMN FRIEND EITHER!
JOE! THAT IS ENOUGH!
IT'S BAD ENOUGH THAT WE HAVE TO GO BY THE SEXIST MONIKER, THE SEX KITTENS..
WE WANTED TO BE THE X-RAY KITTENS.
BUT WE ARE GUESTS HERE, AND I THINK ALL OF US HAVE HAD ENOUGH OF YOUR TANTRUMS TONIGHT!
PLEASE, MY FRIENDS. THERE'S NO NEED TO..HOW YOU SAY.. PEE IN OUR MOUTHS.
PISSING CONTEST, BIG GUY. YOU MEAN PISSING CONTEST.
YES, WELL I FEEL IT'S TIME FOR A STORY THEN...

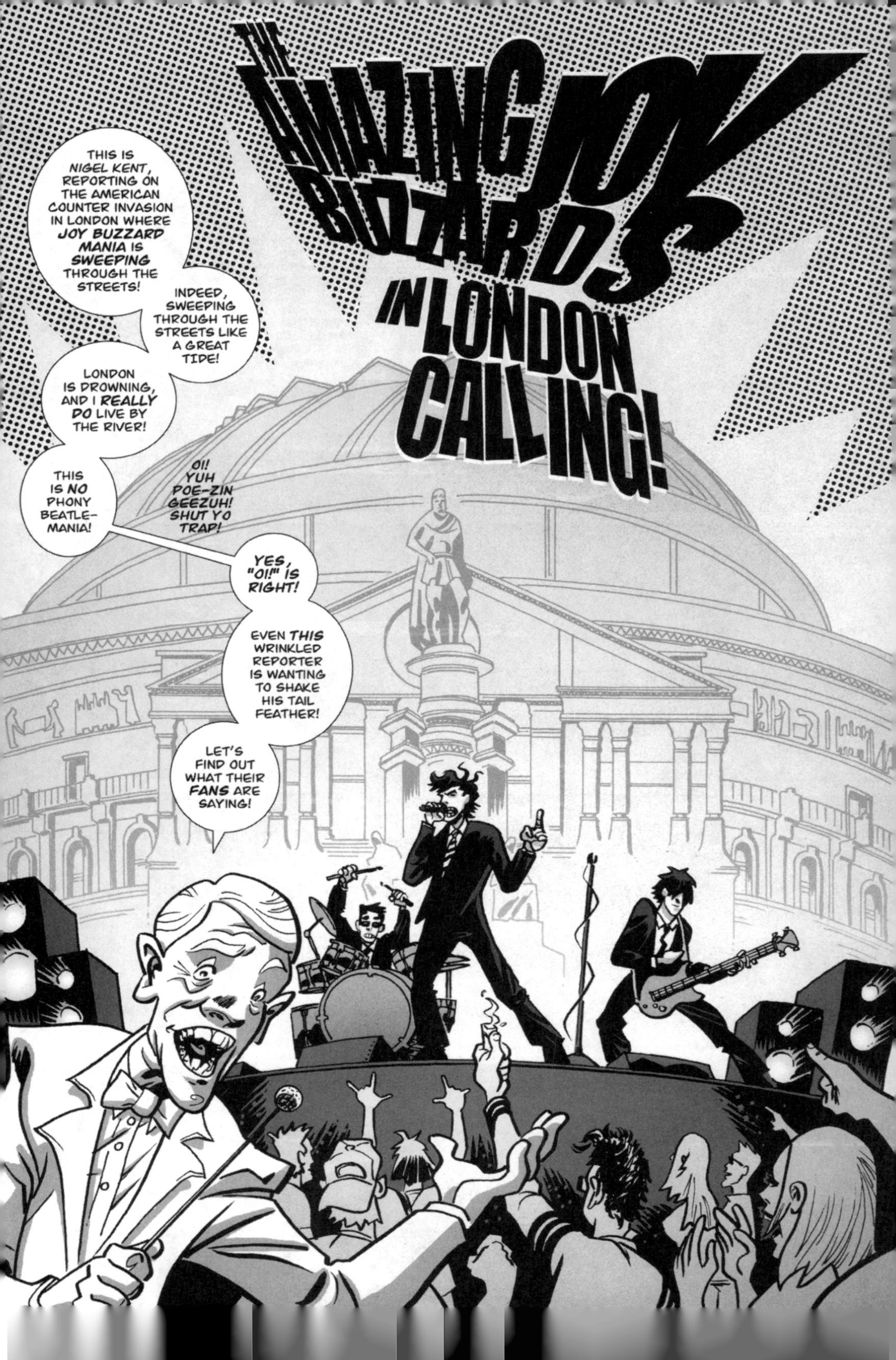

THE AMAZING JOY BUZZARDS IN LONDON CALLING!
THIS IS NIGEL KENT, REPORTING ON THE AMERICAN COUNTER INVASION IN LONDON WHERE JOY BUZZARD MANIA IS SWEEPING THROUGH THE STREETS!
INDEED, SWEEPING THROUGH THE STREETS LIKE A GREAT TIDE!
LONDON IS DROWNING, AND I REALLY DO LIVE BY THE RIVER!
THIS IS NO PHONY BEATLE-MANIA!
OI! YUH POE-ZIN GEEZUH! SHUT YO TRAP!
YES, "OI!" IS RIGHT!
EVEN THIS WRINKLED REPORTER IS WANTING TO SHAKE HIS TAIL FEATHER!
LET'S FIND OUT WHAT THEIR FANS ARE SAYING!

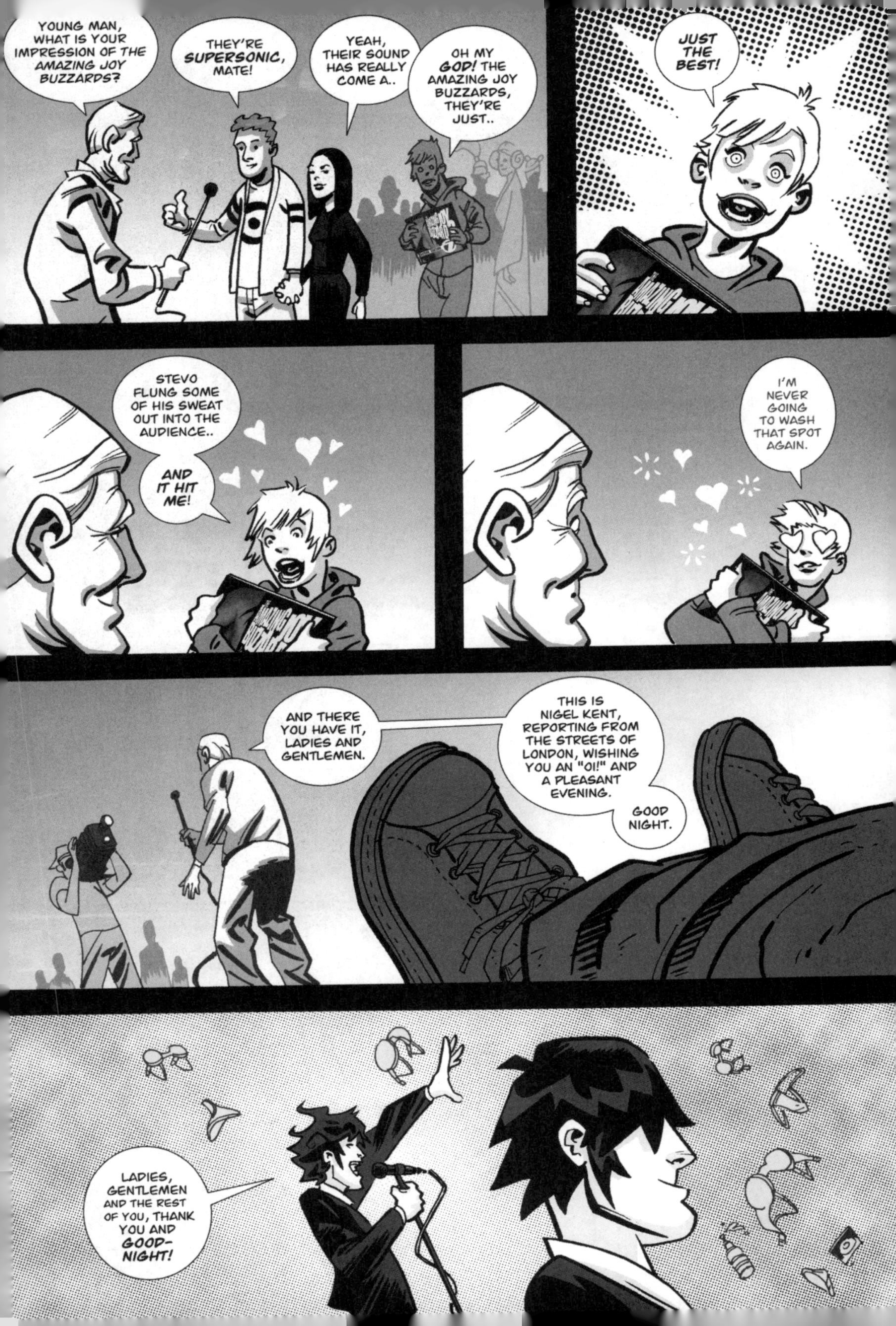
YOUNG MAN, WHAT IS YOUR IMPRESSION OF THE AMAZING JOY BUZZARDS?
THEY'RE **SUPERSONIC**, MATE!
YEAH, THEIR SOUND HAS REALLY COME A..
OH MY **GOD!** THE AMAZING JOY BUZZARDS, THEY'RE JUST..
JUST THE BEST!
STEVO FLUNG SOME OF HIS SWEAT OUT INTO THE AUDIENCE..
AND IT HIT ME!
I'M NEVER GOING TO WASH THAT SPOT AGAIN.
AND THERE YOU HAVE IT, LADIES AND GENTLEMEN.
THIS IS NIGEL KENT, REPORTING FROM THE STREETS OF LONDON, WISHING YOU AN "OI!" AND A PLEASANT EVENING.
GOOD NIGHT.
LADIES, GENTLEMEN AND THE REST OF YOU, THANK YOU AND **GOOD-NIGHT!**

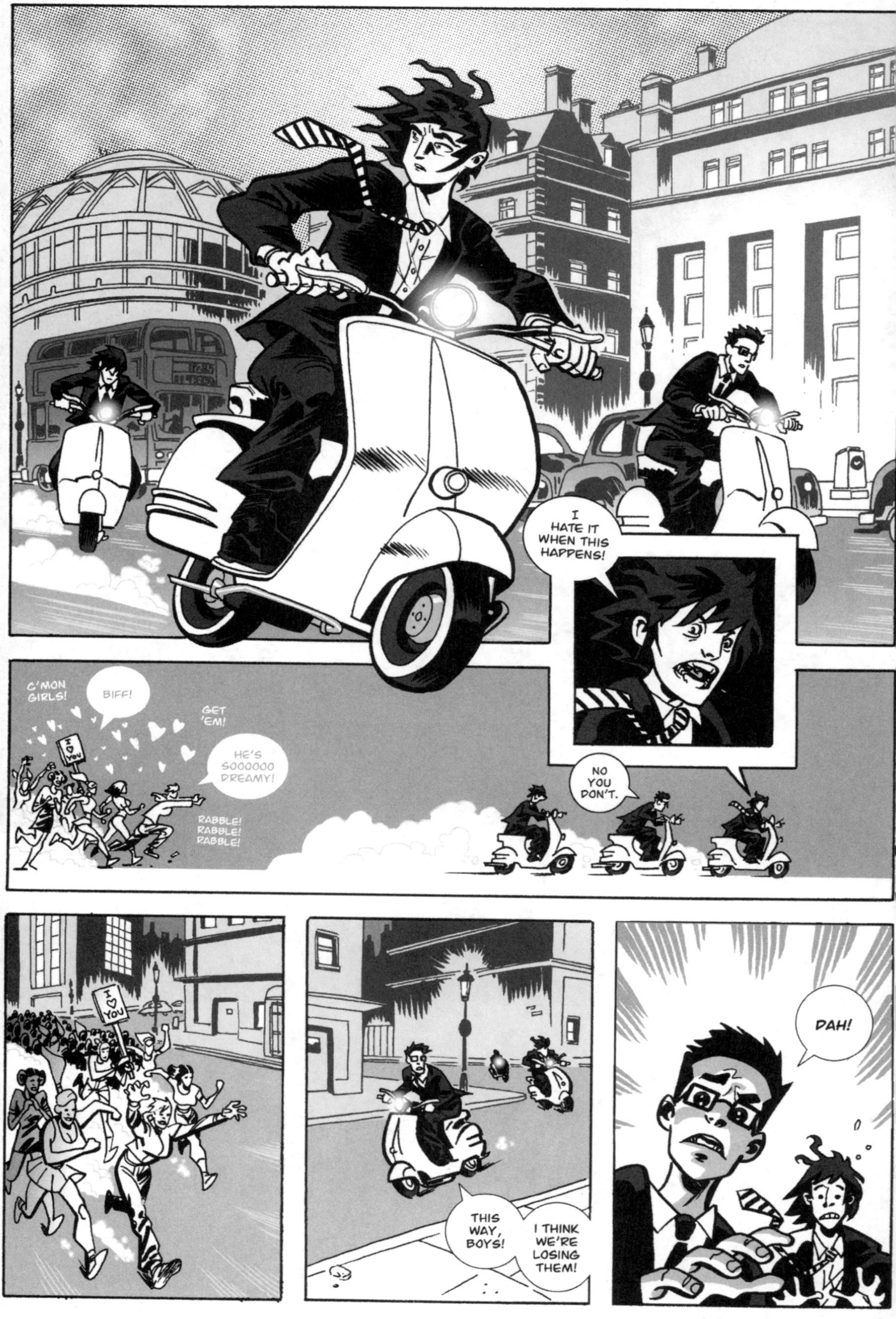
I HATE IT WHEN THIS HAPPENS!
C'MON GIRLS!
BIFF!
GET 'EM!
I ♥ YOU
HE'S SOOOOOO DREAMY!
RABBLE! RABBLE! RABBLE!
NO YOU DON'T.
I ♥ YOU
THIS WAY, BOYS!
I THINK WE'RE LOSING THEM!
DAH!

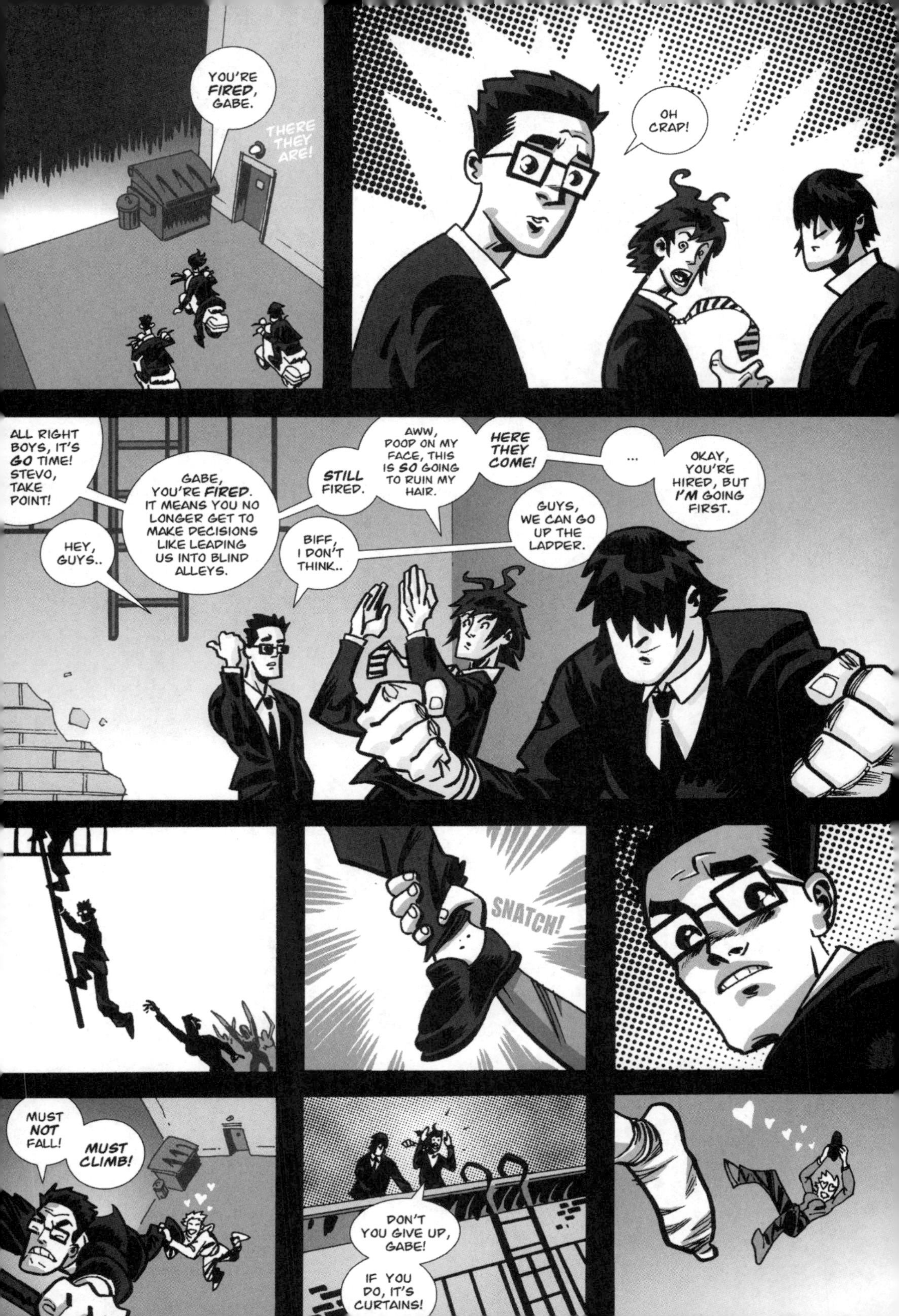
YOU'RE FIRED, GABE.
THERE THEY ARE!
OH CRAP!
ALL RIGHT BOYS, IT'S GO TIME! STEVO, TAKE POINT!
HEY, GUYS..
GABE, YOU'RE FIRED. IT MEANS YOU NO LONGER GET TO MAKE DECISIONS LIKE LEADING US INTO BLIND ALLEYS.
STILL FIRED.
AWW, POOP ON MY FACE, THIS IS SO GOING TO RUIN MY HAIR.
BIFF, I DON'T THINK..
HERE THEY COME!
GUYS, WE CAN GO UP THE LADDER.
...
OKAY, YOU'RE HIRED, BUT I'M GOING FIRST.
SNATCH!
MUST NOT FALL!
MUST CLIMB!
DON'T YOU GIVE UP, GABE!
IF YOU DO, IT'S CURTAINS!

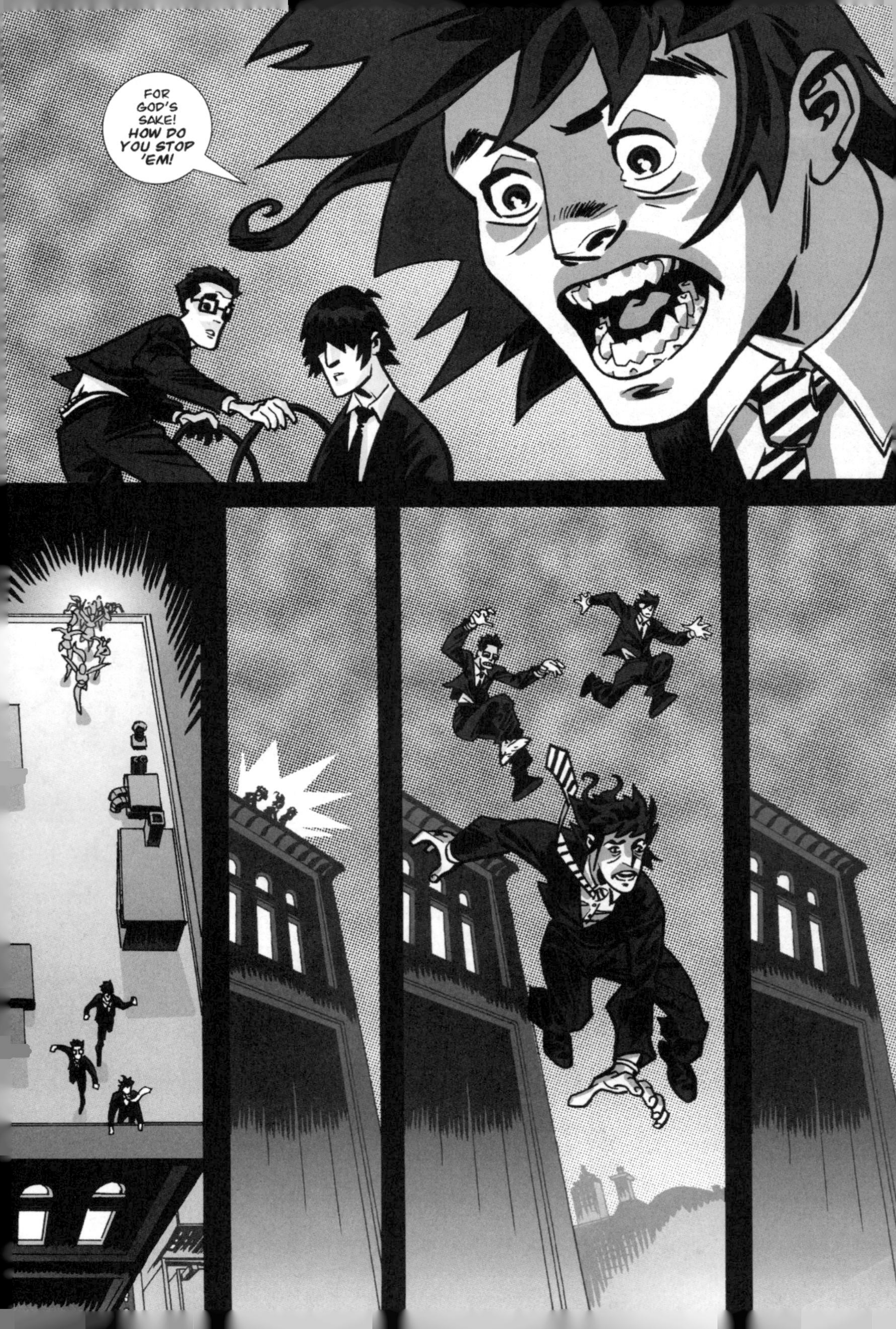
FOR GOD'S SAKE! HOW DO YOU STOP 'EM!

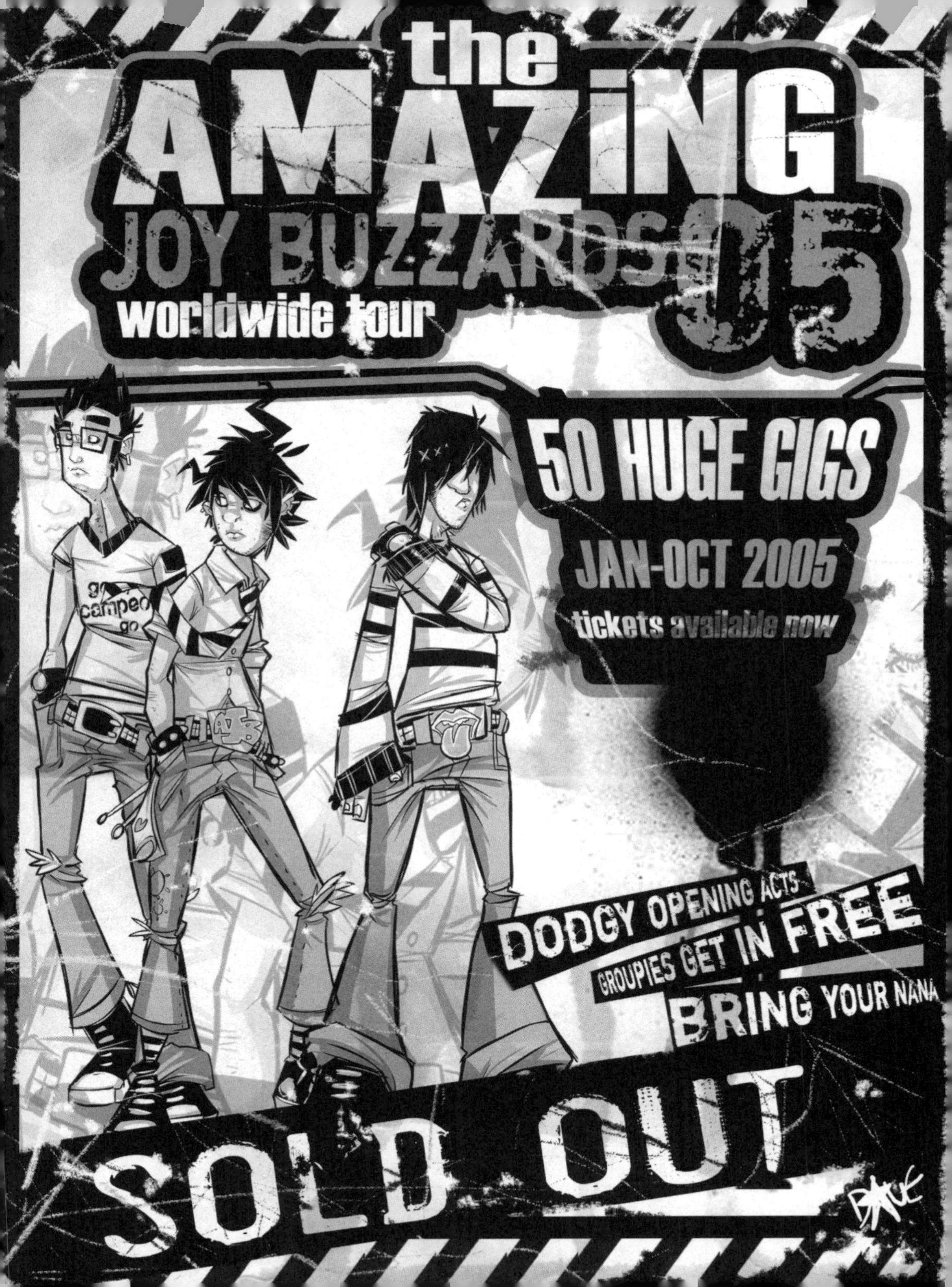
the AMAZING JOY BUZZARDS
worldwide tour
05
50 HUGE GIGS
JAN-OCT 2005
tickets available now
DODGY OPENING ACTS
GROUPIES GET IN FREE
BRING YOUR NANA
SOLD OUT
go campeo go

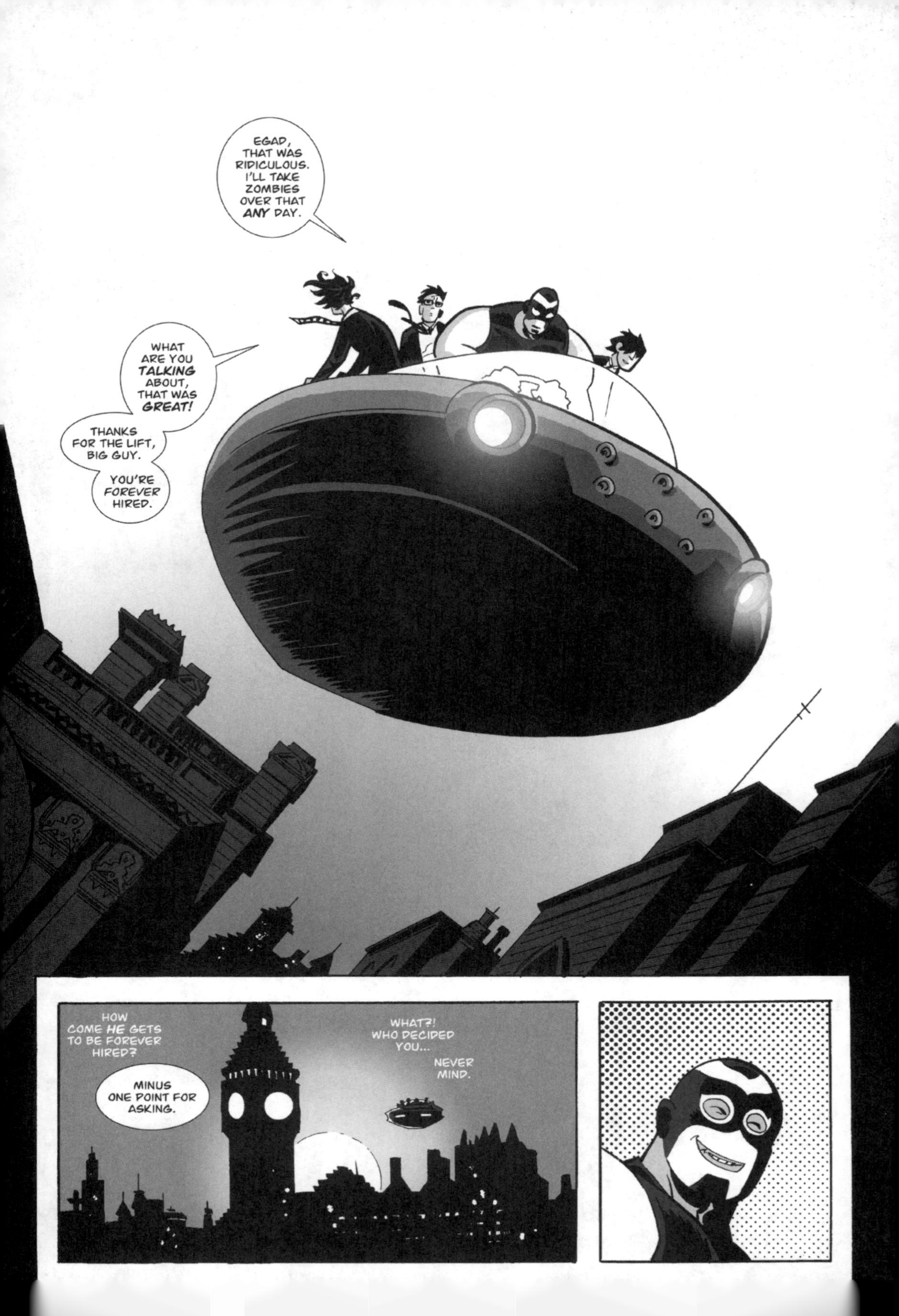

EGAD, THAT WAS RIDICULOUS. I'LL TAKE ZOMBIES OVER THAT ANY DAY.
WHAT ARE YOU TALKING ABOUT, THAT WAS GREAT!
THANKS FOR THE LIFT, BIG GUY.
YOU'RE FOREVER HIRED.
HOW COME HE GETS TO BE FOREVER HIRED?
MINUS ONE POINT FOR ASKING.
WHAT?! WHO DECIDED YOU...
NEVER MIND.

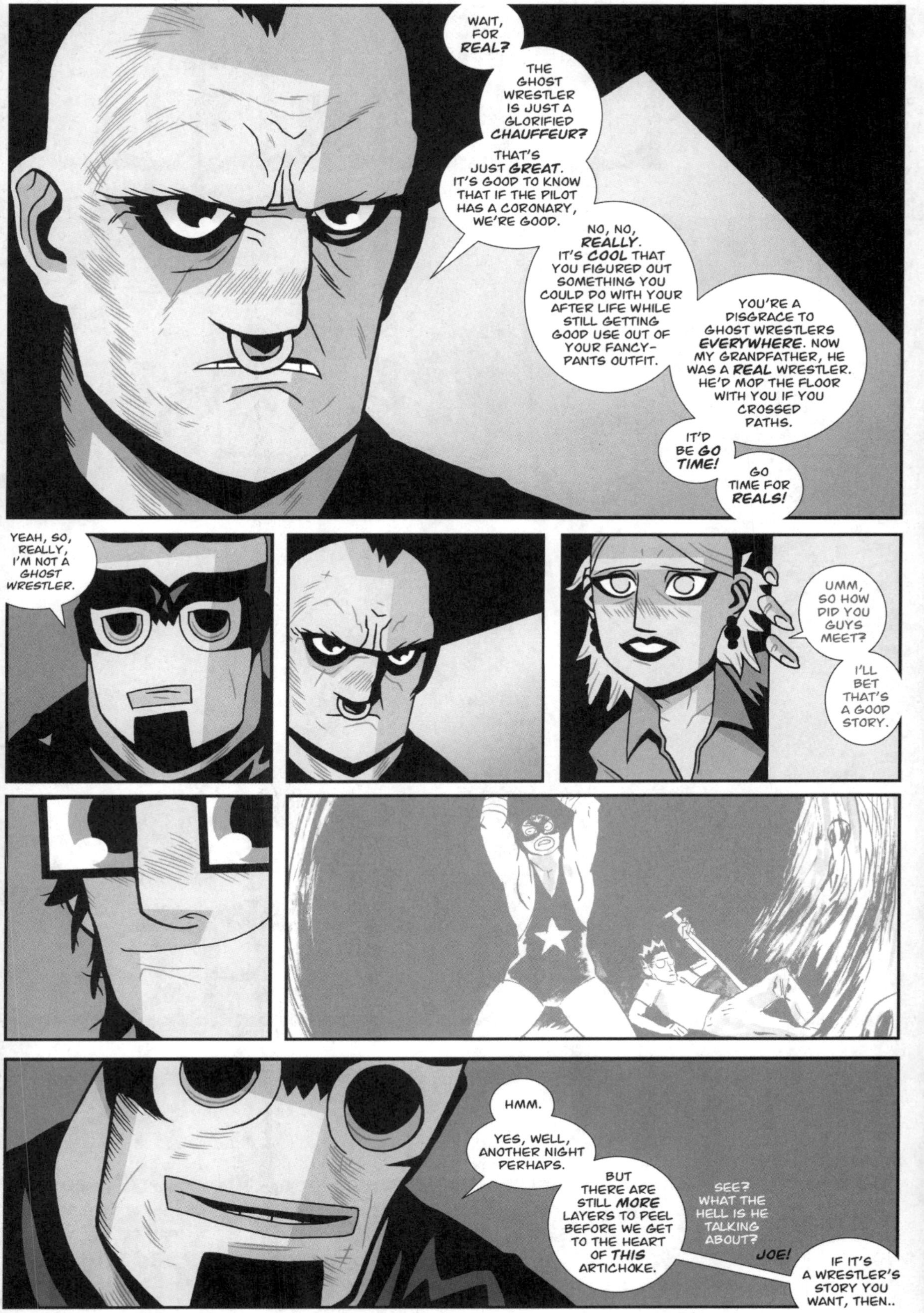
WAIT, FOR REAL?
THE GHOST WRESTLER IS JUST A GLORIFIED CHAUFFEUR?
THAT'S JUST GREAT. IT'S GOOD TO KNOW THAT IF THE PILOT HAS A CORONARY, WE'RE GOOD.
NO, NO, REALLY. IT'S COOL THAT YOU FIGURED OUT SOMETHING YOU COULD DO WITH YOUR AFTER LIFE WHILE STILL GETTING GOOD USE OUT OF YOUR FANCY-PANTS OUTFIT.
YOU'RE A DISGRACE TO GHOST WRESTLERS EVERYWHERE. NOW MY GRANDFATHER, HE WAS A REAL WRESTLER. HE'D MOP THE FLOOR WITH YOU IF YOU CROSSED PATHS.
IT'D BE GO TIME!
GO TIME FOR REALS!
YEAH, SO, REALLY, I'M NOT A GHOST WRESTLER.
UMM, SO HOW DID YOU GUYS MEET?
I'LL BET THAT'S A GOOD STORY.
HMM.
YES, WELL, ANOTHER NIGHT PERHAPS.
BUT THERE ARE STILL MORE LAYERS TO PEEL BEFORE WE GET TO THE HEART OF THIS ARTICHOKE.
SEE? WHAT THE HELL IS HE TALKING ABOUT?
JOE!
IF IT'S A WRESTLER'S STORY YOU WANT, THEN..

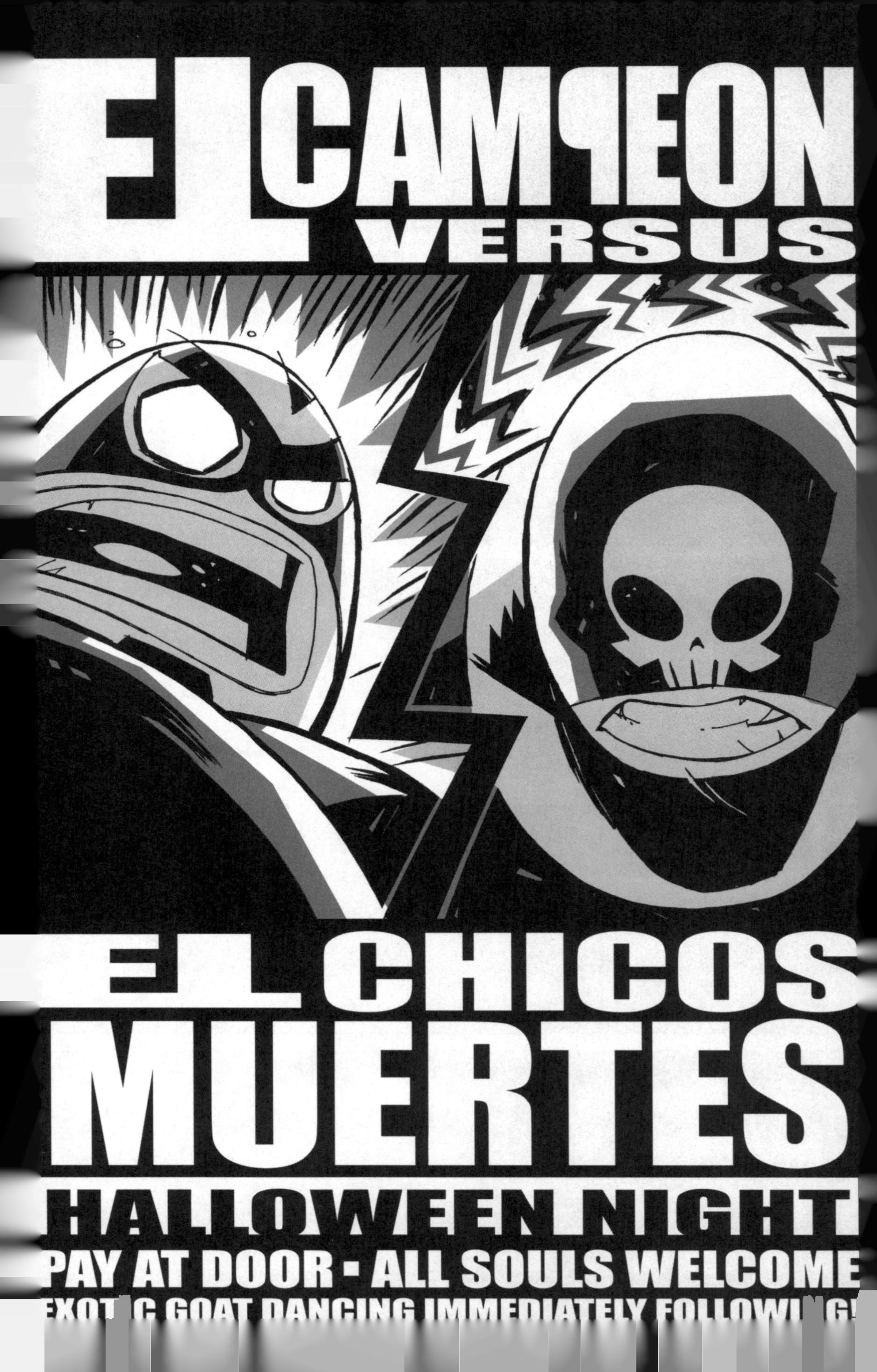
EL CAMPEON
VERSUS
EL CHICOS
MUERTES
HALLOWEEN NIGHT
PAY AT DOOR - ALL SOULS WELCOME
EXOTIC GOAT DANCING IMMEDIATELY FOLLOWING!

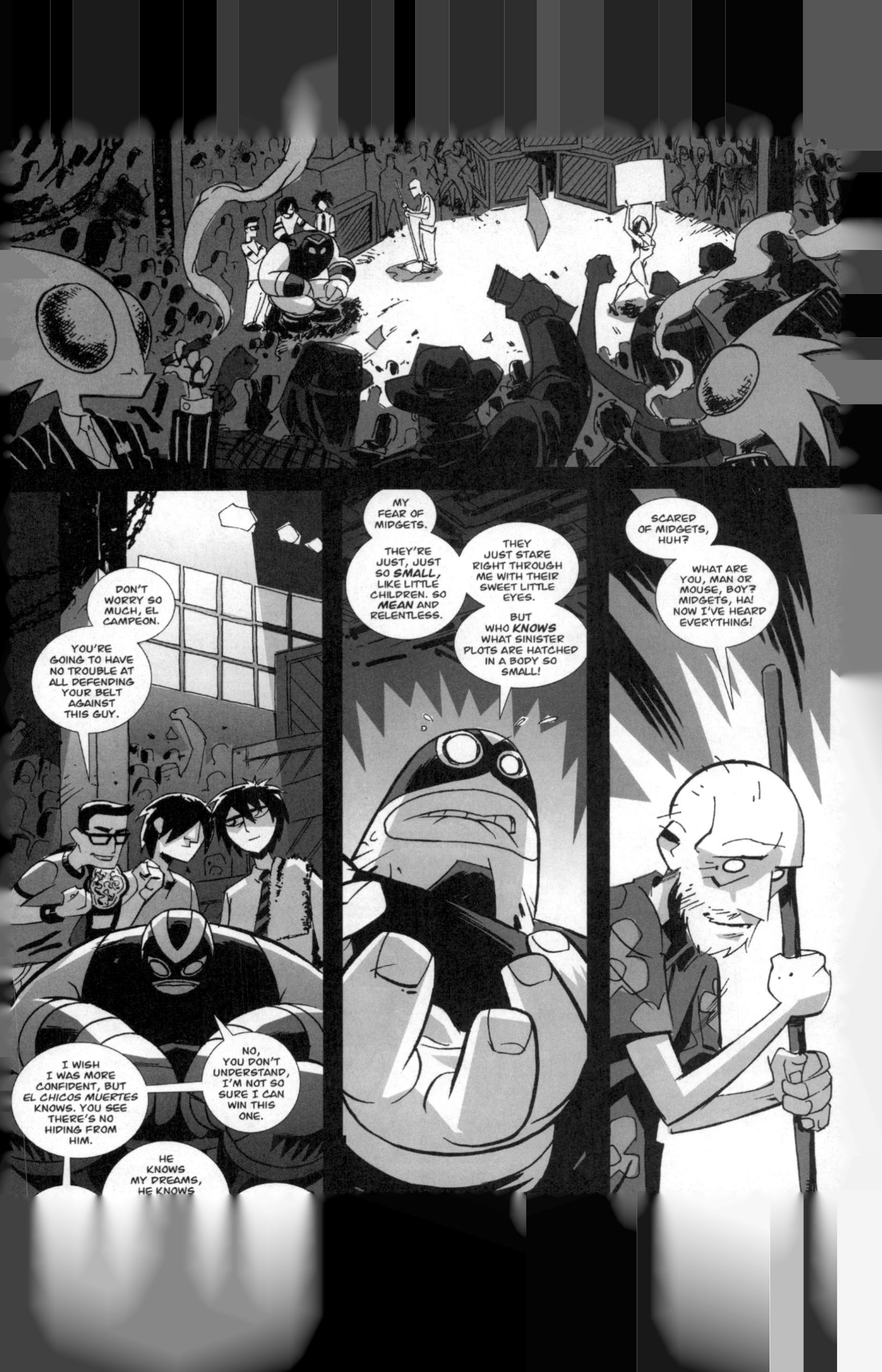

DON'T WORRY SO MUCH, EL CAMPEON.
YOU'RE GOING TO HAVE NO TROUBLE AT ALL DEFENDING YOUR BELT AGAINST THIS GUY.
NO, YOU DON'T UNDERSTAND, I'M NOT SO SURE I CAN WIN THIS ONE.
I WISH I WAS MORE CONFIDENT, BUT EL CHICOS MUERTES KNOWS. YOU SEE THERE'S NO HIDING FROM HIM.
HE KNOWS MY DREAMS, HE KNOWS
MY FEAR OF MIDGETS.
THEY'RE JUST, JUST SO SMALL, LIKE LITTLE CHILDREN. SO MEAN AND RELENTLESS.
THEY JUST STARE RIGHT THROUGH ME WITH THEIR SWEET LITTLE EYES.
BUT WHO KNOWS WHAT SINISTER PLOTS ARE HATCHED IN A BODY SO SMALL!
SCARED OF MIDGETS, HUH?
WHAT ARE YOU, MAN OR MOUSE, BOY? MIDGETS, HA! NOW I'VE HEARD EVERYTHING!

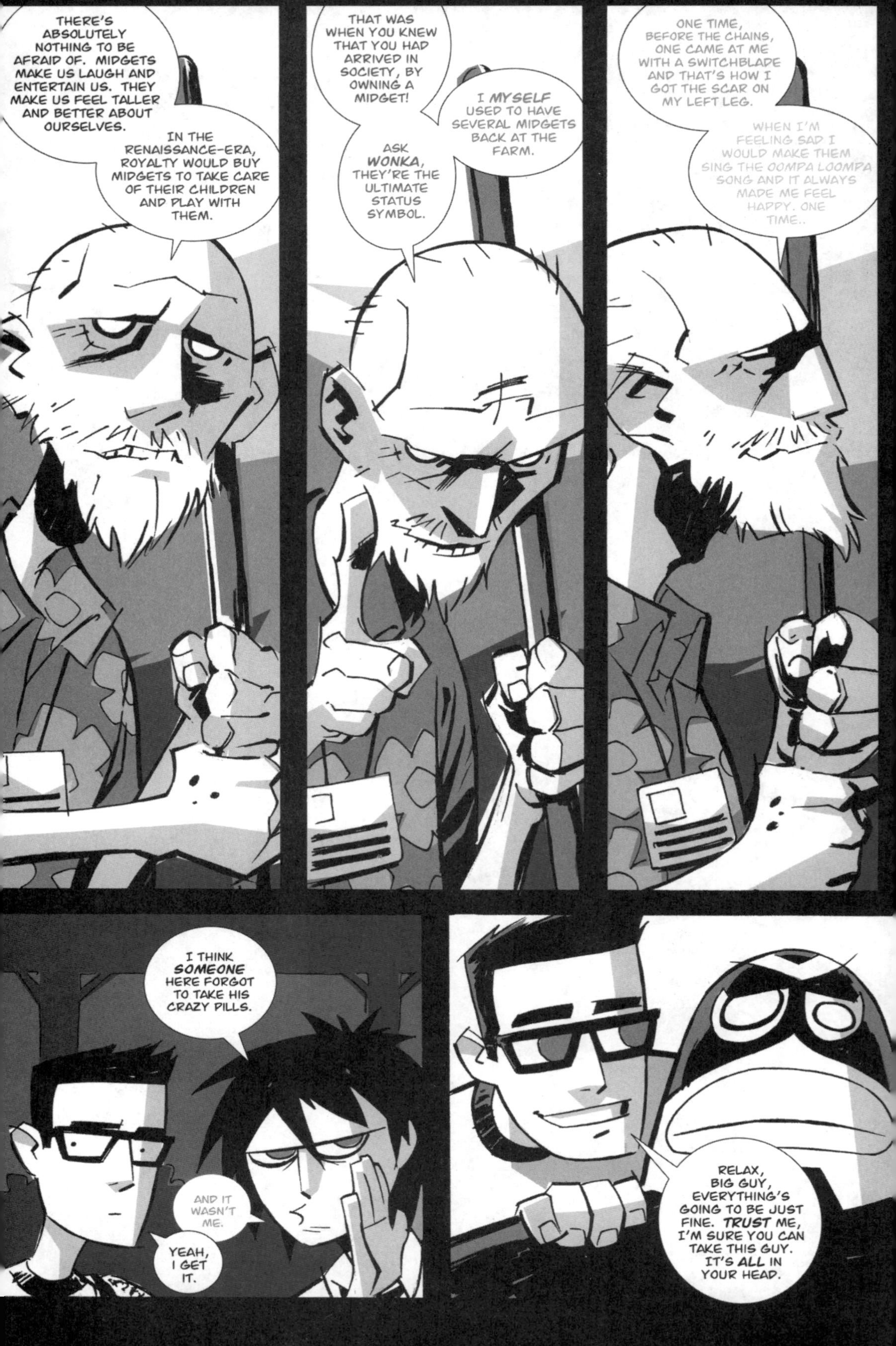
THERE'S ABSOLUTELY NOTHING TO BE AFRAID OF. MIDGETS MAKE US LAUGH AND ENTERTAIN US. THEY MAKE US FEEL TALLER AND BETTER ABOUT OURSELVES.
IN THE RENAISSANCE-ERA, ROYALTY WOULD BUY MIDGETS TO TAKE CARE OF THEIR CHILDREN AND PLAY WITH THEM.
THAT WAS WHEN YOU KNEW THAT YOU HAD ARRIVED IN SOCIETY, BY OWNING A MIDGET!
ASK WONKA, THEY'RE THE ULTIMATE STATUS SYMBOL.
I MYSELF USED TO HAVE SEVERAL MIDGETS BACK AT THE FARM.
ONE TIME, BEFORE THE CHAINS, ONE CAME AT ME WITH A SWITCHBLADE AND THAT'S HOW I GOT THE SCAR ON MY LEFT LEG.
WHEN I'M FEELING SAD I WOULD MAKE THEM SING THE OOMPA LOOMPA SONG AND IT ALWAYS MADE ME FEEL HAPPY. ONE TIME..
I THINK SOMEONE HERE FORGOT TO TAKE HIS CRAZY PILLS.
AND IT WASN'T ME.
YEAH, I GET IT.
RELAX, BIG GUY, EVERYTHING'S GOING TO BE JUST FINE. TRUST ME, I'M SURE YOU CAN TAKE THIS GUY. IT'S ALL IN YOUR HEAD.

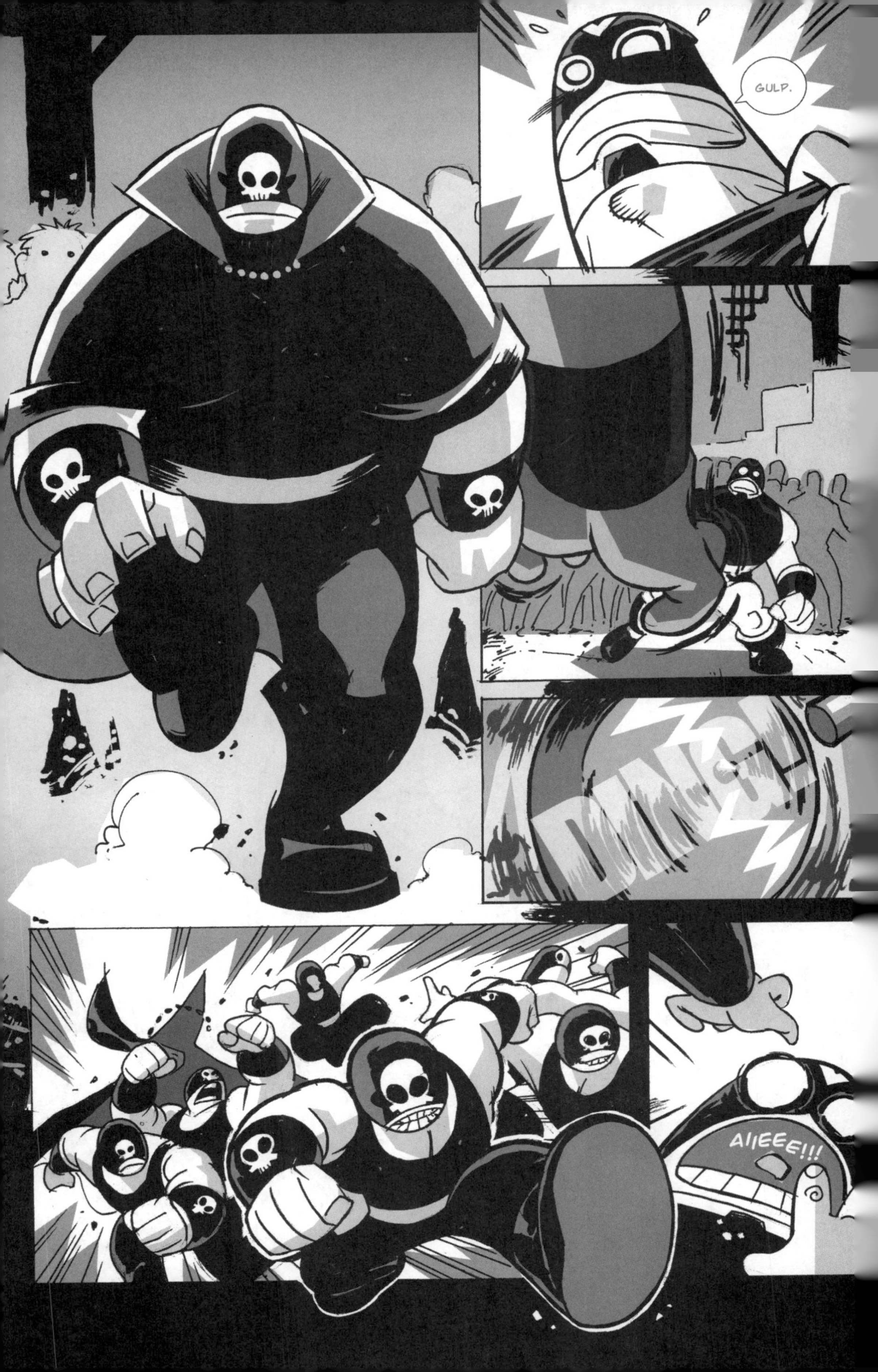
GULP.
AIIEEE!!!

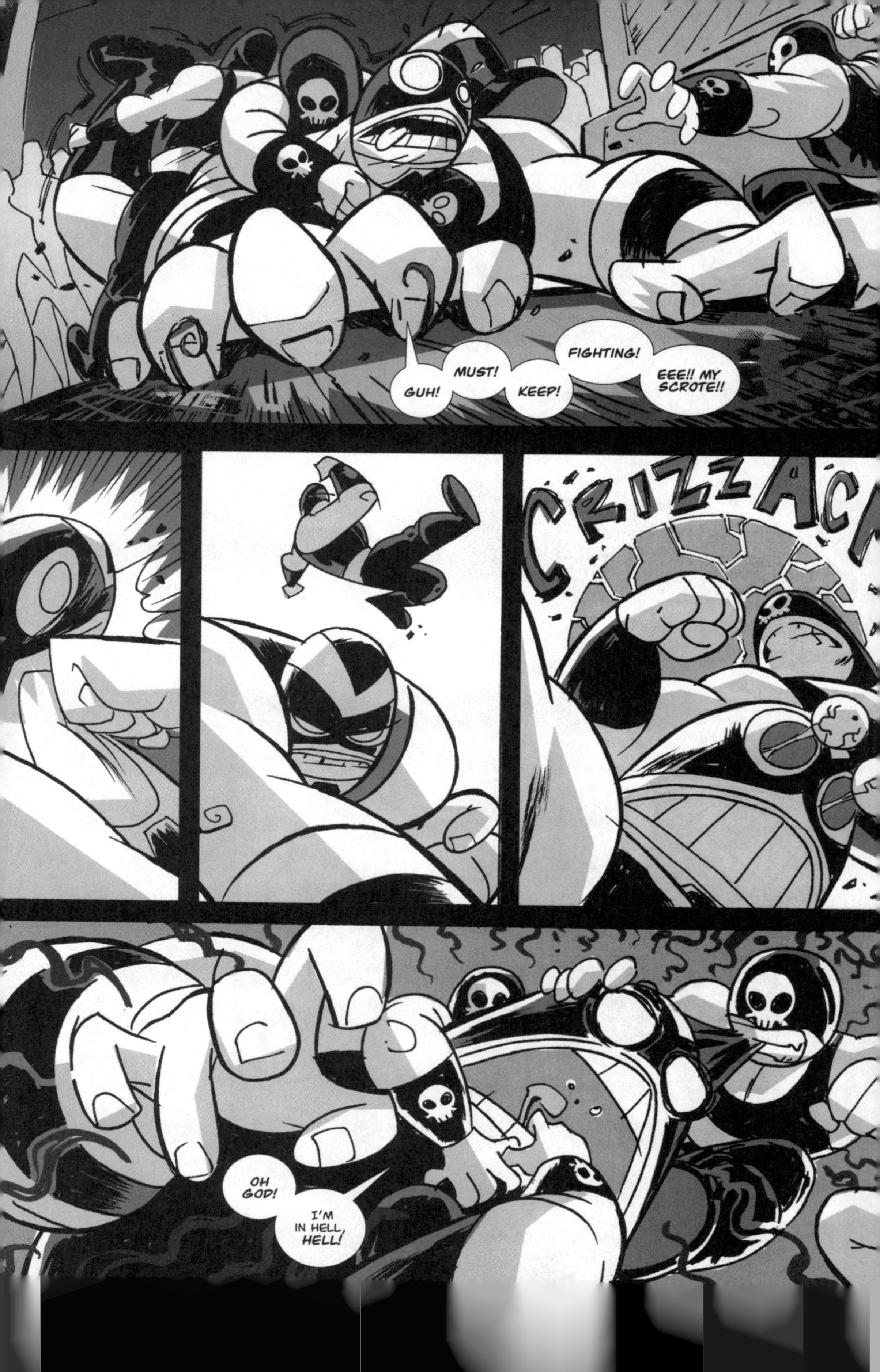

GUH!
MUST!
KEEP!
FIGHTING!
EEE!! MY SCROTE!!
CRIZZACK
OH GOD!
I'M IN HELL, HELL!

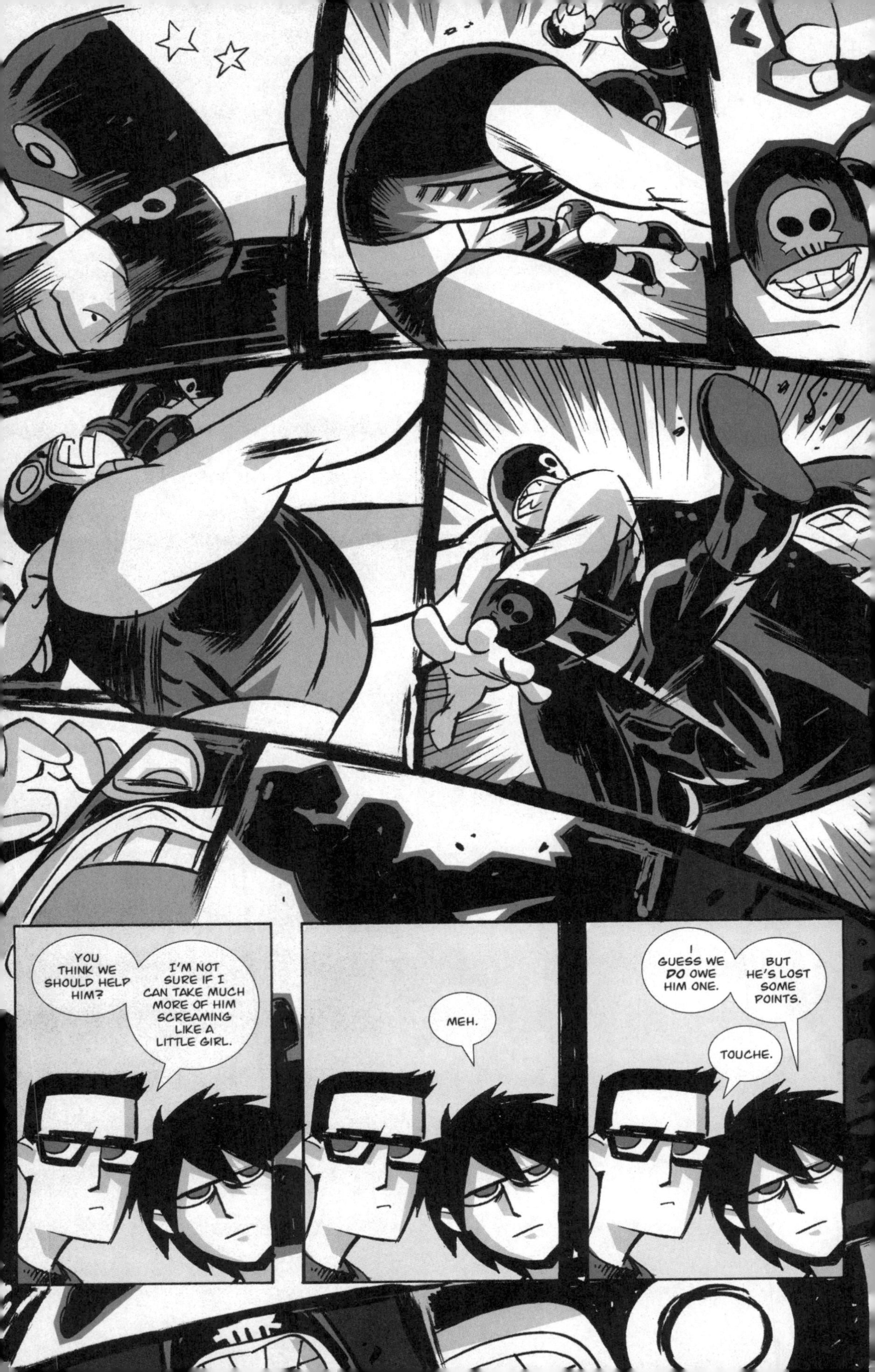
YOU THINK WE SHOULD HELP HIM?
I'M NOT SURE IF I CAN TAKE MUCH MORE OF HIM SCREAMING LIKE A LITTLE GIRL.
MEH.
I GUESS WE DO OWE HIM ONE.
BUT HE'S LOST SOME POINTS.
TOUCHE.

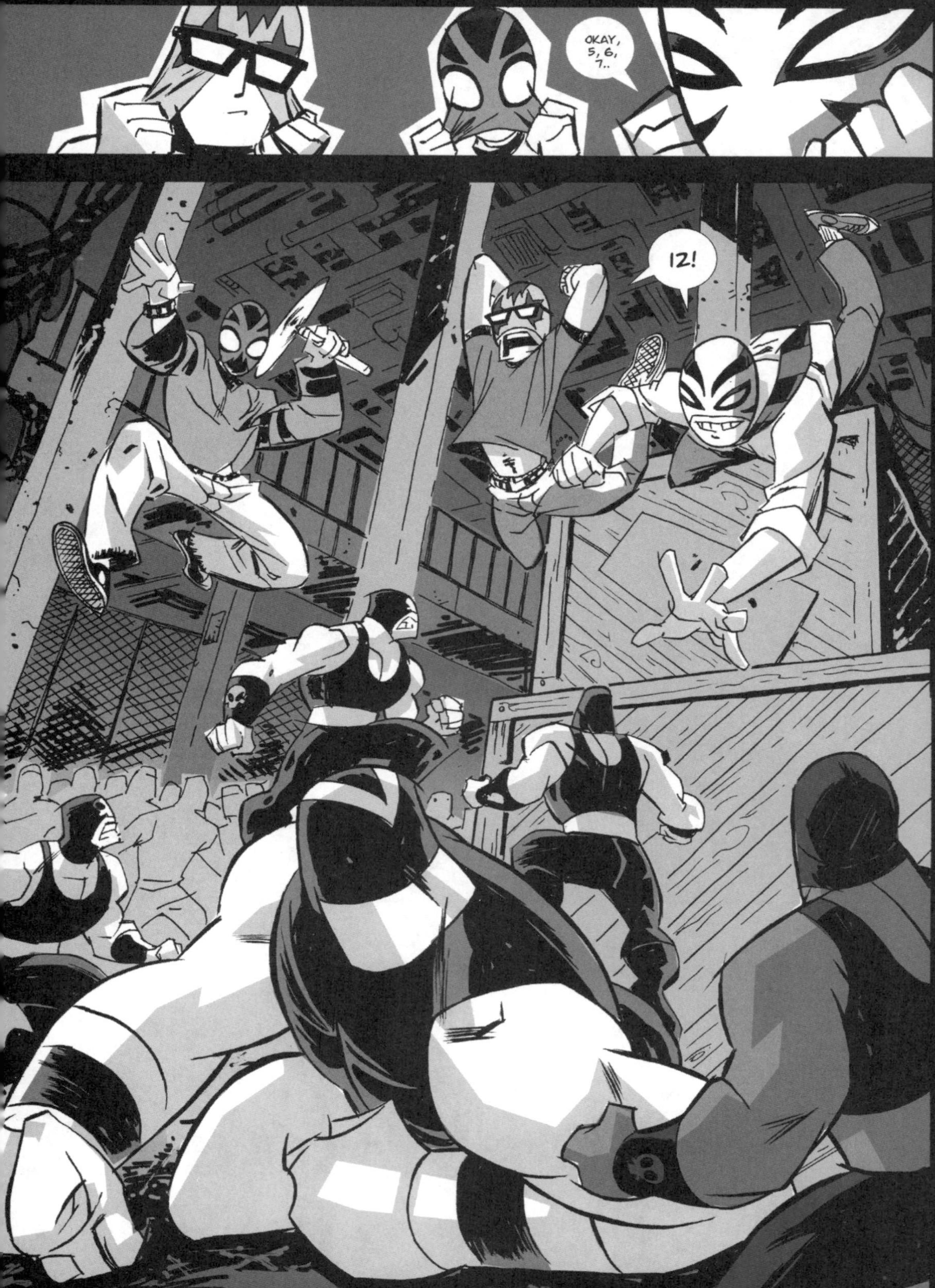
OKAY, 5, 6, 7..
12!

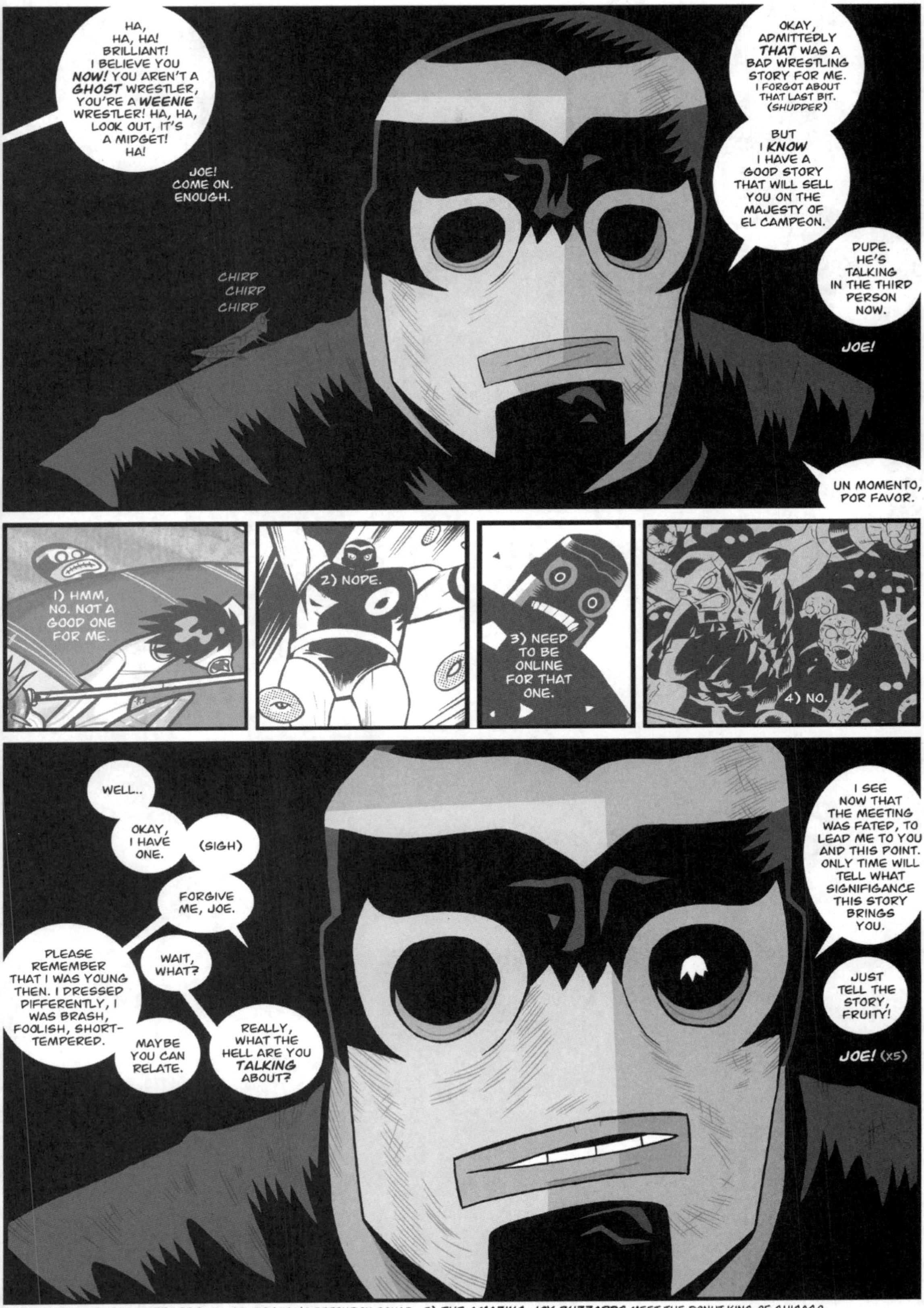
HA, HA, HA! BRILLIANT! I BELIEVE YOU NOW! YOU AREN'T A GHOST WRESTLER, YOU'RE A WEENIE WRESTLER! HA, HA, LOOK OUT, IT'S A MIDGET! HA!
JOE! COME ON. ENOUGH.
OKAY, ADMITTEDLY THAT WAS A BAD WRESTLING STORY FOR ME. I FORGOT ABOUT THAT LAST BIT. (SHUDDER)
BUT I KNOW I HAVE A GOOD STORY THAT WILL SELL YOU ON THE MAJESTY OF EL CAMPEON.
DUDE. HE'S TALKING IN THE THIRD PERSON NOW.
JOE!
CHIRP CHIRP CHIRP
UN MOMENTO, POR FAVOR.
1) HMM, NO. NOT A GOOD ONE FOR ME.
2) NOPE.
3) NEED TO BE ONLINE FOR THAT ONE.
4) NO.
WELL..
OKAY, I HAVE ONE.
(SIGH)
FORGIVE ME, JOE.
PLEASE REMEMBER THAT I WAS YOUNG THEN. I DRESSED DIFFERENTLY, I WAS BRASH, FOOLISH, SHORT-TEMPERED.
MAYBE YOU CAN RELATE.
WAIT, WHAT?
REALLY, WHAT THE HELL ARE YOU TALKING ABOUT?
I SEE NOW THAT THE MEETING WAS FATED, TO LEAD ME TO YOU AND THIS POINT. ONLY TIME WILL TELL WHAT SIGNIFIGANCE THIS STORY BRINGS YOU.
JUST TELL THE STORY, FRUITY!
JOE! (X5)

1) ***THE AMAZING JOY BUZZARDS*** VS. MR. TITICACA'S DETENTION SQUAD. 2) ***THE AMAZING JOY BUZZARDS*** MEET THE DONUT KING OF CHICAGO.
3) ***THE AMAZING JOY BUZZARDS*** GO HOLLYWOOD! (GET BRANNIGAN!) 4) ***THE AMAZING JOY BUZZARDS*** AND THE ROMERO-BBQ-BANDIT-BASH.

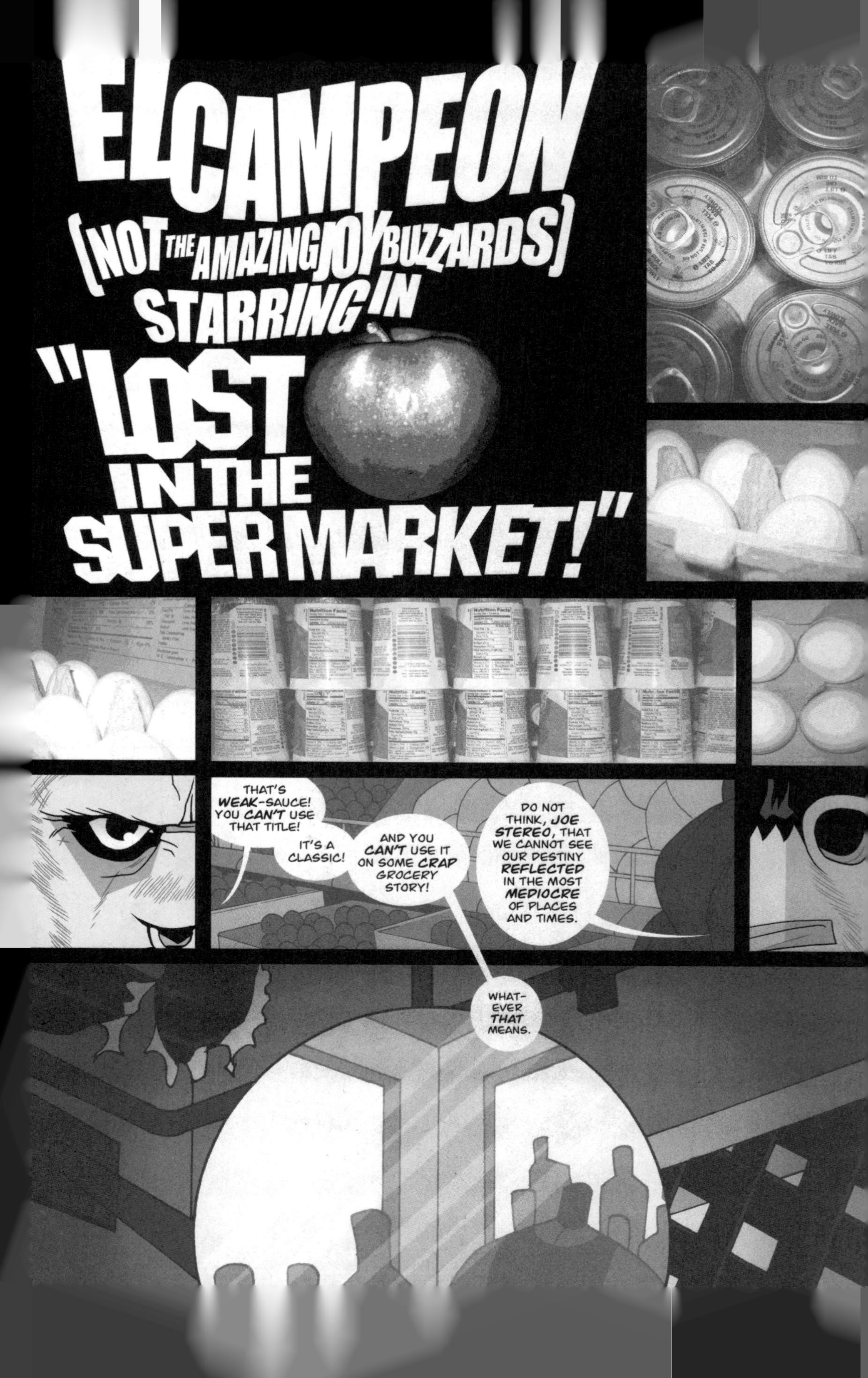
EL CAMPEON
(NOT THE AMAZING JOY BUZZARDS)
STARRING IN
"LOST IN THE SUPERMARKET!"
THAT'S WEAK-SAUCE! YOU CAN'T USE THAT TITLE!
IT'S A CLASSIC!
AND YOU CAN'T USE IT ON SOME CRAP GROCERY STORY!
DO NOT THINK, JOE STEREO, THAT WE CANNOT SEE OUR DESTINY REFLECTED IN THE MOST MEDIOCRE OF PLACES AND TIMES.
WHAT-EVER THAT MEANS.

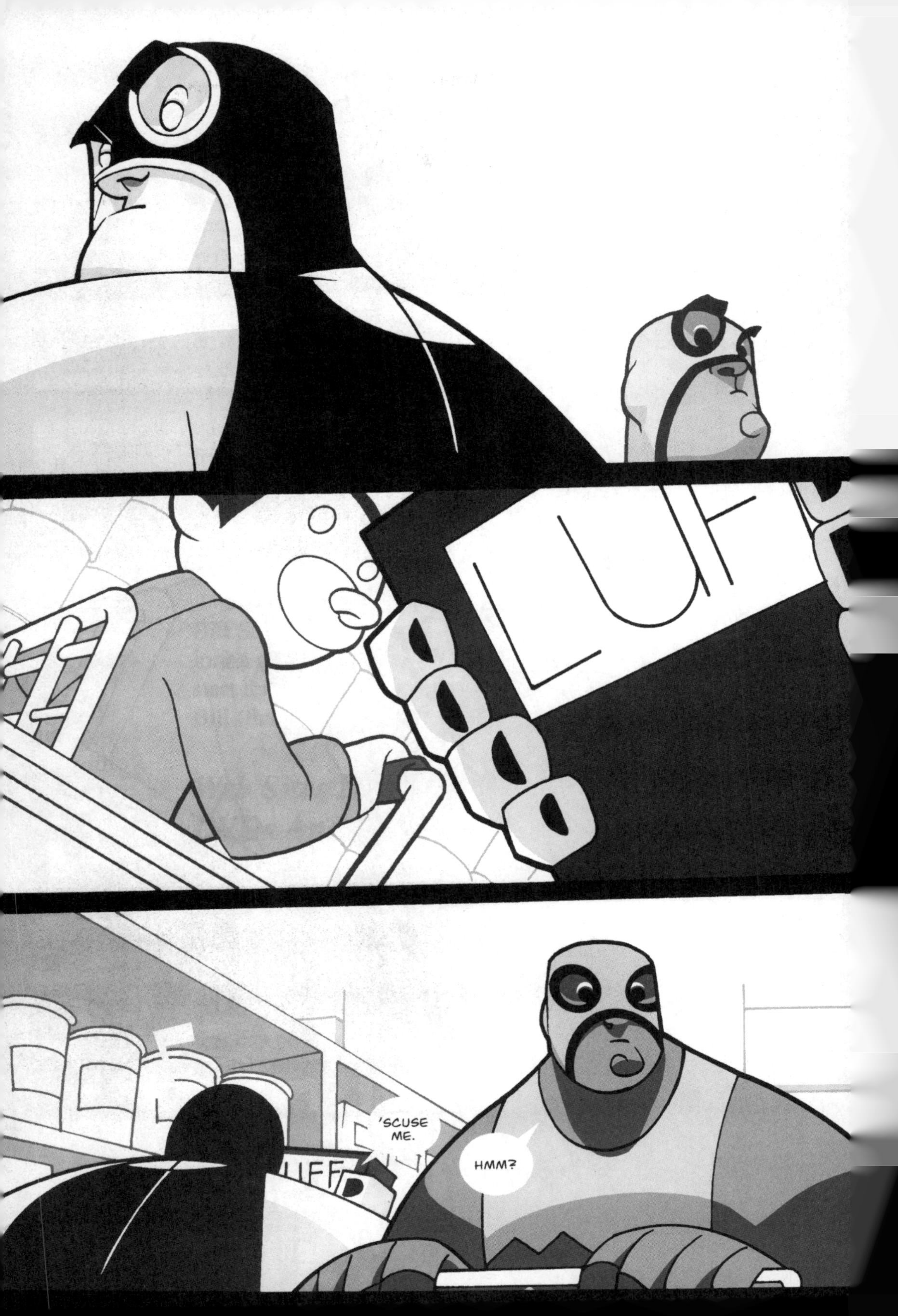
LUFF
'SCUSE ME.
HMM?

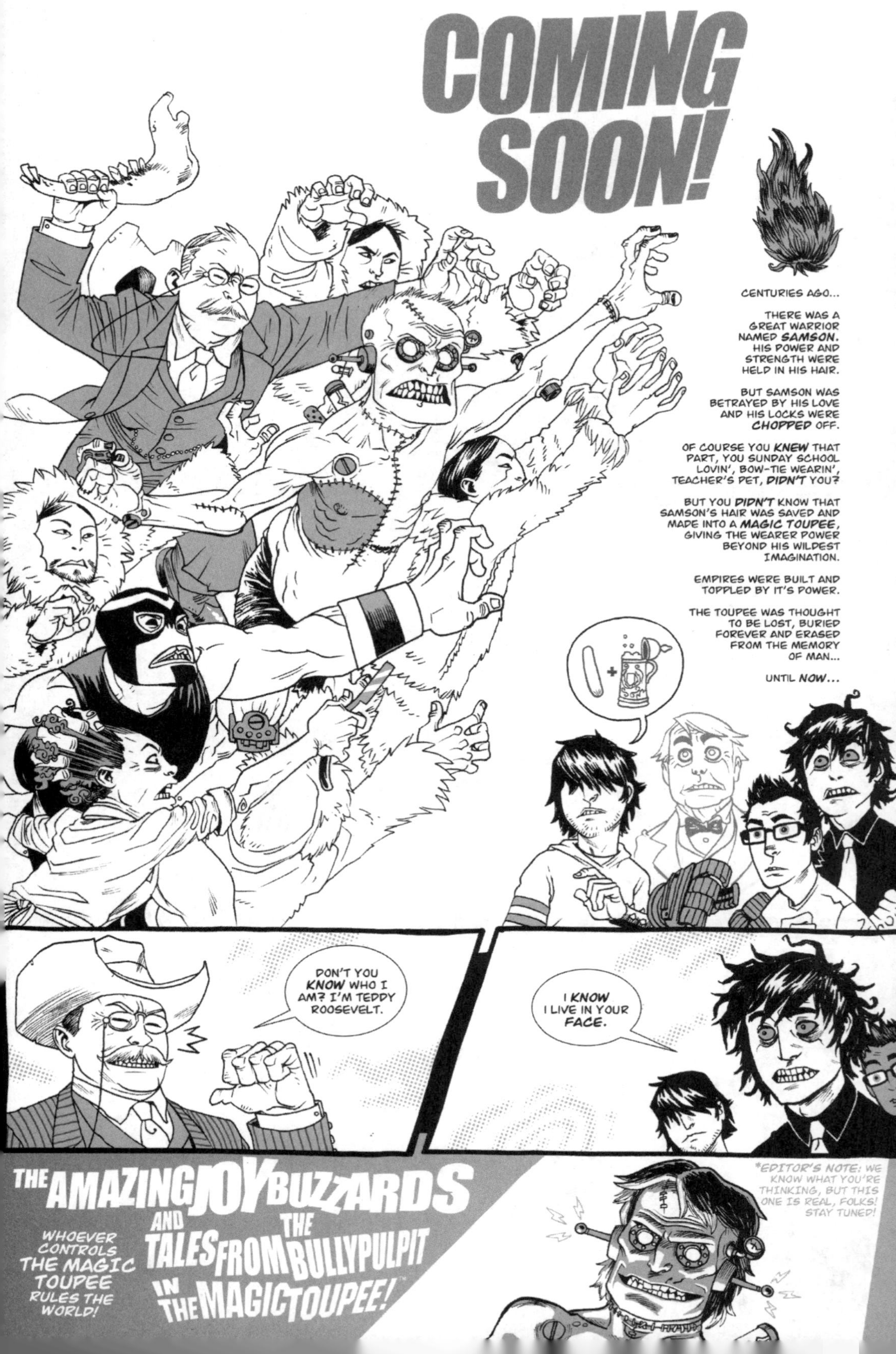
COMING SOON!
CENTURIES AGO...
THERE WAS A GREAT WARRIOR NAMED SAMSON. HIS POWER AND STRENGTH WERE HELD IN HIS HAIR.
BUT SAMSON WAS BETRAYED BY HIS LOVE AND HIS LOCKS WERE CHOPPED OFF.
OF COURSE YOU KNEW THAT PART, YOU SUNDAY SCHOOL LOVIN', BOW-TIE WEARIN', TEACHER'S PET, DIDN'T YOU?
BUT YOU DIDN'T KNOW THAT SAMSON'S HAIR WAS SAVED AND MADE INTO A MAGIC TOUPEE, GIVING THE WEARER POWER BEYOND HIS WILDEST IMAGINATION.
EMPIRES WERE BUILT AND TOPPLED BY IT'S POWER.
THE TOUPEE WAS THOUGHT TO BE LOST, BURIED FOREVER AND ERASED FROM THE MEMORY OF MAN...
UNTIL NOW...
DON'T YOU KNOW WHO I AM? I'M TEDDY ROOSEVELT.
I KNOW I LIVE IN YOUR FACE.
THE AMAZING JOY BUZZARDS AND THE TALES FROM THE BULLYPULPIT IN THE MAGIC TOUPEE!™
WHOEVER CONTROLS THE MAGIC TOUPEE RULES THE WORLD!
*EDITOR'S NOTE: WE KNOW WHAT YOU'RE THINKING, BUT THIS ONE IS REAL, FOLKS! STAY TUNED!

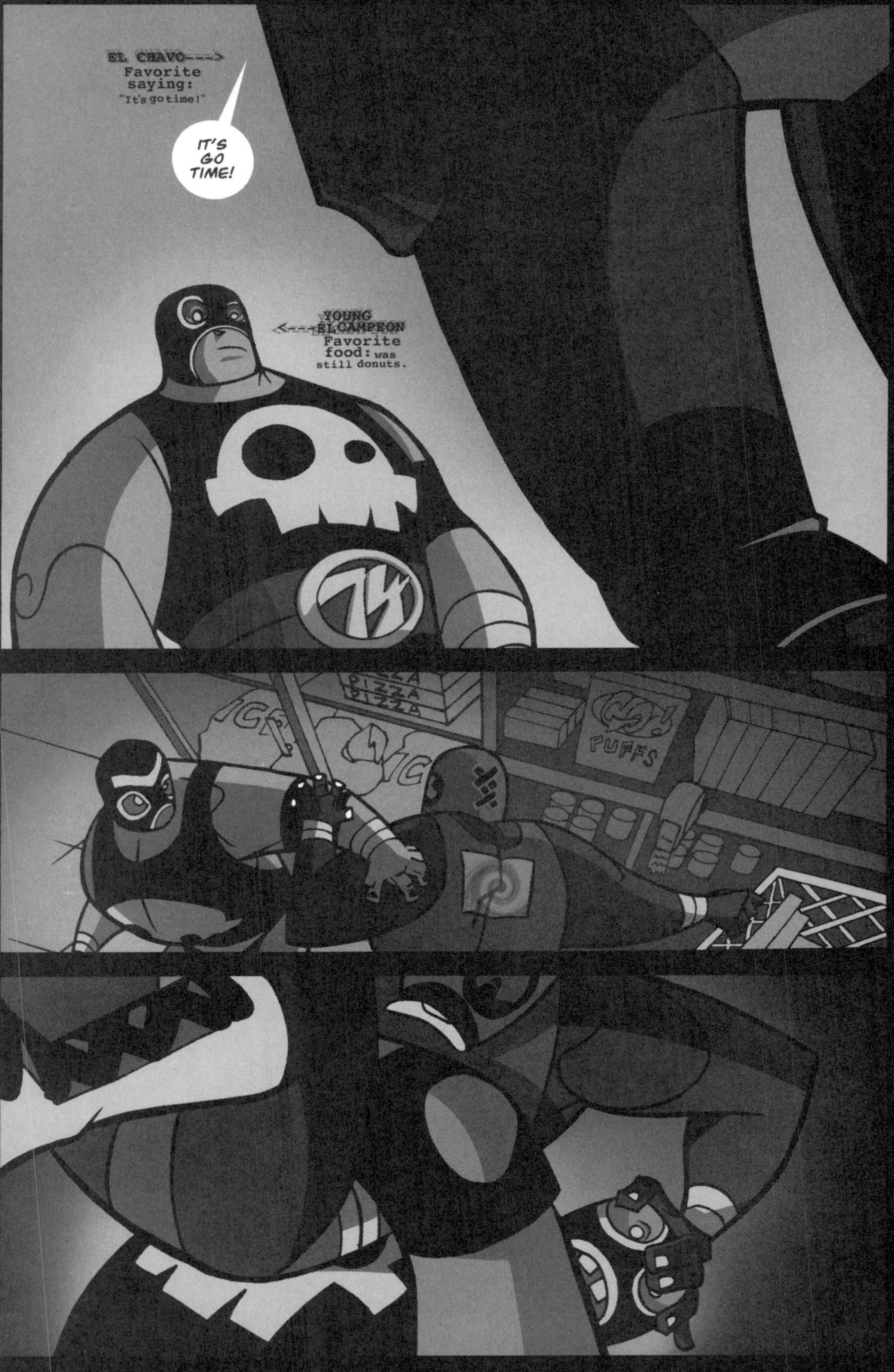
EL CHAVO--->
Favorite saying:
"It's go time!"
IT'S GO TIME!
<---YOUNG EL CAMPEON
Favorite food: was still donuts.
PIZZA
PIZZA
PUFFS

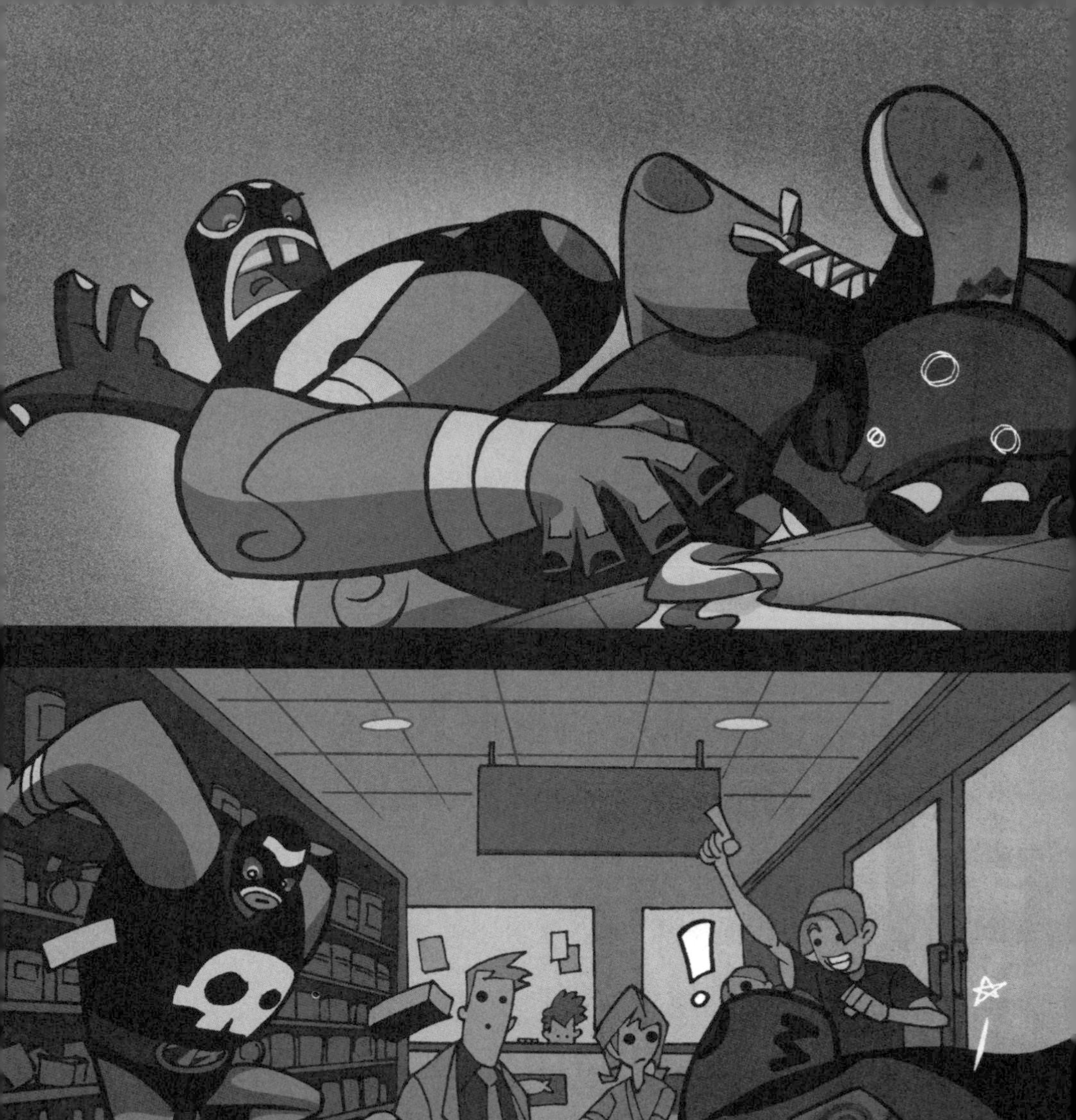
!

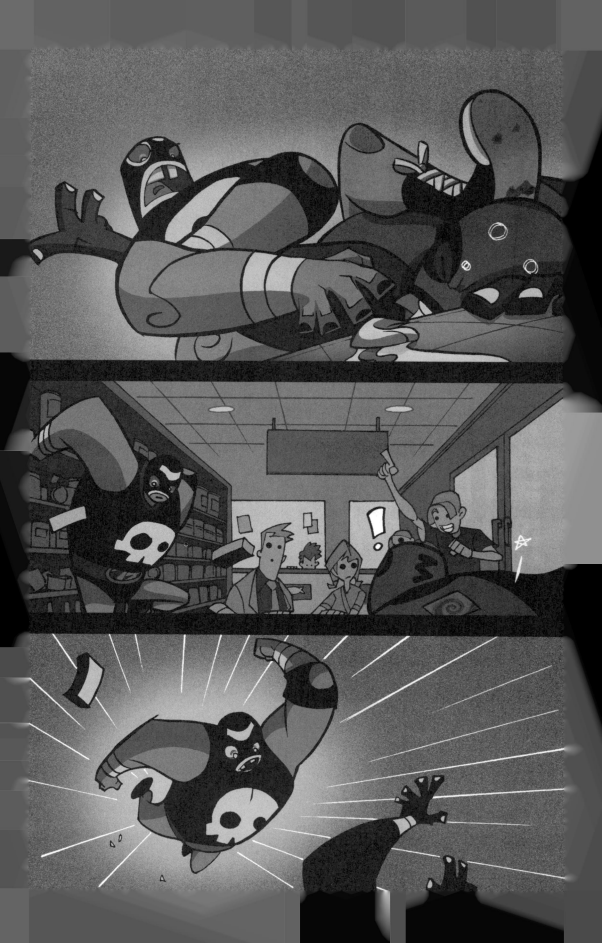

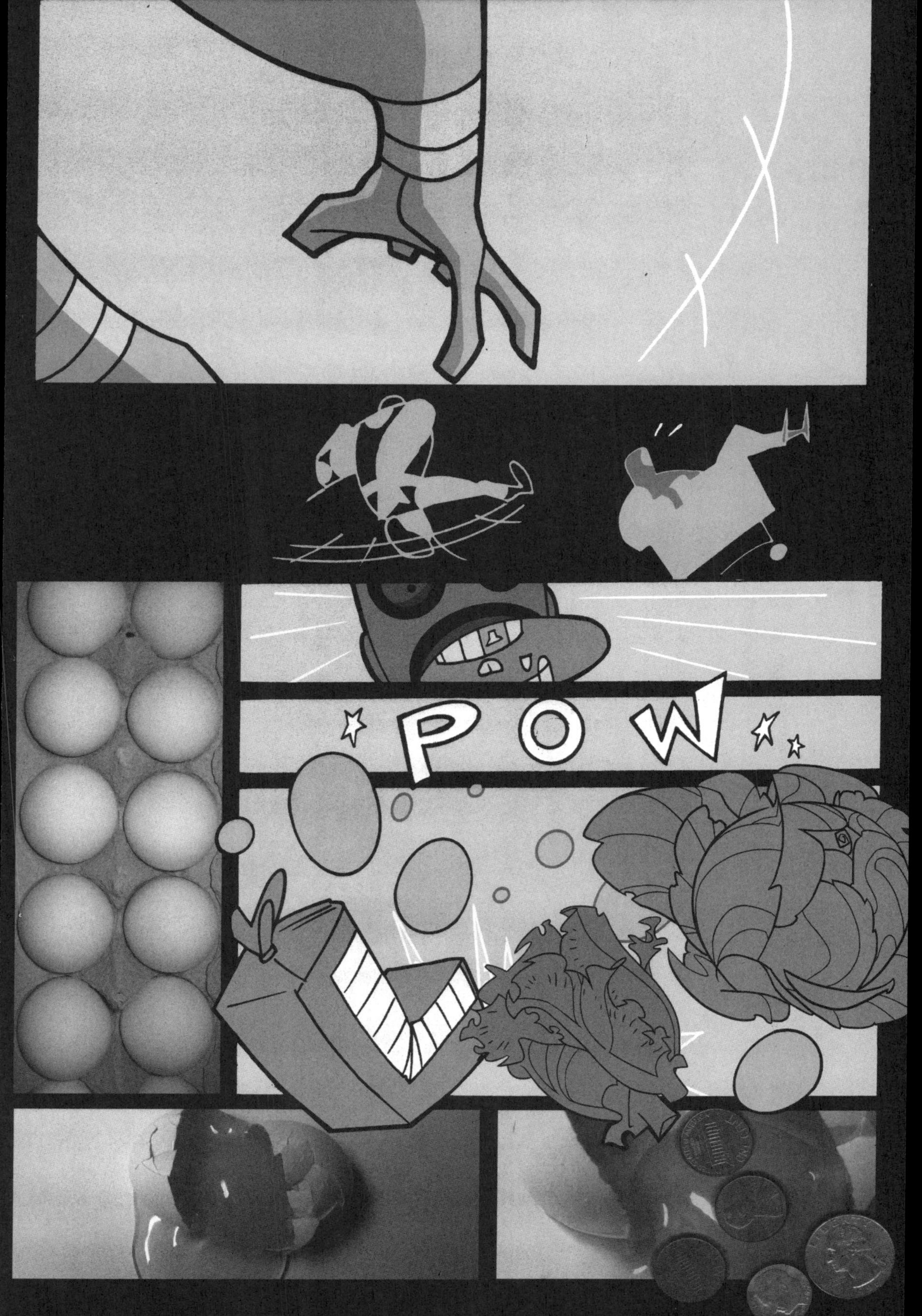
POW

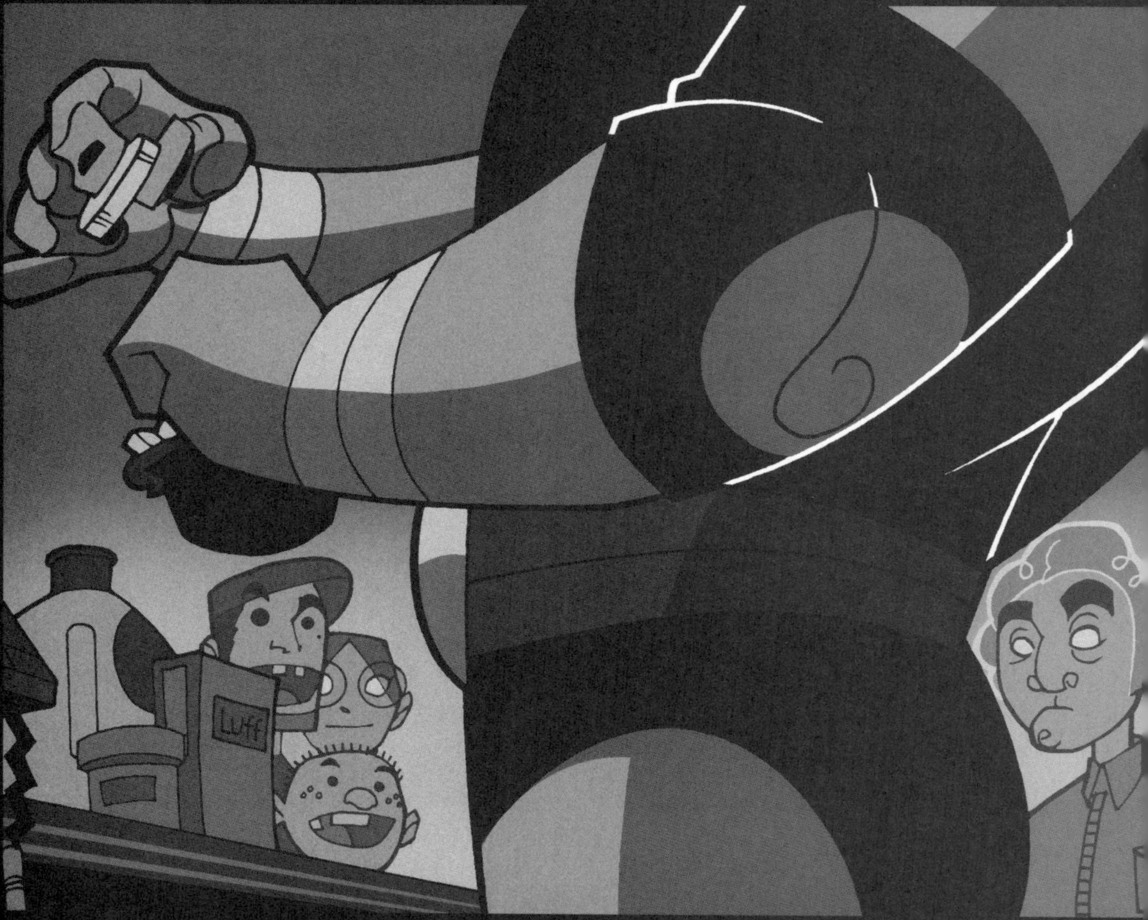
Luff

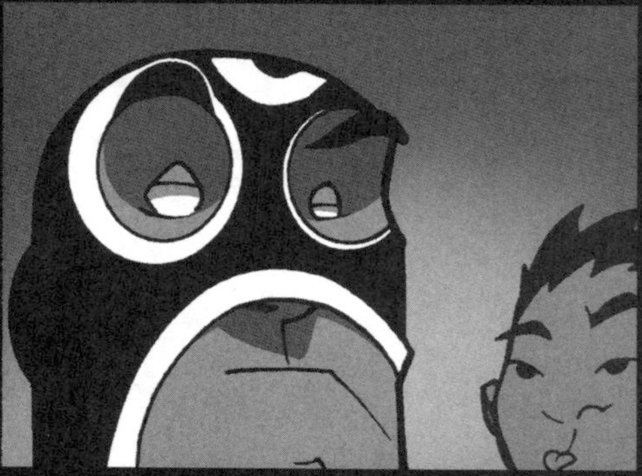

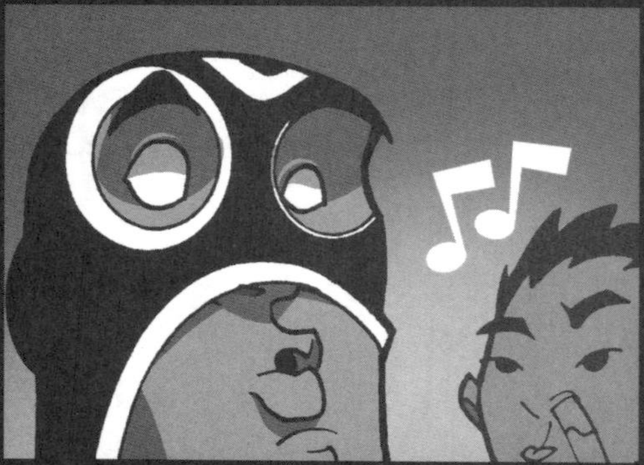

THAT WAS THE ***FIRST*** AND ***LAST*** TIME I EVER SAW ***EL CHAVO.***

BEFORE THAT, I KNEW HIM BY REPUTATION ONLY.

I HEARD THAT SHORTLY AFTER OUR ENCOUNTER HE RETIRED AND STARTED A FAMILY, BUT THAT HE ***STILL*** WANDERS AROUND THE CITY, PICKING FIGHTS.

IT WASN'T UNTIL TONIGHT THAT I REALIZED WHO HE WAS, JOE.

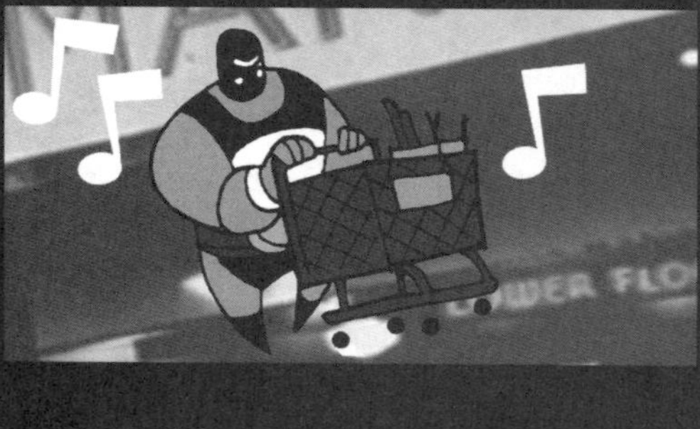

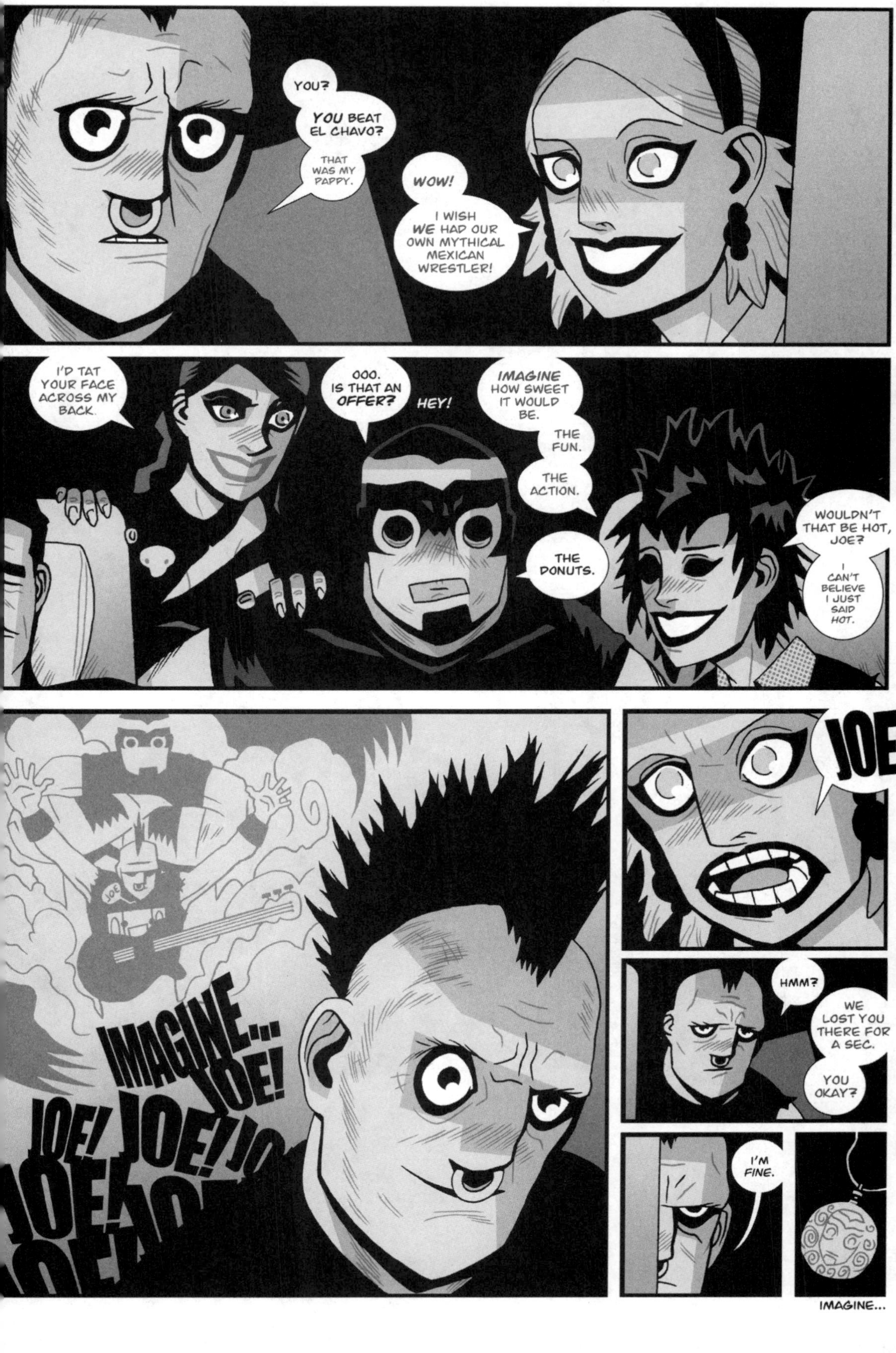
YOU?
YOU BEAT EL CHAVO?
THAT WAS MY PAPPY.
WOW!
I WISH WE HAD OUR OWN MYTHICAL MEXICAN WRESTLER!
I'D TAT YOUR FACE ACROSS MY BACK.
OOO. IS THAT AN OFFER?
HEY!
IMAGINE HOW SWEET IT WOULD BE.
THE FUN.
THE ACTION.
THE DONUTS.
WOULDN'T THAT BE HOT, JOE?
I CAN'T BELIEVE I JUST SAID HOT.
IMAGINE...
JOE!
JOE! JOE! JO
JOE!
JOE!
HMM?
WE LOST YOU THERE FOR A SEC.
YOU OKAY?
I'M FINE.
IMAGINE...

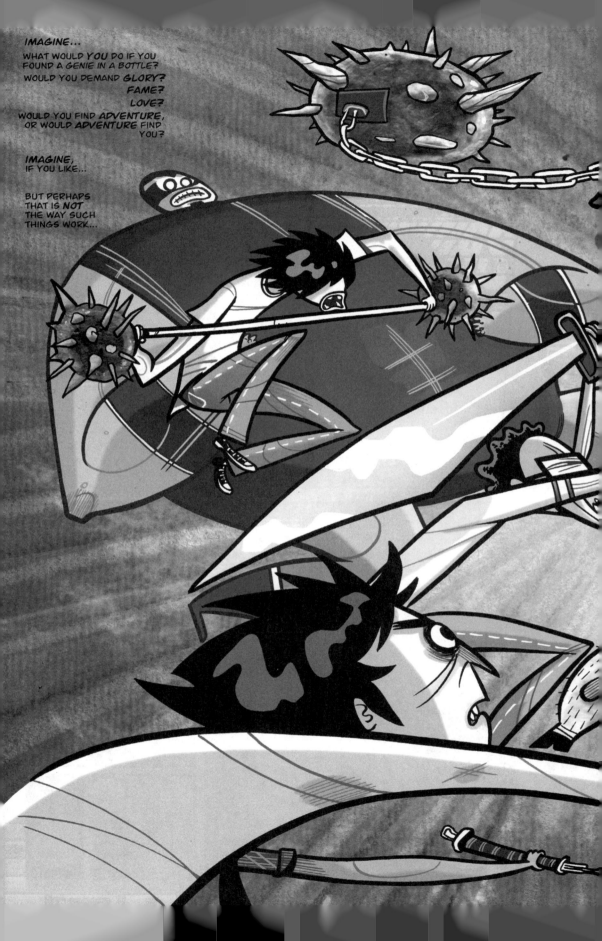

IMAGINE...

WHAT WOULD *YOU* DO IF YOU
FOUND A GENIE IN A BOTTLE?
WOULD YOU DEMAND *GLORY*?
                   FAME?
               LOVE?
WOULD YOU FIND *ADVENTURE*,
OR WOULD *ADVENTURE* FIND
                   YOU?

IMAGINE,
IF YOU LIKE...

BUT PERHAPS
THAT IS *NOT*
THE WAY SUCH
THINGS WORK...

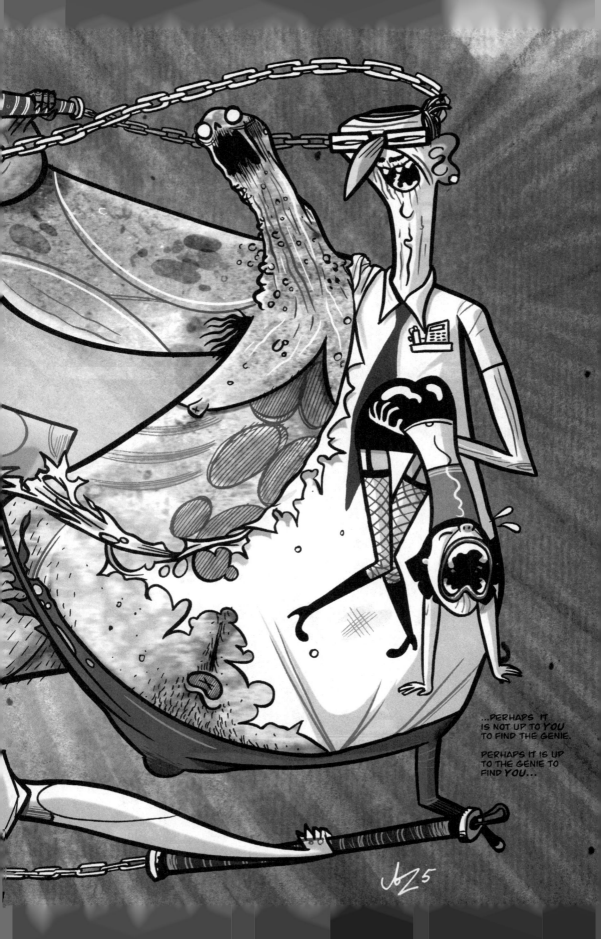

...PERHAPS IT
IS NOT UP TO YOU
TO FIND THE GENIE.

PERHAPS IT IS UP
TO THE GENIE TO
FIND YOU...

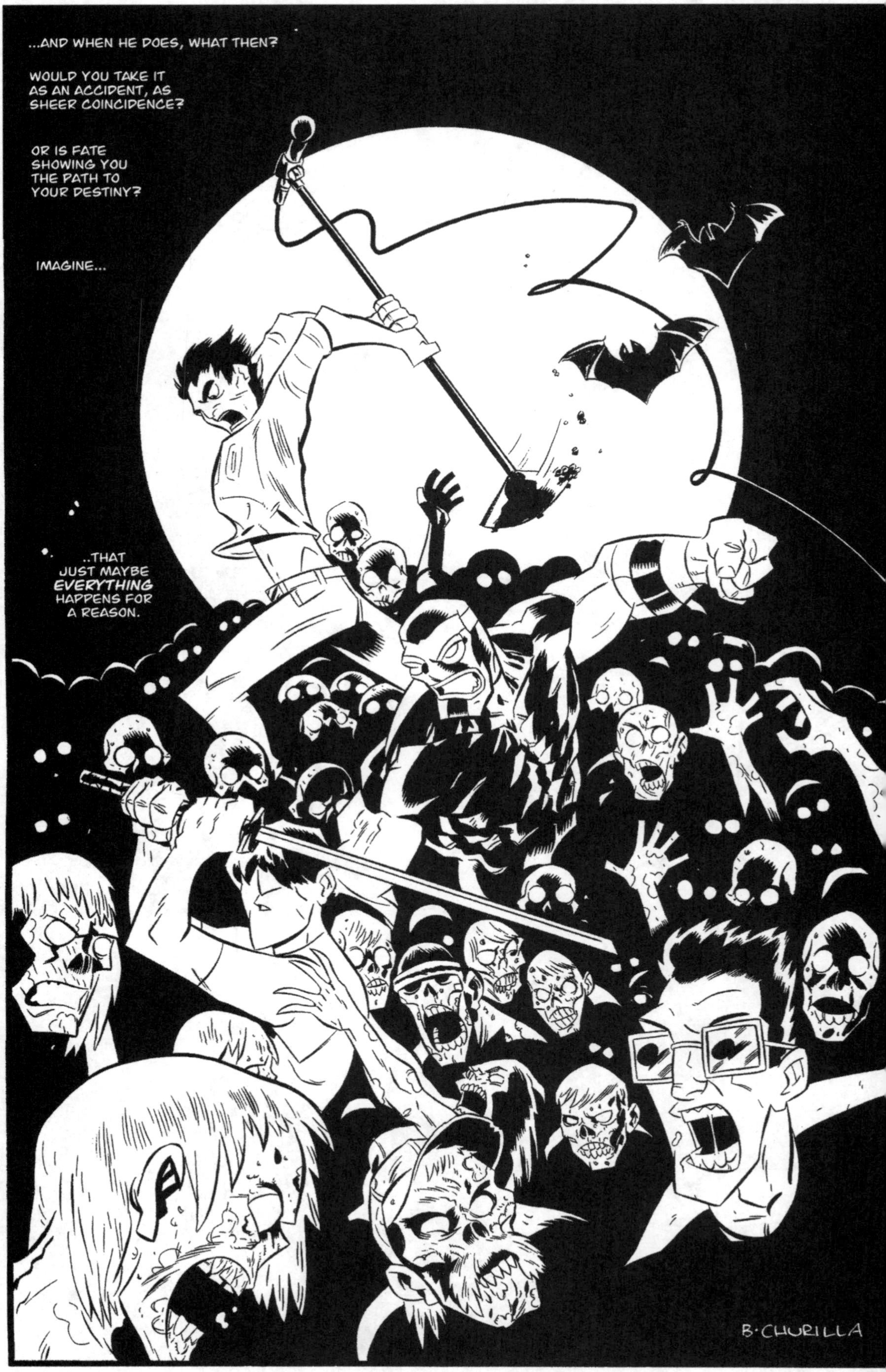

...AND WHEN HE DOES, WHAT THEN?
WOULD YOU TAKE IT AS AN ACCIDENT, AS SHEER COINCIDENCE?
OR IS FATE SHOWING YOU THE PATH TO YOUR DESTINY?
IMAGINE...
..THAT JUST MAYBE *EVERYTHING* HAPPENS FOR A REASON.
B. CHURILLA

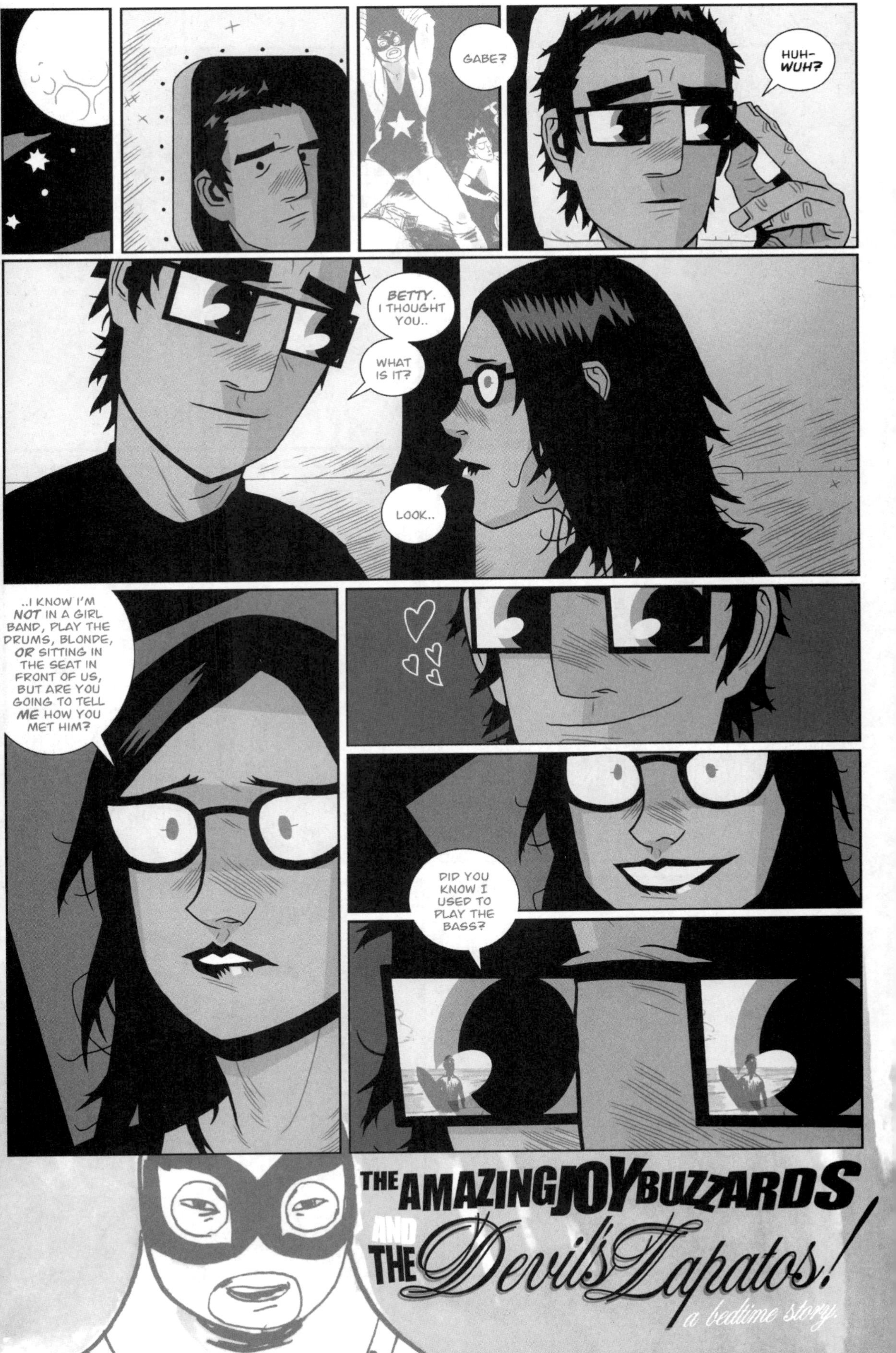
GABE?
HUH-
WUH?
BETTY. I THOUGHT YOU..
WHAT IS IT?
LOOK..
..I KNOW I'M NOT IN A GIRL BAND, PLAY THE DRUMS, BLONDE, OR SITTING IN THE SEAT IN FRONT OF US, BUT ARE YOU GOING TO TELL ME HOW YOU MET HIM?
DID YOU KNOW I USED TO PLAY THE BASS?
THE AMAZING JOY BUZZARDS
AND
THE Devil's Zapatos!
a bedtime story.

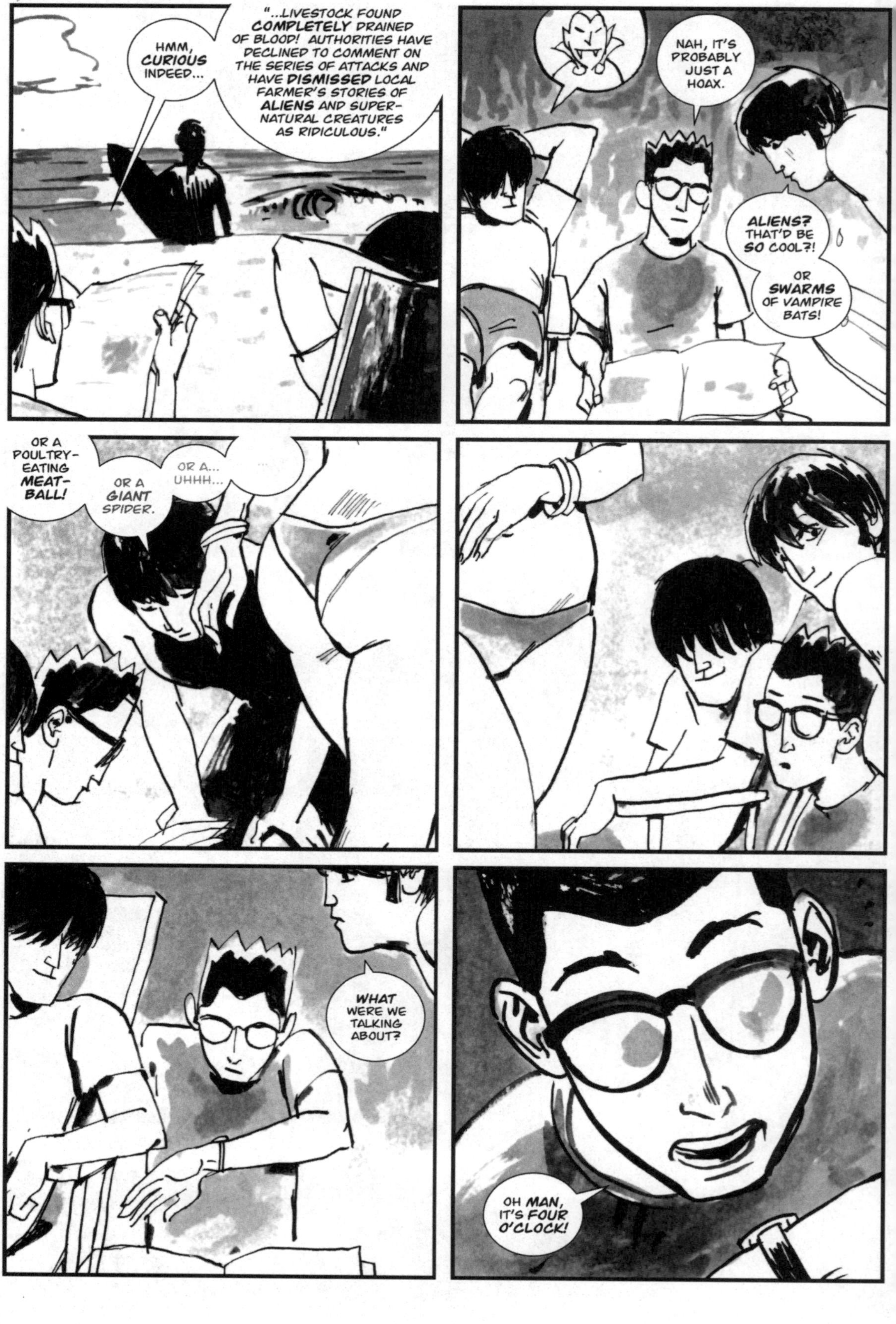
"...LIVESTOCK FOUND COMPLETELY DRAINED OF BLOOD! AUTHORITIES HAVE DECLINED TO COMMENT ON THE SERIES OF ATTACKS AND HAVE DISMISSED LOCAL FARMER'S STORIES OF ALIENS AND SUPER-NATURAL CREATURES AS RIDICULOUS."
HMM, CURIOUS INDEED...
NAH, IT'S PROBABLY JUST A HOAX.
ALIENS? THAT'D BE SO COOL?!
OR SWARMS OF VAMPIRE BATS!
OR A POULTRY-EATING MEAT-BALL!
OR A GIANT SPIDER.
OR A... UHHH...
...
WHAT WERE WE TALKING ABOUT?
OH MAN, IT'S FOUR O'CLOCK!

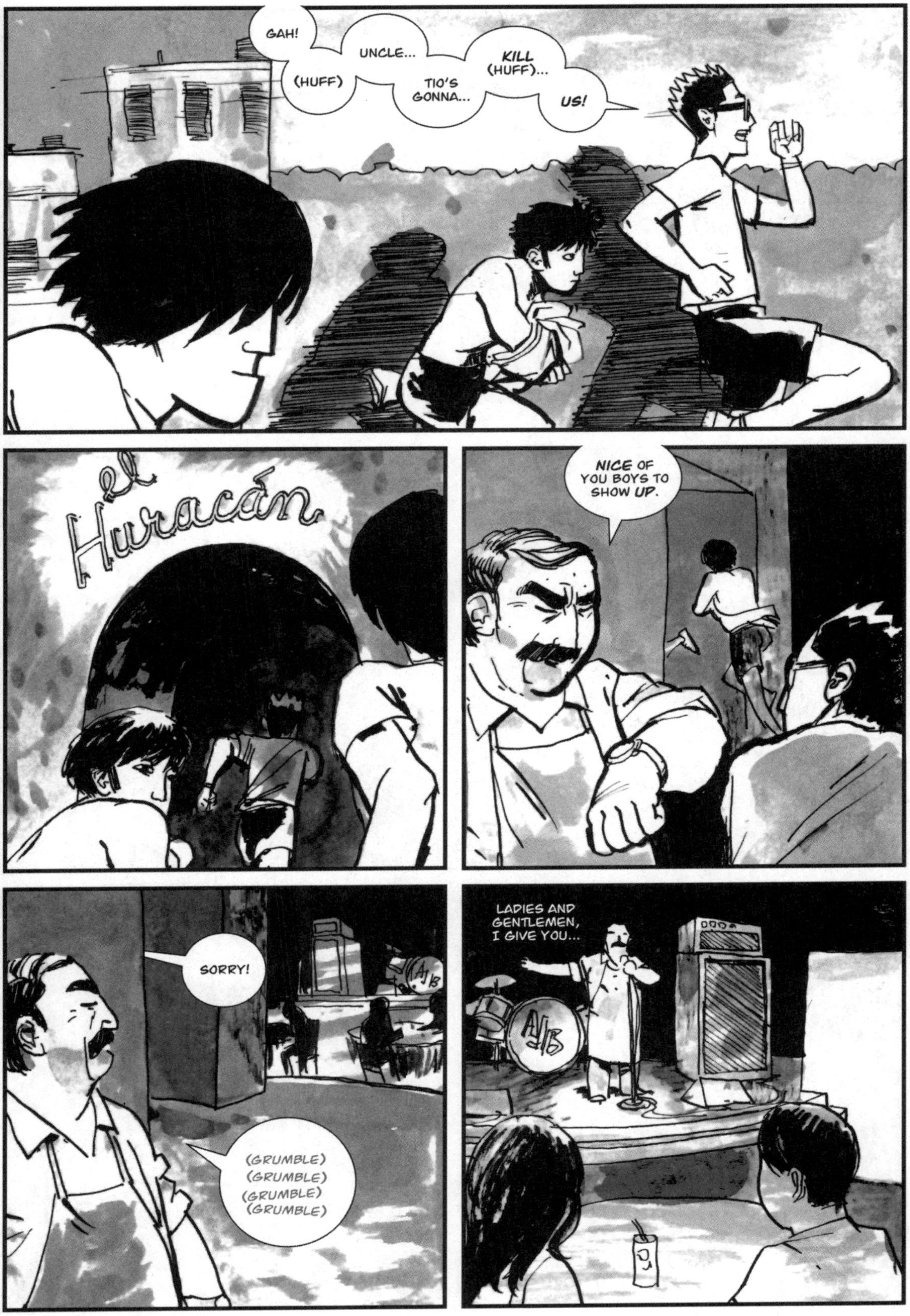
GAH!
(HUFF)
UNCLE...
TIO'S GONNA...
KILL (HUFF)...
US!
el Huracán
NICE OF YOU BOYS TO SHOW UP.
SORRY!
(GRUMBLE) (GRUMBLE) (GRUMBLE) (GRUMBLE)
LADIES AND GENTLEMEN, I GIVE YOU...

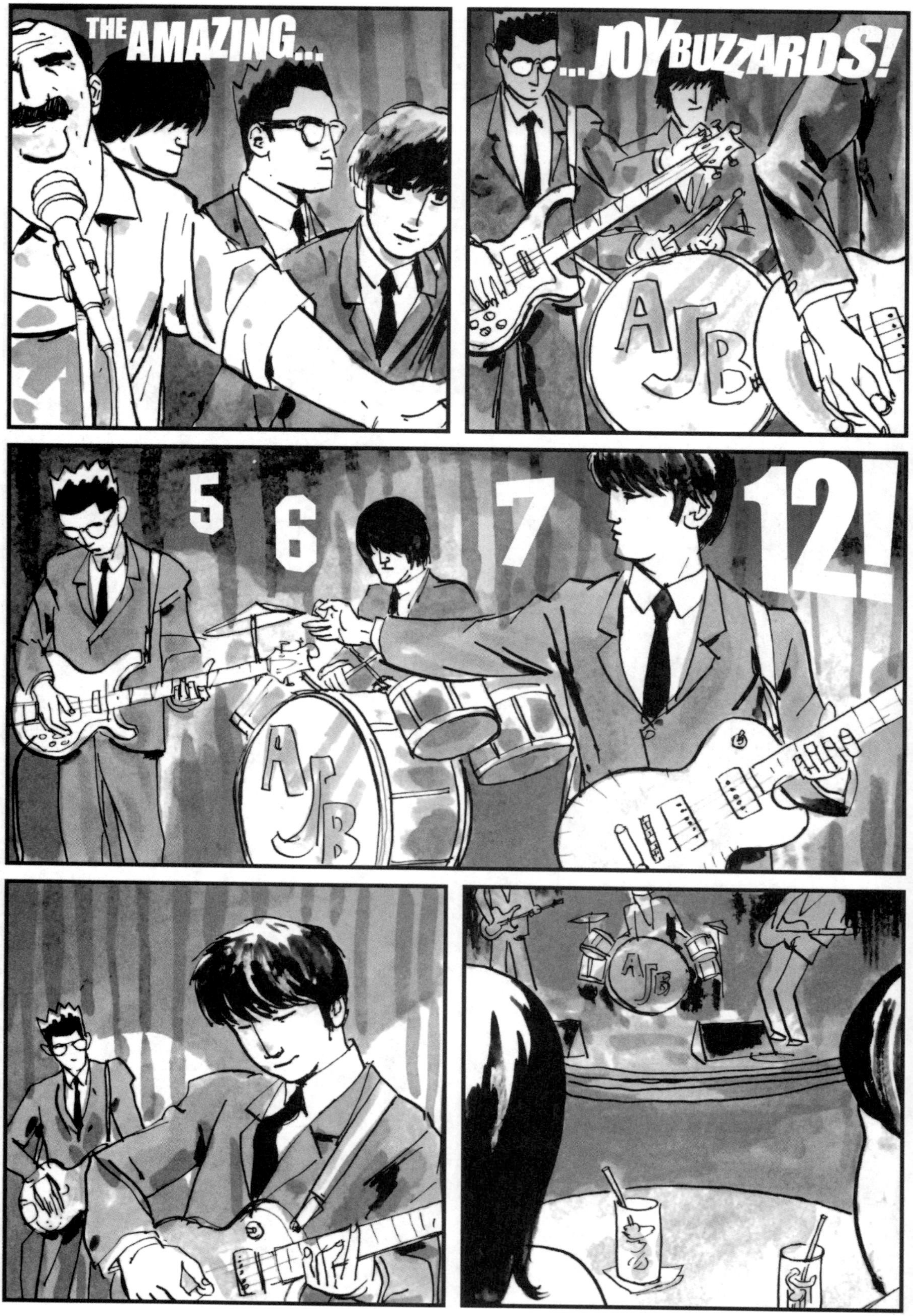
THE AMAZING...
...JOY BUZZARDS!
5
6
7
12!

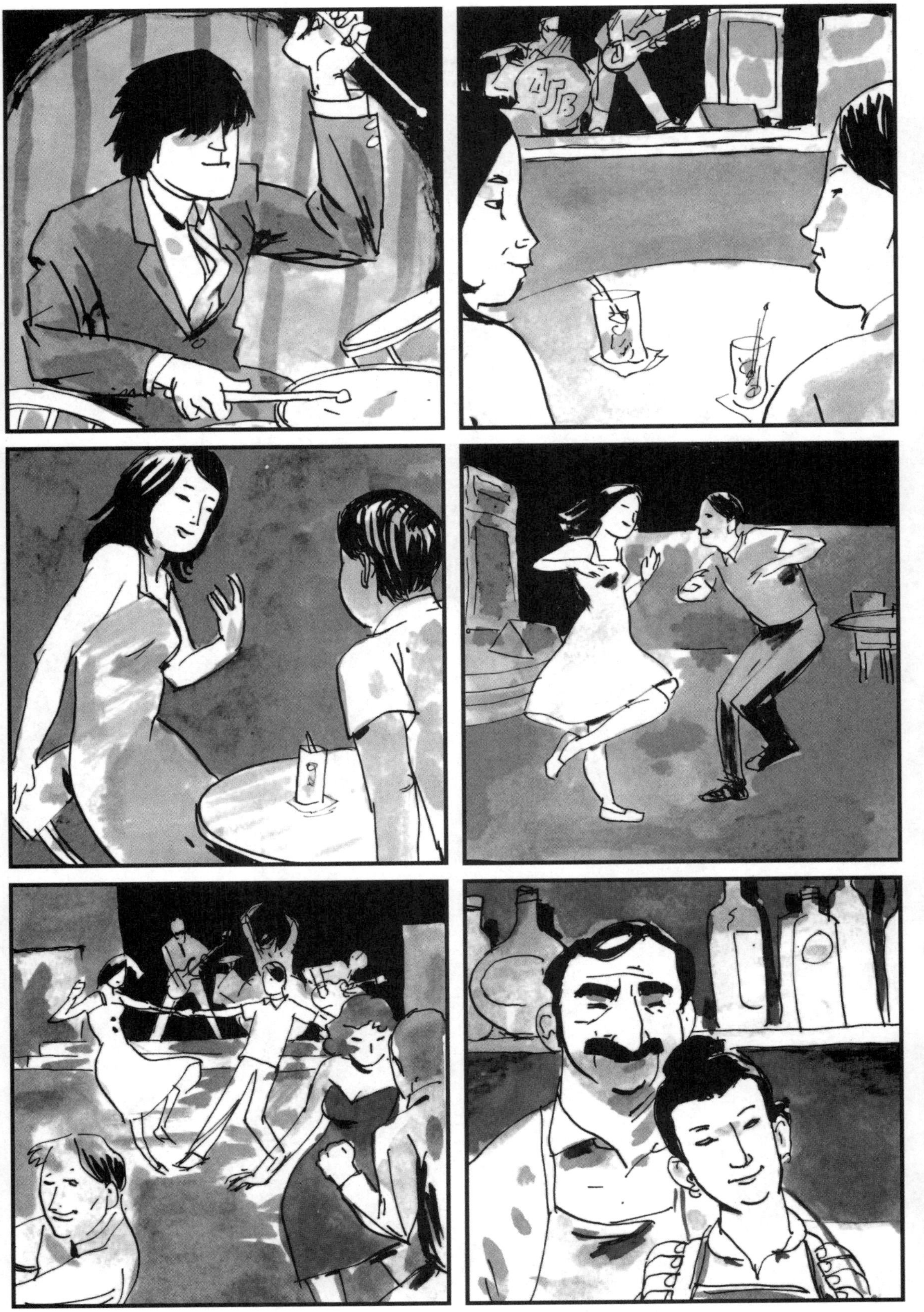

Later

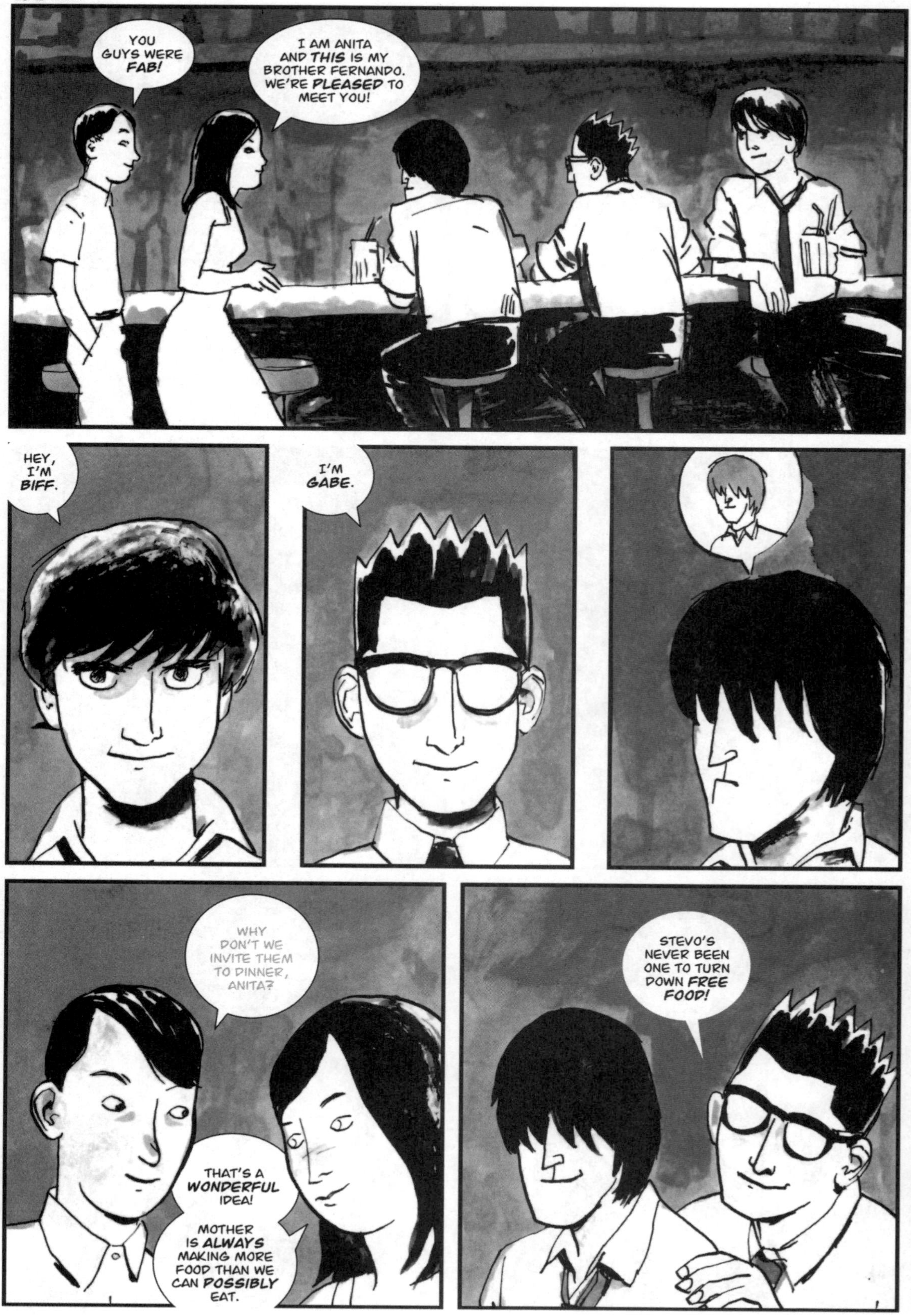
YOU GUYS WERE FAB!
I AM ANITA AND THIS IS MY BROTHER FERNANDO. WE'RE PLEASED TO MEET YOU!
HEY, I'M BIFF.
I'M GABE.
WHY DON'T WE INVITE THEM TO DINNER, ANITA?
THAT'S A WONDERFUL IDEA!
MOTHER IS ALWAYS MAKING MORE FOOD THAN WE CAN POSSIBLY EAT.
STEVO'S NEVER BEEN ONE TO TURN DOWN FREE FOOD!

Later Still

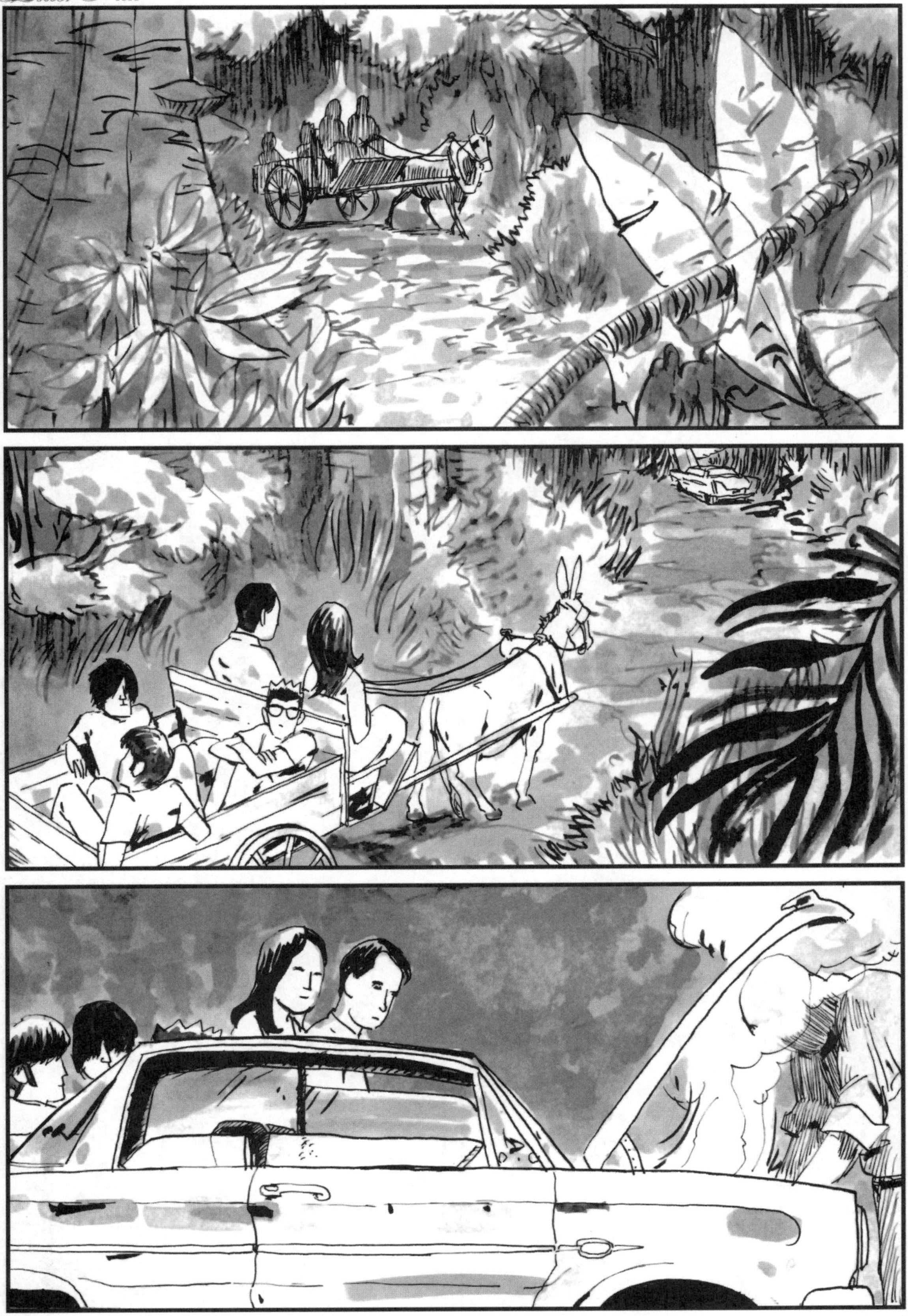

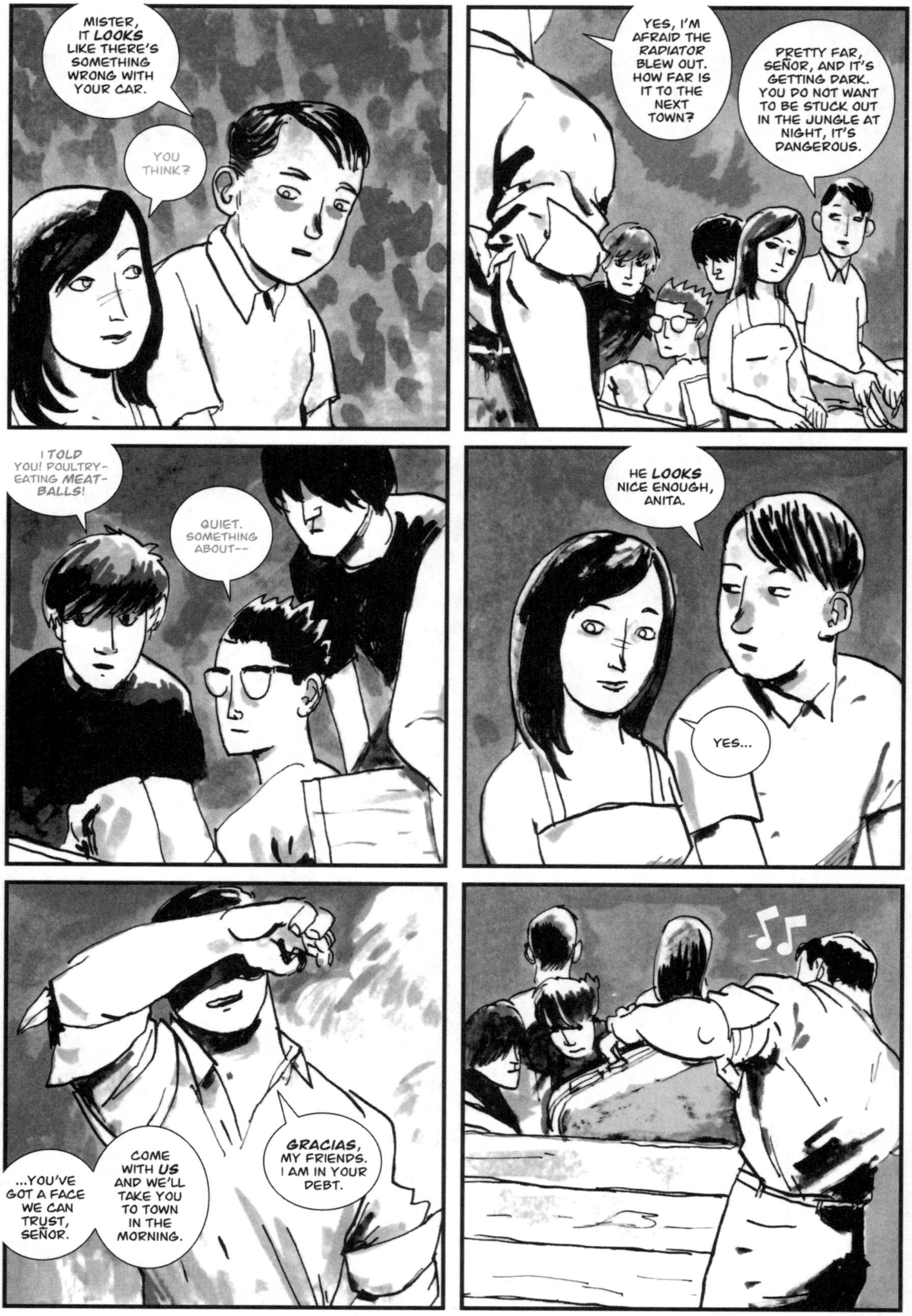
MISTER, IT LOOKS LIKE THERE'S SOMETHING WRONG WITH YOUR CAR.
YOU THINK?
YES, I'M AFRAID THE RADIATOR BLEW OUT. HOW FAR IS IT TO THE NEXT TOWN?
PRETTY FAR, SEÑOR, AND IT'S GETTING DARK. YOU DO NOT WANT TO BE STUCK OUT IN THE JUNGLE AT NIGHT, IT'S DANGEROUS.
I TOLD YOU! POULTRY-EATING MEAT-BALLS!
QUIET. SOMETHING ABOUT--
HE LOOKS NICE ENOUGH, ANITA.
YES...
...YOU'VE GOT A FACE WE CAN TRUST, SEÑOR.
COME WITH US AND WE'LL TAKE YOU TO TOWN IN THE MORNING.
GRACIAS, MY FRIENDS. I AM IN YOUR DEBT.

Even Later Still

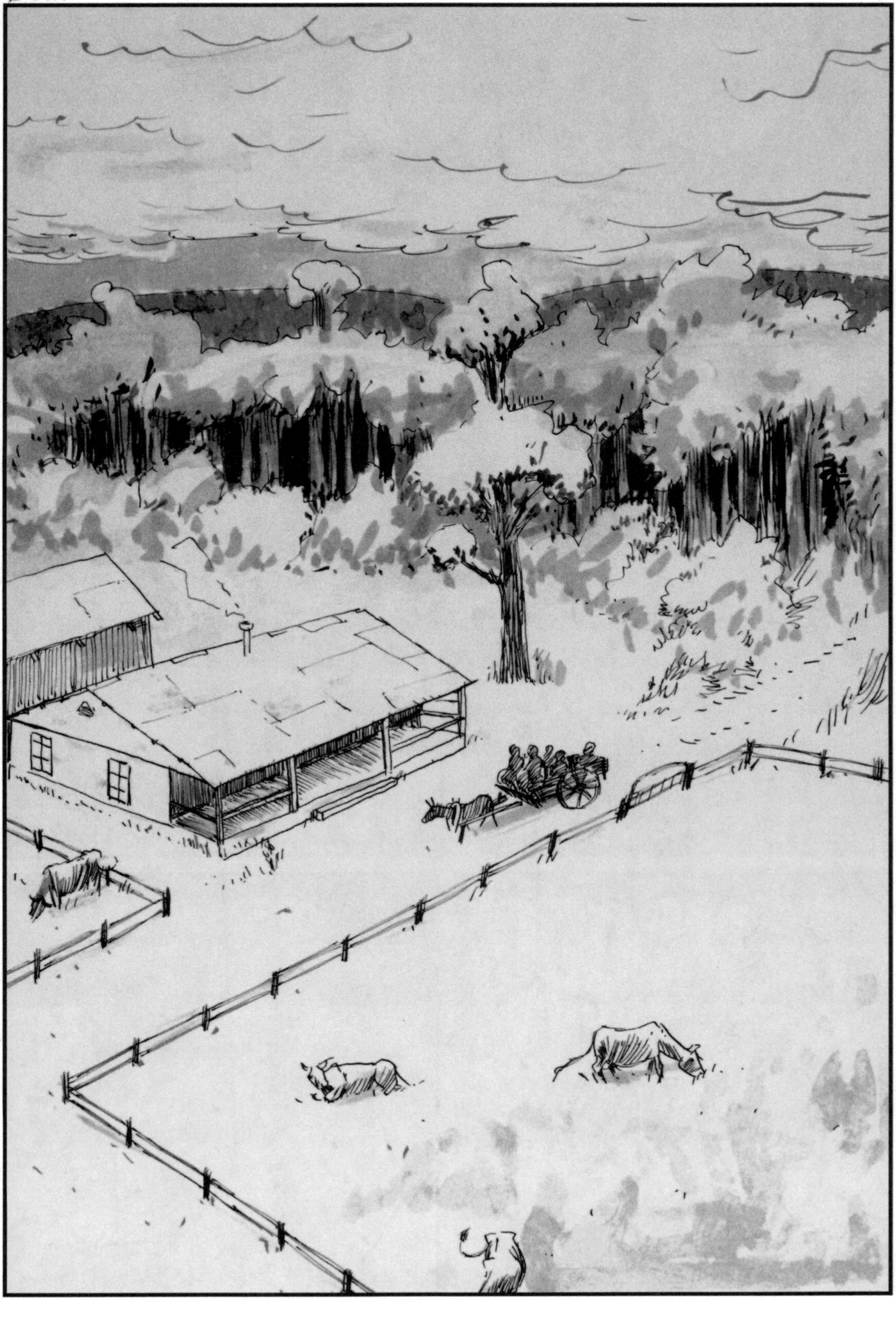

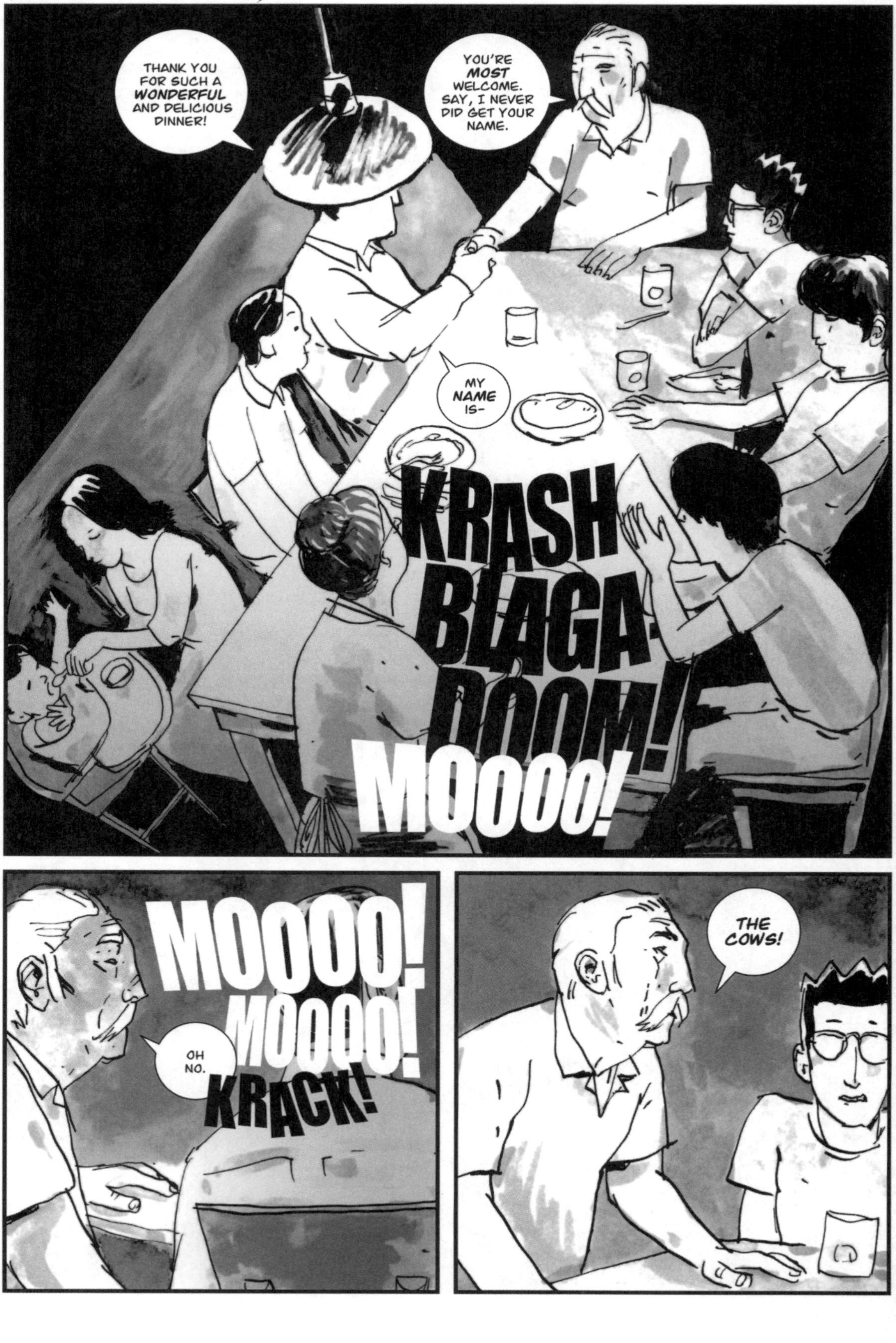
THANK YOU FOR SUCH A WONDERFUL AND DELICIOUS DINNER!
YOU'RE MOST WELCOME. SAY, I NEVER DID GET YOUR NAME.
MY NAME IS-
KRASH BLAGA-DOOM!
MOOOO!
MOOOO!
MOOOO!
OH NO.
KRACK!
THE COWS!

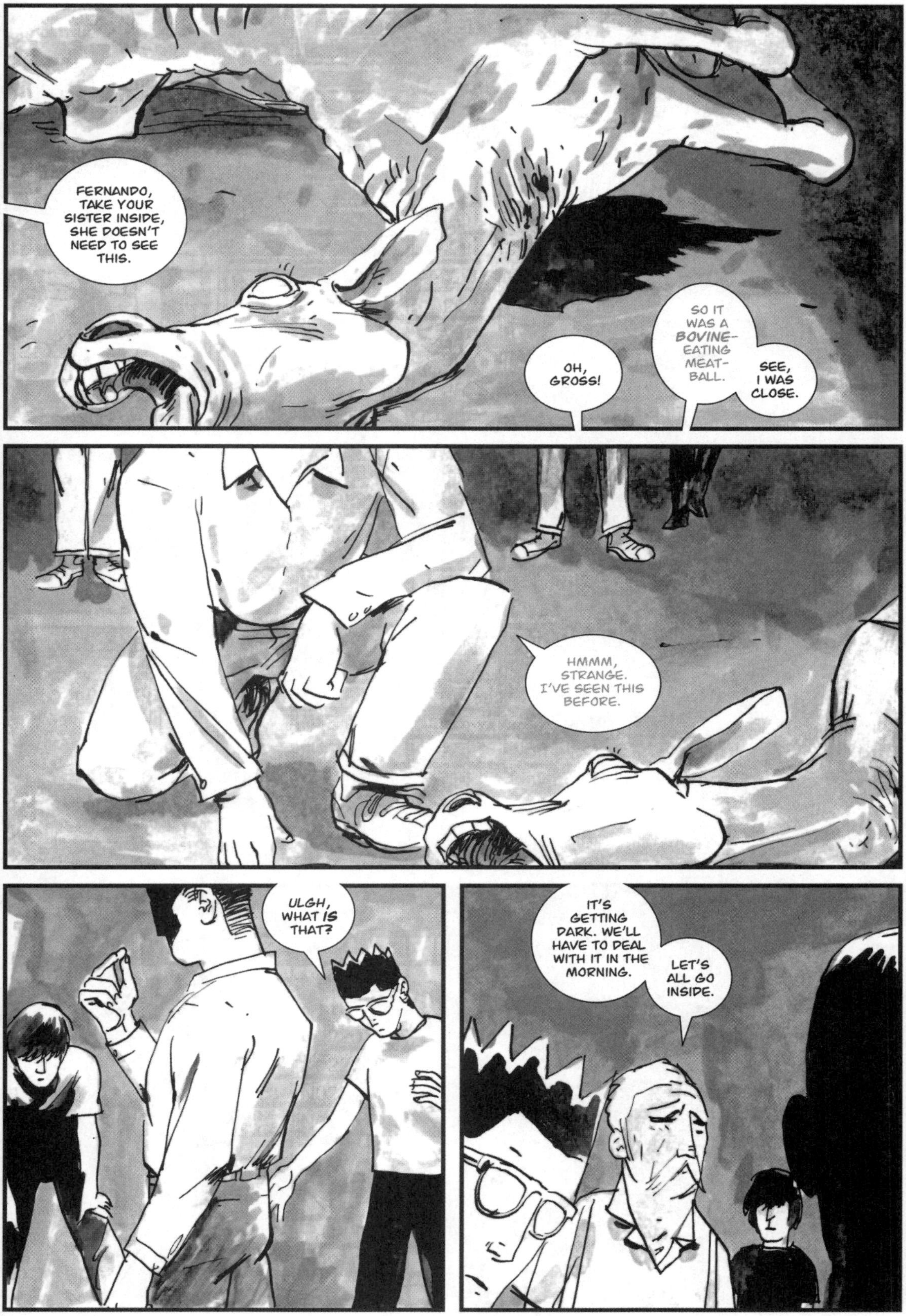
FERNANDO, TAKE YOUR SISTER INSIDE, SHE DOESN'T NEED TO SEE THIS.
OH, GROSS!
SO IT WAS A BOVINE-EATING MEAT-BALL.
SEE, I WAS CLOSE.
HMMM, STRANGE. I'VE SEEN THIS BEFORE.
ULGH, WHAT IS THAT?
IT'S GETTING DARK. WE'LL HAVE TO DEAL WITH IT IN THE MORNING.
LET'S ALL GO INSIDE.

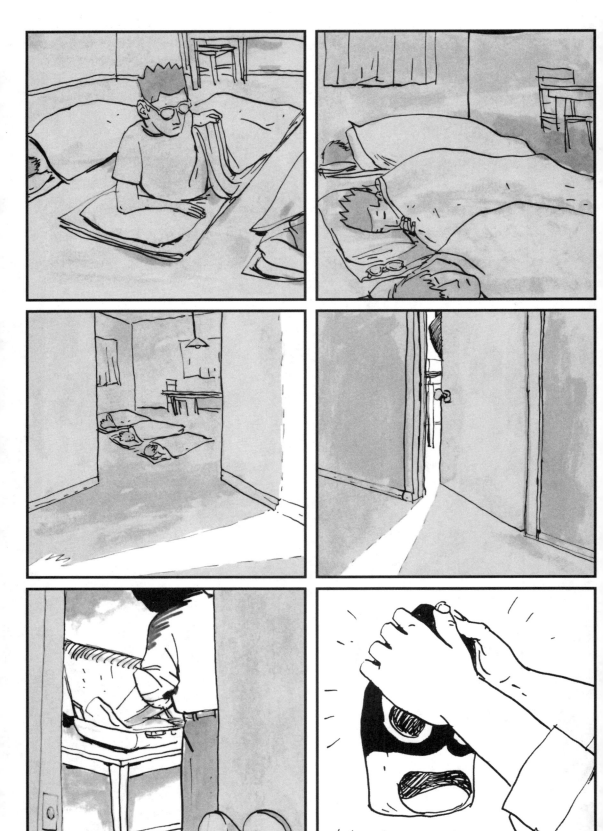

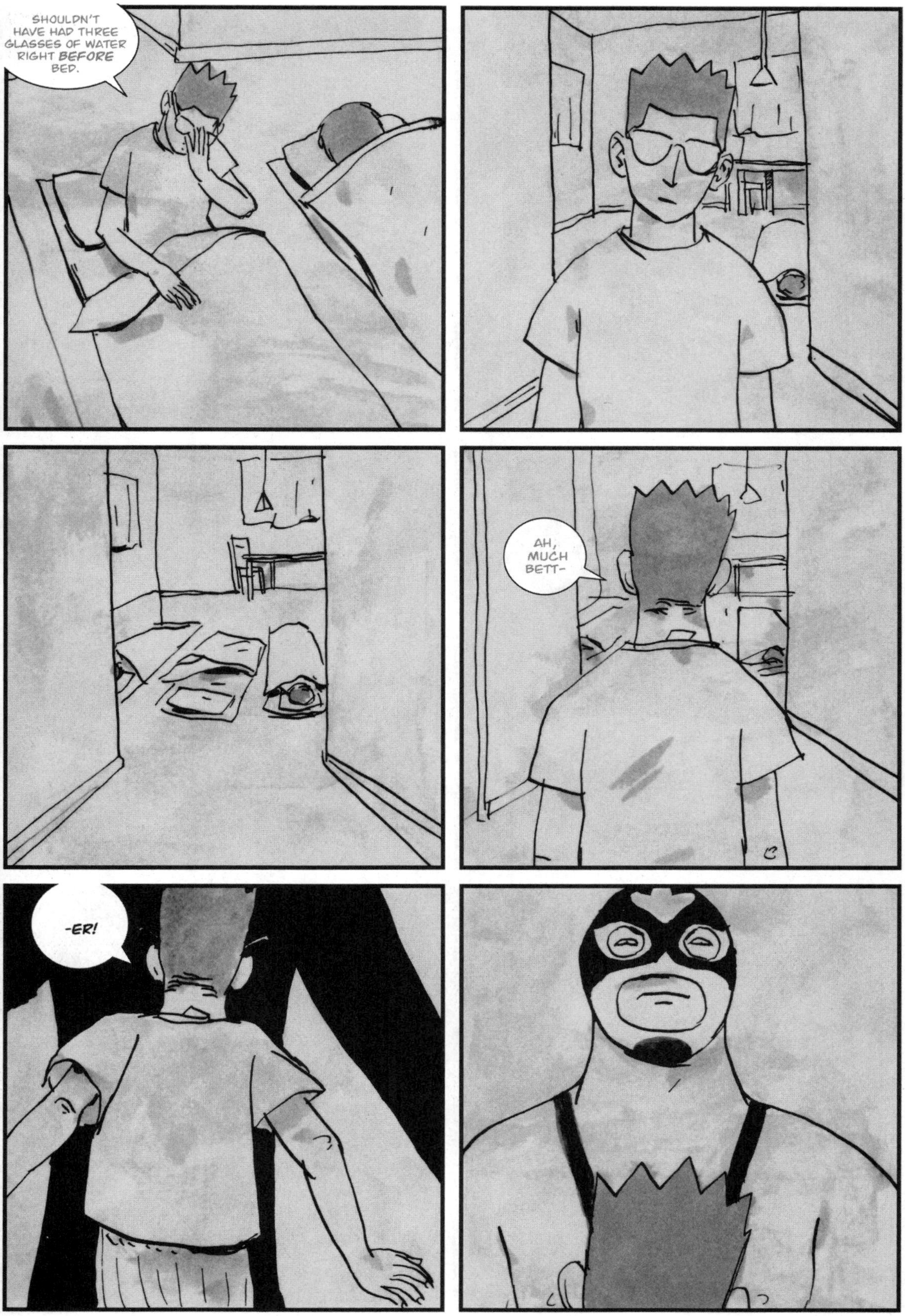
SHOULDN'T HAVE HAD THREE GLASSES OF WATER RIGHT BEFORE BED.
AH, MUCH BETT-
-ER!

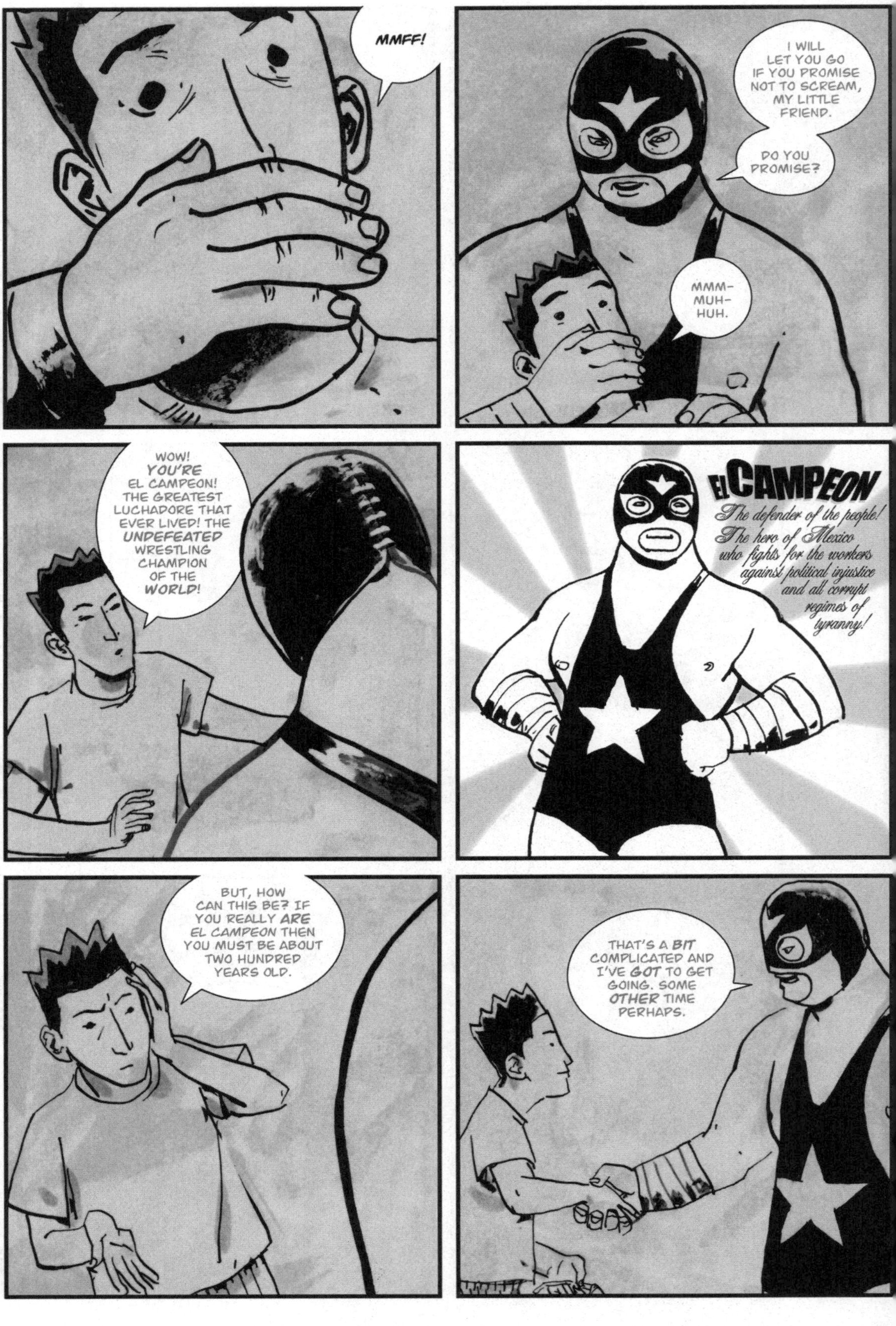

MMFF!
I WILL LET YOU GO IF YOU PROMISE NOT TO SCREAM, MY LITTLE FRIEND.
DO YOU PROMISE?
MMM-MUH-HUH.
WOW! YOU'RE EL CAMPEON! THE GREATEST LUCHADORE THAT EVER LIVED! THE UNDEFEATED WRESTLING CHAMPION OF THE WORLD!
EL CAMPEON
The defender of the people! The hero of Mexico who fights for the workers against political injustice and all corrupt regimes of tyranny!
BUT, HOW CAN THIS BE? IF YOU REALLY ARE EL CAMPEON THEN YOU MUST BE ABOUT TWO HUNDRED YEARS OLD.
THAT'S A BIT COMPLICATED AND I'VE GOT TO GET GOING. SOME OTHER TIME PERHAPS.

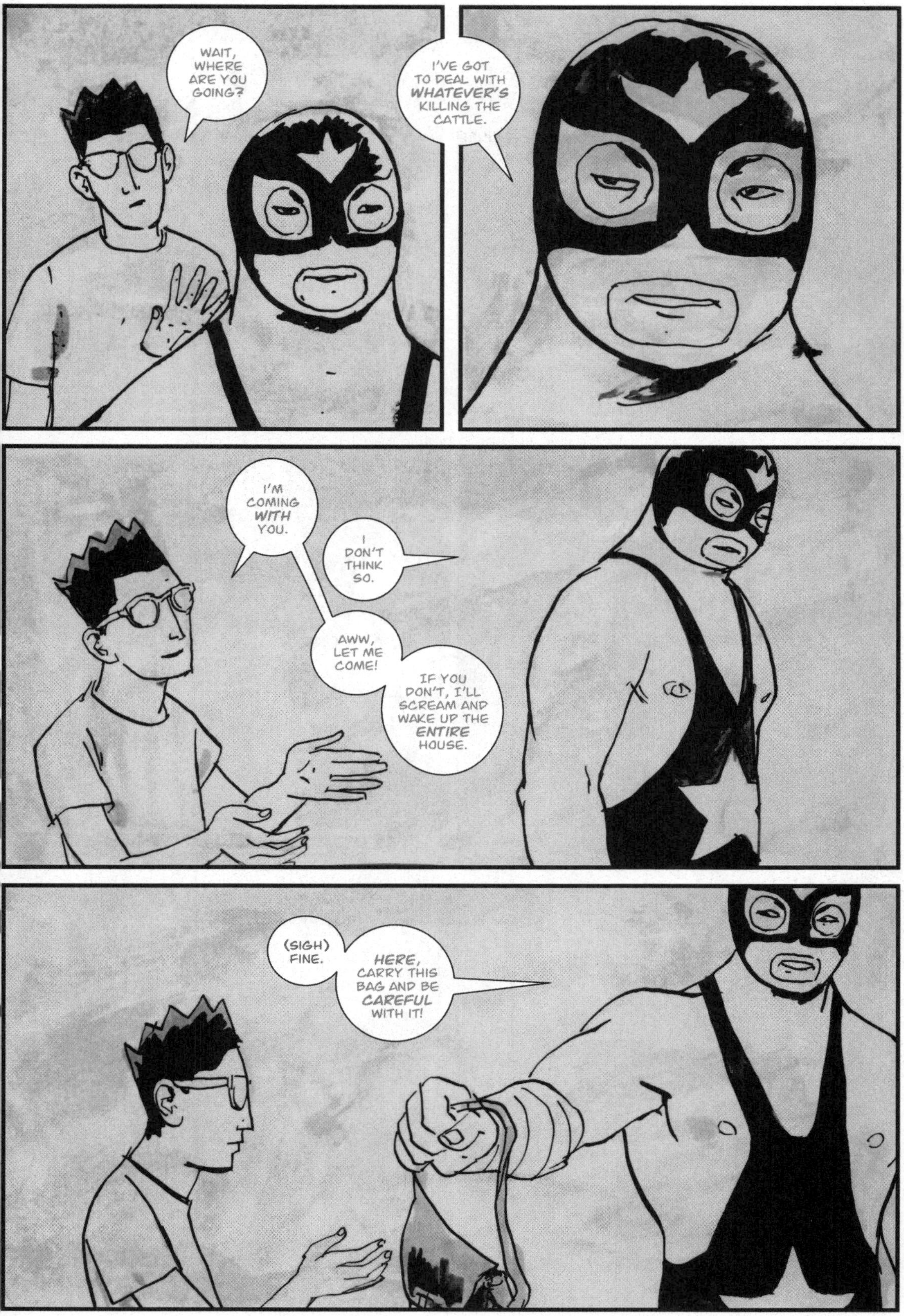

WAIT, WHERE ARE YOU GOING?
I'VE GOT TO DEAL WITH WHATEVER'S KILLING THE CATTLE.
I'M COMING WITH YOU.
I DON'T THINK SO.
AWW, LET ME COME!
IF YOU DON'T, I'LL SCREAM AND WAKE UP THE ENTIRE HOUSE.
(SIGH) FINE.
HERE, CARRY THIS BAG AND BE CAREFUL WITH IT!

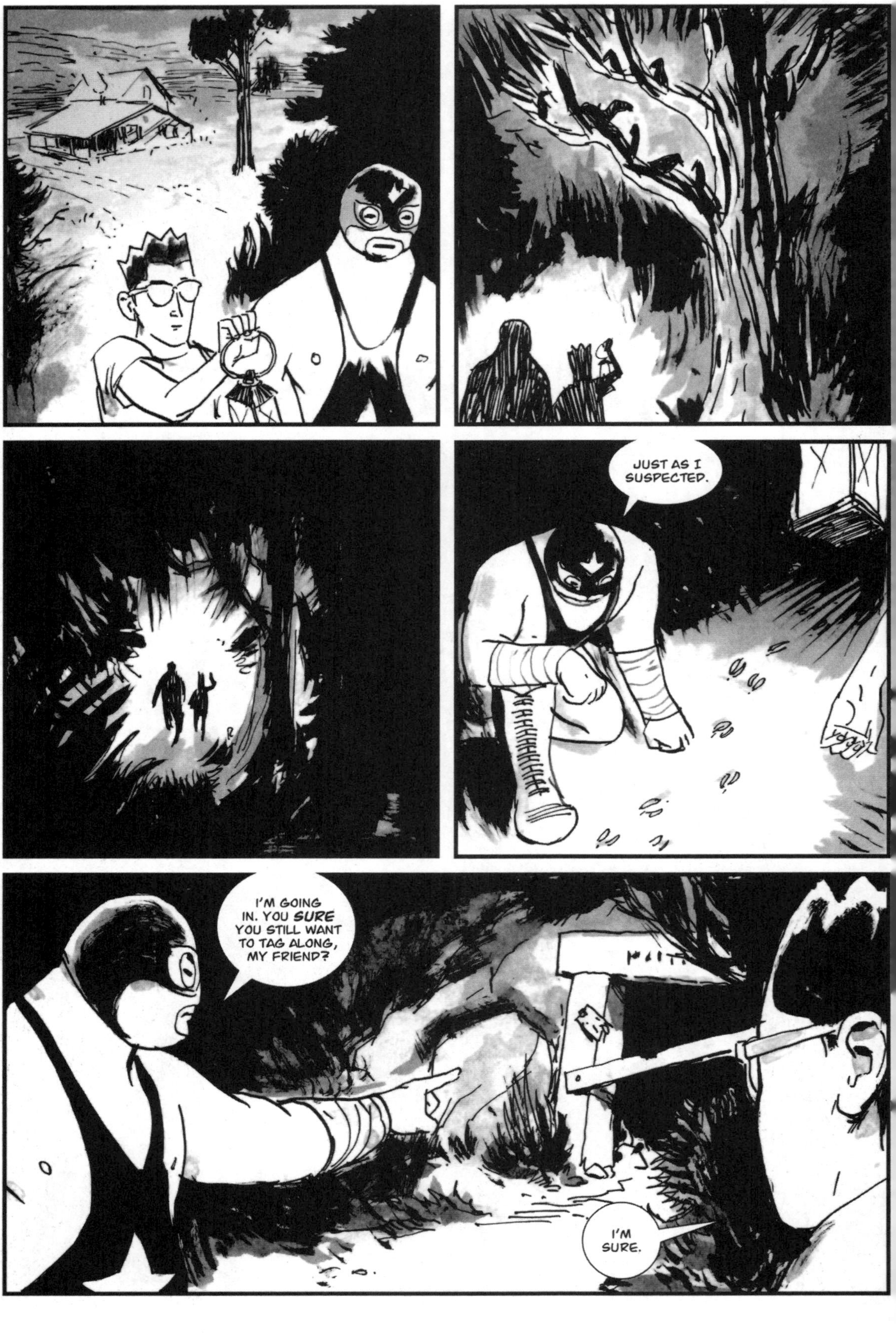
JUST AS I SUSPECTED.
I'M GOING IN. YOU SURE YOU STILL WANT TO TAG ALONG, MY FRIEND?
I'M SURE.

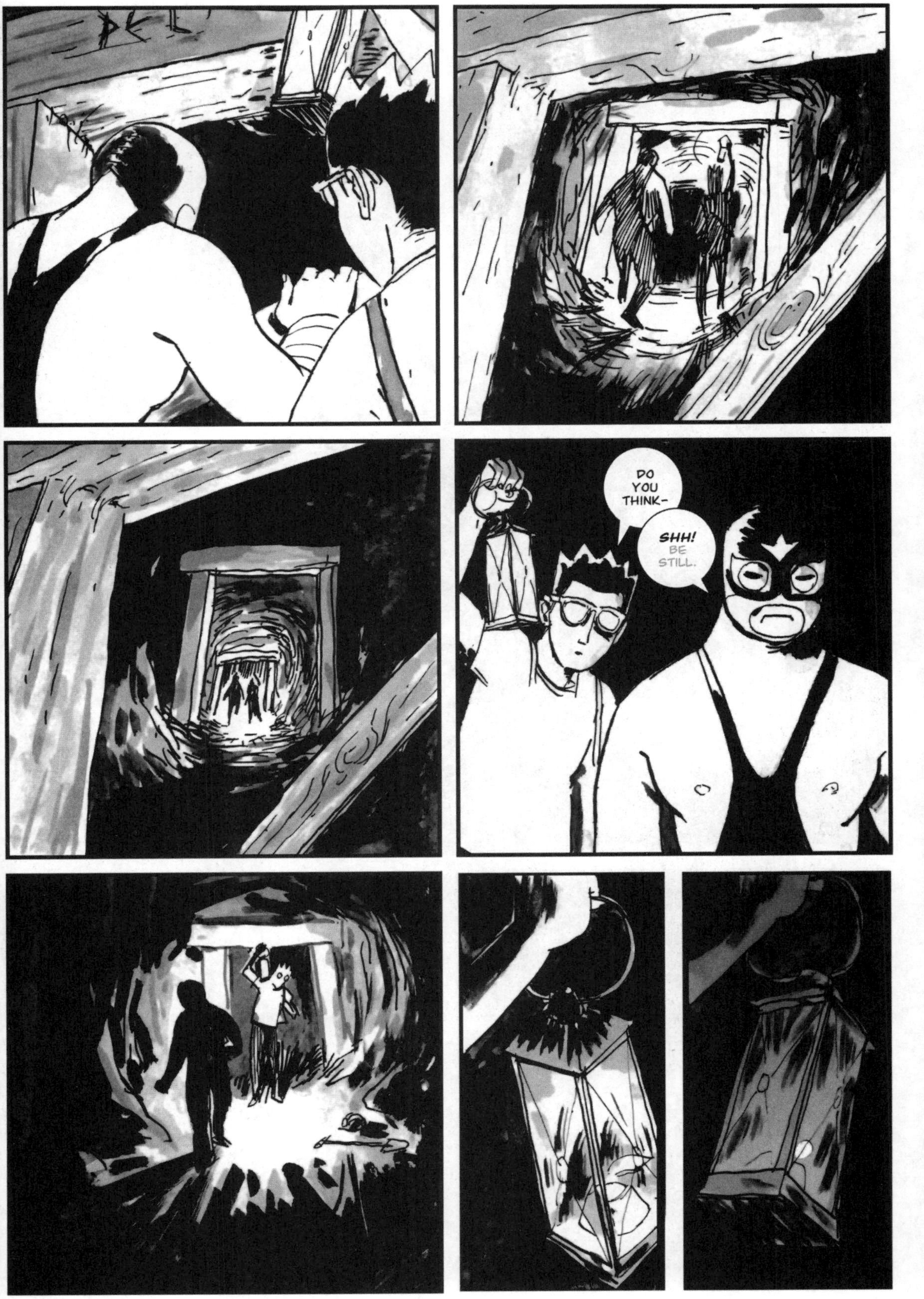
DO YOU THINK-
SHH! BE STILL.

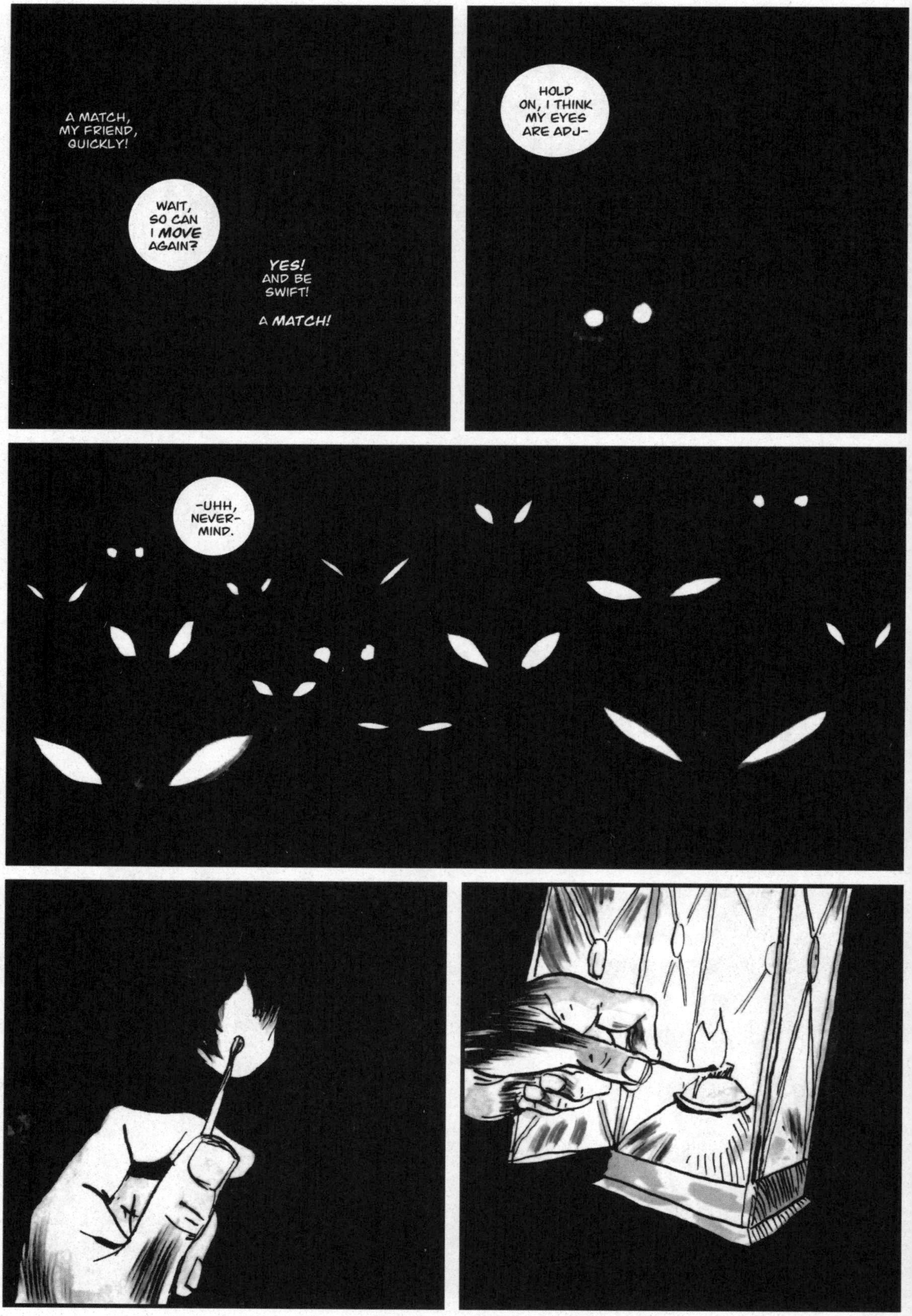
A MATCH, MY FRIEND, QUICKLY!
WAIT, SO CAN I MOVE AGAIN?
YES! AND BE SWIFT!
A MATCH!
HOLD ON, I THINK MY EYES ARE ADJ-
-UHH, NEVER-MIND.

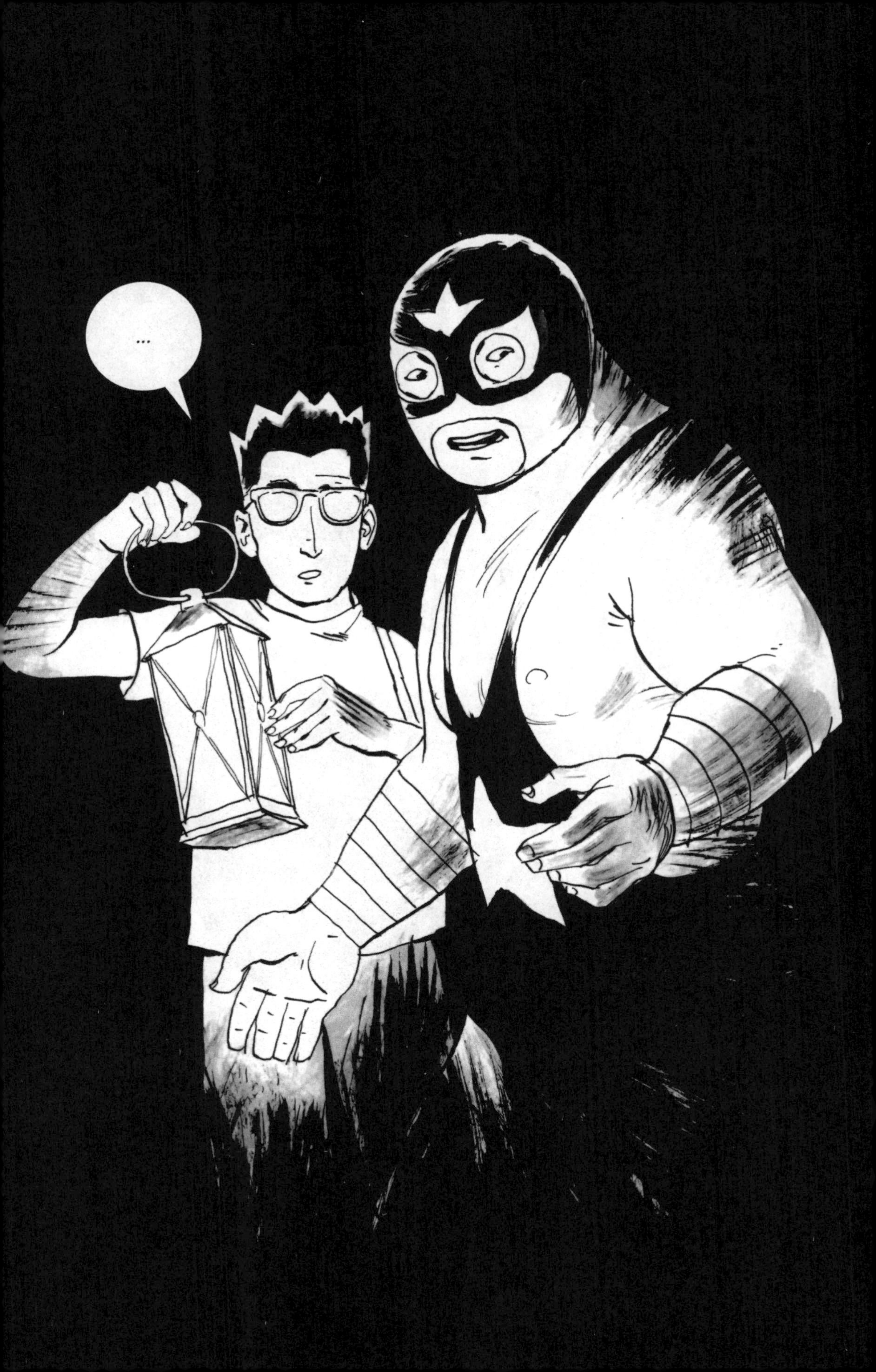
...

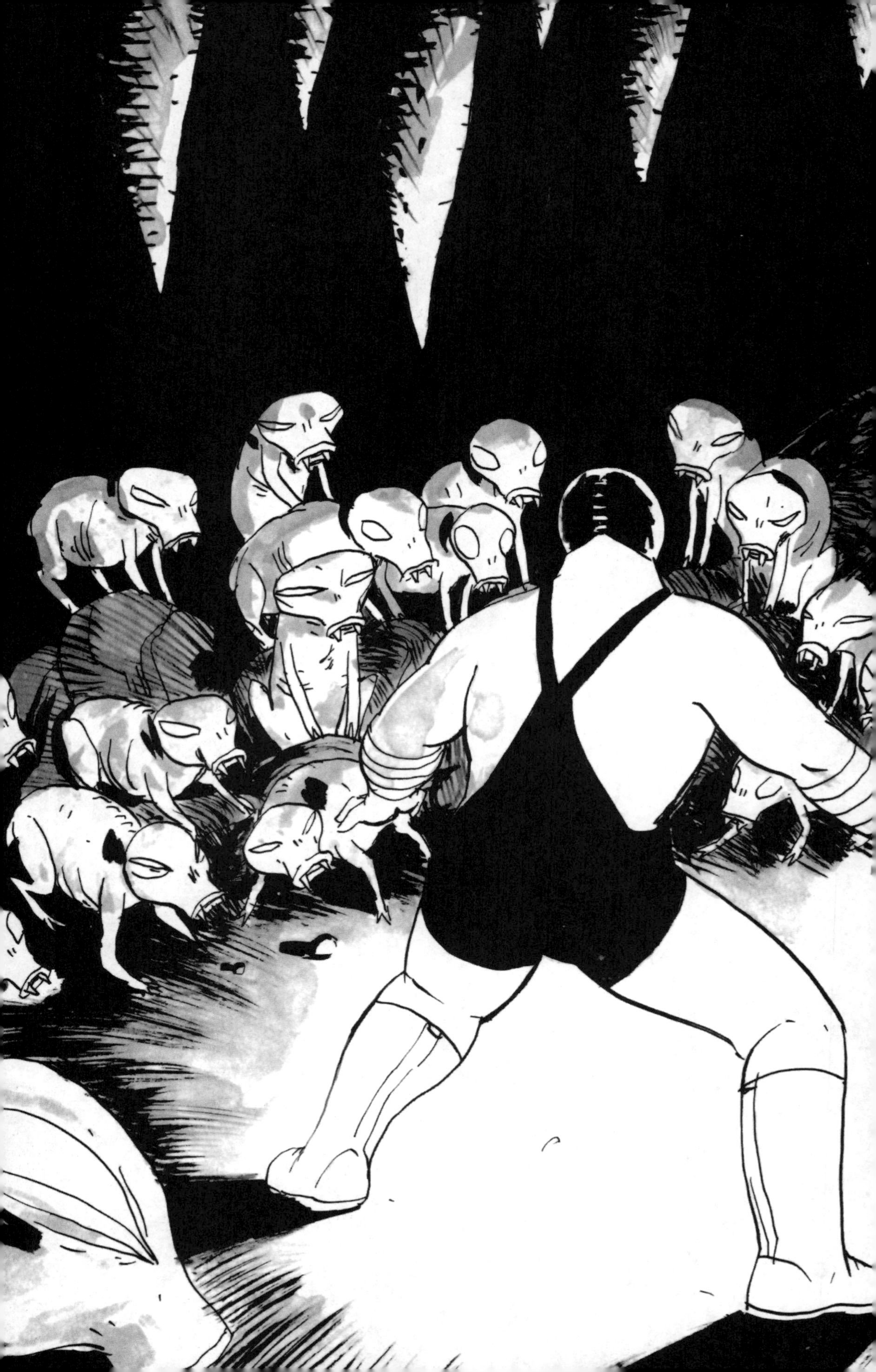

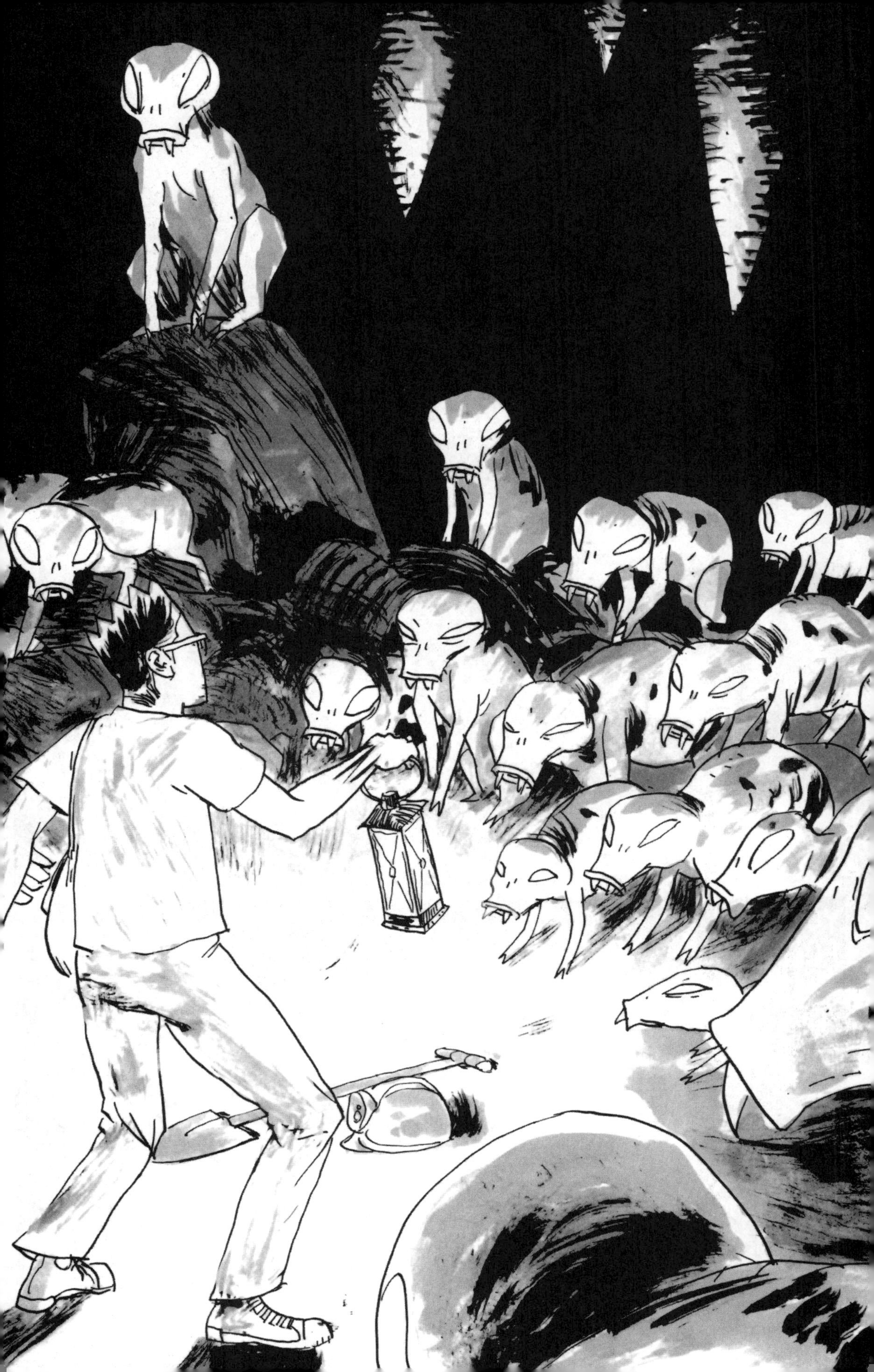

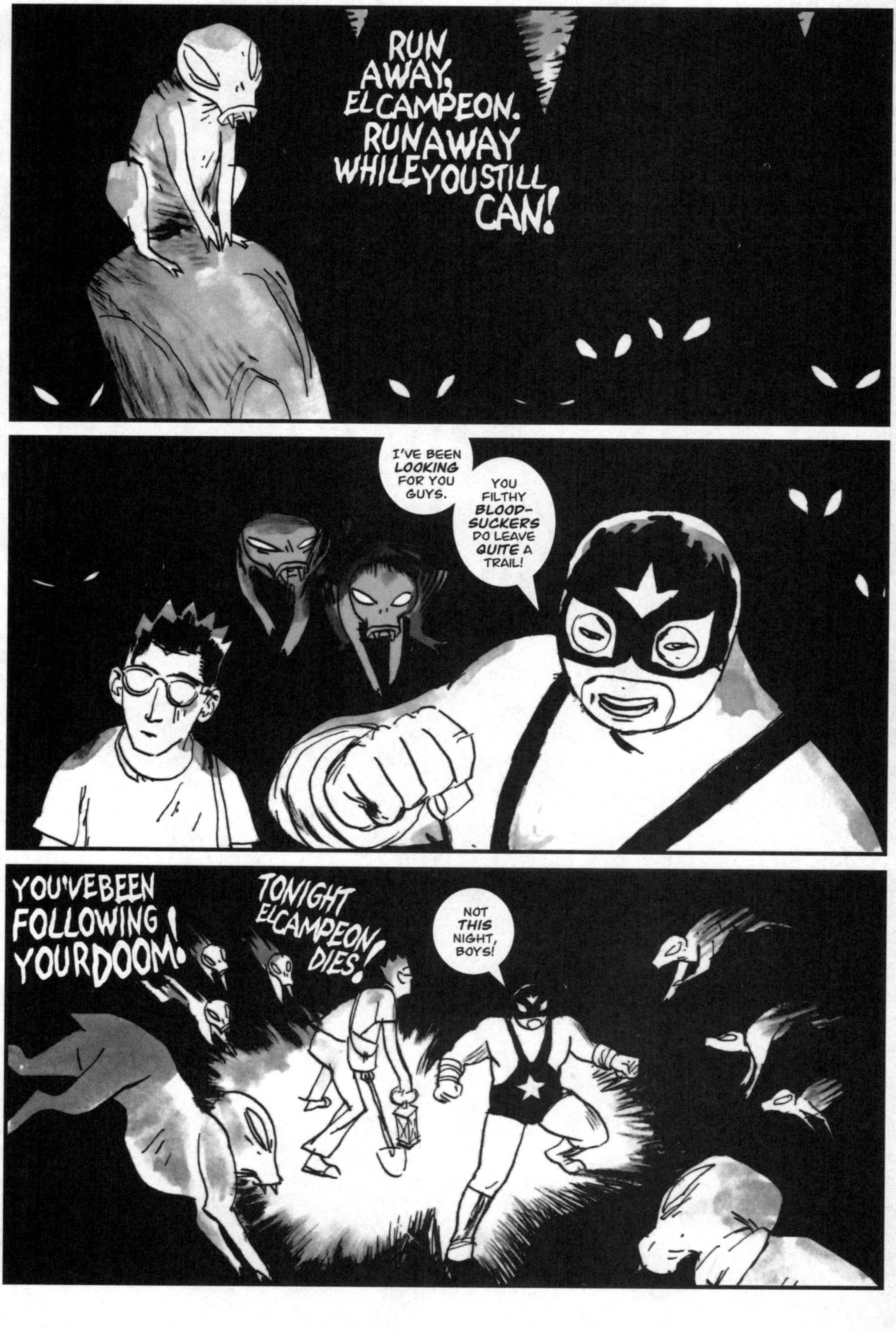
RUN AWAY, EL CAMPEON. RUNAWAY WHILE YOU STILL CAN!
I'VE BEEN LOOKING FOR YOU GUYS.
YOU FILTHY BLOOD-SUCKERS DO LEAVE QUITE A TRAIL!
YOU'VE BEEN FOLLOWING YOUR DOOM!
TONIGHT EL CAMPEON DIES!
NOT THIS NIGHT, BOYS!

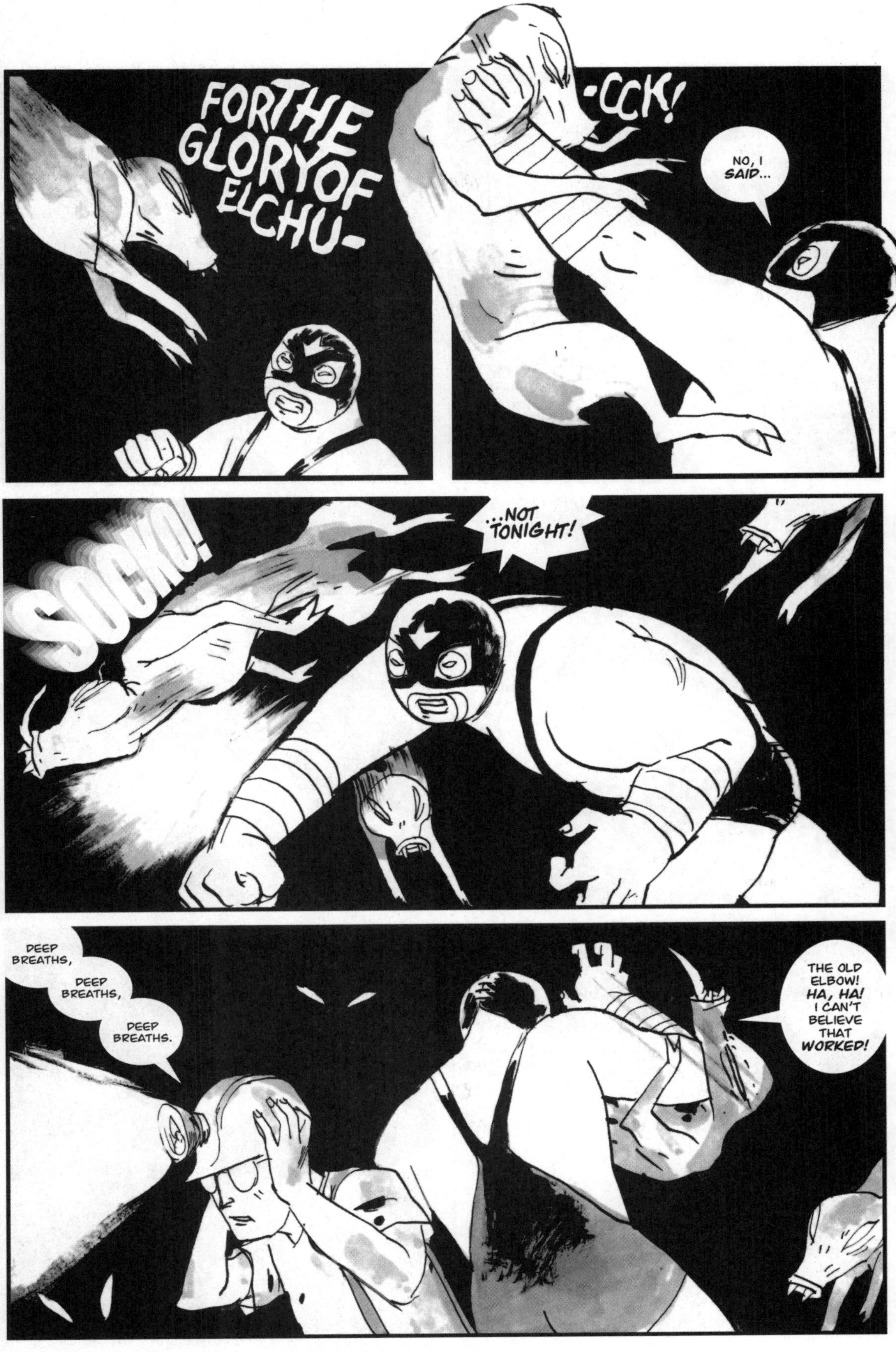
FOR THE GLORY OF ELCHU-
-CCK!
NO, I SAID...
SOCKO!
...NOT TONIGHT!
DEEP BREATHS,
DEEP BREATHS,
DEEP BREATHS.
THE OLD ELBOW! HA, HA! I CAN'T BELIEVE THAT WORKED!

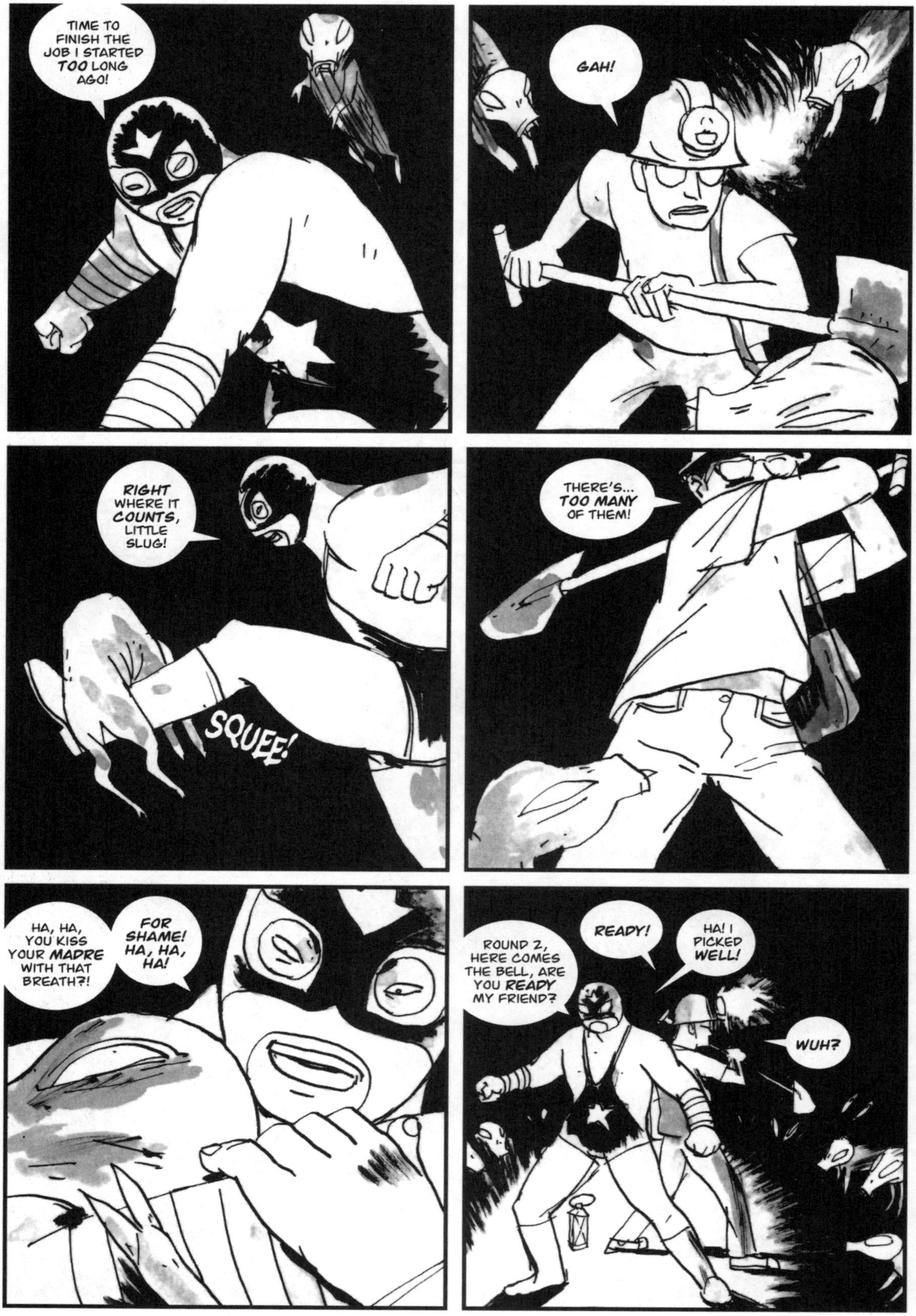
TIME TO FINISH THE JOB I STARTED TOO LONG AGO!
GAH!
RIGHT WHERE IT COUNTS, LITTLE SLUG!
SQUEE!
THERE'S... TOO MANY OF THEM!
HA, HA, YOU KISS YOUR MADRE WITH THAT BREATH?!
FOR SHAME! HA, HA, HA!
ROUND 2, HERE COMES THE BELL, ARE YOU READY MY FRIEND?
READY!
HA! I PICKED WELL!
WUH?

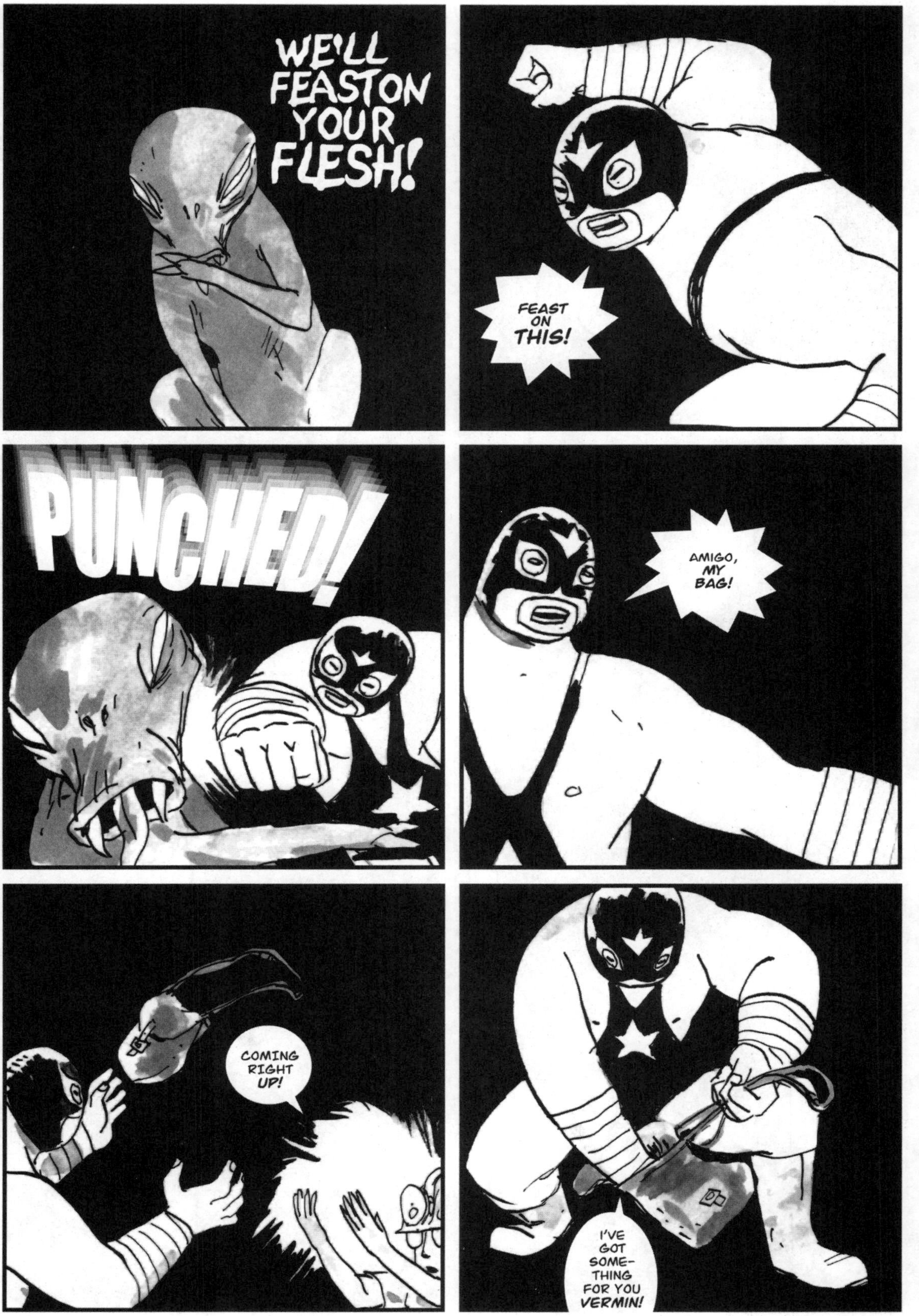
WE'LL FEASTON YOUR FLESH!
FEAST ON THIS!
PUNCHED!
AMIGO, MY BAG!
COMING RIGHT UP!
I'VE GOT SOME-THING FOR YOU VERMIN!

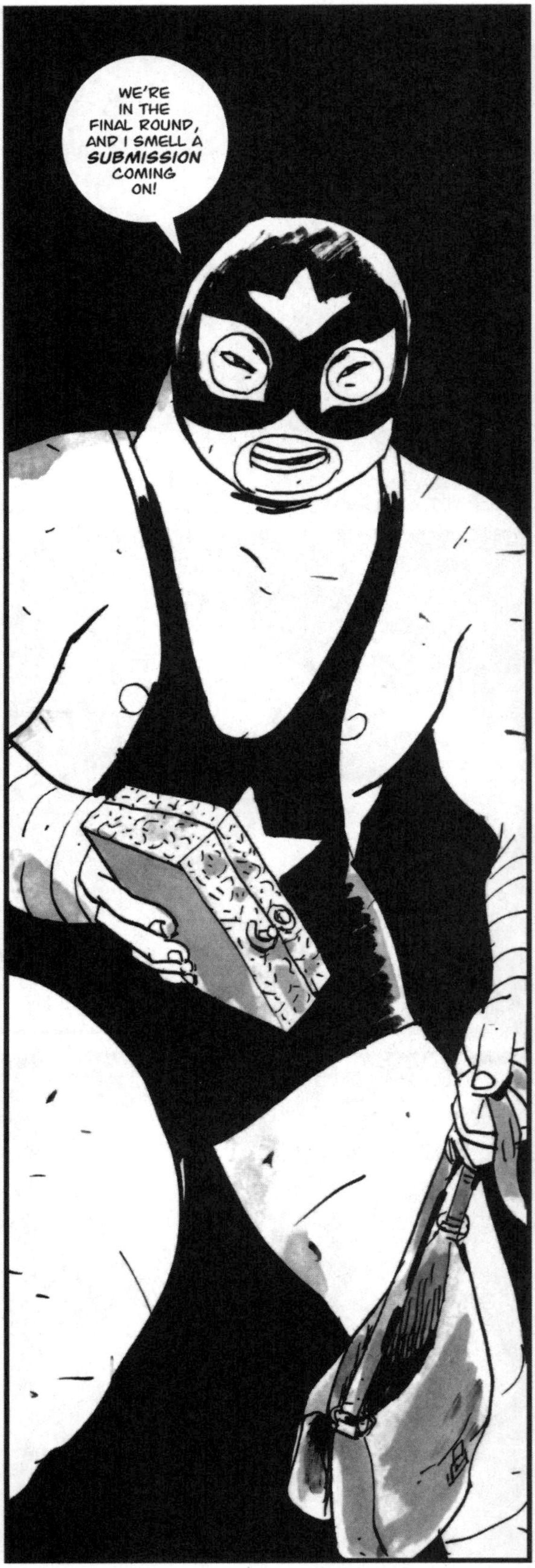
WE'RE IN THE FINAL ROUND, AND I SMELL A **SUBMISSION** COMING ON!

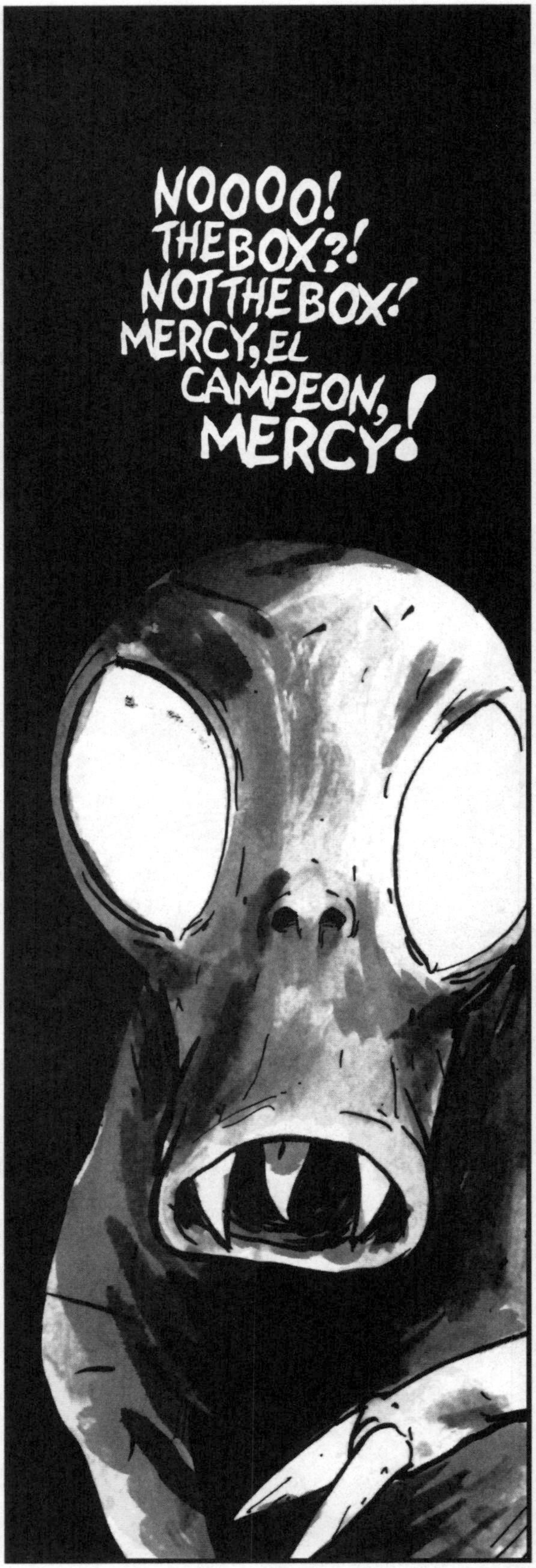
NOOOO! THE BOX?! NOT THE BOX! MERCY, EL CAMPEON, MERCY!

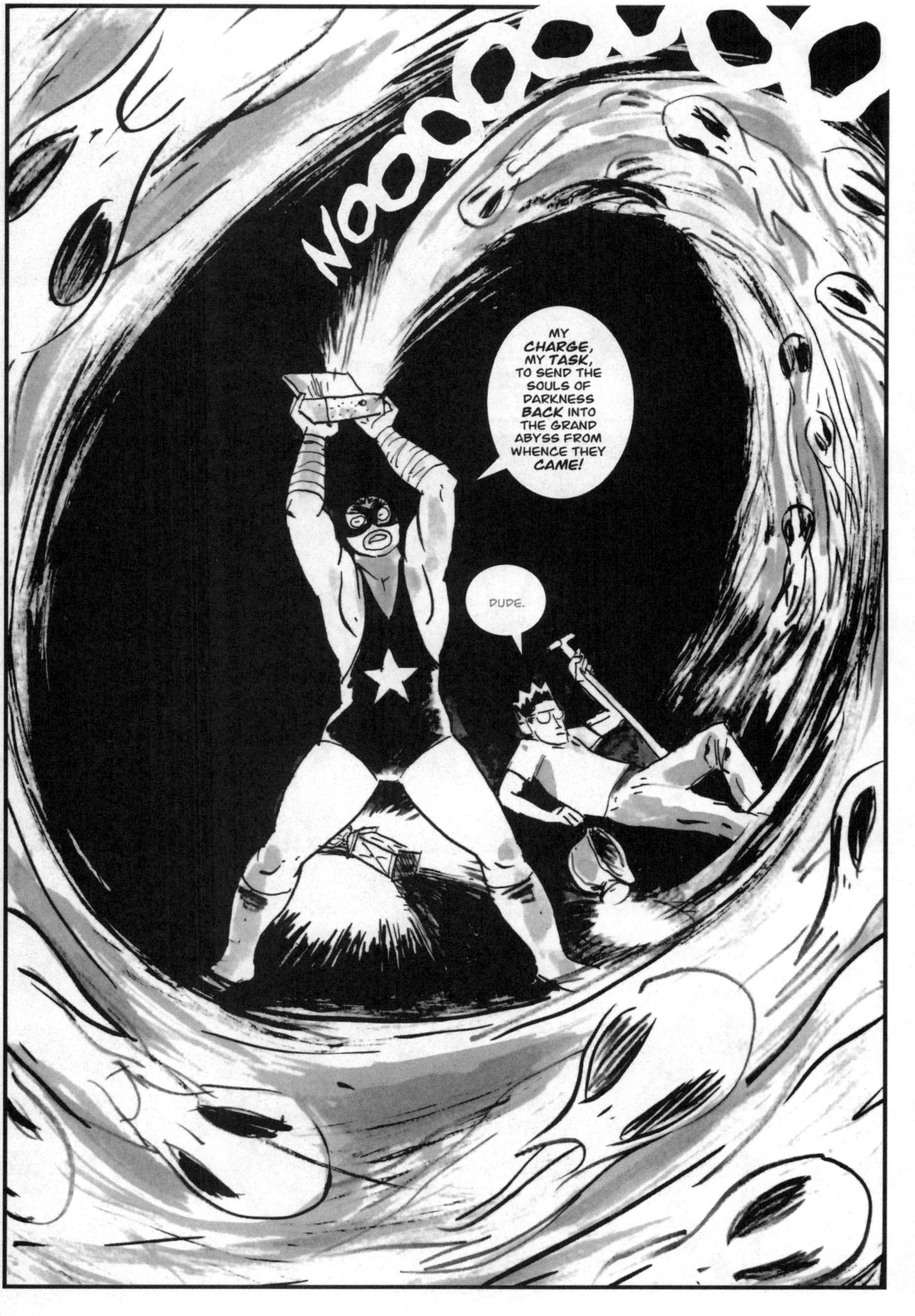
NOOOOOOO
MY CHARGE, MY TASK, TO SEND THE SOULS OF DARKNESS BACK INTO THE GRAND ABYSS FROM WHENCE THEY CAME!
DUDE.

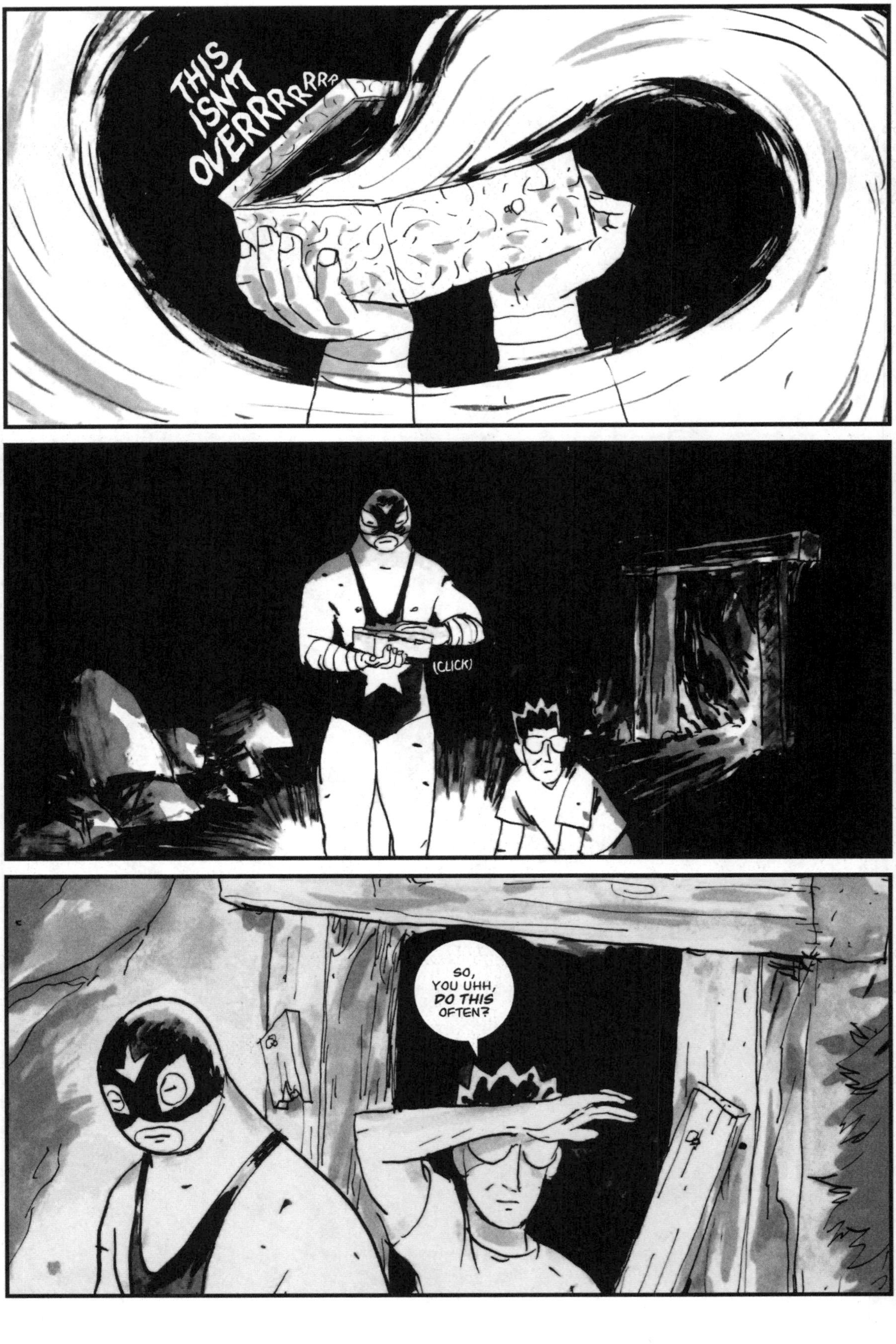
THIS ISN'T OVERRRRRRRR
(CLICK)
SO, YOU UHH, DO THIS OFTEN?

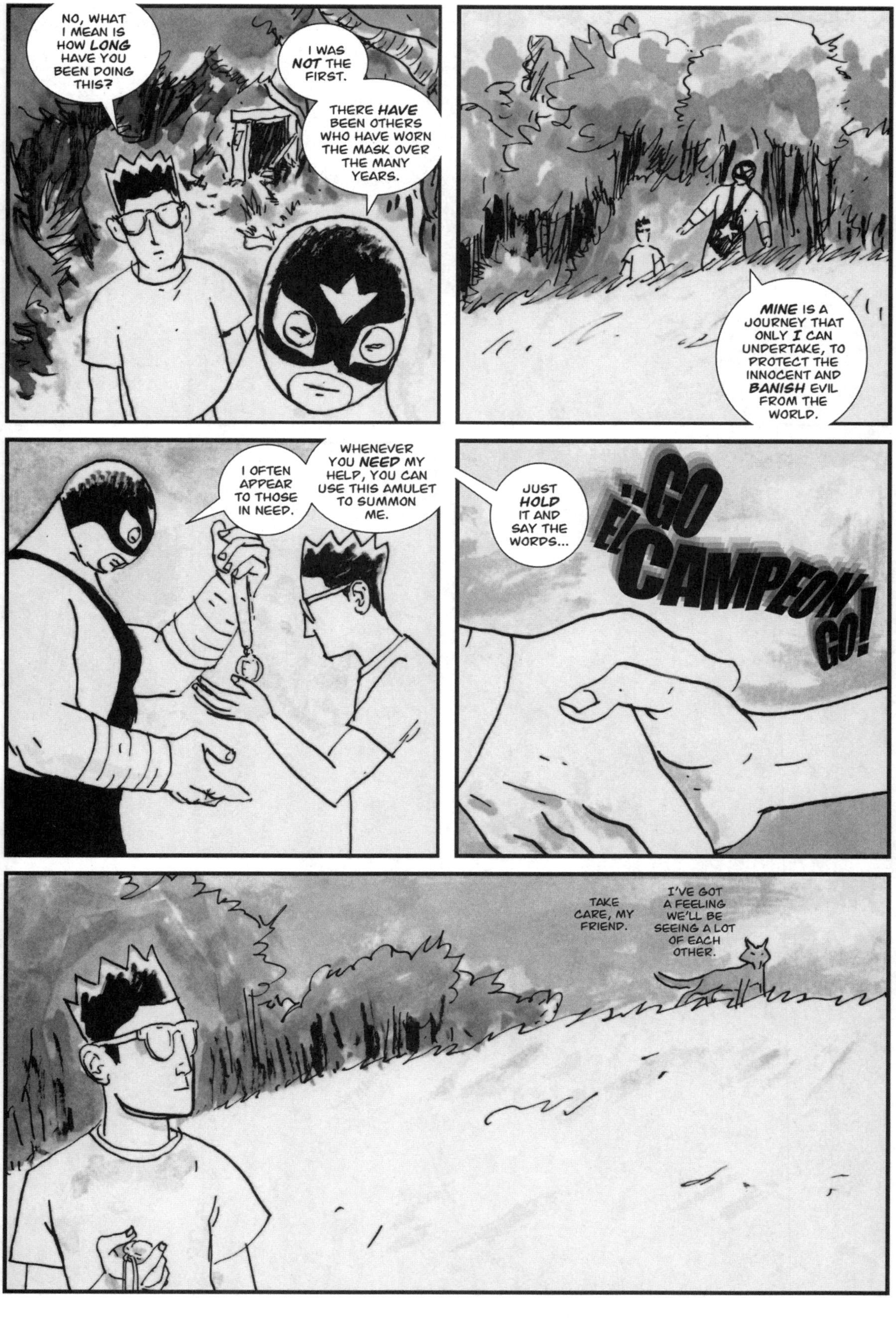
NO, WHAT I MEAN IS HOW LONG HAVE YOU BEEN DOING THIS?
I WAS NOT THE FIRST.
THERE HAVE BEEN OTHERS WHO HAVE WORN THE MASK OVER THE MANY YEARS.
MINE IS A JOURNEY THAT ONLY I CAN UNDERTAKE, TO PROTECT THE INNOCENT AND BANISH EVIL FROM THE WORLD.
I OFTEN APPEAR TO THOSE IN NEED.
WHENEVER YOU NEED MY HELP, YOU CAN USE THIS AMULET TO SUMMON ME.
JUST HOLD IT AND SAY THE WORDS...
¡¡GO El CAMPEON GO!
TAKE CARE, MY FRIEND.
I'VE GOT A FEELING WE'LL BE SEEING A LOT OF EACH OTHER.

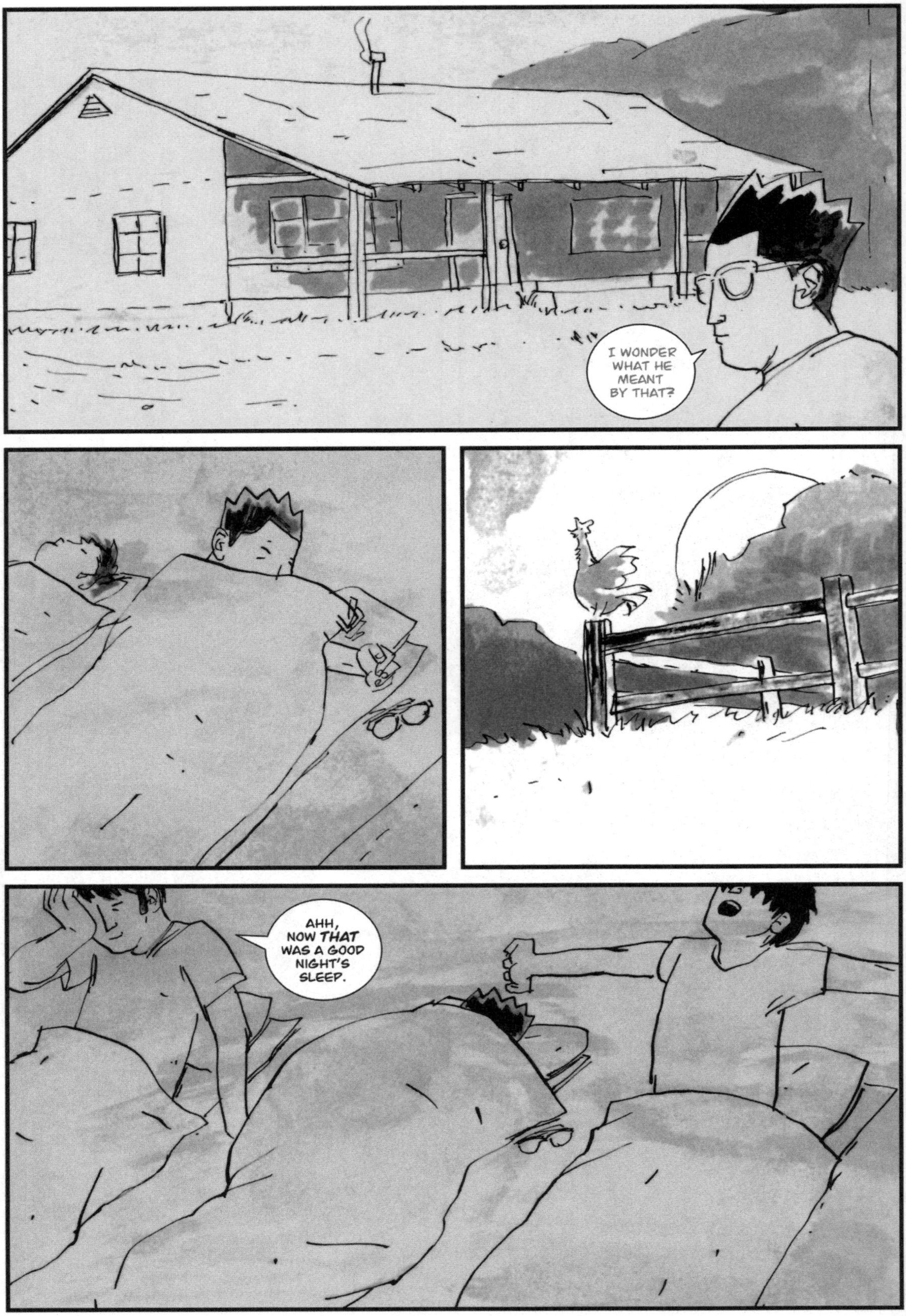
I WONDER WHAT HE MEANT BY THAT?
AHH, NOW THAT WAS A GOOD NIGHT'S SLEEP.

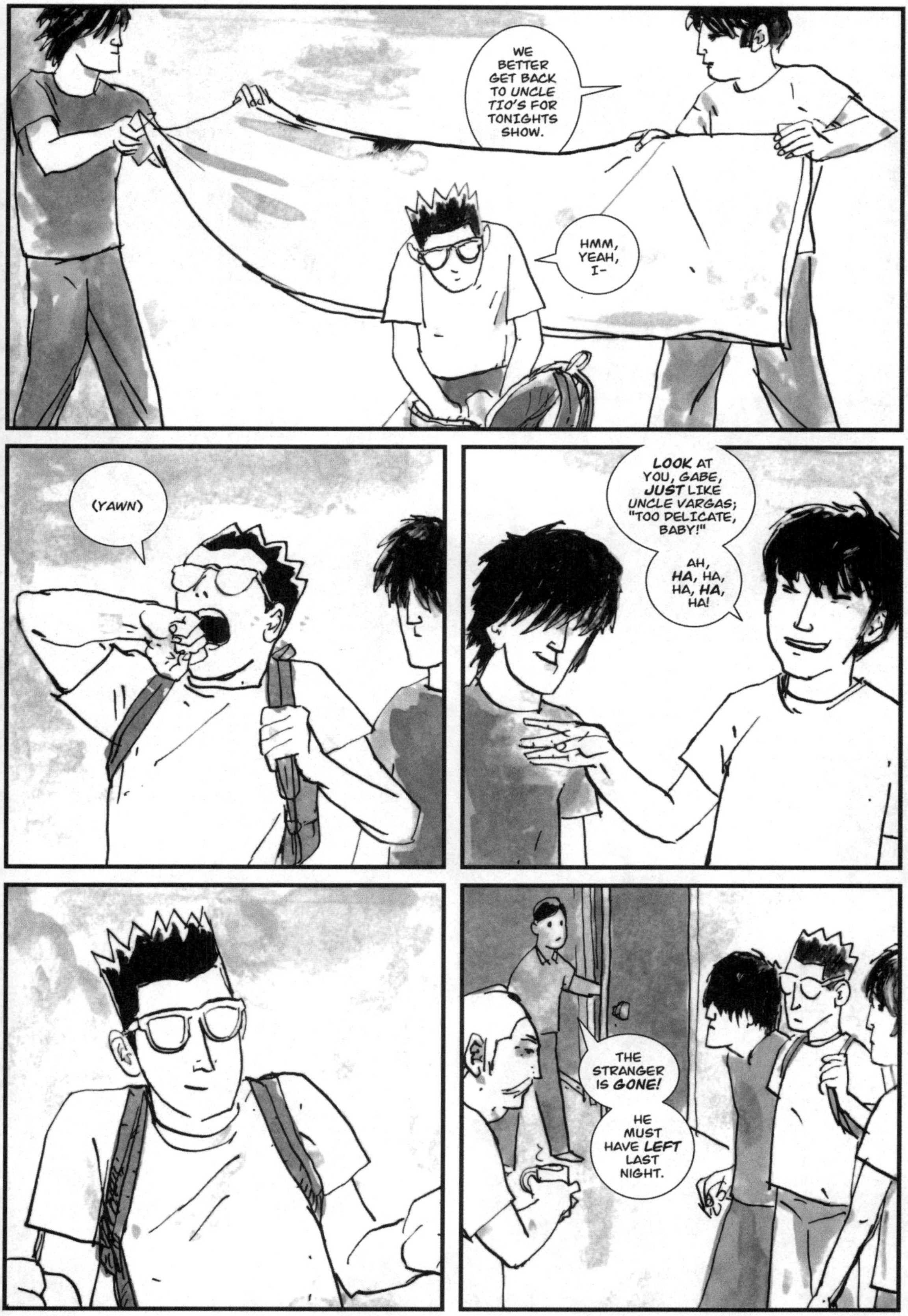
WE BETTER GET BACK TO UNCLE TIO'S FOR TONIGHTS SHOW.
HMM, YEAH, I-
(YAWN)
LOOK AT YOU, GABE, JUST LIKE UNCLE VARGAS; "TOO DELICATE, BABY!"
AH, HA, HA, HA, HA, HA!
THE STRANGER IS GONE!
HE MUST HAVE LEFT LAST NIGHT.

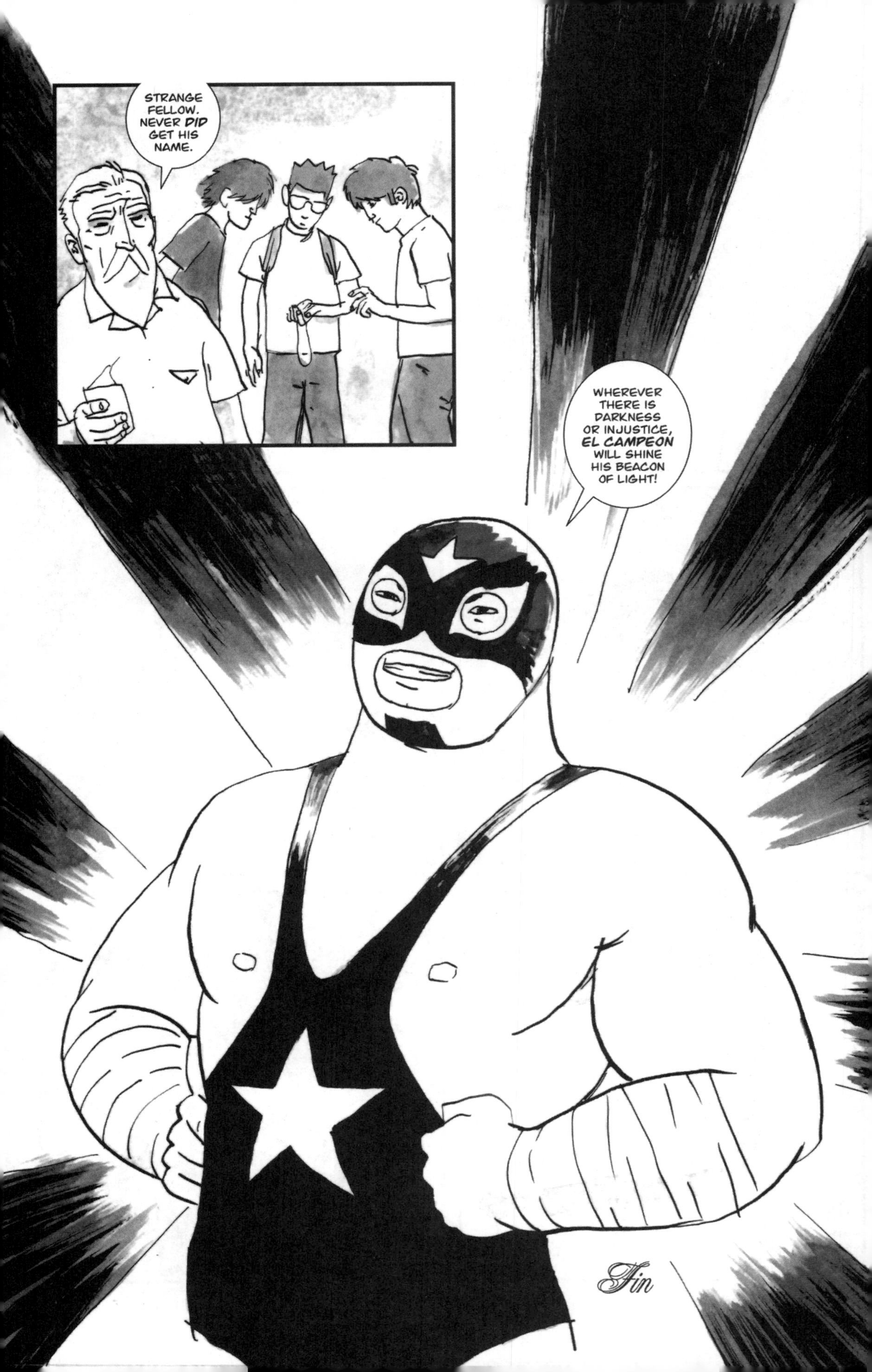
STRANGE FELLOW. NEVER DID GET HIS NAME.
WHEREVER THERE IS DARKNESS OR INJUSTICE, EL CAMPEON WILL SHINE HIS BEACON OF LIGHT!
Fin

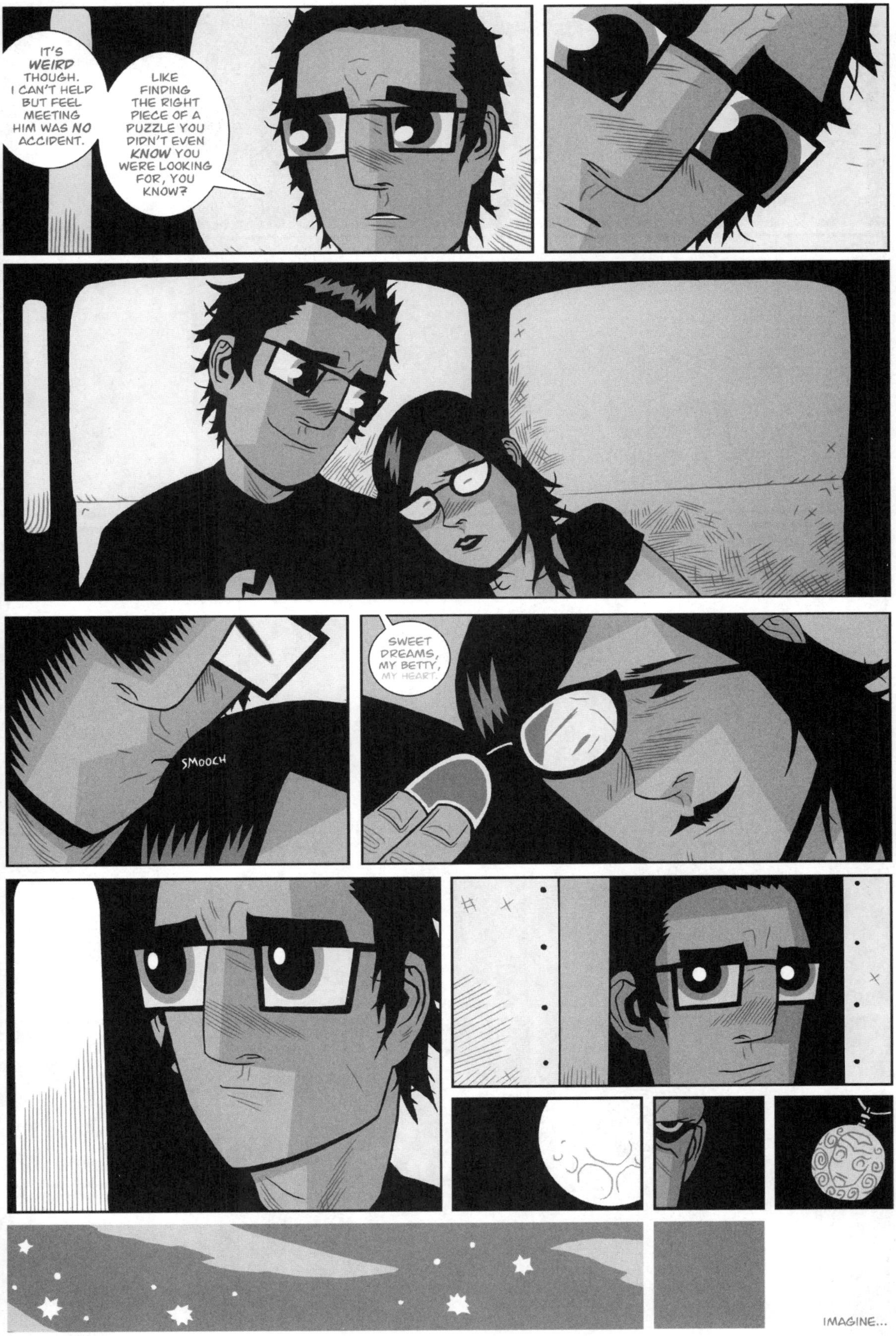
IT'S WEIRD THOUGH. I CAN'T HELP BUT FEEL MEETING HIM WAS NO ACCIDENT.
LIKE FINDING THE RIGHT PIECE OF A PUZZLE YOU DIDN'T EVEN KNOW YOU WERE LOOKING FOR, YOU KNOW?
SMOOCH
SWEET DREAMS, MY BETTY, MY HEART.
IMAGINE...

EPILOGUE

THE MIRACLE...

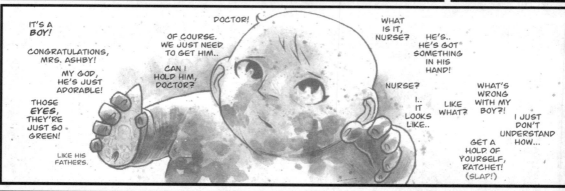

IT'S A **BOY**!

DOCTOR!

OF COURSE. WE JUST NEED TO GET HIM..

CAN I HOLD HIM, DOCTOR?

WHAT IS IT, NURSE?

HE'S.. HE'S GOT SOMETHING IN HIS HAND!

CONGRATULATIONS, MRS. ASHBY!

MY GOD, HE'S JUST ADORABLE!

THOSE **EYES**, THEY'RE JUST SO GREEN!

LIKE HIS FATHERS.

NURSE?

I.. IT LOOKS LIKE..

LIKE WHAT?

WHAT'S WRONG WITH MY BOY?!

I JUST DON'T UNDERSTAND HOW...

GET A HOLD OF YOURSELF, RATCHET! (SLAP!)

WHAT IS IT, NURSE, WHAT IS HE HOLDING?!

WHAT'S WRONG WITH MY BOY?!! ANSWER ME!!!

MY GOD..

HE'S HOLDING A...

(GASP)

WHY DOES IT SMELL LIKE PEE IN HERE?

ARE YOU FOLLOWING **YOUR** PATH?

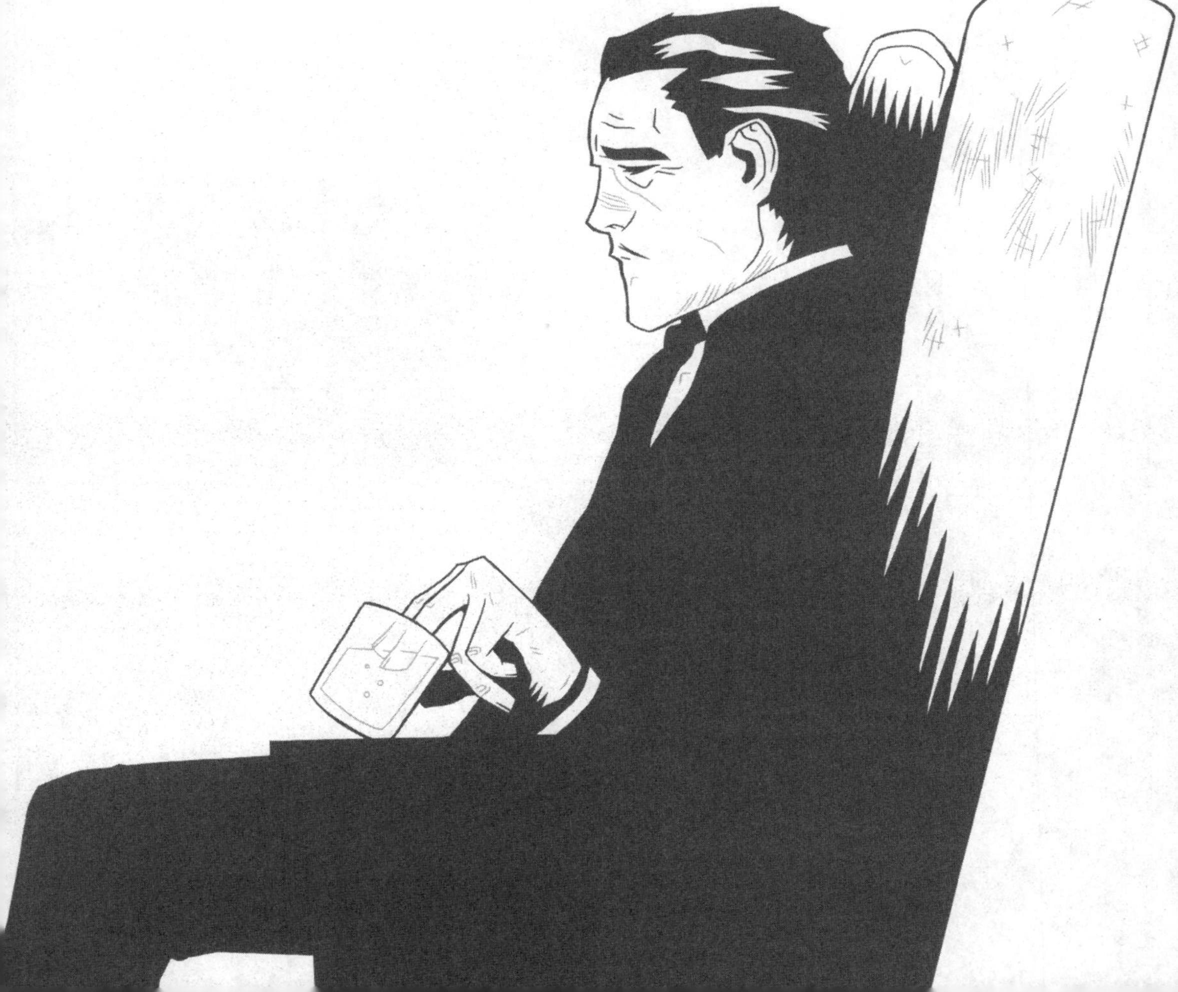

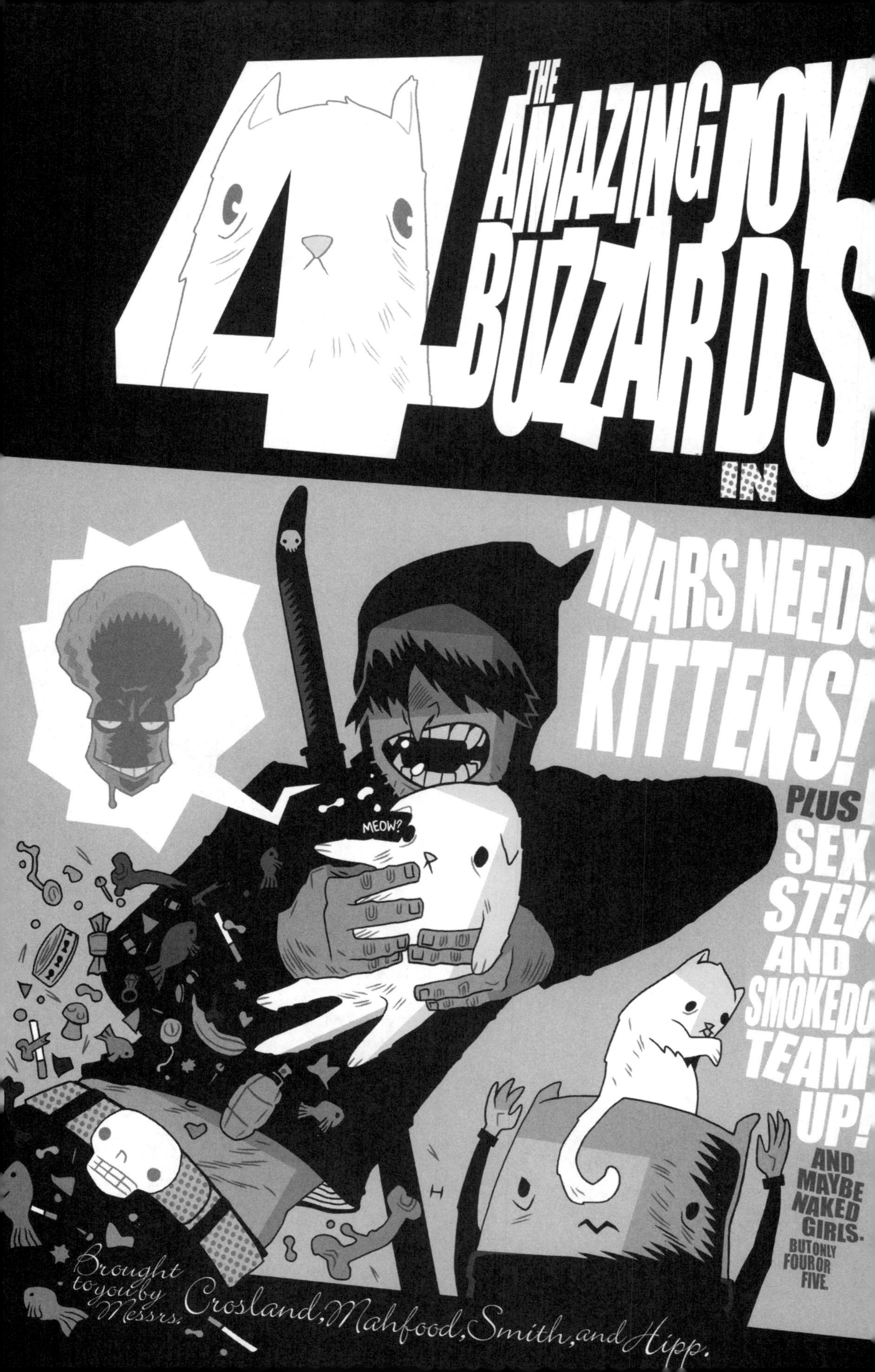
4
THE AMAZING JOY BUZZARDS
IN
"MARS NEEDS KITTENS!
MEOW?
PLUS SEX, STEV[E] AND SMOKEDO[G] TEAM UP!
AND MAYBE NAKED GIRLS.
BUT ONLY FOUR OR FIVE.
Brought to you by Messrs. Crosland, Mahfood, Smith, and Hipp.

NOW FOR AN AMAZING JOY BUZZARDS *Masterpiece Moment...*

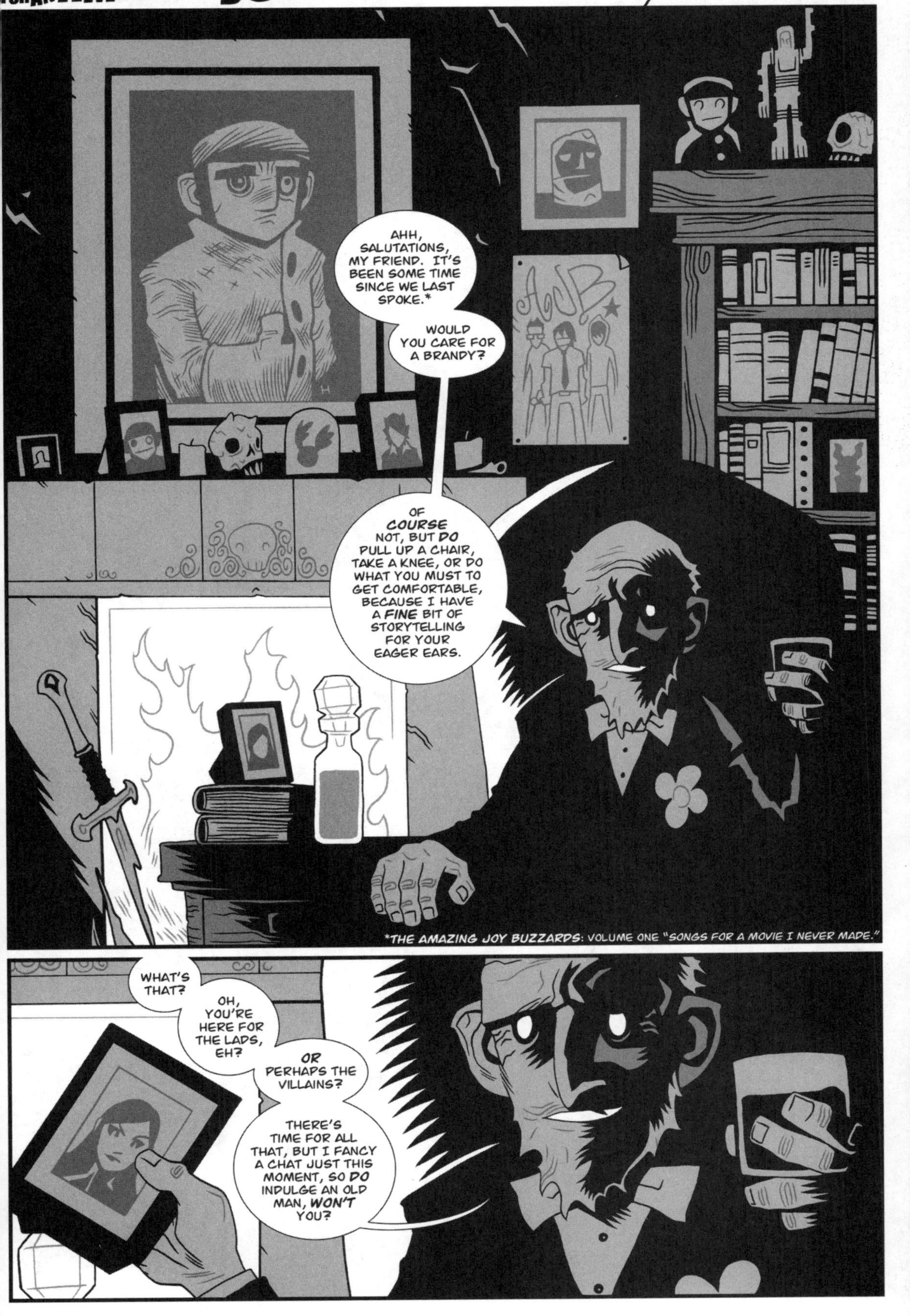
AHH, SALUTATIONS, MY FRIEND. IT'S BEEN SOME TIME SINCE WE LAST SPOKE.*
WOULD YOU CARE FOR A BRANDY?
OF COURSE NOT, BUT DO PULL UP A CHAIR, TAKE A KNEE, OR DO WHAT YOU MUST TO GET COMFORTABLE, BECAUSE I HAVE A FINE BIT OF STORYTELLING FOR YOUR EAGER EARS.
*THE AMAZING JOY BUZZARDS: VOLUME ONE "SONGS FOR A MOVIE I NEVER MADE."
WHAT'S THAT?
OH, YOU'RE HERE FOR THE LADS, EH?
OR PERHAPS THE VILLAINS?
THERE'S TIME FOR ALL THAT, BUT I FANCY A CHAT JUST THIS MOMENT, SO DO INDULGE AN OLD MAN, WON'T YOU?

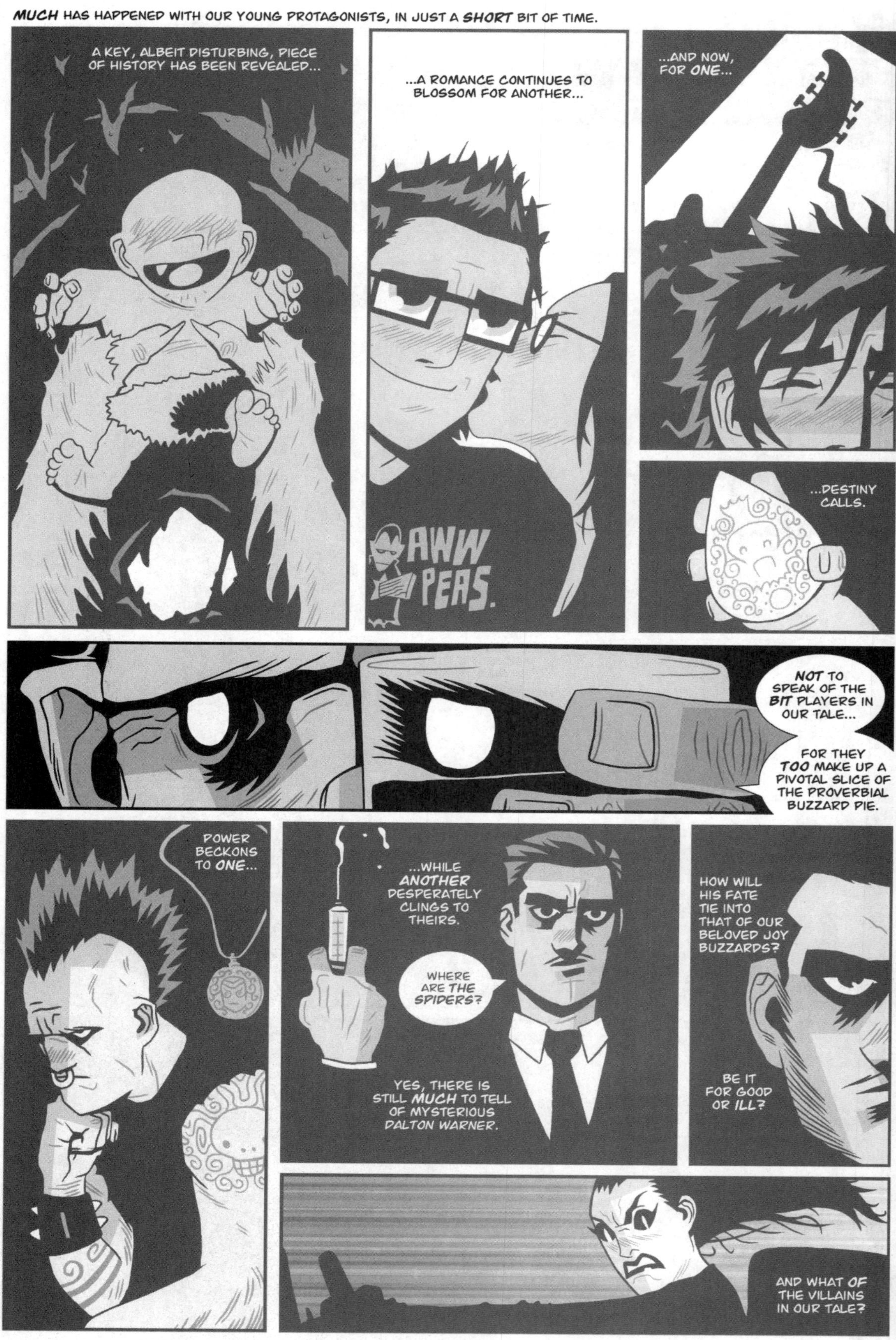
MUCH HAS HAPPENED WITH OUR YOUNG PROTAGONISTS, IN JUST A SHORT BIT OF TIME.
A KEY, ALBEIT DISTURBING, PIECE OF HISTORY HAS BEEN REVEALED...
...A ROMANCE CONTINUES TO BLOSSOM FOR ANOTHER...
AWW PEAS.
...AND NOW, FOR ONE...
...DESTINY CALLS.
NOT TO SPEAK OF THE BIT PLAYERS IN OUR TALE...
FOR THEY TOO MAKE UP A PIVOTAL SLICE OF THE PROVERBIAL BUZZARD PIE.
POWER BECKONS TO ONE...
...WHILE ANOTHER DESPERATELY CLINGS TO THEIRS.
WHERE ARE THE SPIDERS?
YES, THERE IS STILL MUCH TO TELL OF MYSTERIOUS DALTON WARNER.
HOW WILL HIS FATE TIE INTO THAT OF OUR BELOVED JOY BUZZARDS?
BE IT FOR GOOD OR ILL?
AND WHAT OF THE VILLAINS IN OUR TALE?

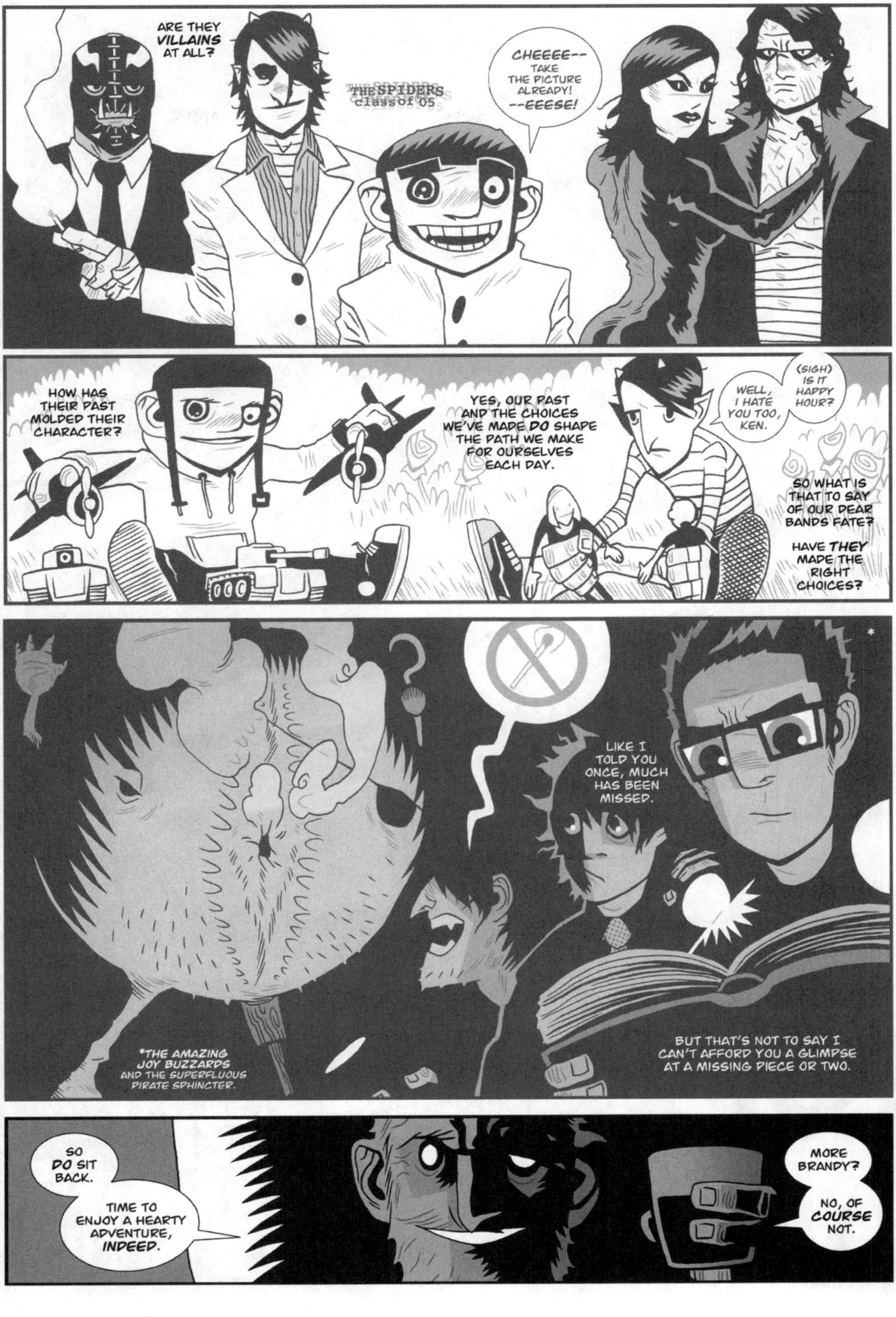

ARE THEY VILLAINS AT ALL?
THE SPIDERS class of 05
CHEEEE-- TAKE THE PICTURE ALREADY! --EEESE!
HOW HAS THEIR PAST MOLDED THEIR CHARACTER?
YES, OUR PAST AND THE CHOICES WE'VE MADE DO SHAPE THE PATH WE MAKE FOR OURSELVES EACH DAY.
WELL, I HATE YOU TOO, KEN.
(SIGH) IS IT HAPPY HOUR?
SO WHAT IS THAT TO SAY OF OUR DEAR BANDS FATE?
HAVE THEY MADE THE RIGHT CHOICES?
*
LIKE I TOLD YOU ONCE, MUCH HAS BEEN MISSED.
*THE AMAZING JOY BUZZARDS AND THE SUPERFLUOUS PIRATE SPHINCTER.
BUT THAT'S NOT TO SAY I CAN'T AFFORD YOU A GLIMPSE AT A MISSING PIECE OR TWO.
SO DO SIT BACK.
TIME TO ENJOY A HEARTY ADVENTURE, INDEED.
MORE BRANDY?
NO, OF COURSE NOT.

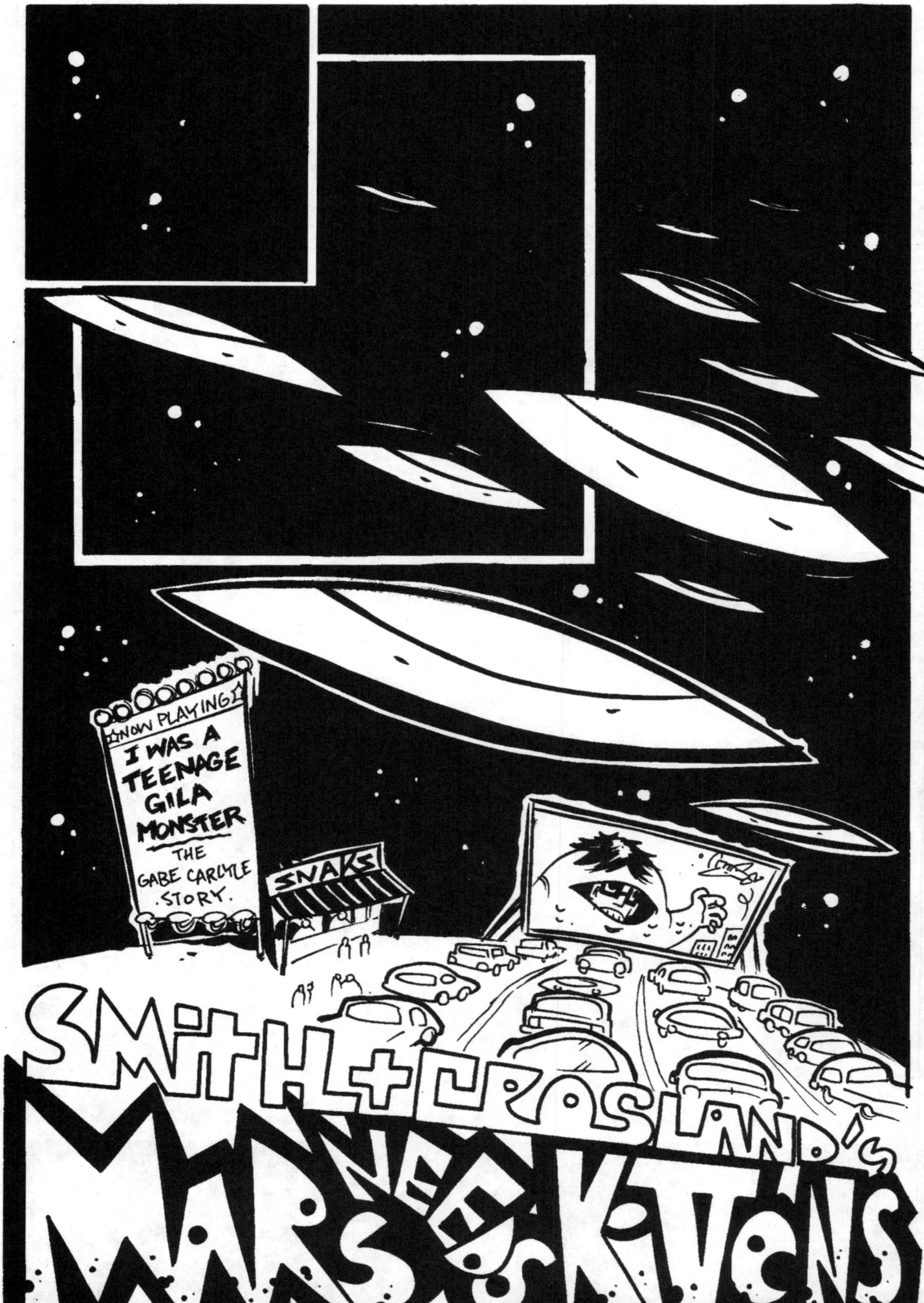

NOW PLAYING
I WAS A TEENAGE GILA MONSTER
THE GABE CARLYLE STORY.
SNAKS
SMITH + CROSLAND'S
MARS NEEDS KITTENS

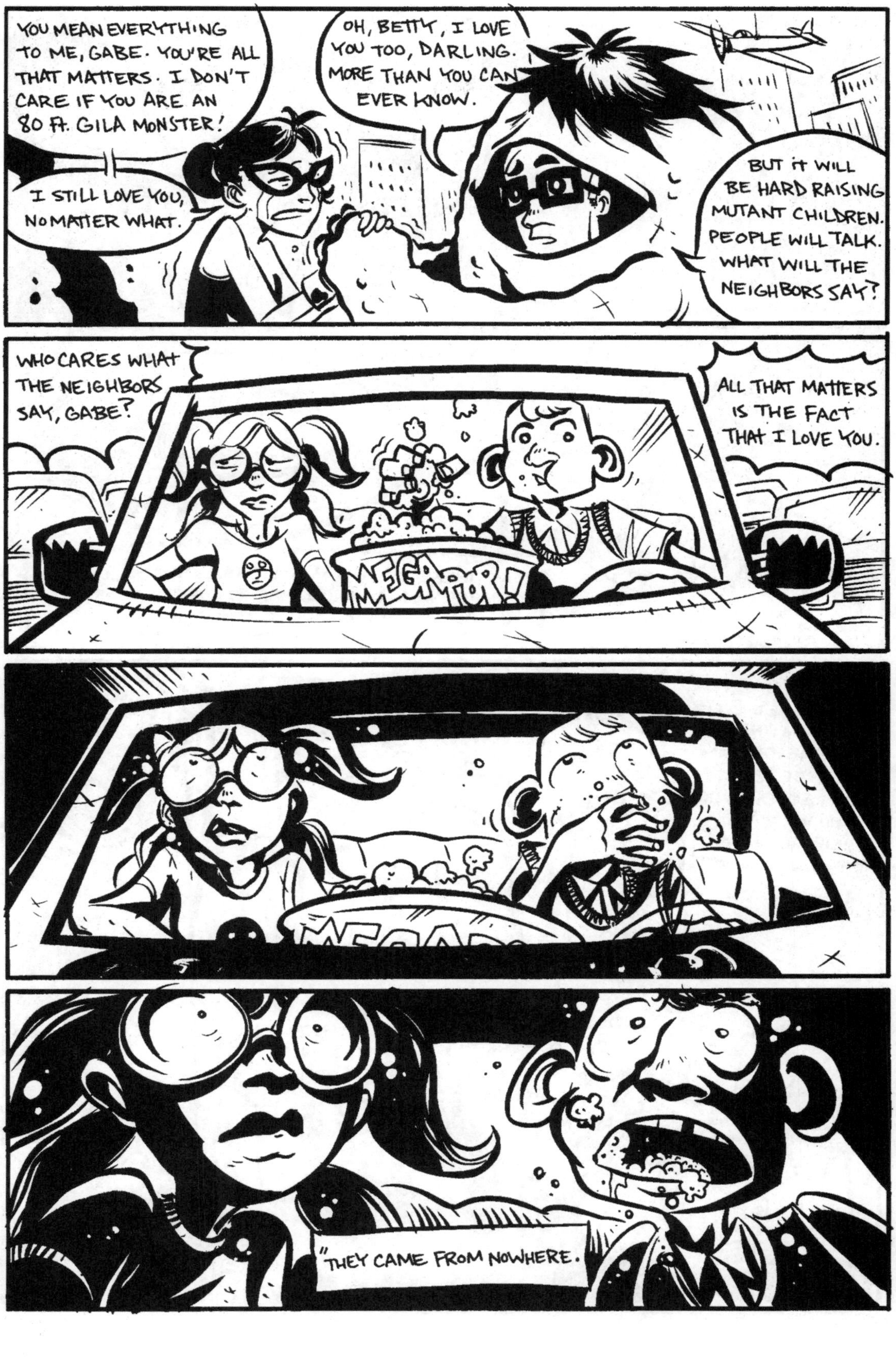
YOU MEAN EVERYTHING TO ME, GABE. YOU'RE ALL THAT MATTERS. I DON'T CARE IF YOU ARE AN 80 FT. GILA MONSTER!
I STILL LOVE YOU, NO MATTER WHAT.
OH, BETTY, I LOVE YOU TOO, DARLING. MORE THAN YOU CAN EVER KNOW.
BUT IT WILL BE HARD RAISING MUTANT CHILDREN. PEOPLE WILL TALK. WHAT WILL THE NEIGHBORS SAY?
WHO CARES WHAT THE NEIGHBORS SAY, GABE?
ALL THAT MATTERS IS THE FACT THAT I LOVE YOU.
MEGAPOP!
"THEY CAME FROM NOWHERE.

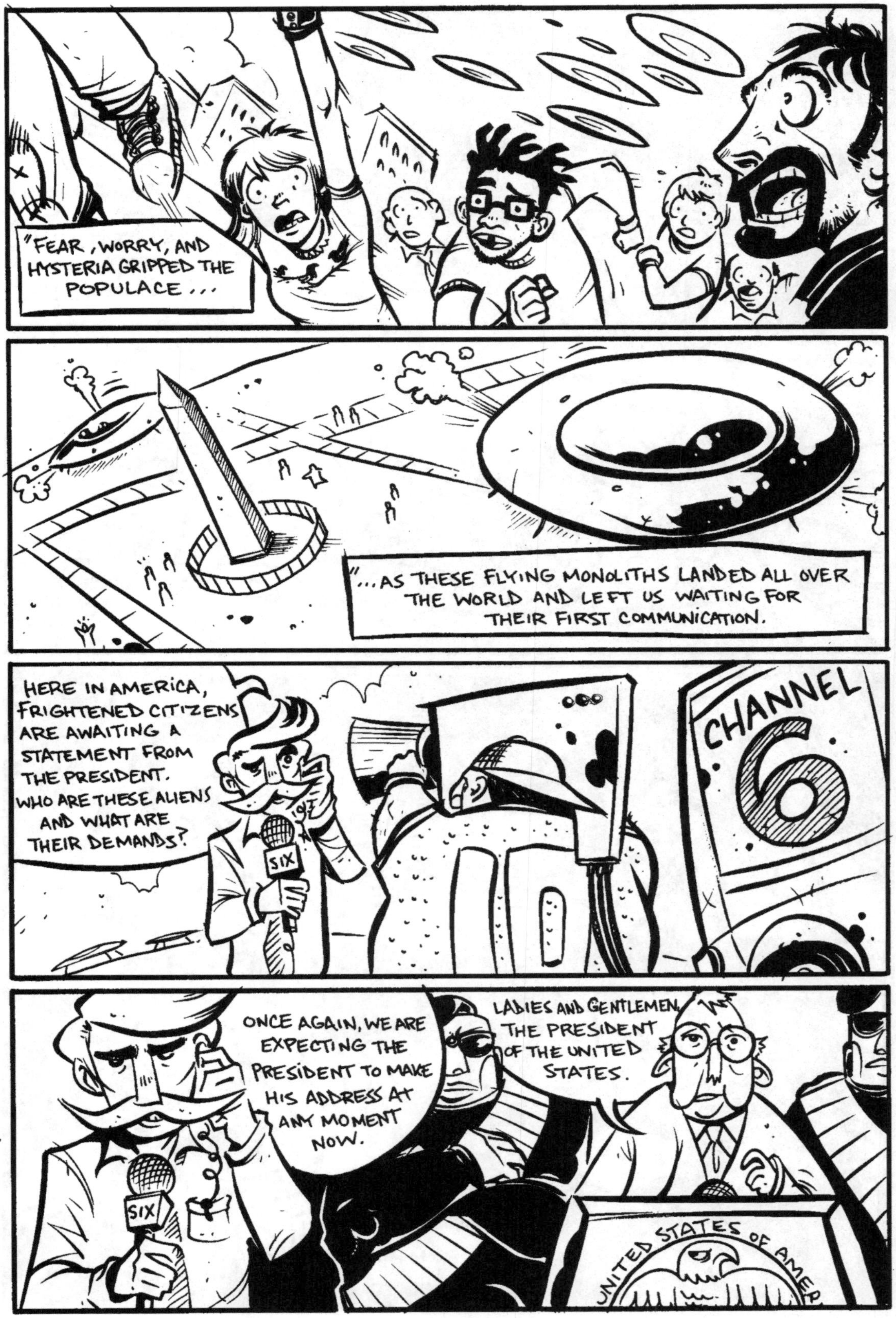
"FEAR, WORRY, AND HYSTERIA GRIPPED THE POPULACE...
"...AS THESE FLYING MONOLITHS LANDED ALL OVER THE WORLD AND LEFT US WAITING FOR THEIR FIRST COMMUNICATION.
HERE IN AMERICA, FRIGHTENED CITIZENS ARE AWAITING A STATEMENT FROM THE PRESIDENT. WHO ARE THESE ALIENS AND WHAT ARE THEIR DEMANDS?
SIX
CHANNEL 6
SIX
ONCE AGAIN, WE ARE EXPECTING THE PRESIDENT TO MAKE HIS ADDRESS AT ANY MOMENT NOW.
LADIES AND GENTLEMEN, THE PRESIDENT OF THE UNITED STATES.
UNITED STATES OF AMER

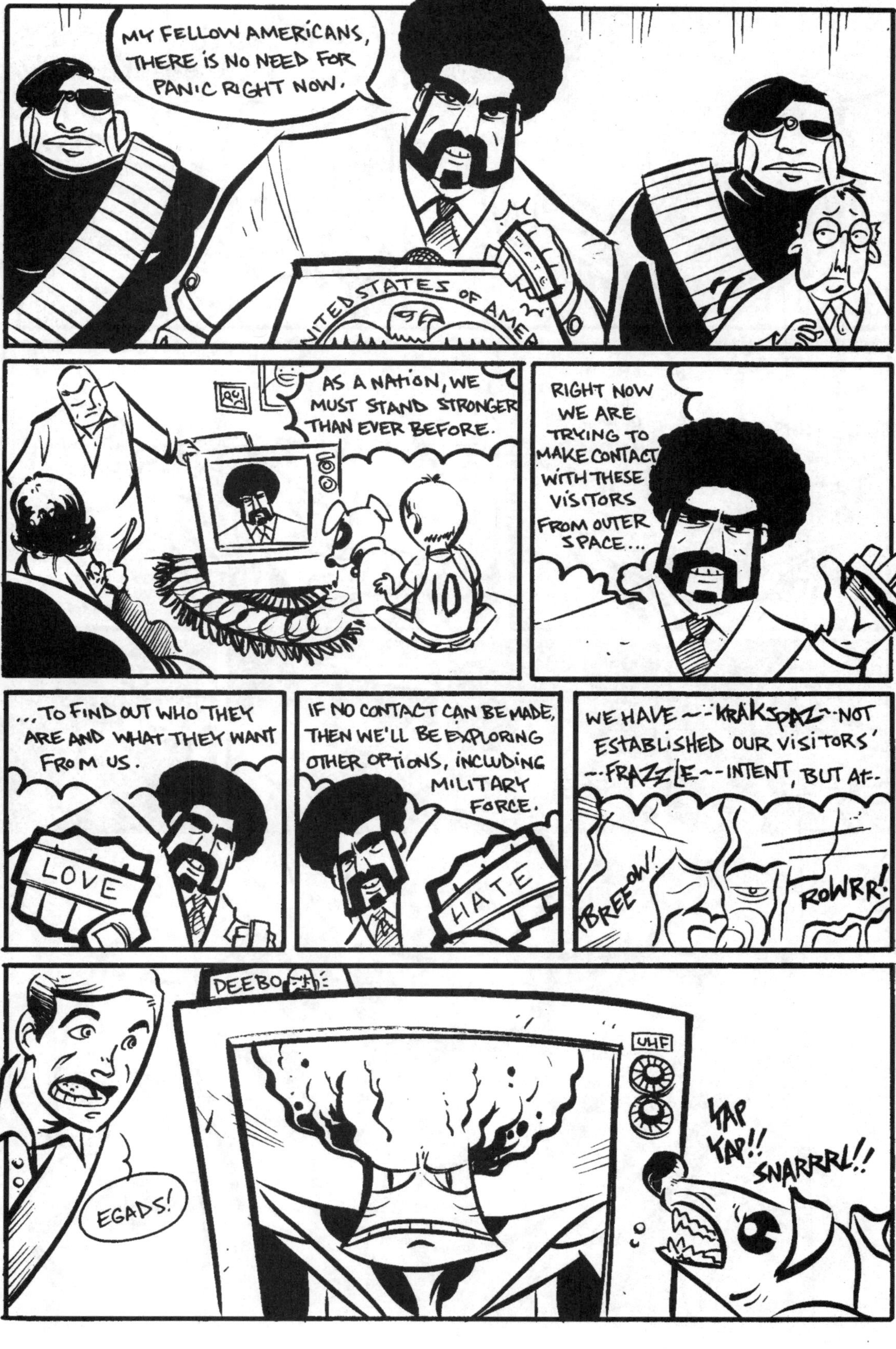
MY FELLOW AMERICANS, THERE IS NO NEED FOR PANIC RIGHT NOW.
UNITED STATES OF AMER
AS A NATION, WE MUST STAND STRONGER THAN EVER BEFORE.
10
RIGHT NOW WE ARE TRYING TO MAKE CONTACT WITH THESE VISITORS FROM OUTER SPACE...
...TO FIND OUT WHO THEY ARE AND WHAT THEY WANT FROM US.
LOVE
IF NO CONTACT CAN BE MADE, THEN WE'LL BE EXPLORING OTHER OPTIONS, INCLUDING MILITARY FORCE.
HATE
WE HAVE ~~KRAKSPAZ~~NOT ESTABLISHED OUR VISITORS' ~~FRAZZLE~~INTENT, BUT AT-
BREEOW!
ROWRR!
DEEBO
UHF
EGADS!
YAP YAP!!
SNARRRL!!

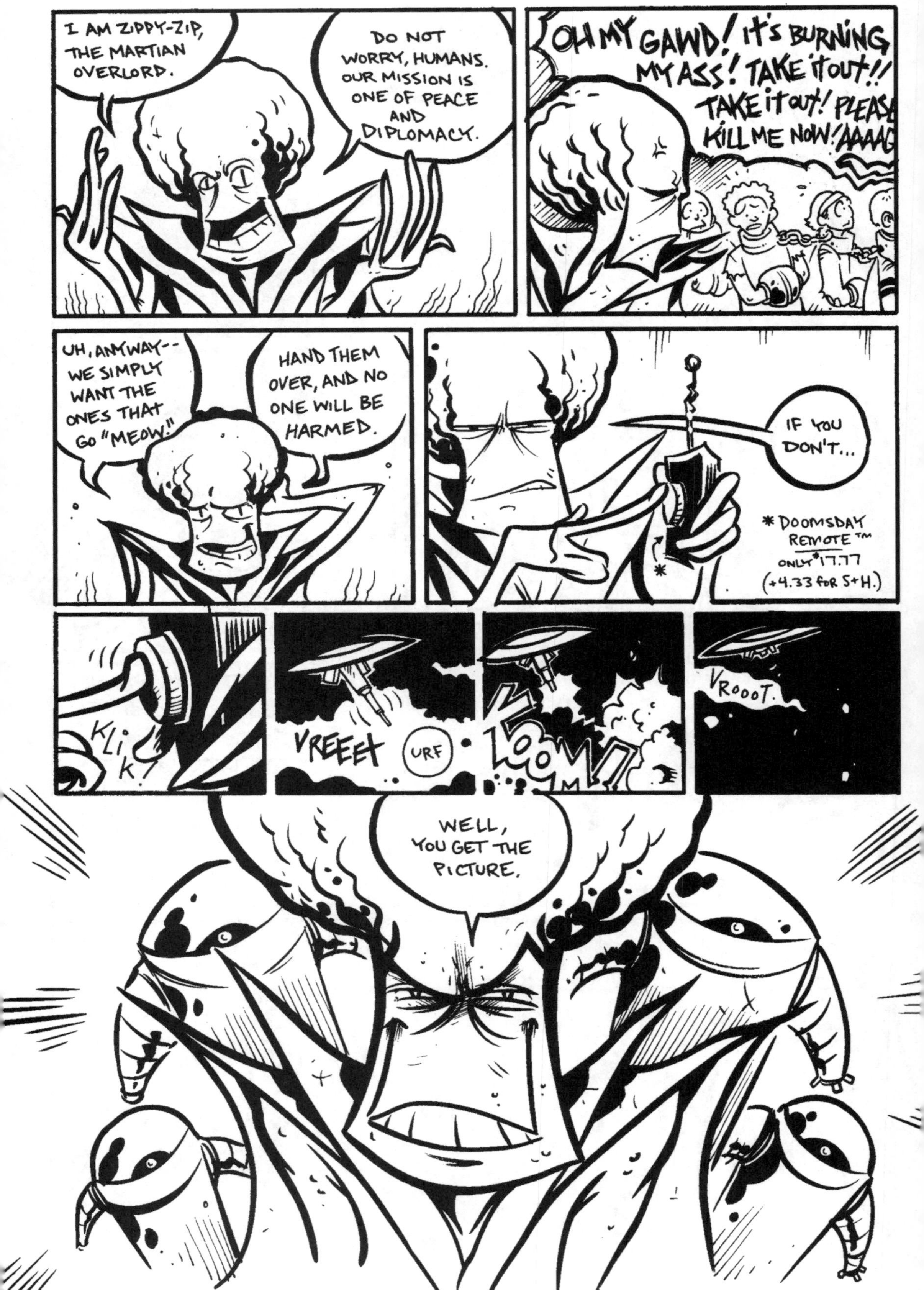
I AM ZIPPY-ZIP, THE MARTIAN OVERLORD.
DO NOT WORRY, HUMANS. OUR MISSION IS ONE OF PEACE AND DIPLOMACY.
OH MY GAWD! IT'S BURNING MY ASS! TAKE IT OUT!! TAKE IT OUT! PLEASE KILL ME NOW! AAAAG
UH, ANYWAY-- WE SIMPLY WANT THE ONES THAT GO "MEOW."
HAND THEM OVER, AND NO ONE WILL BE HARMED.
IF YOU DON'T...
* DOOMSDAY REMOTE™ ONLY $17.77 (+4.33 FOR S+H.)
KLIK!
VREEEH
URF
BOOM!
VROOOT.
WELL, YOU GET THE PICTURE.

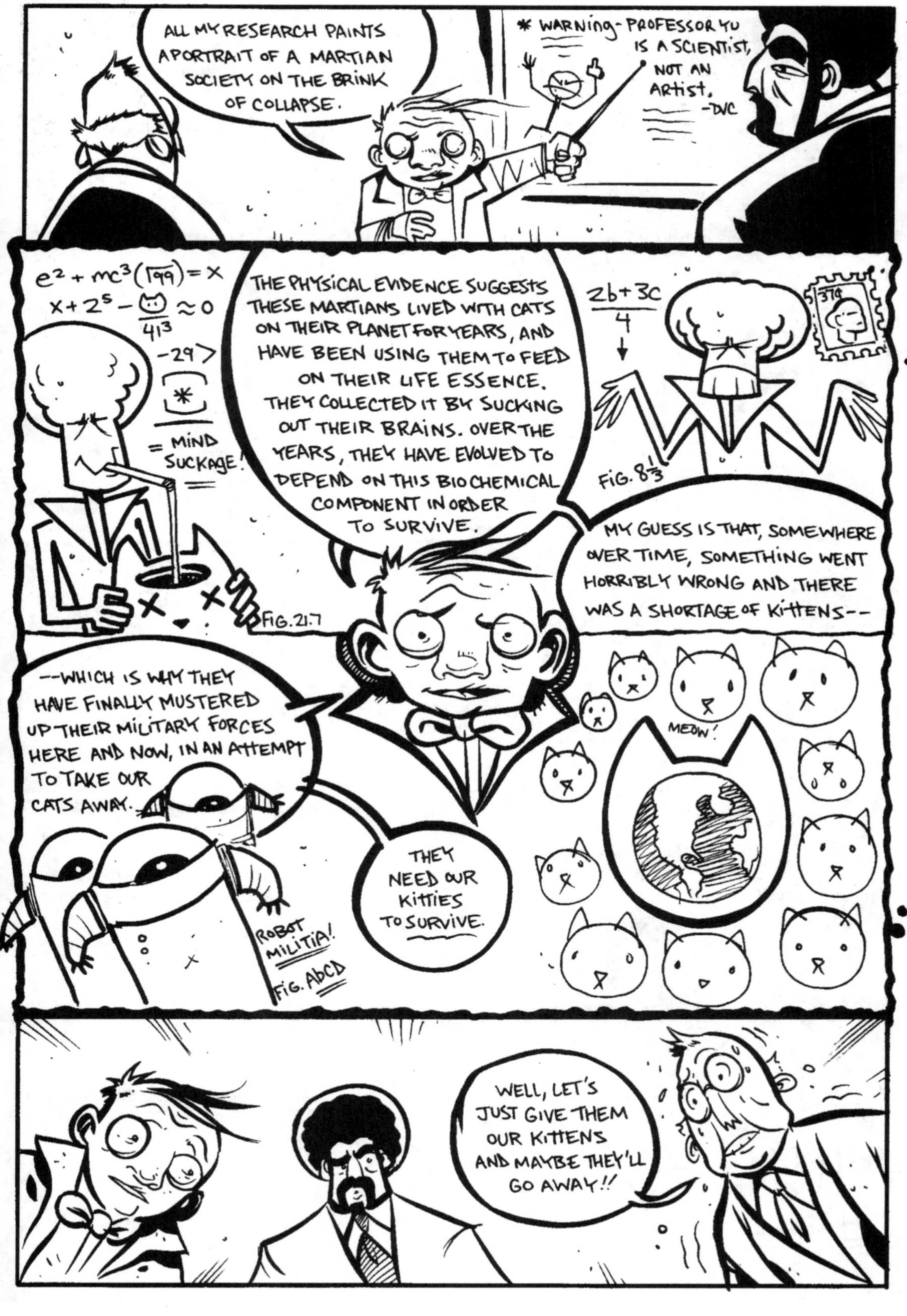
ALL MY RESEARCH PAINTS A PORTRAIT OF A MARTIAN SOCIETY ON THE BRINK OF COLLAPSE.
* WARNING - PROFESSOR YU IS A SCIENTIST, NOT AN ARTIST. -DVC
e2 + mc3 (√99) = X
X + 25 - 41^3 ≈ 0
-29 >
= MIND SUCKAGE!
FIG. 21.7
THE PHYSICAL EVIDENCE SUGGESTS THESE MARTIANS LIVED WITH CATS ON THEIR PLANET FOR YEARS, AND HAVE BEEN USING THEM TO FEED ON THEIR LIFE ESSENCE. THEY COLLECTED IT BY SUCKING OUT THEIR BRAINS. OVER THE YEARS, THEY HAVE EVOLVED TO DEPEND ON THIS BIOCHEMICAL COMPONENT IN ORDER TO SURVIVE.
2b + 3c / 4
37¢
FIG. 8 1/3
MY GUESS IS THAT, SOMEWHERE OVER TIME, SOMETHING WENT HORRIBLY WRONG AND THERE WAS A SHORTAGE OF KITTENS--
--WHICH IS WHY THEY HAVE FINALLY MUSTERED UP THEIR MILITARY FORCES HERE AND NOW, IN AN ATTEMPT TO TAKE OUR CATS AWAY.
ROBOT MILITIA!
FIG. AbCD
THEY NEED OUR KITTIES TO SURVIVE.
MEOW!
WELL, LET'S JUST GIVE THEM OUR KITTENS AND MAYBE THEY'LL GO AWAY!!

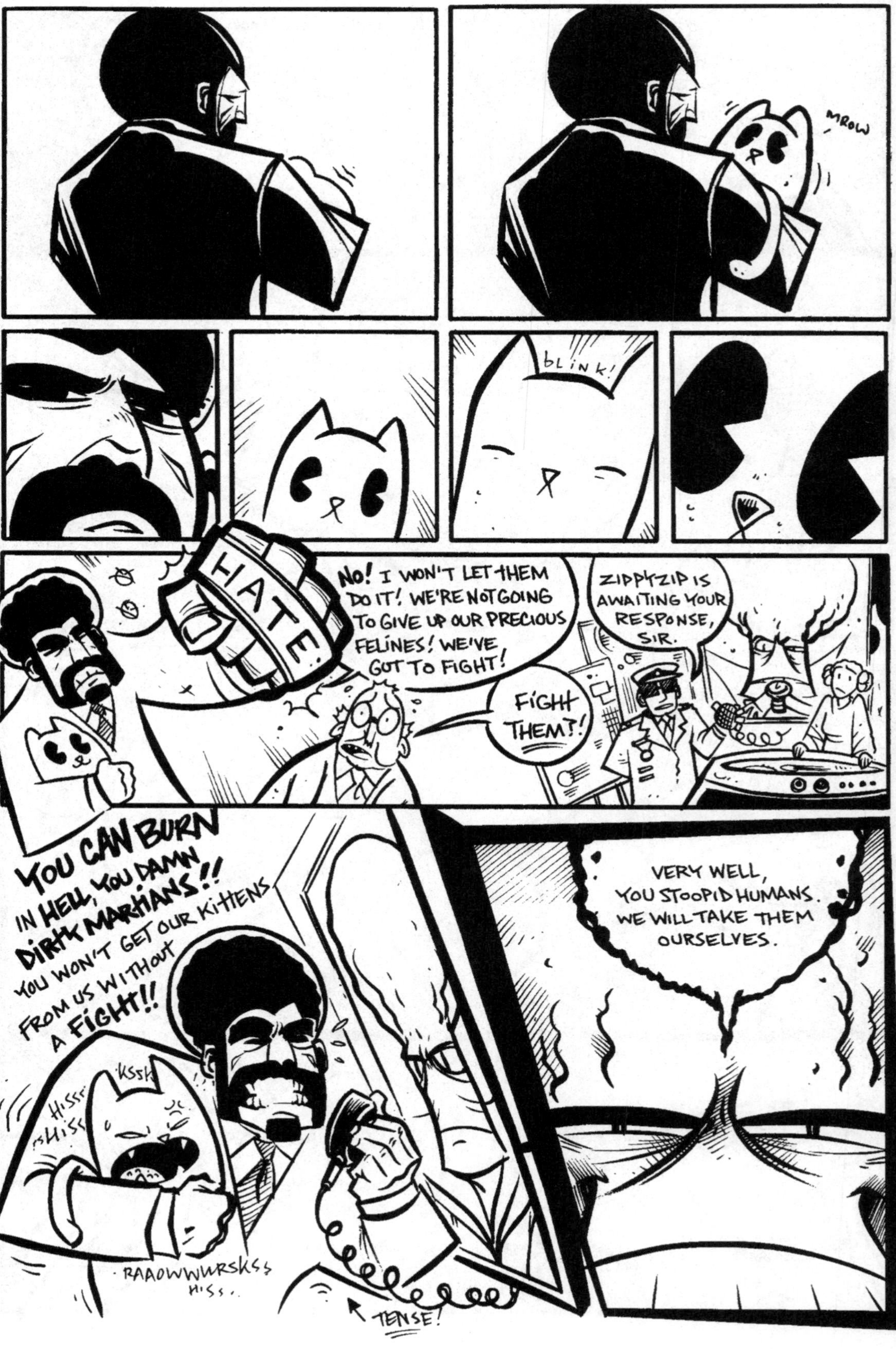
MROW
BLINK!
HATE
NO! I WON'T LET THEM DO IT! WE'RE NOT GOING TO GIVE UP OUR PRECIOUS FELINES! WE'VE GOT TO FIGHT!
FIGHT THEM?!
ZIPPYZIP IS AWAITING YOUR RESPONSE, SIR.
YOU CAN BURN IN HELL, YOU DAMN DIRTY MARTIANS!! YOU WON'T GET OUR KITTENS FROM US WITHOUT A FIGHT!!
VERY WELL, YOU STOOPID HUMANS. WE WILL TAKE THEM OURSELVES.
HISS HISS
KSSH
RAAOWWURSKSS HISS.
TENSE!

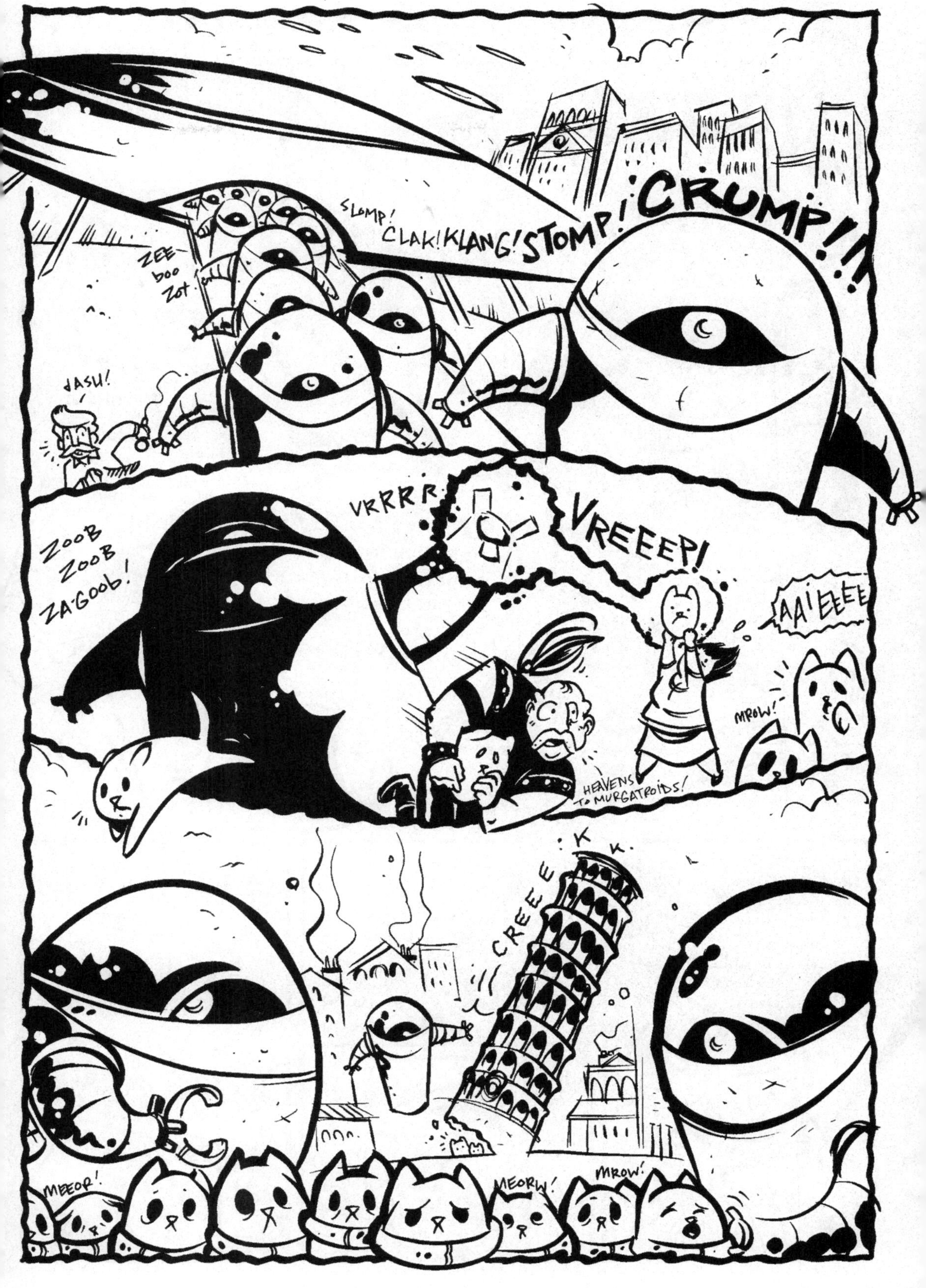
SLOMP!
CLAK! KLANG! STOMP! CRUMP!!!
ZEE boo Zot
DASH!
VRRRR
VREEEP!
ZOOB ZOOB ZA-GOOB!
AAIEEEE
MROW!
HEAVENS TO MURGATROIDS!
CREEEKK.
MEEOR!
MEORW!
MROW!

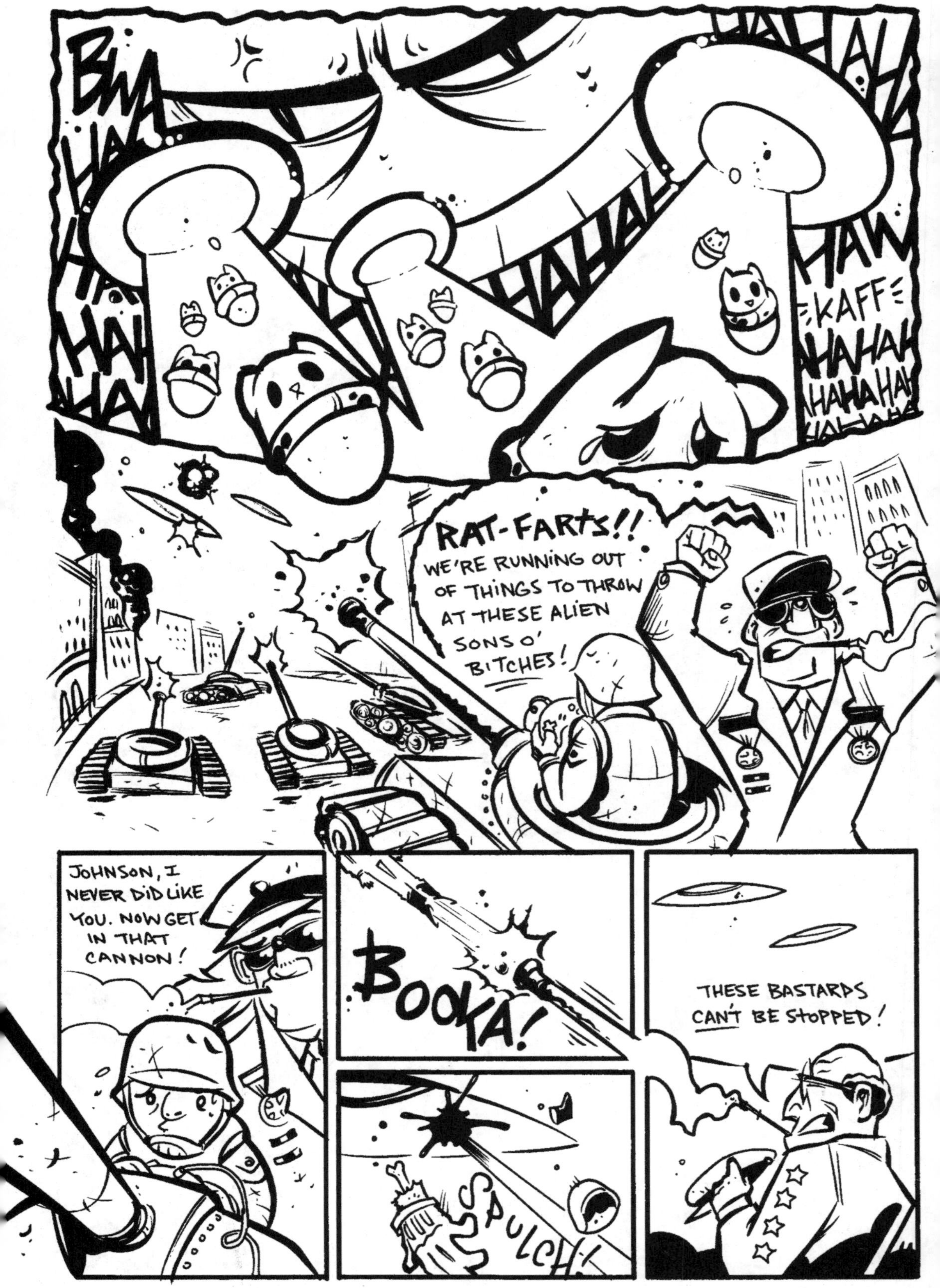

BWAHAHAHAHAHA
HAHAHAHAH
KAFF
HAHAHAHAHAHA
RAT-FARTS!! WE'RE RUNNING OUT OF THINGS TO THROW AT THESE ALIEN SONS O' BITCHES!
JOHNSON, I NEVER DID LIKE YOU. NOW GET IN THAT CANNON!
BOOKA!
SPULCH!
THESE BASTARDS CAN'T BE STOPPED!

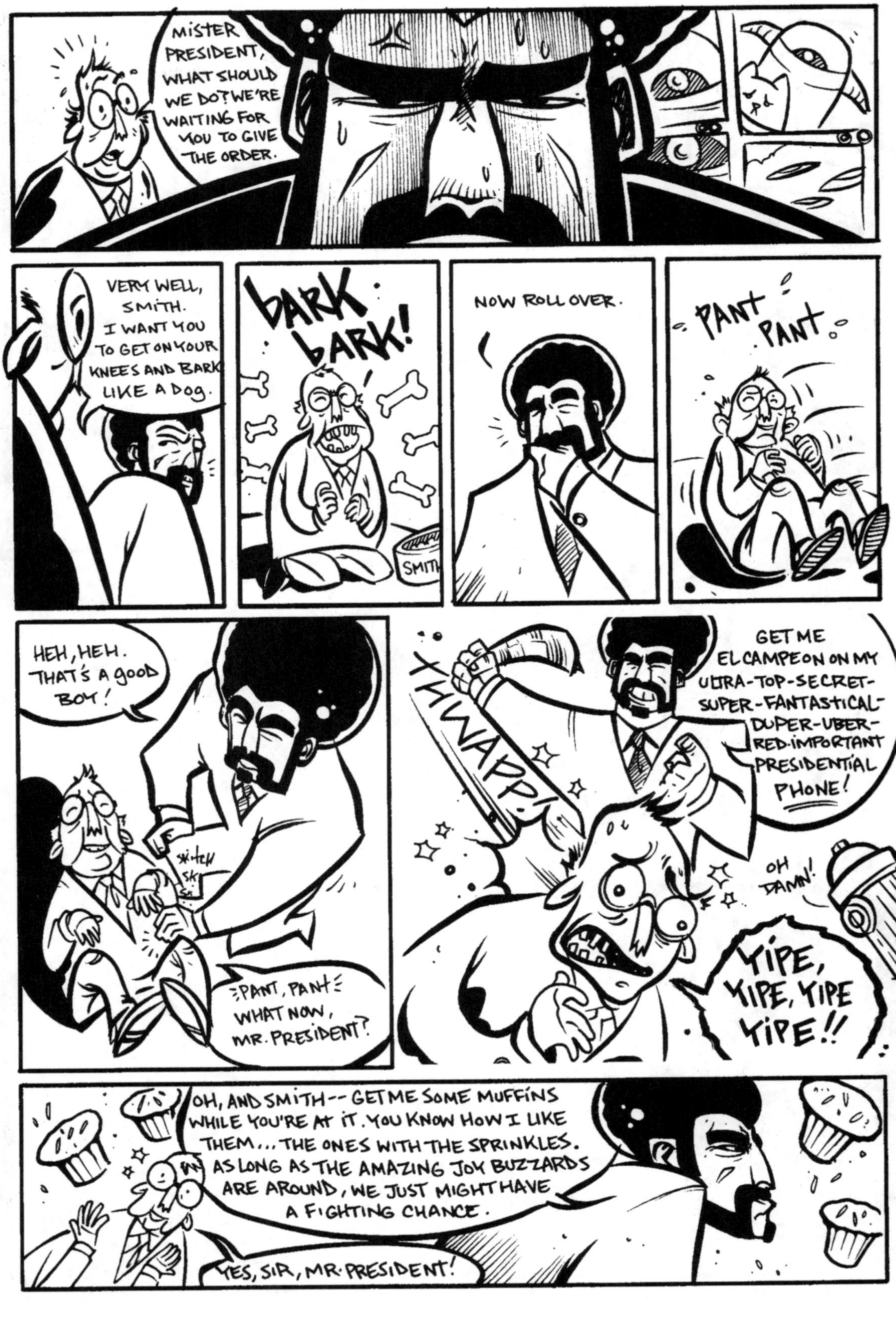
MISTER PRESIDENT, WHAT SHOULD WE DO? WE'RE WAITING FOR YOU TO GIVE THE ORDER.
VERY WELL, SMITH. I WANT YOU TO GET ON YOUR KNEES AND BARK LIKE A DOG.
BARK BARK!
SMITH
NOW ROLL OVER.
PANT PANT
HEH, HEH. THAT'S A GOOD BOY!
PANT, PANT WHAT NOW, MR. PRESIDENT?
THWAPP!
GET ME EL CAMPEON ON MY ULTRA-TOP-SECRET-SUPER-FANTASTICAL-DUPER-UBER-RED-IMPORTANT PRESIDENTIAL PHONE!
OH DAMN!
YIPE, YIPE, YIPE YIPE!!
OH, AND SMITH-- GET ME SOME MUFFINS WHILE YOU'RE AT IT. YOU KNOW HOW I LIKE THEM... THE ONES WITH THE SPRINKLES. AS LONG AS THE AMAZING JOY BUZZARDS ARE AROUND, WE JUST MIGHT HAVE A FIGHTING CHANCE.
YES, SIR, MR. PRESIDENT!

Mt. RUSHMORE...

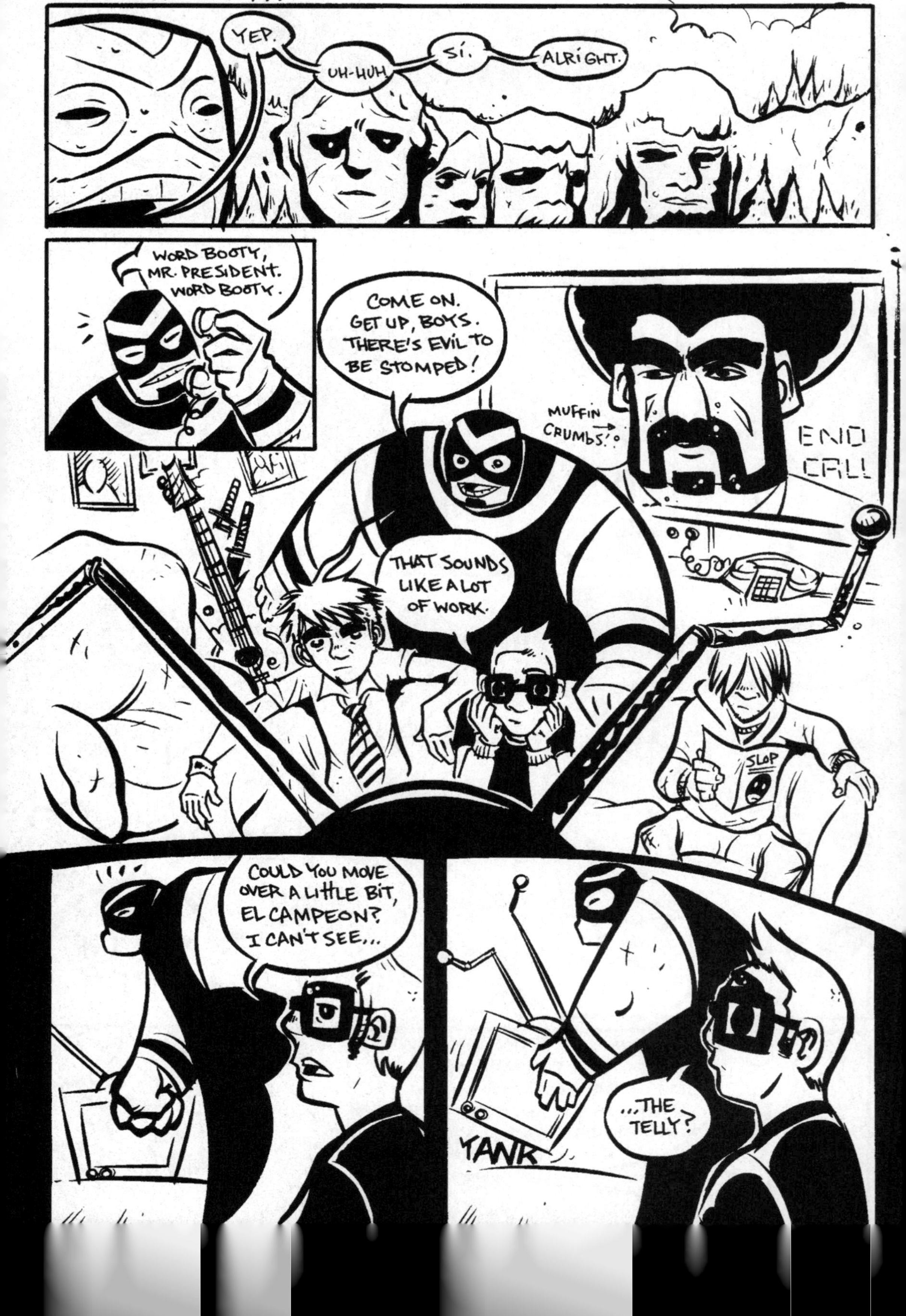
YEP.
UH-HUH
SÍ.
ALRIGHT.
WORD BOOTY, MR. PRESIDENT. WORD BOOTY.
COME ON. GET UP, BOYS. THERE'S EVIL TO BE STOMPED!
MUFFIN CRUMBS!
END CALL
THAT SOUNDS LIKE A LOT OF WORK.
SLOP
COULD YOU MOVE OVER A LITTLE BIT, EL CAMPEON? I CAN'T SEE...
YANK
...THE TELLY?

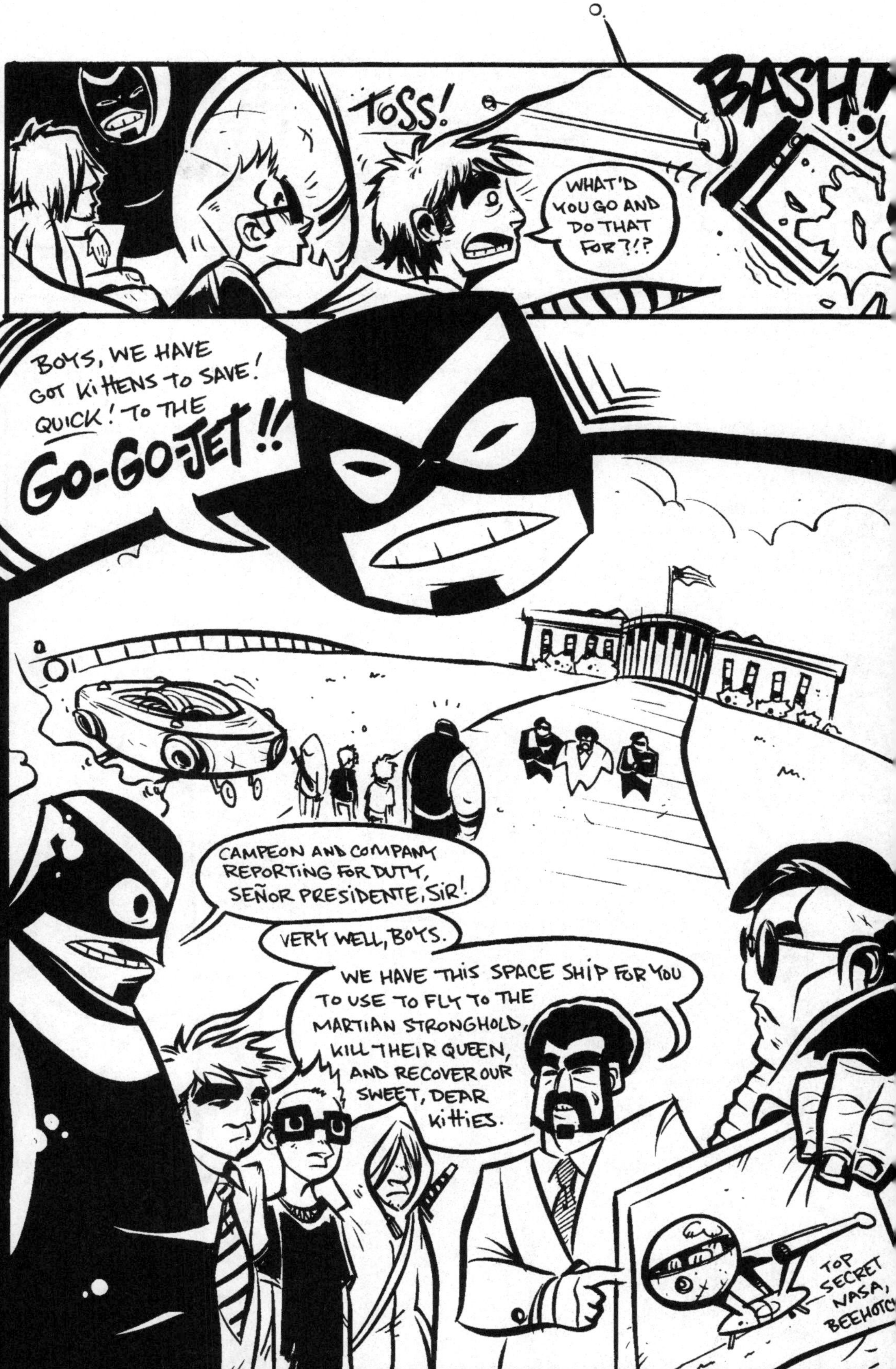
TOSS!
BASH!!
WHAT'D YOU GO AND DO THAT FOR?!?
BOYS, WE HAVE GOT KITTENS TO SAVE! QUICK! TO THE
GO-GO-JET!!
CAMPEON AND COMPANY REPORTING FOR DUTY, SEÑOR PRESIDENTE, SIR!
VERY WELL, BOYS.
WE HAVE THIS SPACE SHIP FOR YOU TO USE TO FLY TO THE MARTIAN STRONGHOLD, KILL THEIR QUEEN, AND RECOVER OUR SWEET, DEAR KITTIES.
TOP SECRET NASA, BEEHOTCH

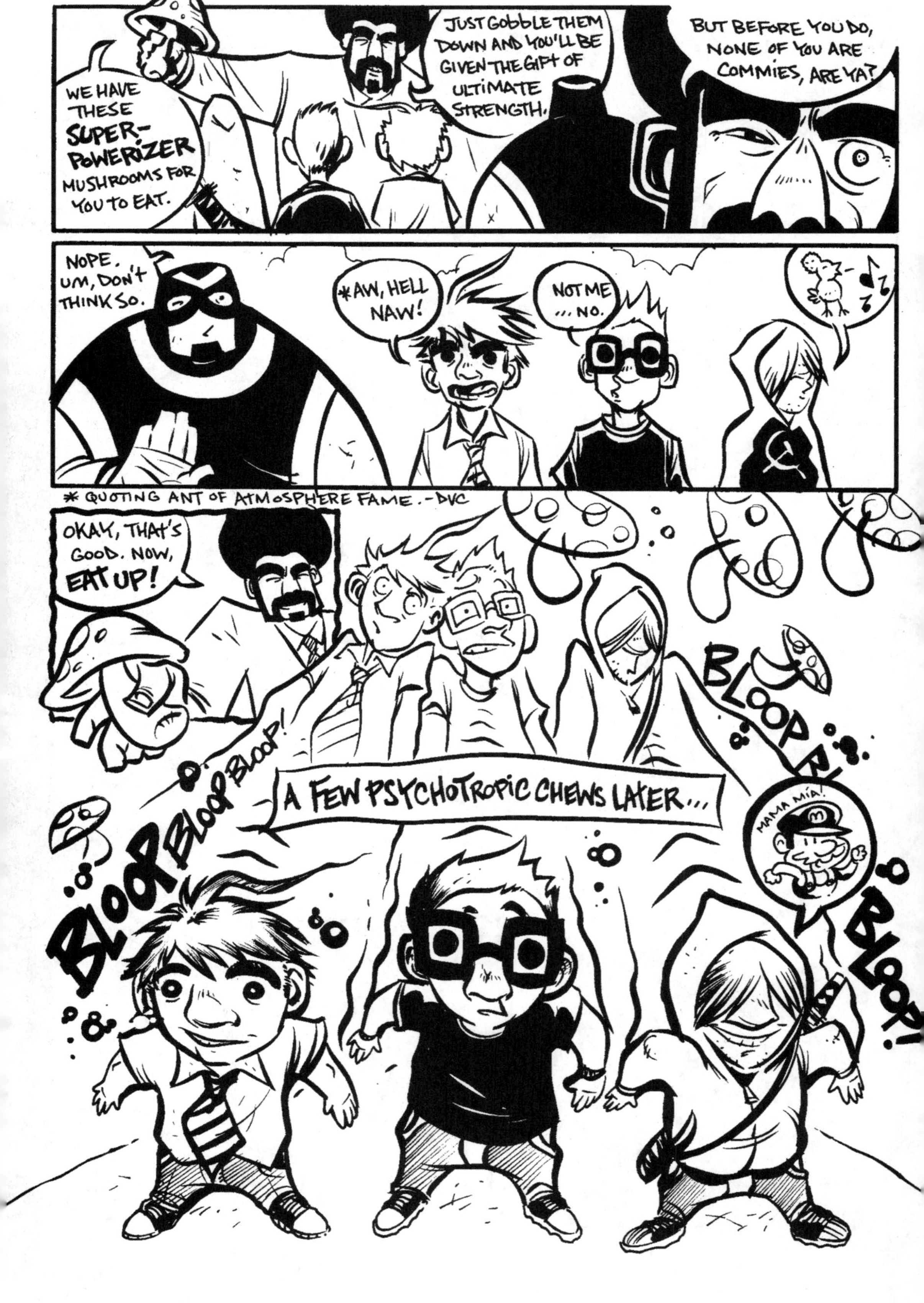
WE HAVE THESE SUPER-POWERIZER MUSHROOMS FOR YOU TO EAT.
JUST GOBBLE THEM DOWN AND YOU'LL BE GIVEN THE GIFT OF ULTIMATE STRENGTH.
BUT BEFORE YOU DO, NONE OF YOU ARE COMMIES, ARE YA?
NOPE. UM, DON'T THINK SO.
*AW, HELL NAW!
NOT ME ... NO.
* QUOTING ANT OF ATMOSPHERE FAME. -DVC
OKAY, THAT'S GOOD. NOW, EAT UP!
BLOOP BLOOP BLOOP!
A FEW PSYCHOTROPIC CHEWS LATER...
BLOOP BL-
MAMA MIA!
BLOOP BLOOP!

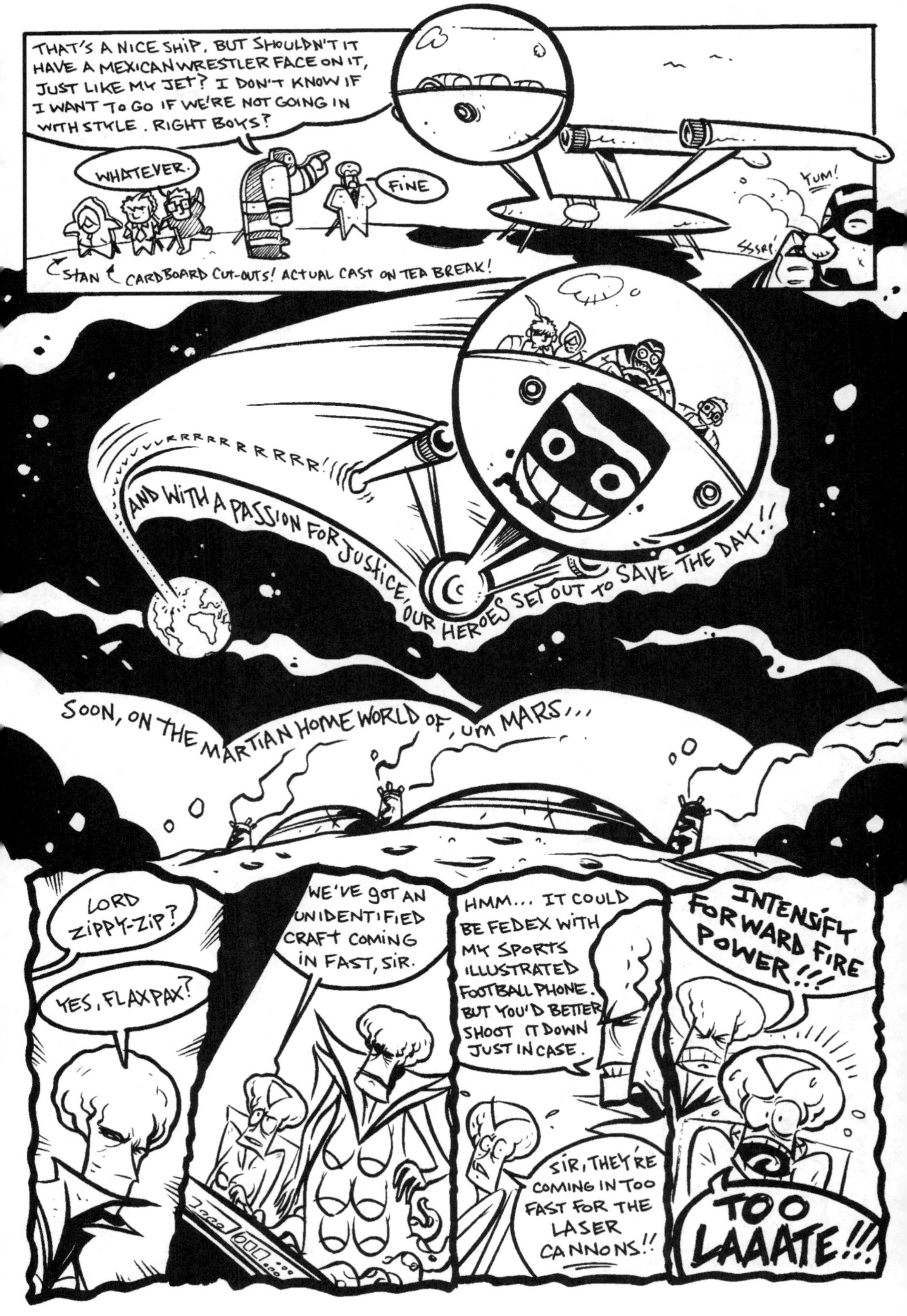
THAT'S A NICE SHIP. BUT SHOULDN'T IT HAVE A MEXICAN WRESTLER FACE ON IT, JUST LIKE MY JET? I DON'T KNOW IF I WANT TO GO IF WE'RE NOT GOING IN WITH STYLE. RIGHT BOYS?
WHATEVER.
FINE
YUM!
SSSRP!
STAN
CARDBOARD CUT-OUTS! ACTUAL CAST ON TEA BREAK!
VVVVRRRRRRRRRRRRR!
AND WITH A PASSION FOR JUSTICE, OUR HEROES SET OUT TO SAVE THE DAY!!
SOON, ON THE MARTIAN HOME WORLD OF, UM MARS...
LORD ZIPPY-ZIP?
YES, FLAXPAX?
WE'VE GOT AN UNIDENTIFIED CRAFT COMING IN FAST, SIR.
HMM... IT COULD BE FEDEX WITH MY SPORTS ILLUSTRATED FOOTBALL PHONE. BUT YOU'D BETTER SHOOT IT DOWN JUST IN CASE.
SIR, THEY'RE COMING IN TOO FAST FOR THE LASER CANNONS!!
INTENSIFY FORWARD FIRE POWER!!!
TOO LAAATE!!!

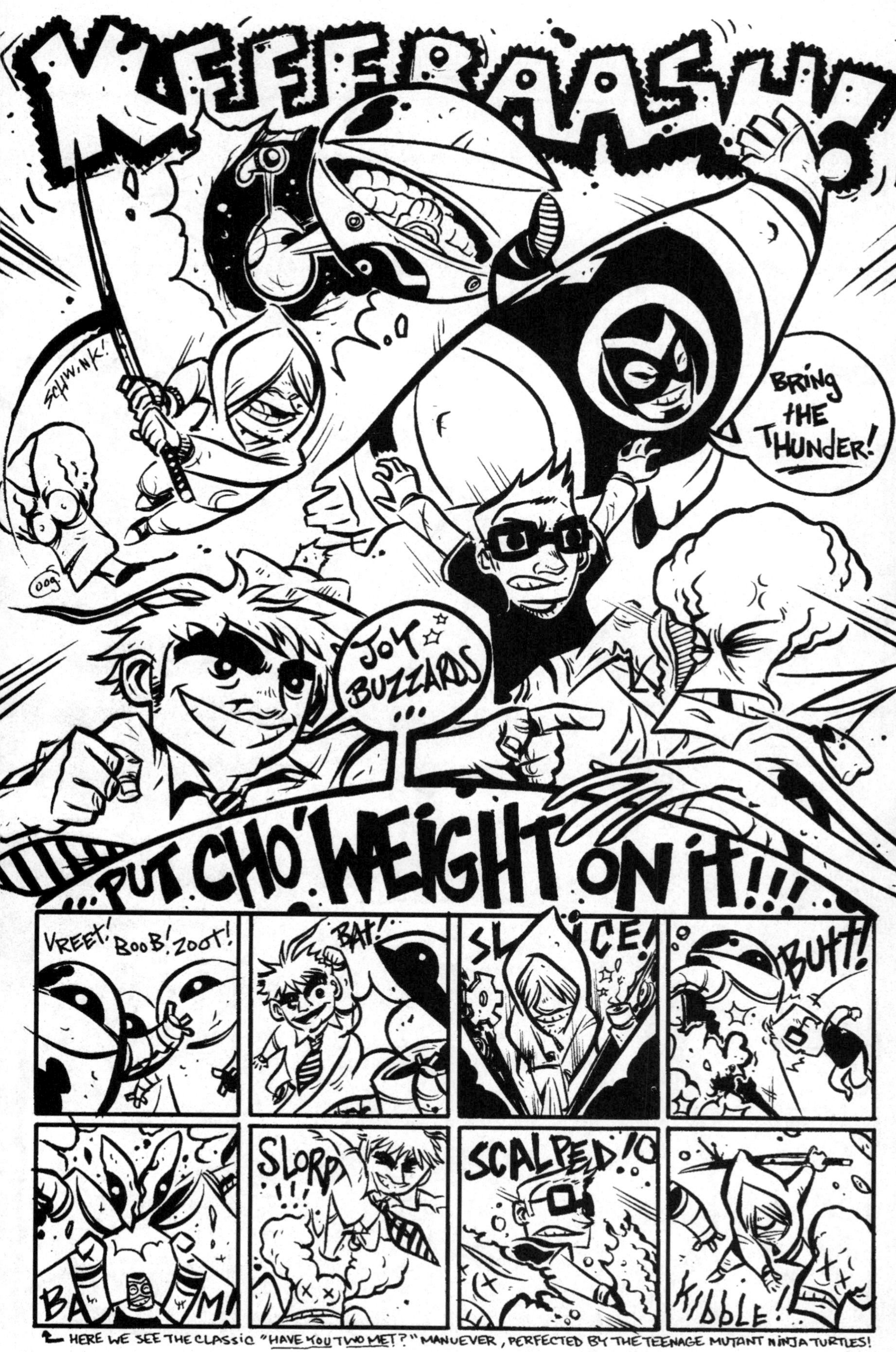
KEEERAASH!
SCHWINK!
OOG.
BRING THE THUNDER!
JOY BUZZARDS...
...PUT CHO' WEIGHT ON IT!!!
VREET! BOOB! ZOOT!
BAT!
BUTT!
BA M!
SLORP!!!
SCALPED!
KIBBLE!

HERE WE SEE THE CLASSIC "HAVE YOU TWO MET?" MANUEVER, PERFECTED BY THE TEENAGE MUTANT NINJA TURTLES!

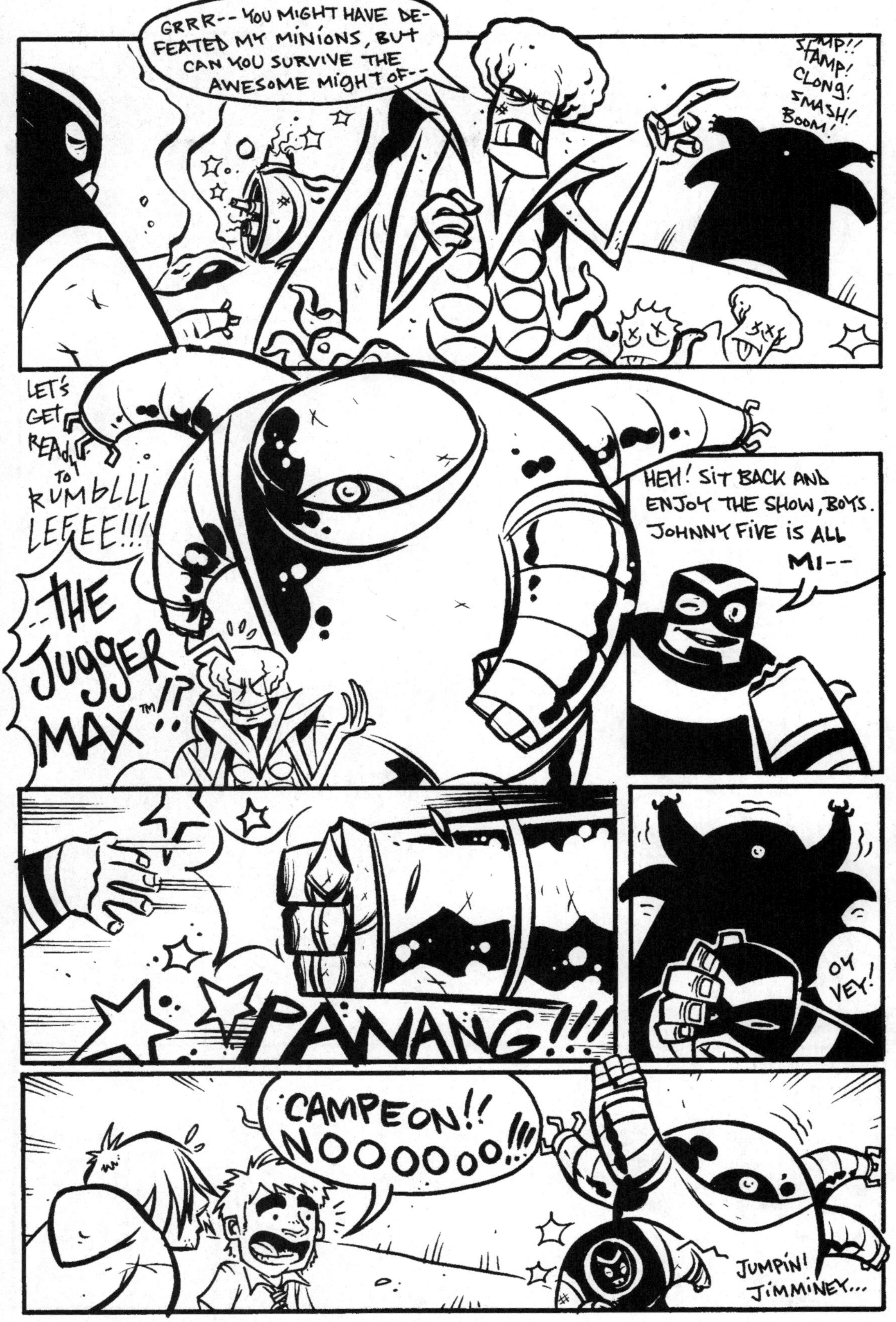
GRRR-- YOU MIGHT HAVE DEFEATED MY MINIONS, BUT CAN YOU SURVIVE THE AWESOME MIGHT OF--
STOMP!! STAMP! CLONG! SMASH! BOOM!
LET'S GET READY TO RUMBLLL LEEEE!!!
--THE JUGGER MAX™!?
HEH! SIT BACK AND ENJOY THE SHOW, BOYS. JOHNNY FIVE IS ALL MI--
PANANG!!!
OY VEY!
CAMPEON!! NOOOOOO!!!
JUMPIN' JIMMINEY...

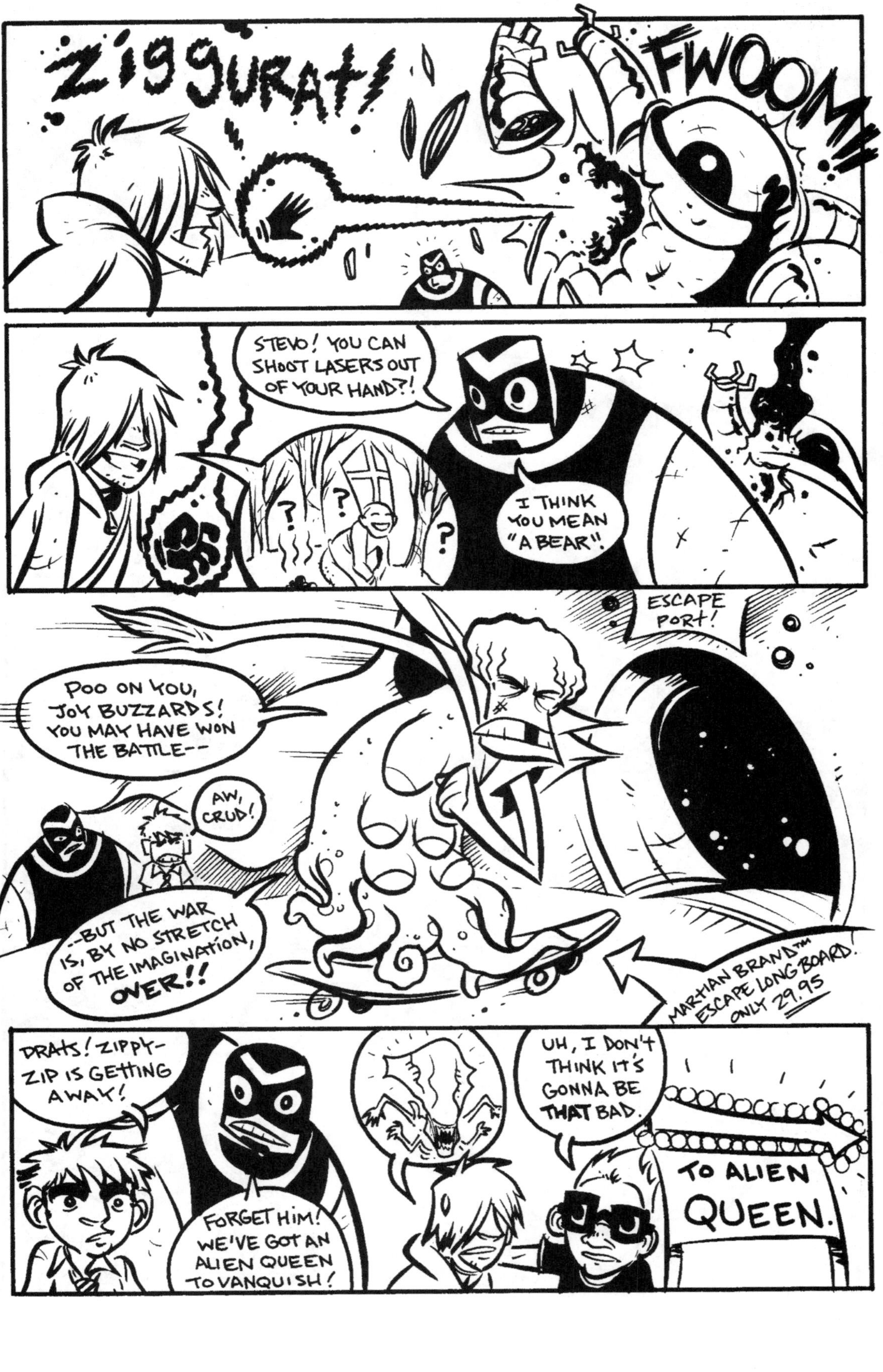
ZIGGURAT!
FWOOM!!
STEVO! YOU CAN SHOOT LASERS OUT OF YOUR HAND?!
I THINK YOU MEAN "A BEAR".
ESCAPE PORT!
POO ON YOU, JOY BUZZARDS! YOU MAY HAVE WON THE BATTLE--
AW, CRUD!
--BUT THE WAR IS, BY NO STRETCH OF THE IMAGINATION, OVER!!
MARTIAN BRAND™ ESCAPE LONG BOARD! ONLY 29.95
DRATS! ZIPPY-ZIP IS GETTING AWAY!
FORGET HIM! WE'VE GOT AN ALIEN QUEEN TO VANQUISH!
UH, I DON'T THINK IT'S GONNA BE THAT BAD.
TO ALIEN QUEEN.

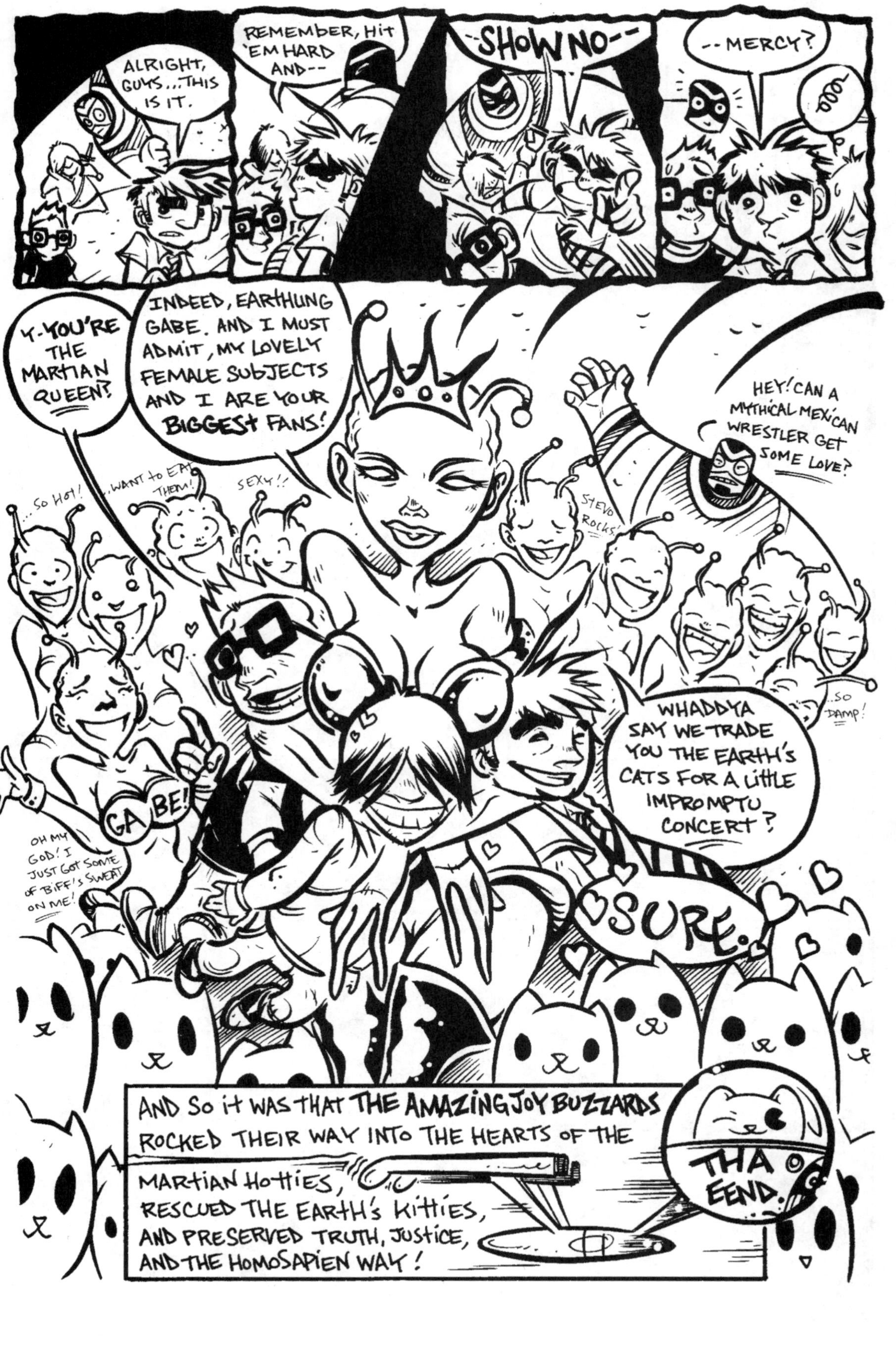

ALRIGHT, GUYS... THIS IS IT.
REMEMBER, HIT 'EM HARD AND--
--SHOW NO--
--MERCY?
Y-YOU'RE THE MARTIAN QUEEN?
INDEED, EARTHLING GABE. AND I MUST ADMIT, MY LOVELY FEMALE SUBJECTS AND I ARE YOUR BIGGEST FANS!
HEY! CAN A MYTHICAL MEXICAN WRESTLER GET SOME LOVE?
...SO HOT!
...WANT TO EAT THEM!
SEXY!!
STEVO ROCKS!
...SO DAMP!
GA BE!
WHADDYA SAY WE TRADE YOU THE EARTH'S CATS FOR A LITTLE IMPROMPTU CONCERT?
OH MY GOD! I JUST GOT SOME OF BIFF'S SWEAT ON ME!
SURE.
AND SO IT WAS THAT THE AMAZING JOY BUZZARDS ROCKED THEIR WAY INTO THE HEARTS OF THE MARTIAN HOTTIES, RESCUED THE EARTH'S KITTIES, AND PRESERVED TRUTH, JUSTICE, AND THE HOMOSAPIEN WAY!
THA EEND.

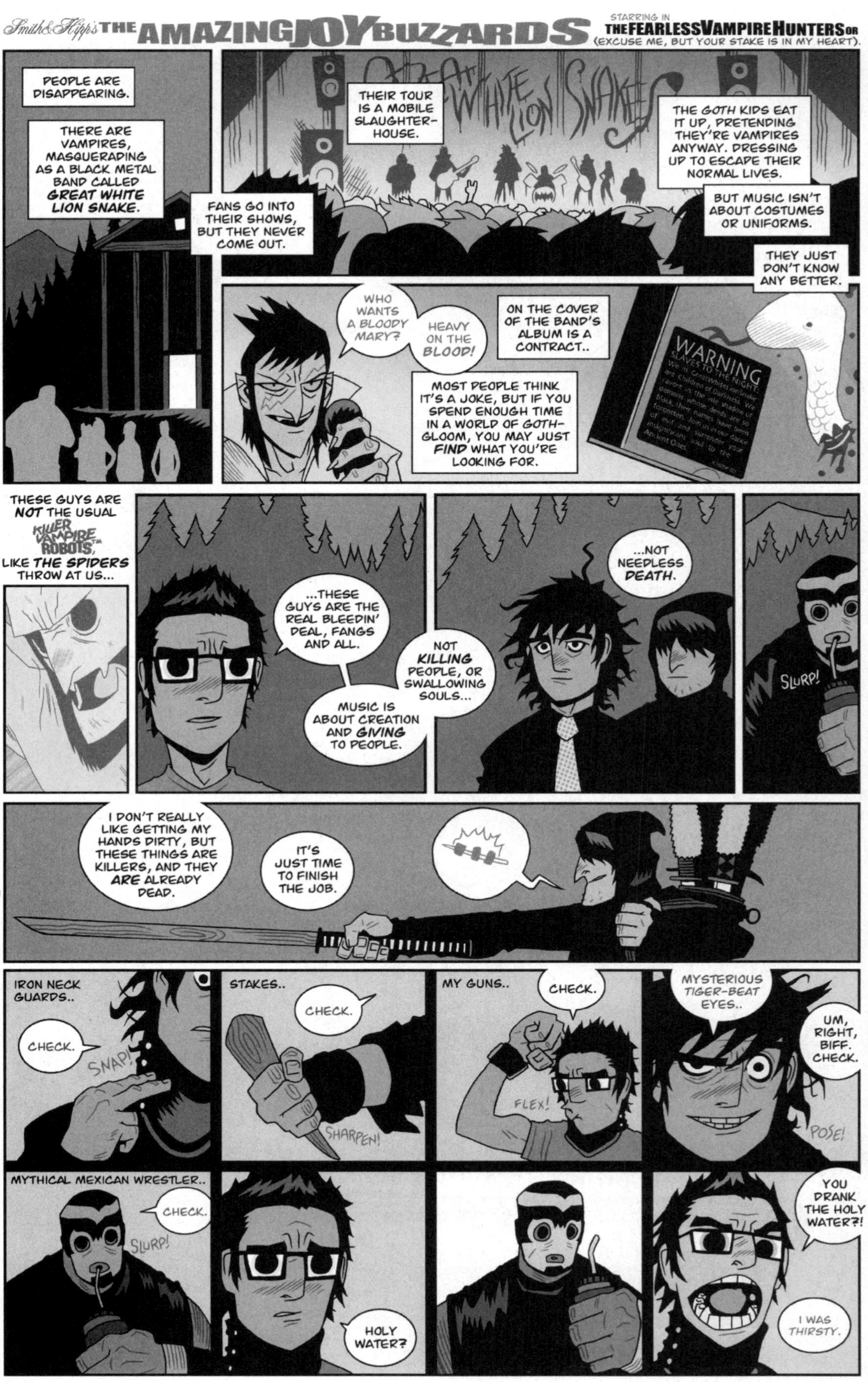
Smith & Hipp's THE AMAZING JOY BUZZARDS
STARRING IN THE FEARLESS VAMPIRE HUNTERS OR (EXCUSE ME, BUT YOUR STAKE IS IN MY HEART).
PEOPLE ARE DISAPPEARING.
THERE ARE VAMPIRES, MASQUERADING AS A BLACK METAL BAND CALLED GREAT WHITE LION SNAKE.
FANS GO INTO THEIR SHOWS, BUT THEY NEVER COME OUT.
THEIR TOUR IS A MOBILE SLAUGHTER-HOUSE.
GREAT WHITE LION SNAKE
THE GOTH KIDS EAT IT UP, PRETENDING THEY'RE VAMPIRES ANYWAY. DRESSING UP TO ESCAPE THEIR NORMAL LIVES.
BUT MUSIC ISN'T ABOUT COSTUMES OR UNIFORMS.
THEY JUST DON'T KNOW ANY BETTER.
WHO WANTS A BLOODY MARY?
HEAVY ON THE BLOOD!
ON THE COVER OF THE BAND'S ALBUM IS A CONTRACT..
MOST PEOPLE THINK IT'S A JOKE, BUT IF YOU SPEND ENOUGH TIME IN A WORLD OF GOTH-GLOOM, YOU MAY JUST FIND WHAT YOU'RE LOOKING FOR.
WARNING
SLAVES TO THE NIGHT
THESE GUYS ARE NOT THE USUAL KILLER VAMPIRE ROBOTS™, LIKE THE SPIDERS THROW AT US...
...THESE GUYS ARE THE REAL BLEEDIN' DEAL, FANGS AND ALL.
MUSIC IS ABOUT CREATION AND GIVING TO PEOPLE.
NOT KILLING PEOPLE, OR SWALLOWING SOULS...
...NOT NEEDLESS DEATH.
SLURP!
I DON'T REALLY LIKE GETTING MY HANDS DIRTY, BUT THESE THINGS ARE KILLERS, AND THEY ARE ALREADY DEAD.
IT'S JUST TIME TO FINISH THE JOB.
IRON NECK GUARDS..
CHECK.
SNAP!
STAKES..
CHECK.
SHARPEN!
MY GUNS..
CHECK.
FLEX!
MYSTERIOUS TIGER-BEAT EYES..
UM, RIGHT, BIFF. CHECK.
POSE!
MYTHICAL MEXICAN WRESTLER..
CHECK.
SLURP!
HOLY WATER?
YOU DRANK THE HOLY WATER?!
I WAS THIRSTY.

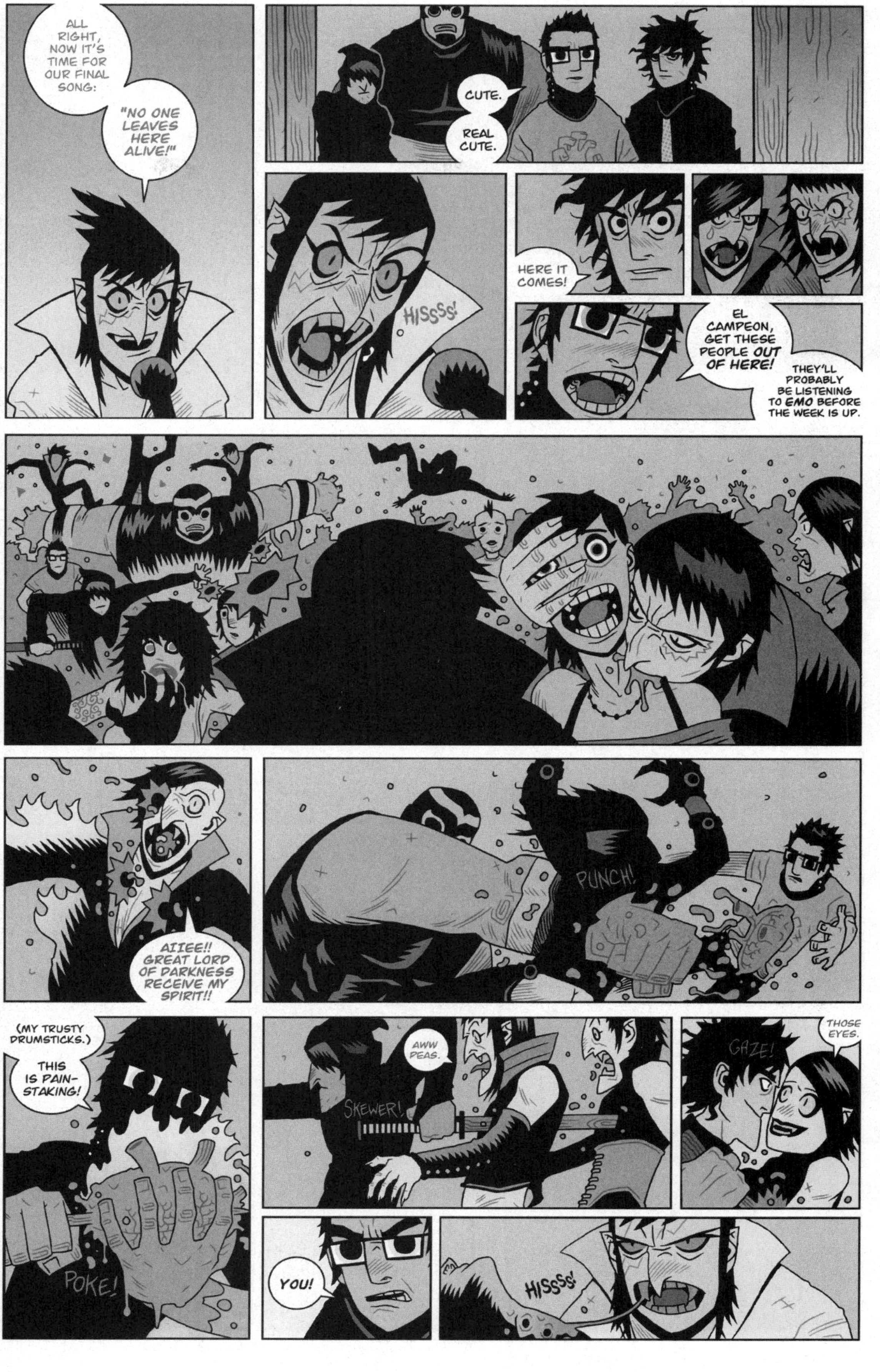
ALL RIGHT, NOW IT'S TIME FOR OUR FINAL SONG:
"NO ONE LEAVES HERE ALIVE!"
CUTE.
REAL CUTE.
HISSSS!
HERE IT COMES!
EL CAMPEON, GET THESE PEOPLE OUT OF HERE!
THEY'LL PROBABLY BE LISTENING TO EMO BEFORE THE WEEK IS UP.
AIIEE!! GREAT LORD OF DARKNESS RECEIVE MY SPIRIT!!
PUNCH!
(MY TRUSTY DRUMSTICKS.)
THIS IS PAIN-STAKING!
POKE!
AWW PEAS.
SKEWER!
THOSE EYES.
GAZE!
YOU!
HISSSS!

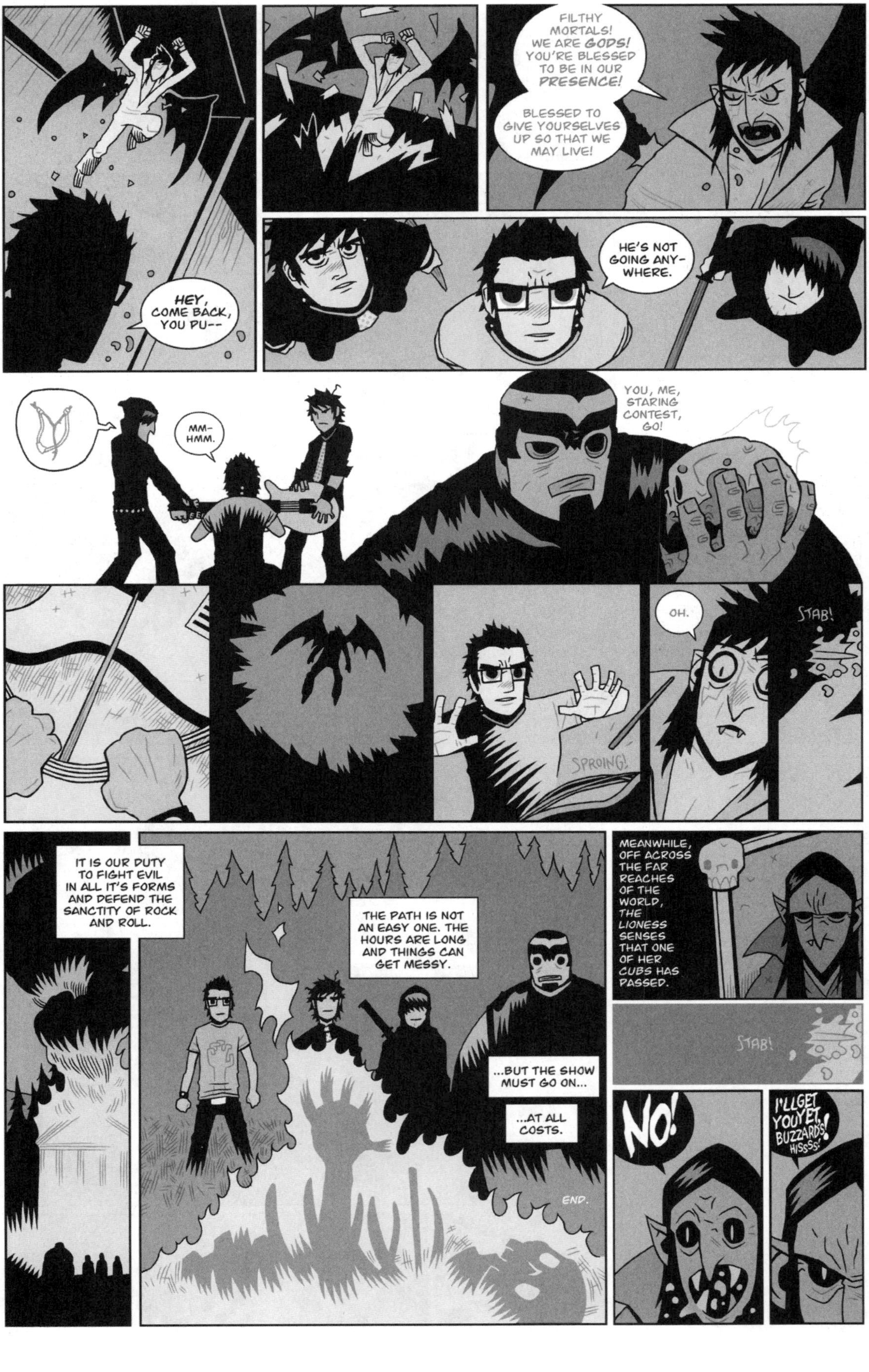
FILTHY MORTALS! WE ARE GODS! YOU'RE BLESSED TO BE IN OUR PRESENCE!
BLESSED TO GIVE YOURSELVES UP SO THAT WE MAY LIVE!
HEY, COME BACK, YOU PU--
HE'S NOT GOING ANY-WHERE.
MM-HMM.
YOU, ME, STARING CONTEST, GO!
SPROING!
OH.
STAB!
IT IS OUR DUTY TO FIGHT EVIL IN ALL IT'S FORMS AND DEFEND THE SANCTITY OF ROCK AND ROLL.
THE PATH IS NOT AN EASY ONE. THE HOURS ARE LONG AND THINGS CAN GET MESSY.
...BUT THE SHOW MUST GO ON...
...AT ALL COSTS.
END.
MEANWHILE, OFF ACROSS THE FAR REACHES OF THE WORLD, THE LIONESS SENSES THAT ONE OF HER CUBS HAS PASSED.
STAB!
NO!
I'LL GET YOU YET, BUZZARDS! HISSSS!

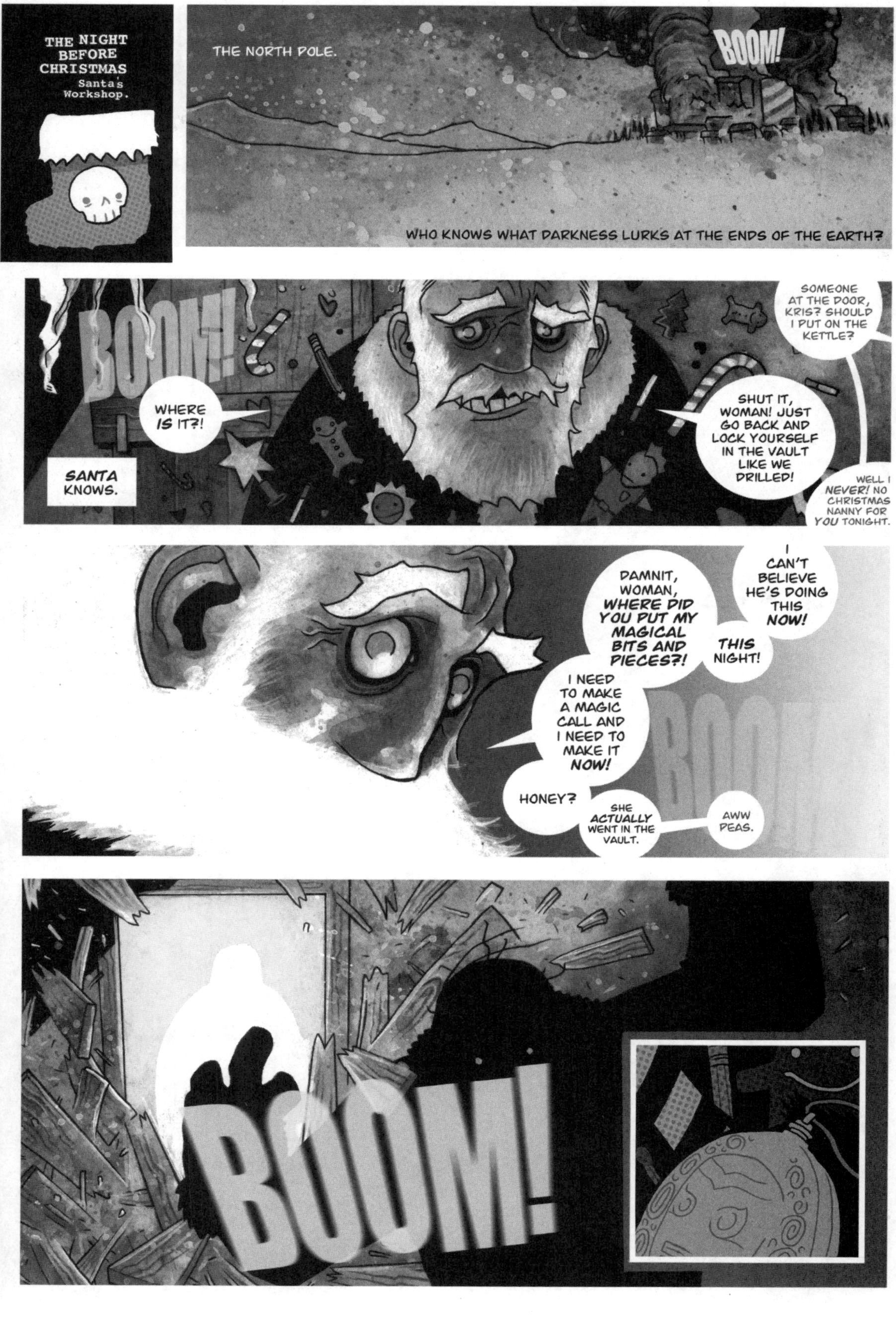
THE NIGHT BEFORE CHRISTMAS
Santa's Workshop.
THE NORTH POLE.
BOOM!
WHO KNOWS WHAT DARKNESS LURKS AT THE ENDS OF THE EARTH?
BOOM!
WHERE IS IT?!
SANTA KNOWS.
SOMEONE AT THE DOOR, KRIS? SHOULD I PUT ON THE KETTLE?
SHUT IT, WOMAN! JUST GO BACK AND LOCK YOURSELF IN THE VAULT LIKE WE DRILLED!
WELL I NEVER! NO CHRISTMAS NANNY FOR YOU TONIGHT.
DAMNIT, WOMAN, WHERE DID YOU PUT MY MAGICAL BITS AND PIECES?!
I CAN'T BELIEVE HE'S DOING THIS NOW!
THIS NIGHT!
I NEED TO MAKE A MAGIC CALL AND I NEED TO MAKE IT NOW!
HONEY?
SHE ACTUALLY WENT IN THE VAULT.
AWW PEAS.
BOOM!

SOMEWHERE ELSE ENTIRELY, in the middle of a snowstorm, the show must go on...

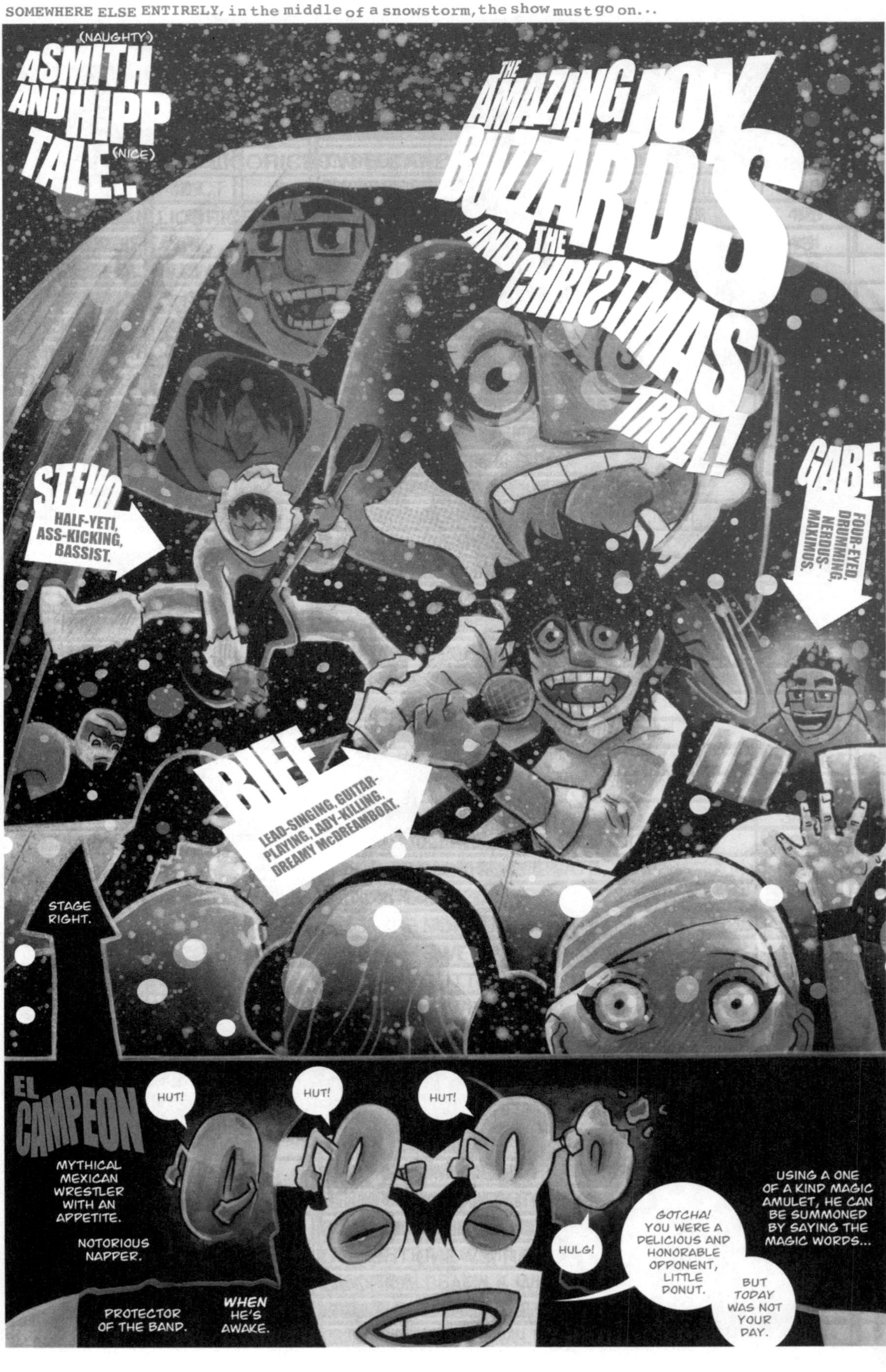
(NAUGHTY)
A SMITH AND HIPP TALE..
(NICE)
THE AMAZING JOY BUZZARDS AND THE CHRISTMAS TROLL!
STEVO
HALF-YETI, ASS-KICKING, BASSIST.
GABE
FOUR-EYED, DRUMMING, NERDUS-MAXIMUS.
RIFF
LEAD-SINGING, GUITAR-PLAYING, LADY-KILLING, DREAMY McDREAMBOAT.
STAGE RIGHT.
EL CAMPEON
MYTHICAL MEXICAN WRESTLER WITH AN APPETITE.
NOTORIOUS NAPPER.
PROTECTOR OF THE BAND.
WHEN HE'S AWAKE.
HUT!
HUT!
HUT!
HULG!
GOTCHA! YOU WERE A DELICIOUS AND HONORABLE OPPONENT, LITTLE DONUT.
BUT TODAY WAS NOT YOUR DAY.
USING A ONE OF A KIND MAGIC AMULET, HE CAN BE SUMMONED BY SAYING THE MAGIC WORDS...

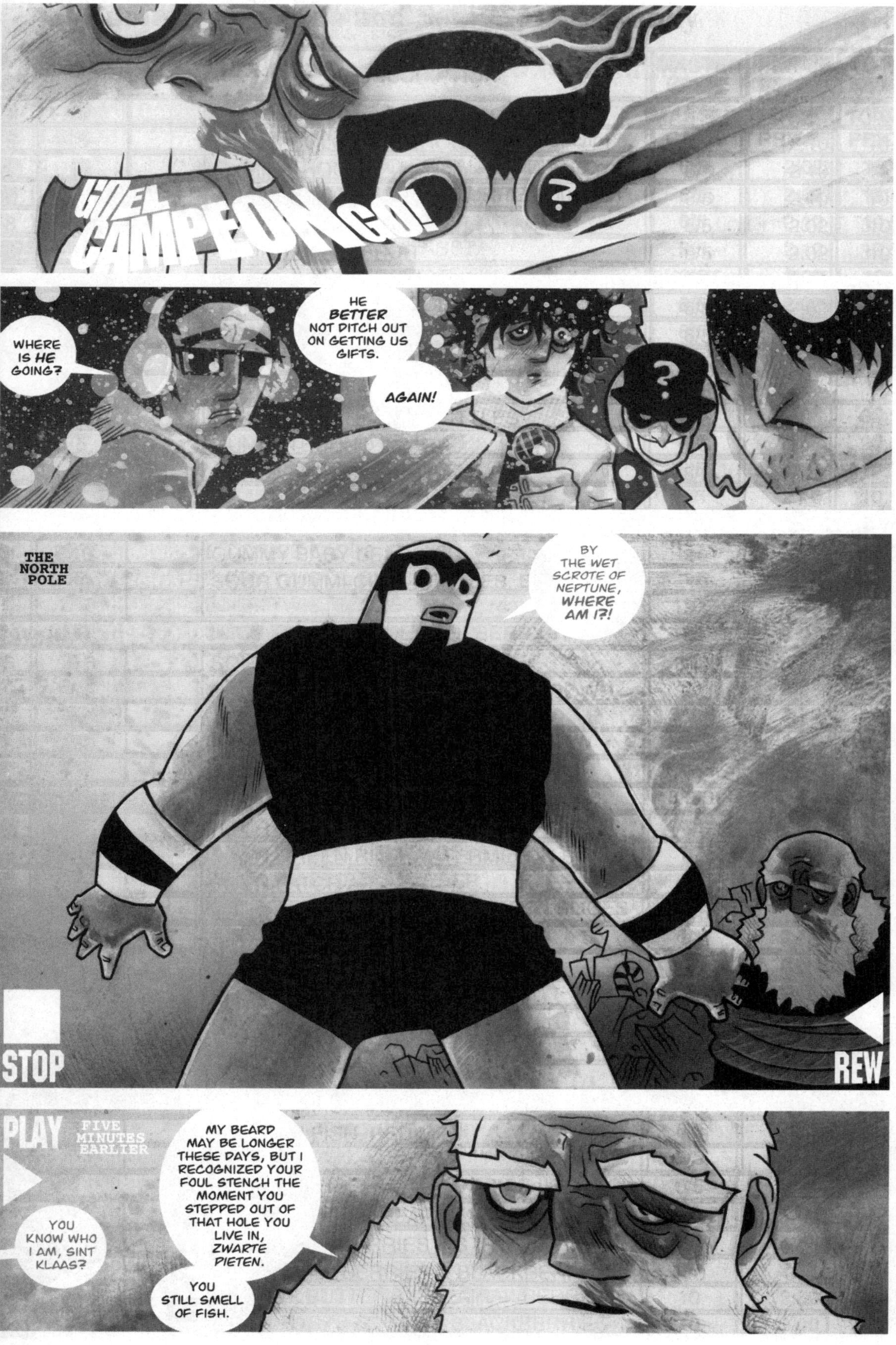
GO EL CAMPEON GO!
WHERE IS HE GOING?
HE BETTER NOT DITCH OUT ON GETTING US GIFTS.
AGAIN!
THE NORTH POLE
BY THE WET SCROTE OF NEPTUNE, WHERE AM I?!
STOP
REW
PLAY
FIVE MINUTES EARLIER
YOU KNOW WHO I AM, SINT KLAAS?
MY BEARD MAY BE LONGER THESE DAYS, BUT I RECOGNIZED YOUR FOUL STENCH THE MOMENT YOU STEPPED OUT OF THAT HOLE YOU LIVE IN, ZWARTE PIETEN.
YOU STILL SMELL OF FISH.

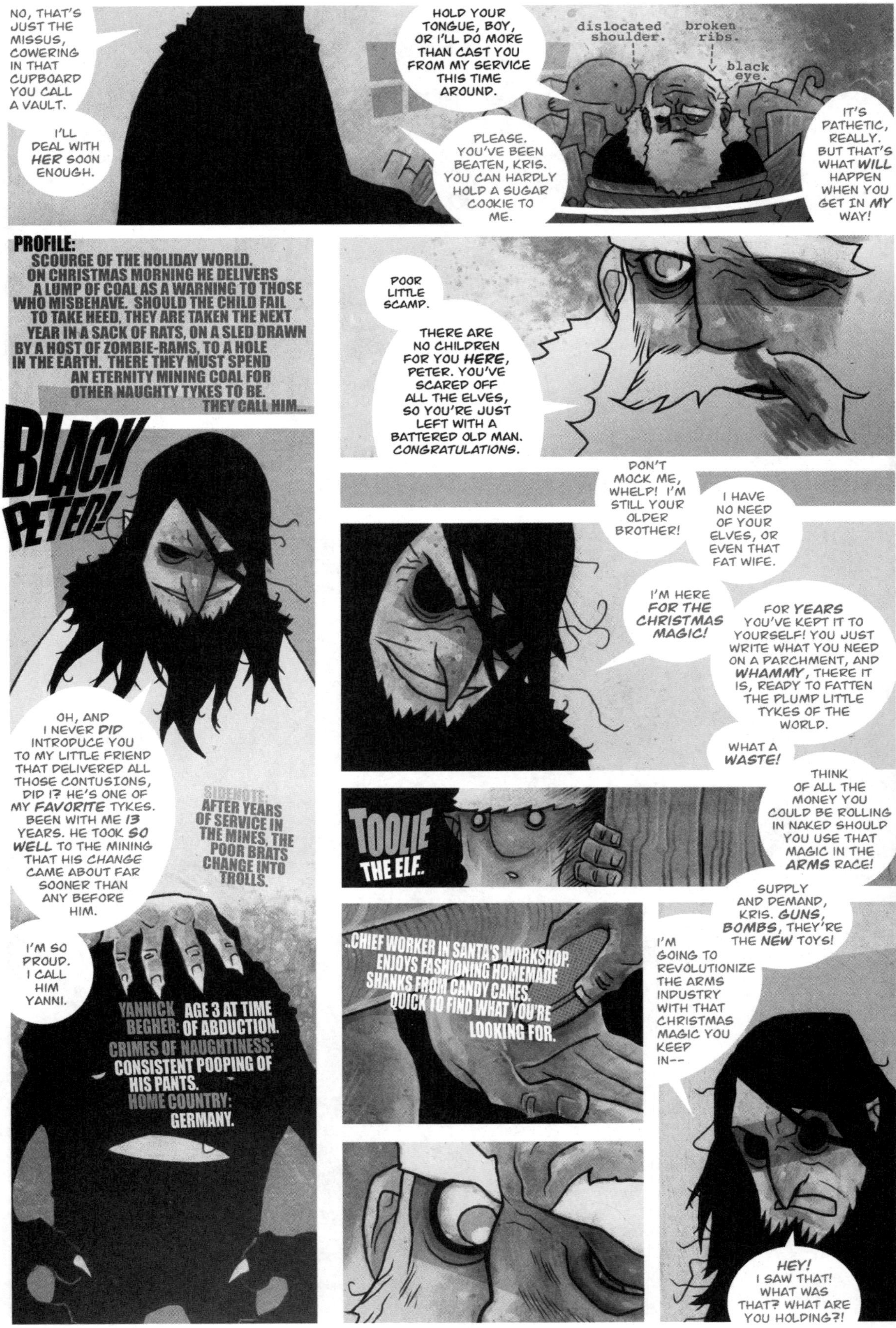
NO, THAT'S JUST THE MISSUS, COWERING IN THAT CUPBOARD YOU CALL A VAULT.
I'LL DEAL WITH HER SOON ENOUGH.
HOLD YOUR TONGUE, BOY, OR I'LL DO MORE THAN CAST YOU FROM MY SERVICE THIS TIME AROUND.
dislocated shoulder.
broken ribs.
black eye.
PLEASE. YOU'VE BEEN BEATEN, KRIS. YOU CAN HARDLY HOLD A SUGAR COOKIE TO ME.
IT'S PATHETIC, REALLY. BUT THAT'S WHAT WILL HAPPEN WHEN YOU GET IN MY WAY!
PROFILE: SCOURGE OF THE HOLIDAY WORLD. ON CHRISTMAS MORNING HE DELIVERS A LUMP OF COAL AS A WARNING TO THOSE WHO MISBEHAVE. SHOULD THE CHILD FAIL TO TAKE HEED, THEY ARE TAKEN THE NEXT YEAR IN A SACK OF RATS, ON A SLED DRAWN BY A HOST OF ZOMBIE-RAMS, TO A HOLE IN THE EARTH. THERE THEY MUST SPEND AN ETERNITY MINING COAL FOR OTHER NAUGHTY TYKES TO BE. THEY CALL HIM...
BLACK PETER!
POOR LITTLE SCAMP.
THERE ARE NO CHILDREN FOR YOU HERE, PETER. YOU'VE SCARED OFF ALL THE ELVES, SO YOU'RE JUST LEFT WITH A BATTERED OLD MAN. CONGRATULATIONS.
DON'T MOCK ME, WHELP! I'M STILL YOUR OLDER BROTHER!
I HAVE NO NEED OF YOUR ELVES, OR EVEN THAT FAT WIFE.
I'M HERE FOR THE CHRISTMAS MAGIC!
FOR YEARS YOU'VE KEPT IT TO YOURSELF! YOU JUST WRITE WHAT YOU NEED ON A PARCHMENT, AND WHAMMY, THERE IT IS, READY TO FATTEN THE PLUMP LITTLE TYKES OF THE WORLD.
WHAT A WASTE!
OH, AND I NEVER DID INTRODUCE YOU TO MY LITTLE FRIEND THAT DELIVERED ALL THOSE CONTUSIONS, DID I? HE'S ONE OF MY FAVORITE TYKES. BEEN WITH ME 13 YEARS. HE TOOK SO WELL TO THE MINING THAT HIS CHANGE CAME ABOUT FAR SOONER THAN ANY BEFORE HIM.
SIDENOTE: AFTER YEARS OF SERVICE IN THE MINES, THE POOR BRATS CHANGE INTO TROLLS.
I'M SO PROUD. I CALL HIM YANNI.
YANNICK BEGHER: AGE 3 AT TIME OF ABDUCTION.
CRIMES OF NAUGHTINESS: CONSISTENT POOPING OF HIS PANTS.
HOME COUNTRY: GERMANY.
THINK OF ALL THE MONEY YOU COULD BE ROLLING IN NAKED SHOULD YOU USE THAT MAGIC IN THE ARMS RACE!
TOOLIE THE ELF..
..CHIEF WORKER IN SANTA'S WORKSHOP. ENJOYS FASHIONING HOMEMADE SHANKS FROM CANDY CANES. QUICK TO FIND WHAT YOU'RE LOOKING FOR.
SUPPLY AND DEMAND, KRIS. GUNS, BOMBS, THEY'RE THE NEW TOYS!
I'M GOING TO REVOLUTIONIZE THE ARMS INDUSTRY WITH THAT CHRISTMAS MAGIC YOU KEEP IN--
HEY! I SAW THAT! WHAT WAS THAT? WHAT ARE YOU HOLDING?!

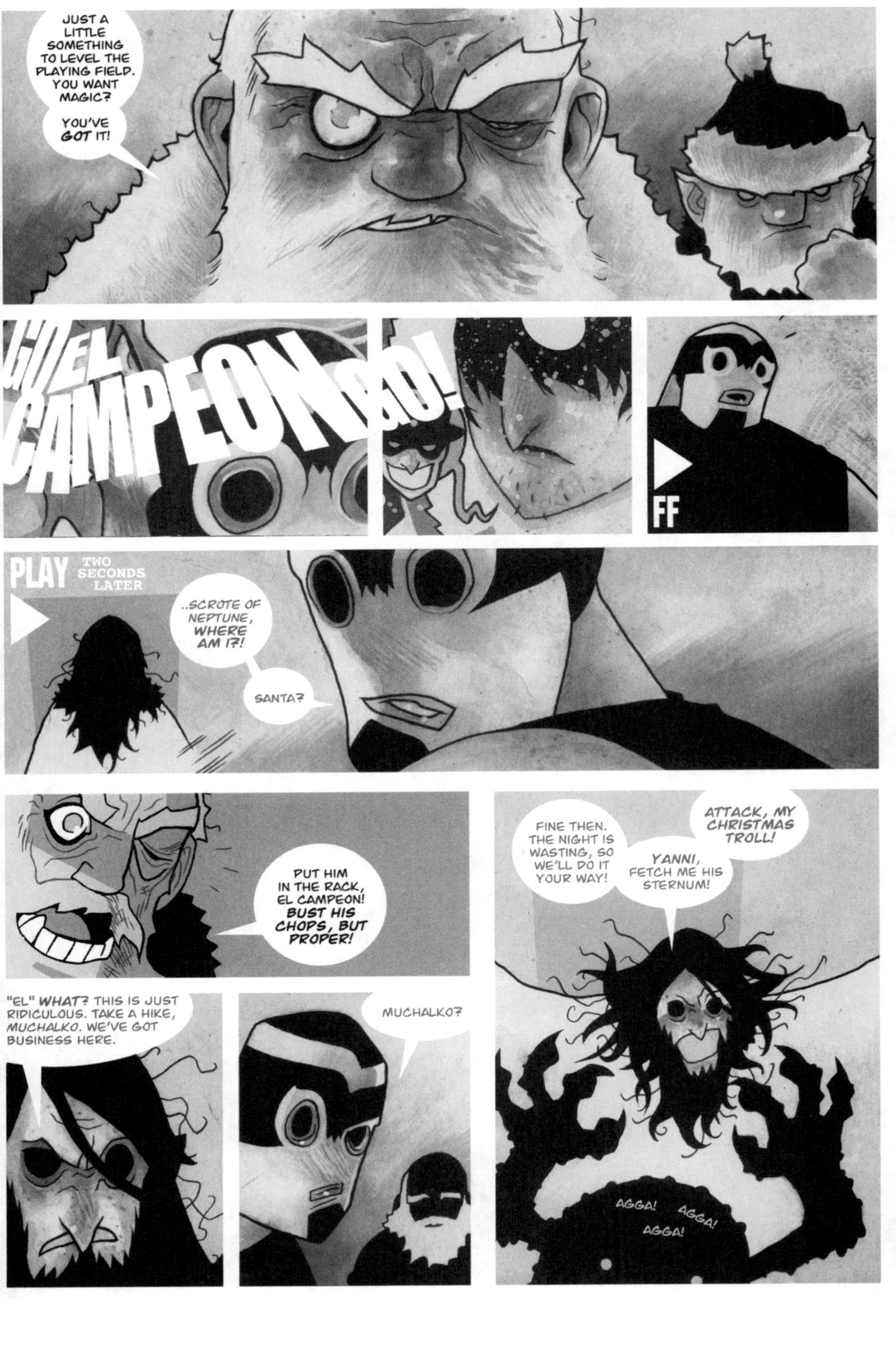
JUST A LITTLE SOMETHING TO LEVEL THE PLAYING FIELD. YOU WANT MAGIC?
YOU'VE GOT IT!
GO EL CAMPEON GO!
FF
PLAY
TWO SECONDS LATER
..SCROTE OF NEPTUNE, WHERE AM I?!
SANTA?
PUT HIM IN THE RACK, EL CAMPEON! BUST HIS CHOPS, BUT PROPER!
"EL" WHAT? THIS IS JUST RIDICULOUS. TAKE A HIKE, MUCHALKO. WE'VE GOT BUSINESS HERE.
MUCHALKO?
FINE THEN. THE NIGHT IS WASTING, SO WE'LL DO IT YOUR WAY!
ATTACK, MY CHRISTMAS TROLL!
YANNI, FETCH ME HIS STERNUM!
AGGA! AGGA! AGGA!

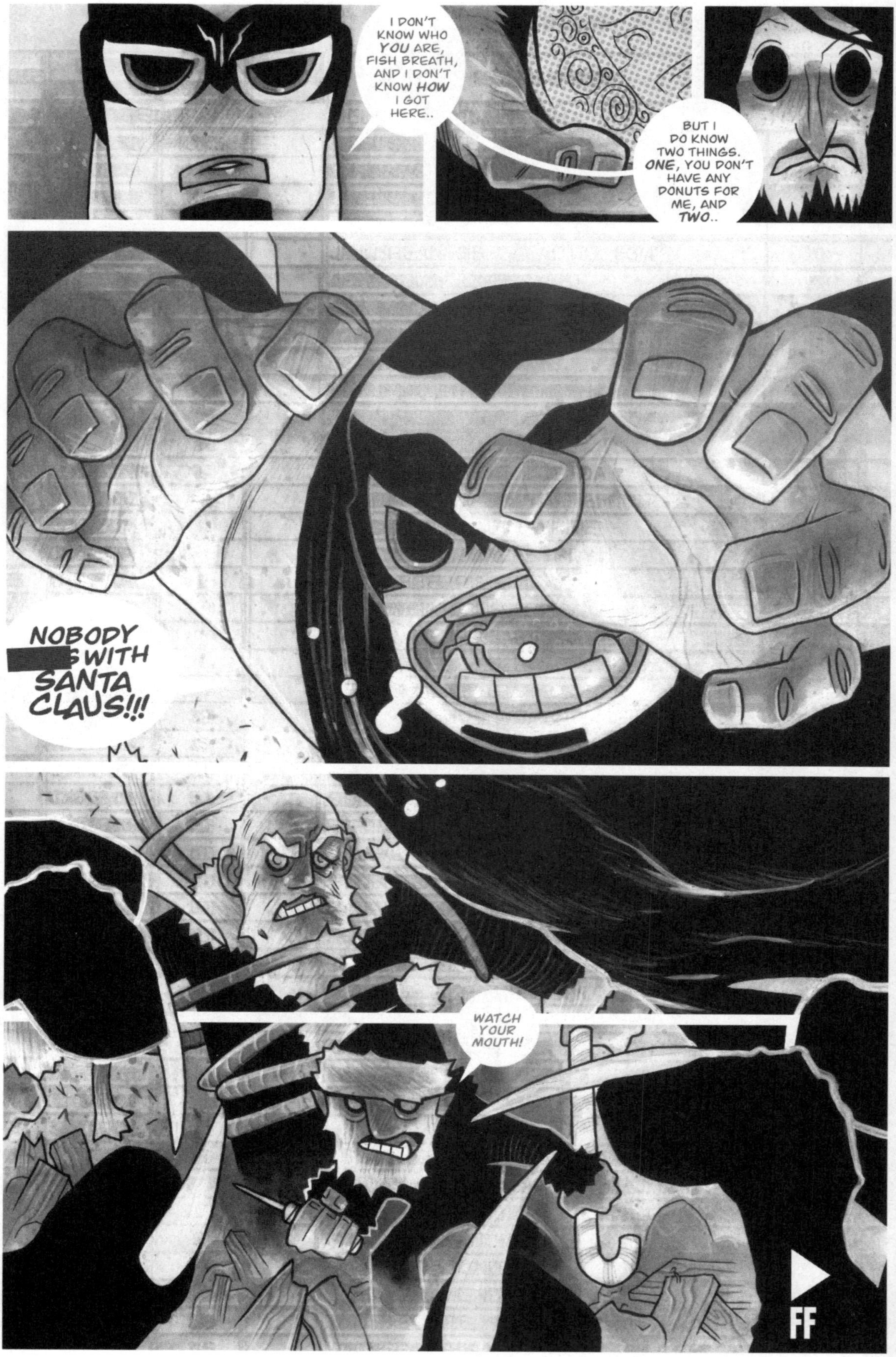
I DON'T KNOW WHO YOU ARE, FISH BREATH, AND I DON'T KNOW HOW I GOT HERE..
BUT I DO KNOW TWO THINGS. ONE, YOU DON'T HAVE ANY DONUTS FOR ME, AND TWO..
NOBODY [redacted] WITH SANTA CLAUS!!!
WATCH YOUR MOUTH!
FF

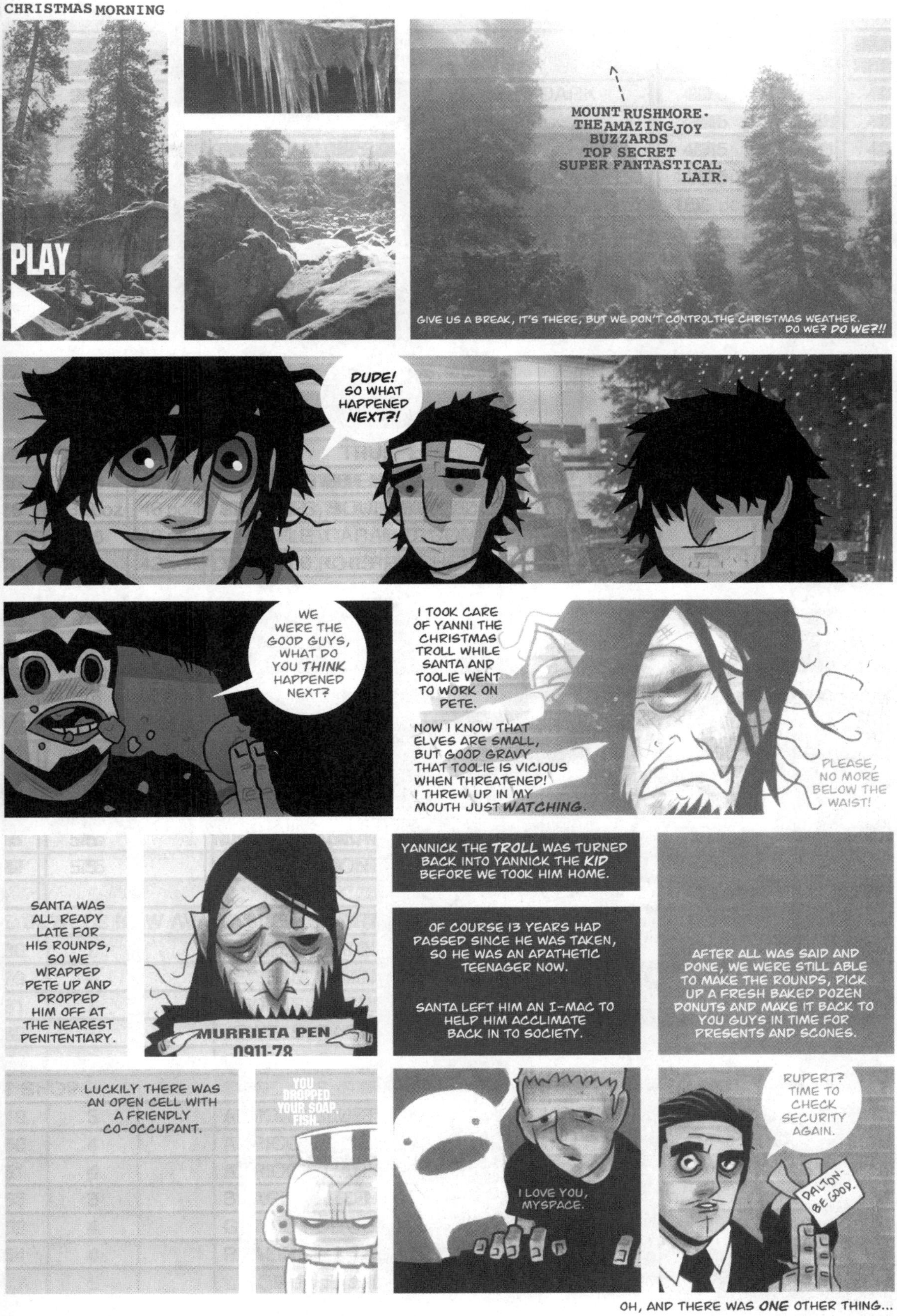
CHRISTMAS MORNING
PLAY
MOUNT RUSHMORE. THE AMAZING JOY BUZZARDS TOP SECRET SUPER FANTASTICAL LAIR.
GIVE US A BREAK, IT'S THERE, BUT WE DON'T CONTROL THE CHRISTMAS WEATHER. DO WE? DO WE?!!
DUDE! SO WHAT HAPPENED NEXT?!
WE WERE THE GOOD GUYS, WHAT DO YOU THINK HAPPENED NEXT?
I TOOK CARE OF YANNI THE CHRISTMAS TROLL WHILE SANTA AND TOOLIE WENT TO WORK ON PETE.
NOW I KNOW THAT ELVES ARE SMALL, BUT GOOD GRAVY THAT TOOLIE IS VICIOUS WHEN THREATENED! I THREW UP IN MY MOUTH JUST WATCHING.
PLEASE, NO MORE BELOW THE WAIST!
SANTA WAS ALL READY LATE FOR HIS ROUNDS, SO WE WRAPPED PETE UP AND DROPPED HIM OFF AT THE NEAREST PENITENTIARY.
MURRIETA PEN
0911-78
YANNICK THE TROLL WAS TURNED BACK INTO YANNICK THE KID BEFORE WE TOOK HIM HOME.
OF COURSE 13 YEARS HAD PASSED SINCE HE WAS TAKEN, SO HE WAS AN APATHETIC TEENAGER NOW.
SANTA LEFT HIM AN I-MAC TO HELP HIM ACCLIMATE BACK IN TO SOCIETY.
AFTER ALL WAS SAID AND DONE, WE WERE STILL ABLE TO MAKE THE ROUNDS, PICK UP A FRESH BAKED DOZEN DONUTS AND MAKE IT BACK TO YOU GUYS IN TIME FOR PRESENTS AND SCONES.
LUCKILY THERE WAS AN OPEN CELL WITH A FRIENDLY CO-OCCUPANT.
YOU DROPPED YOUR SOAP, FISH.
I LOVE YOU, MYSPACE.
RUPERT? TIME TO CHECK SECURITY AGAIN.
DALTON- BE GOOD.
OH, AND THERE WAS ONE OTHER THING...

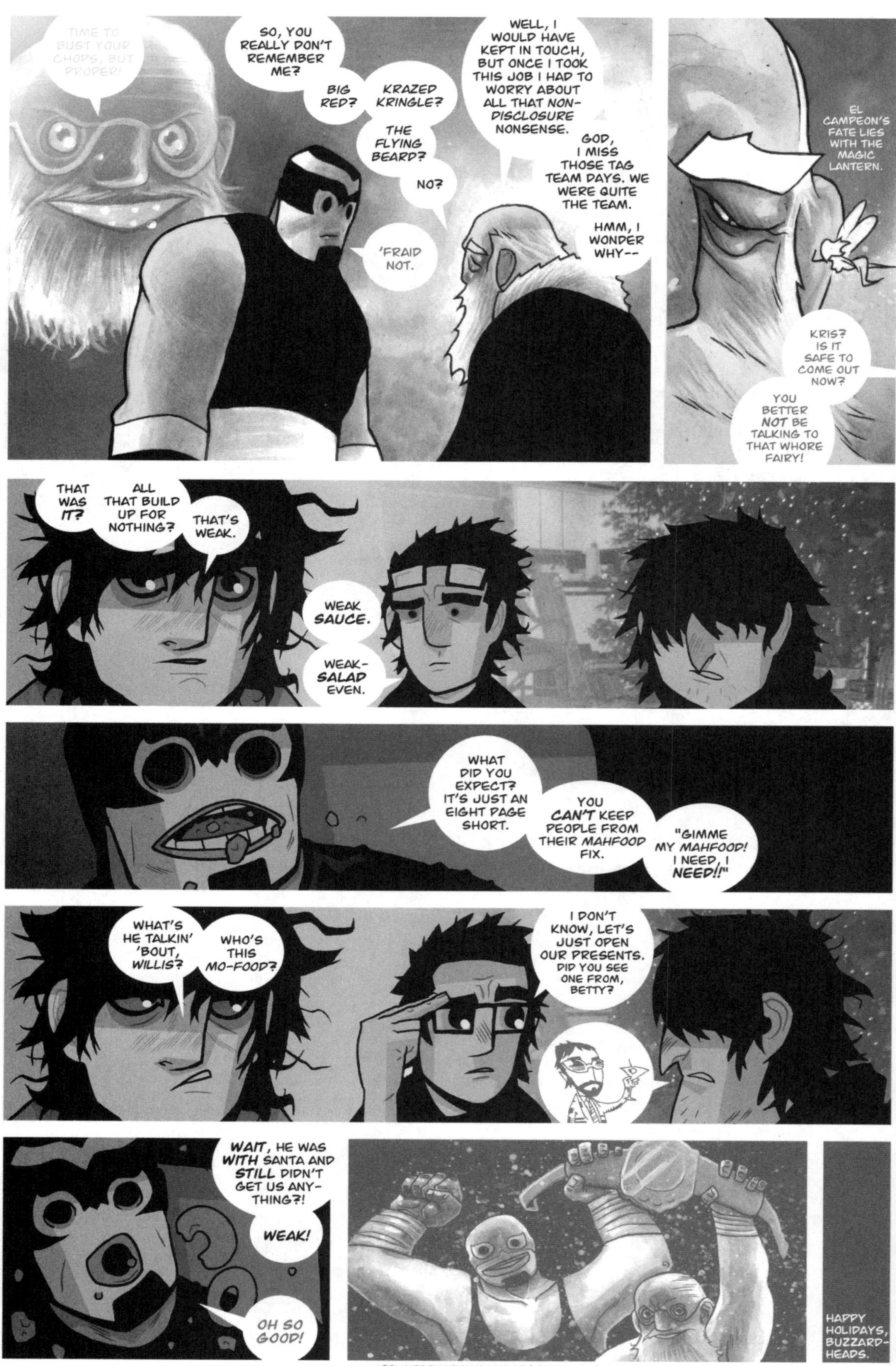
TIME TO BUST YOUR CHOPS, BUT PROPER!
SO, YOU REALLY DON'T REMEMBER ME?
BIG RED?
KRAZED KRINGLE?
THE FLYING BEARD?
NO?
'FRAID NOT.
WELL, I WOULD HAVE KEPT IN TOUCH, BUT ONCE I TOOK THIS JOB I HAD TO WORRY ABOUT ALL THAT NON-DISCLOSURE NONSENSE.
GOD, I MISS THOSE TAG TEAM DAYS. WE WERE QUITE THE TEAM.
HMM, I WONDER WHY--
EL CAMPEON'S FATE LIES WITH THE MAGIC LANTERN.
KRIS? IS IT SAFE TO COME OUT NOW?
YOU BETTER NOT BE TALKING TO THAT WHORE FAIRY!
THAT WAS IT?
ALL THAT BUILD UP FOR NOTHING?
THAT'S WEAK.
WEAK SAUCE.
WEAK-SALAD EVEN.
WHAT DID YOU EXPECT? IT'S JUST AN EIGHT PAGE SHORT.
YOU CAN'T KEEP PEOPLE FROM THEIR MAHFOOD FIX.
"GIMME MY MAHFOOD! I NEED, I NEED!!"
WHAT'S HE TALKIN' 'BOUT, WILLIS?
WHO'S THIS MO-FOOD?
I DON'T KNOW, LET'S JUST OPEN OUR PRESENTS. DID YOU SEE ONE FROM, BETTY?
WAIT, HE WAS WITH SANTA AND STILL DIDN'T GET US ANYTHING?!
WEAK!
OH SO GOOD!
HAPPY HOLIDAYS, BUZZARD-HEADS.
1951 INTERNATIONALUNDERGROUND TAG-TEAM WRESTLING CHAMPIONSHIPS.

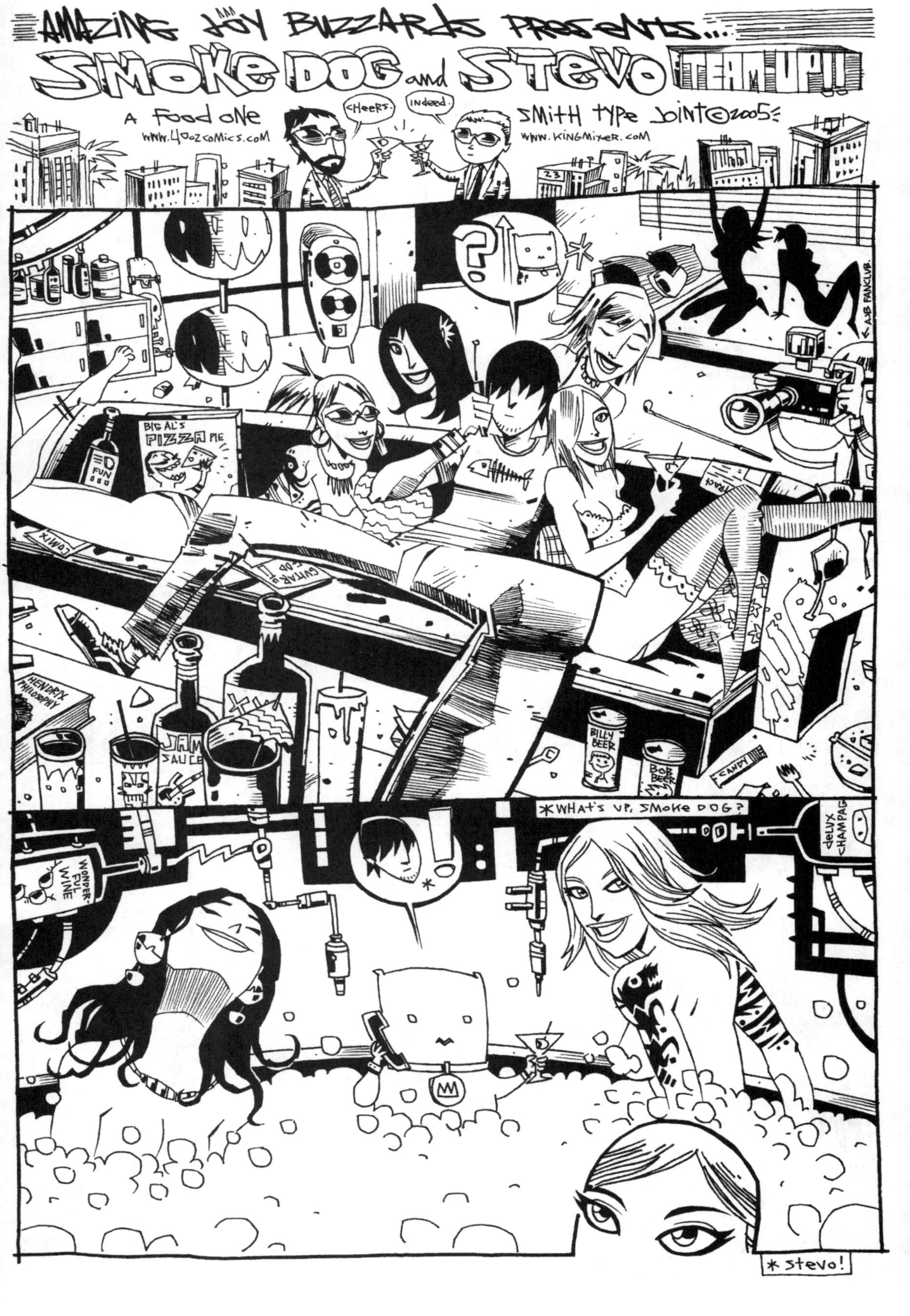
AMAZING JOY BUZZARDS PRESENTS...
SMOKE DOG and STEVO TEAM UP!!
A FOOD ONE
www.40ozcomics.com
CHEERS.
INDEED.
SMITH TYPE JOINT ©2005
www.kingmixer.com
BIG AL'S PIZZA PIE
FUN
AJB FANCLUB
COMIX
GUITAR GOD
TRACK
HENDRIX PHILOSOPHY
JAM SAUCE
BILLY BEER
BOB BEER
CANDY
*WHAT'S UP, SMOKE DOG?
DELUX CHAMPAG
WONDER-FUL WINE
*STEVO!

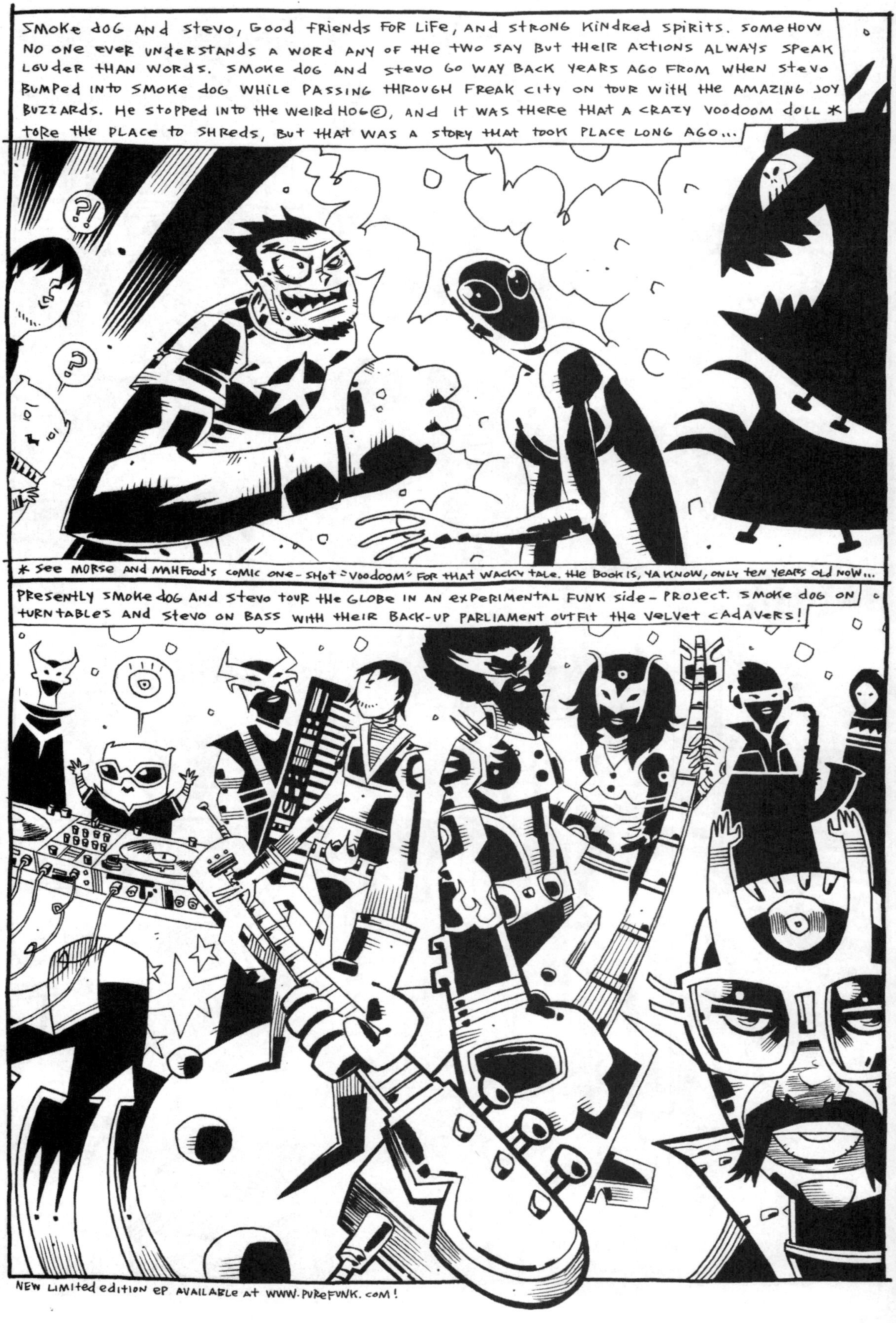
SMOKE DOG AND STEVO, GOOD FRIENDS FOR LIFE, AND STRONG KINDRED SPIRITS. SOMEHOW NO ONE EVER UNDERSTANDS A WORD ANY OF THE TWO SAY BUT THEIR ACTIONS ALWAYS SPEAK LOUDER THAN WORDS. SMOKE DOG AND STEVO GO WAY BACK YEARS AGO FROM WHEN STEVO BUMPED INTO SMOKE DOG WHILE PASSING THROUGH FREAK CITY ON TOUR WITH THE AMAZING JOY BUZZARDS. HE STOPPED INTO THE WEIRD HOG©, AND IT WAS THERE THAT A CRAZY VOODOOM DOLL * TORE THE PLACE TO SHREDS, BUT THAT WAS A STORY THAT TOOK PLACE LONG AGO...
?!
?
* SEE MORSE AND MAHFOOD'S COMIC ONE-SHOT "VOODOOM" FOR THAT WACKY TALE. THE BOOK IS, YA KNOW, ONLY TEN YEARS OLD NOW...
PRESENTLY SMOKE DOG AND STEVO TOUR THE GLOBE IN AN EXPERIMENTAL FUNK SIDE-PROJECT. SMOKE DOG ON TURNTABLES AND STEVO ON BASS WITH THEIR BACK-UP PARLIAMENT OUTFIT THE VELVET CADAVERS!

NEW LIMITED EDITION EP AVAILABLE AT WWW.PUREFUNK.COM!

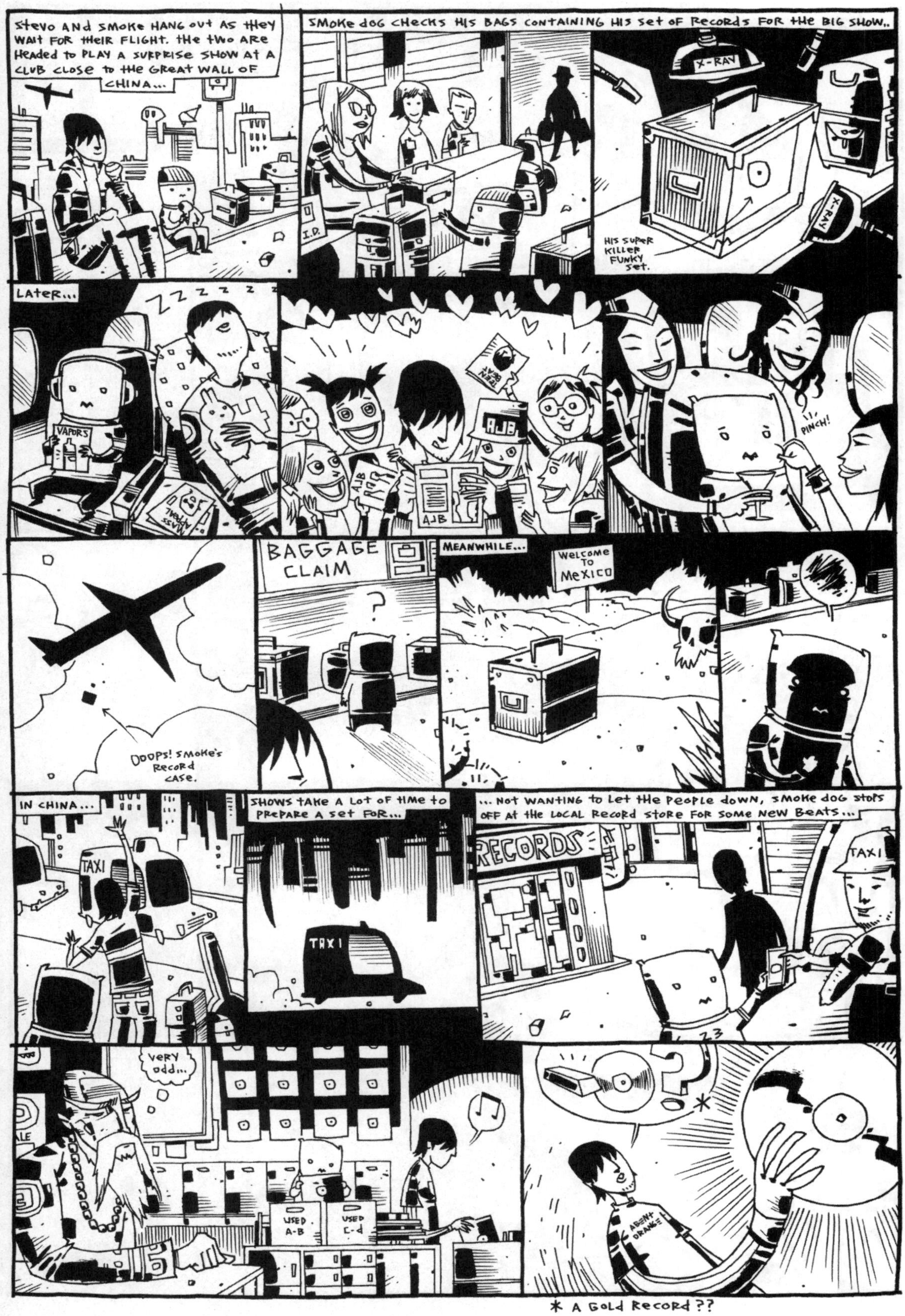

Stevo and Smoke hang out as they wait for their flight. The two are headed to play a surprise show at a club close to the Great Wall of China...
Smoke dog checks his bags containing his set of records for the big show..
I.D.
X-RAY
X-RAY
His super killer funky set.
Later...
Z Z Z Z Z Z Z
VAPORS
MASS APPEAL
TEEN BEAT
AJB
AJB
AJB
PINCH!
OOPS! Smoke's record case.
BAGGAGE CLAIM
?
Meanwhile...
Welcome to Mexico
In China...
TAXI
Shows take a lot of time to prepare a set for...
TAXI
...Not wanting to let the people down, Smoke dog stops off at the local record store for some new beats...
RECORDS
TAXI
Very odd...
USED A-B
USED C-D
AGENT ORANGE
* A Gold Record??

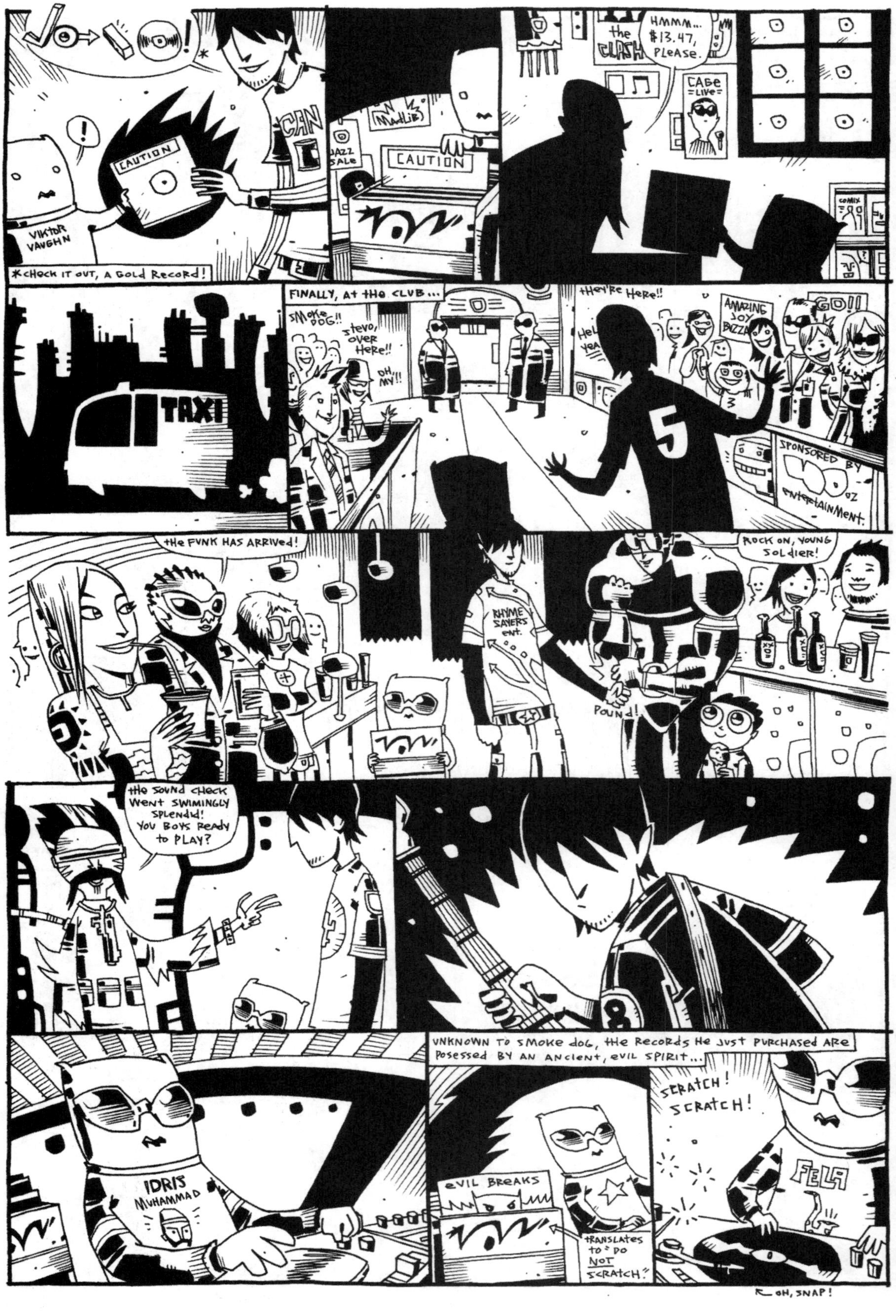

JO → ! *
*CHECK IT OUT, A GOLD RECORD!
!
VIKTOR VAUGHN
CAUTION
CAN
MADLIB
JAZZ SALE
CAUTION
the CLASH
HMMM... $13.47, PLEASE.
CAGE LIVE
COMIX
TAXI
FINALLY, AT THE CLUB...
SMOKE DOG!!
STEVO, OVER HERE!!
OH, MY!!
THEY'RE HERE!!
AMAZING JOY BUZZARDS
GO!!
SPONSORED BY 40 OZ ENTERTAINMENT.
THE FUNK HAS ARRIVED!
RHYME SAYERS ENT.
ROCK ON, YOUNG SOLDIER!
POUND!
THE SOUND CHECK WENT SWIMINGLY SPLENDID! YOU BOYS READY TO PLAY?
UNKNOWN TO SMOKE DOG, THE RECORDS HE JUST PURCHASED ARE POSESSED BY AN ANCIENT, EVIL SPIRIT...
IDRIS MUHAMMAD
EVIL BREAKS
TRANSLATES TO: DO NOT SCRATCH!
SCRATCH! SCRATCH!
FELA
OH, SNAP!

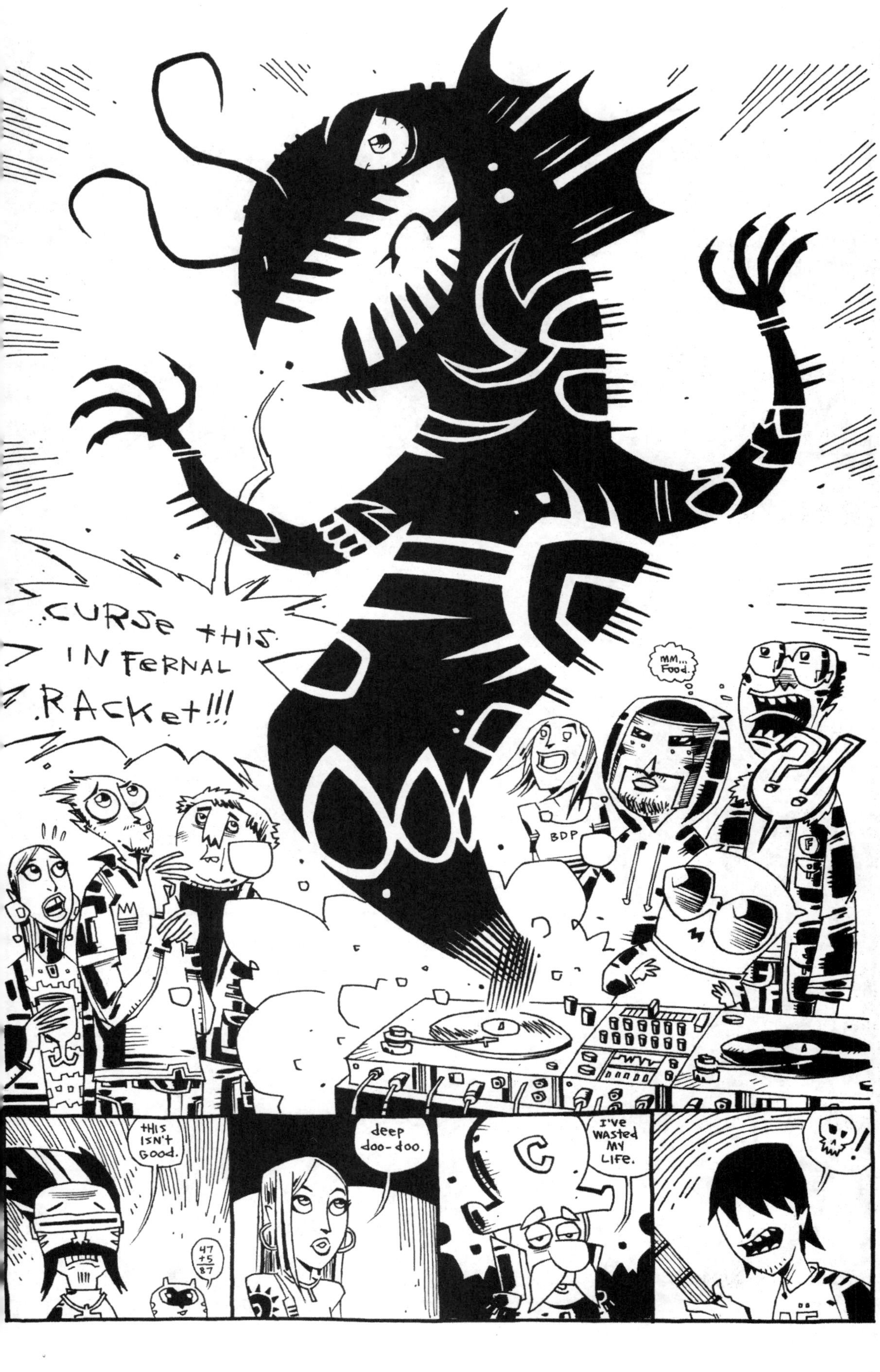

CURSE THIS INFERNAL RACKET!!!
MM... FOOD.
?!
BDP
THIS ISN'T GOOD.
47 +5 87
deep doo-doo.
I'VE WASTED MY LIFE.
!

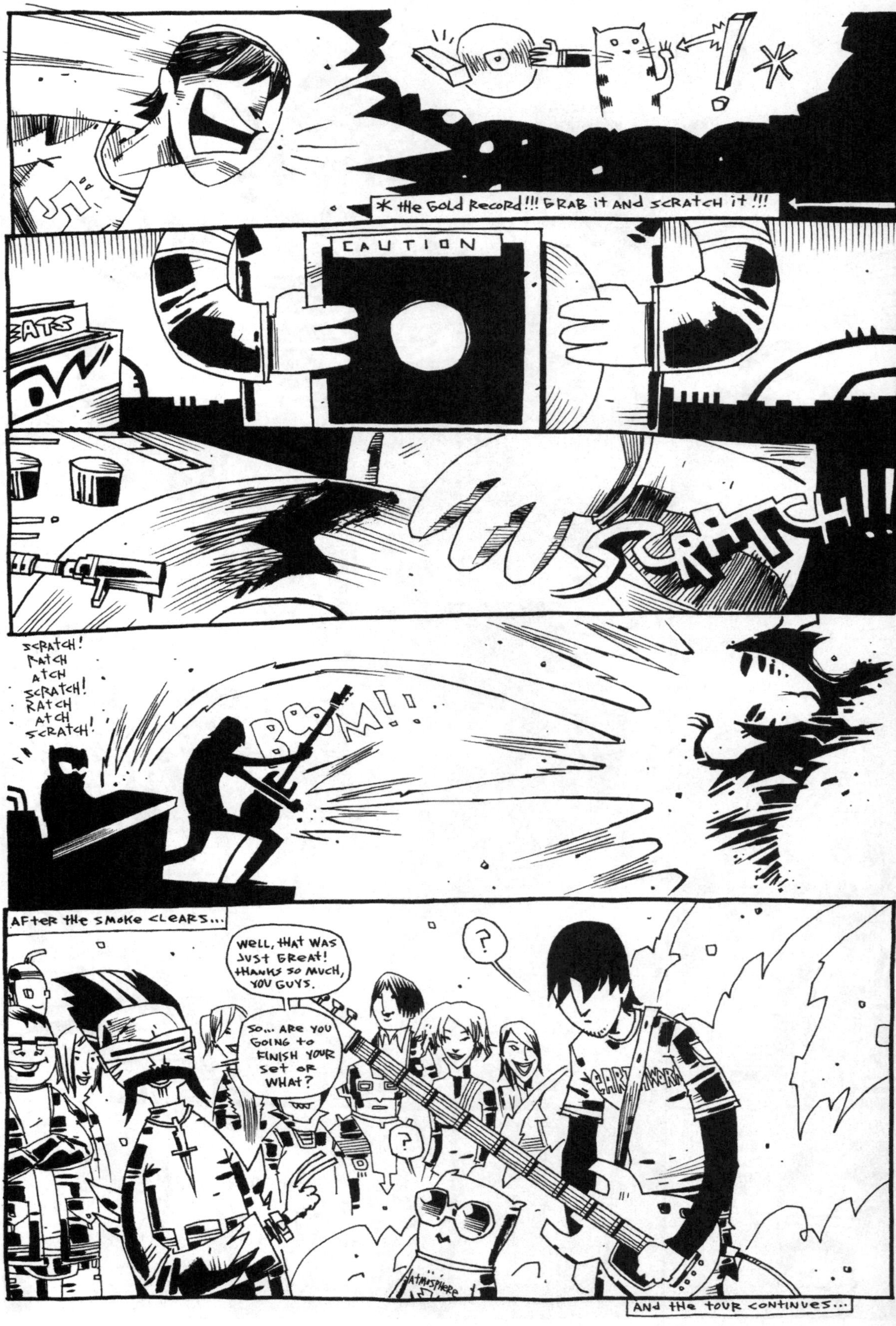
* the Gold Record!!! GRAB it AND scratch it!!!
CAUTION
SCRATCH!!!
scratch!
RATCH
ATCH
scratch!
RATCH
ATCH
scratch!
BOOM!!
After the smoke clears...
WELL, THAT WAS JUST GREAT! THANKS SO MUCH, YOU GUYS.
?
SO... ARE YOU GOING TO FINISH YOUR SET OR WHAT?
?
atmosphere
And the tour continues...

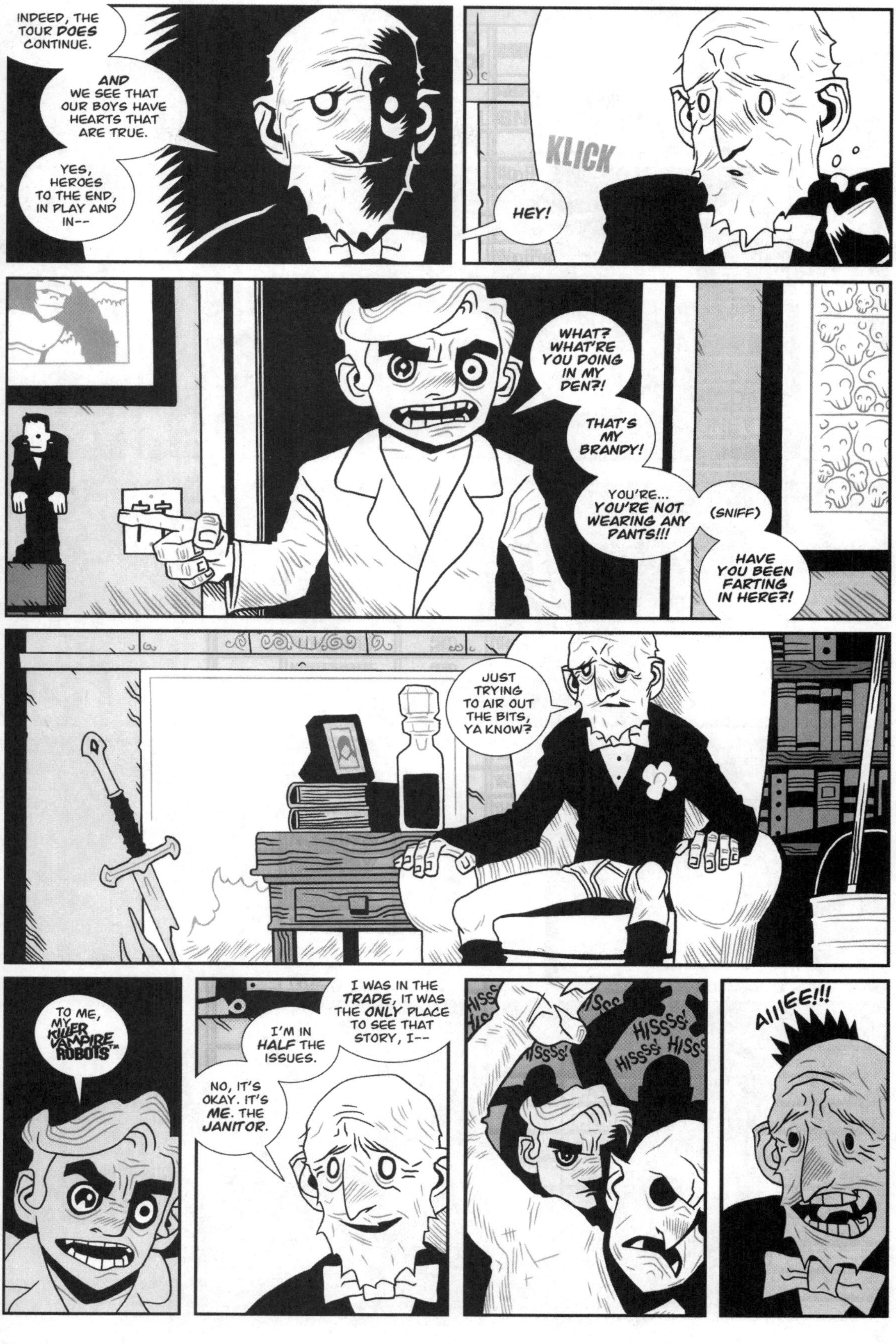
INDEED, THE TOUR **DOES** CONTINUE.
AND WE SEE THAT OUR BOYS HAVE HEARTS THAT ARE TRUE.
YES, HEROES TO THE END, IN PLAY AND IN--
KLICK
HEY!
WHAT? WHAT'RE YOU DOING IN MY DEN?!
THAT'S MY BRANDY!
YOU'RE... **YOU'RE NOT WEARING ANY PANTS!!!**
(SNIFF)
HAVE YOU BEEN FARTING IN HERE?!
JUST TRYING TO AIR OUT THE BITS, YA KNOW?
TO ME, MY KILLER VAMPIRE ROBOTS™
I'M IN **HALF** THE ISSUES.
I WAS IN THE **TRADE**, IT WAS THE **ONLY** PLACE TO SEE THAT STORY, I--
NO, IT'S OKAY. IT'S **ME**. THE **JANITOR**.
HISSS! HISSSS! HISSSS! HISSSS! HISSS
AIIIEE!!!

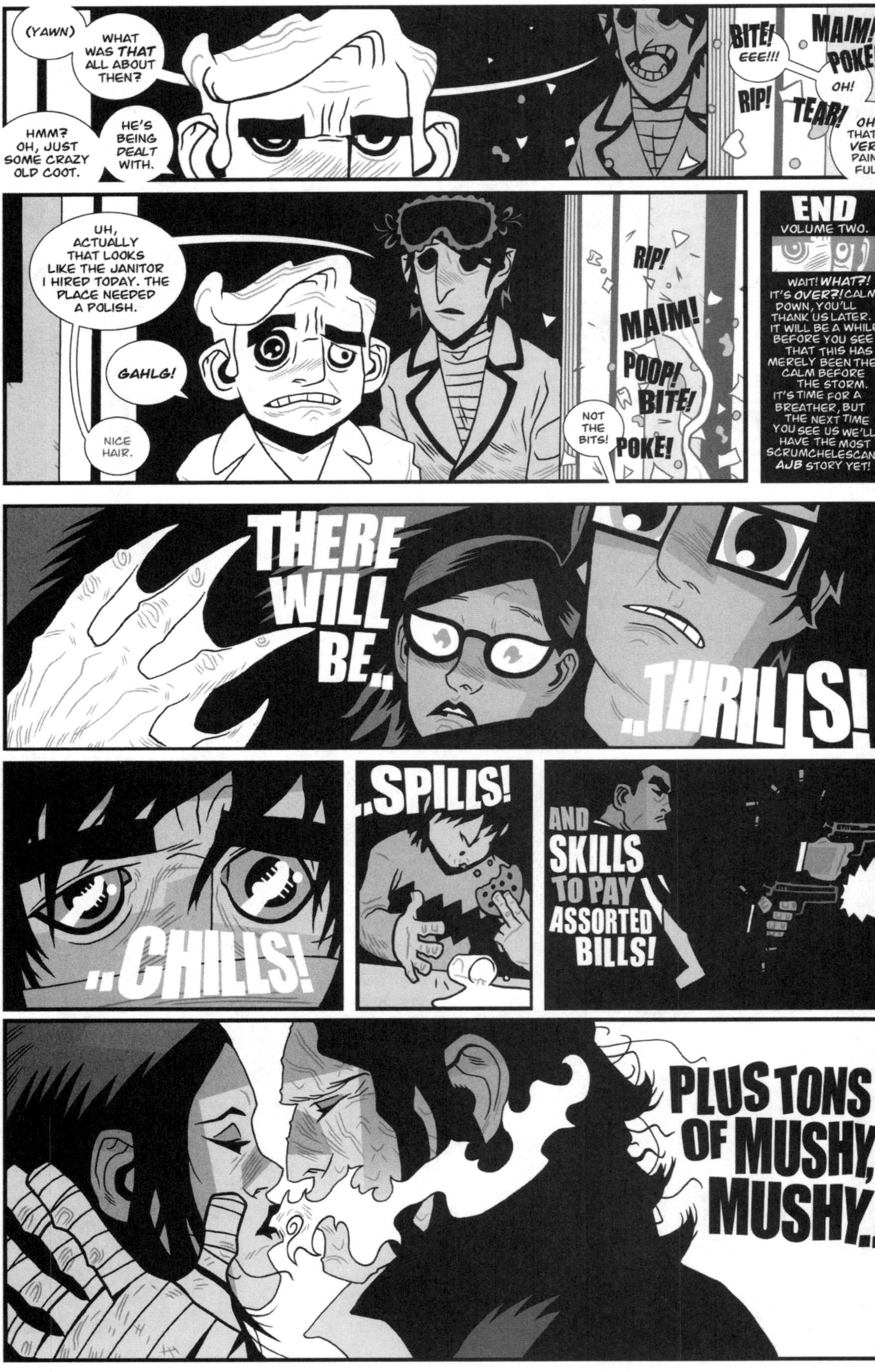
(YAWN)
WHAT WAS THAT ALL ABOUT THEN?
HMM? OH, JUST SOME CRAZY OLD COOT.
HE'S BEING DEALT WITH.
BITE!
EEE!!!
MAIM!
POKE!
OH!
RIP!
TEAR!
OH! THAT'S VERY PAIN-FUL!
UH, ACTUALLY THAT LOOKS LIKE THE JANITOR I HIRED TODAY. THE PLACE NEEDED A POLISH.
GAHLG!
NICE HAIR.
RIP!
MAIM!
POOP!
BITE!
POKE!
NOT THE BITS!
END
VOLUME TWO.
WAIT! WHAT?! IT'S OVER?! CALM DOWN, YOU'LL THANK US LATER. IT WILL BE A WHILE BEFORE YOU SEE THAT THIS HAS MERELY BEEN THE CALM BEFORE THE STORM. IT'S TIME FOR A BREATHER, BUT THE NEXT TIME YOU SEE US WE'LL HAVE THE MOST SCRUMCHELESCANT AJB STORY YET!
THERE WILL BE..
..THRILLS!
..CHILLS!
..SPILLS!
AND SKILLS TO PAY ASSORTED BILLS!
PLUS TONS OF MUSHY, MUSHY..

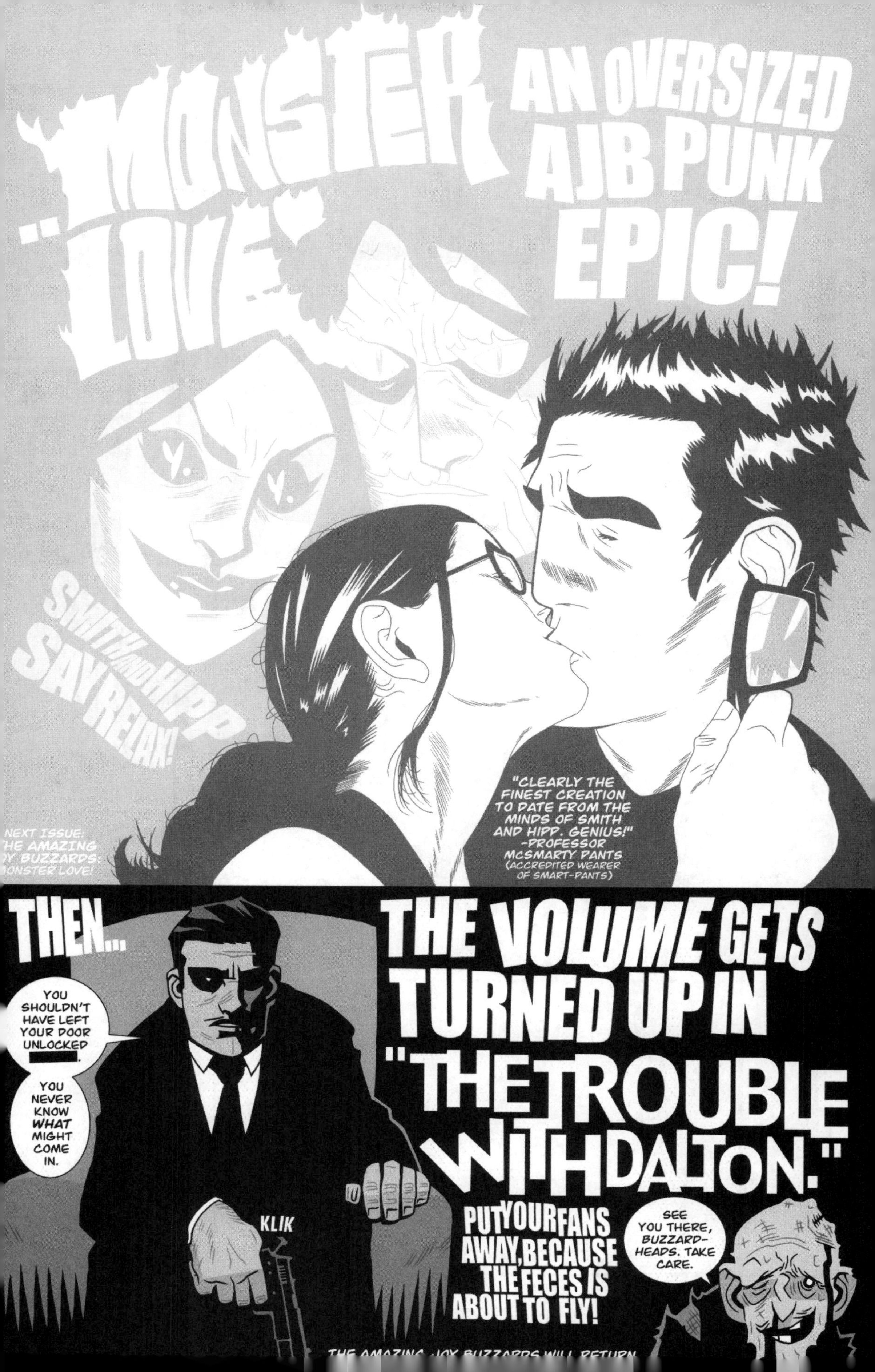
"MONSTER LOVE"
AN OVERSIZED AJB PUNK EPIC!
SMITH AND HIPP SAY RELAX!
NEXT ISSUE: THE AMAZING JOY BUZZARDS: MONSTER LOVE!
"CLEARLY THE FINEST CREATION TO DATE FROM THE MINDS OF SMITH AND HIPP. GENIUS!" -PROFESSOR McSMARTY PANTS (ACCREDITED WEARER OF SMART-PANTS)
THEN...
THE VOLUME GETS TURNED UP IN "THE TROUBLE WITH DALTON."
YOU SHOULDN'T HAVE LEFT YOUR DOOR UNLOCKED [redacted].
YOU NEVER KNOW WHAT MIGHT COME IN.
KLIK
PUT YOUR FANS AWAY, BECAUSE THE FECES IS ABOUT TO FLY!
SEE YOU THERE, BUZZARD-HEADS. TAKE CARE.
THE AMAZING JOY BUZZARDS WILL RETURN

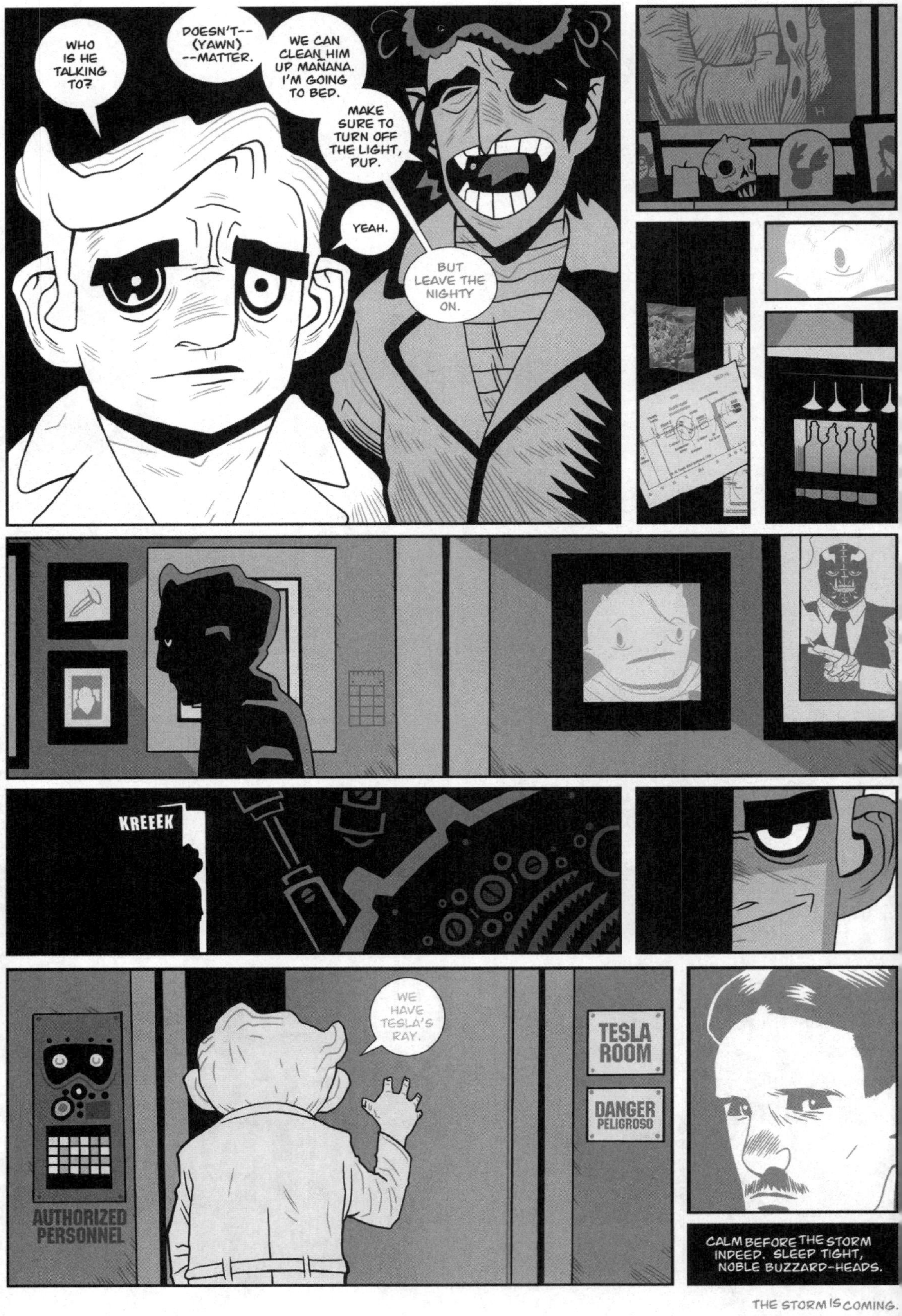
WHO IS HE TALKING TO?
DOESN'T-- (YAWN) --MATTER.
WE CAN CLEAN HIM UP MAÑANA. I'M GOING TO BED.
MAKE SURE TO TURN OFF THE LIGHT, PUP.
YEAH.
BUT LEAVE THE NIGHTY ON.
KREEEK
AUTHORIZED PERSONNEL
WE HAVE TESLA'S RAY.
TESLA ROOM
DANGER PELIGROSO
CALM BEFORE THE STORM INDEED. SLEEP TIGHT, NOBLE BUZZARD-HEADS.

THE STORM IS COMING.

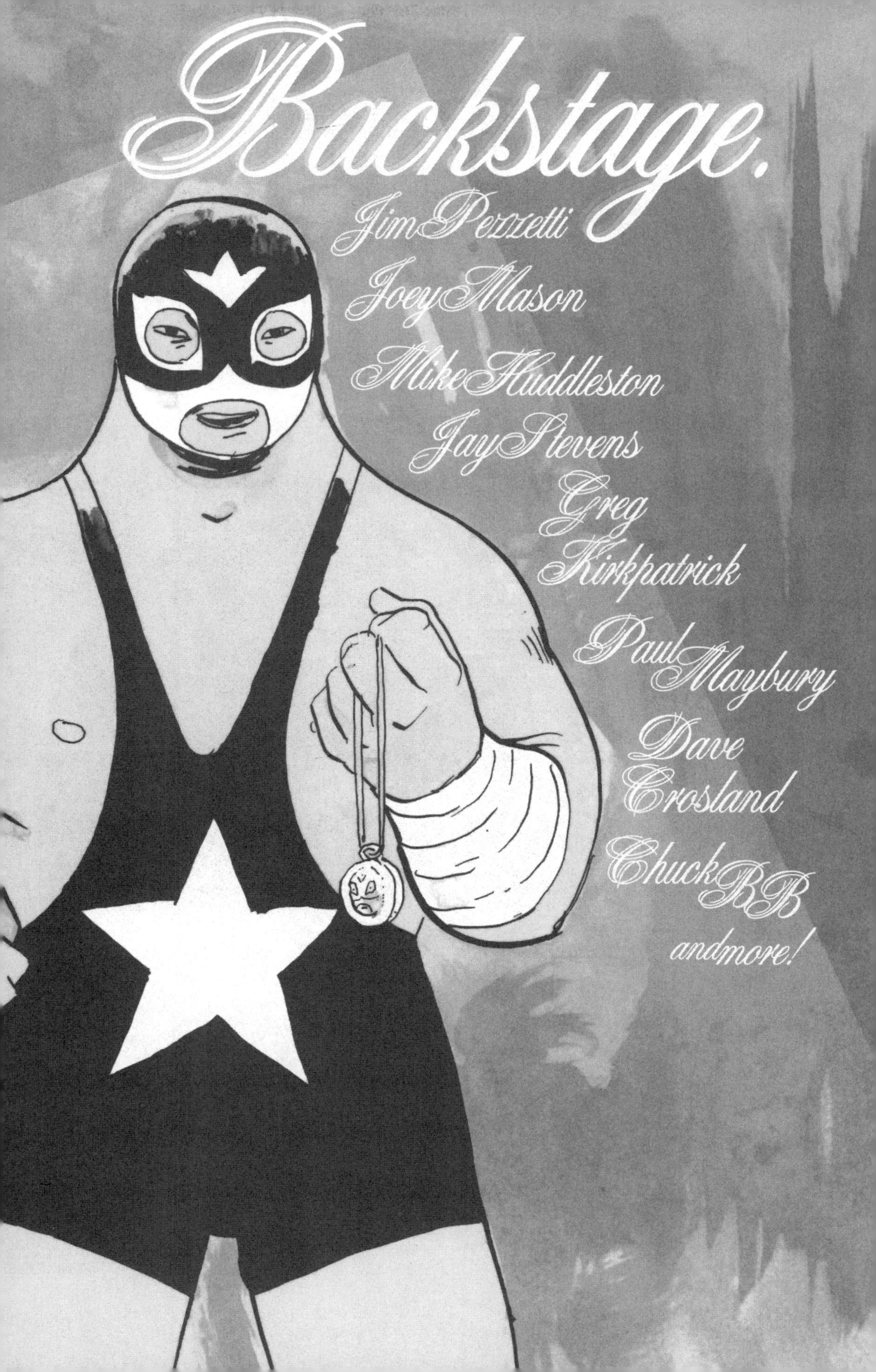
Backstage.
Jim Pezzetti
Joey Mason
Mike Huddleston
Jay Stevens
Greg Kirkpatrick
Paul Maybury
Dave Crosland
Chuck BB
and more!

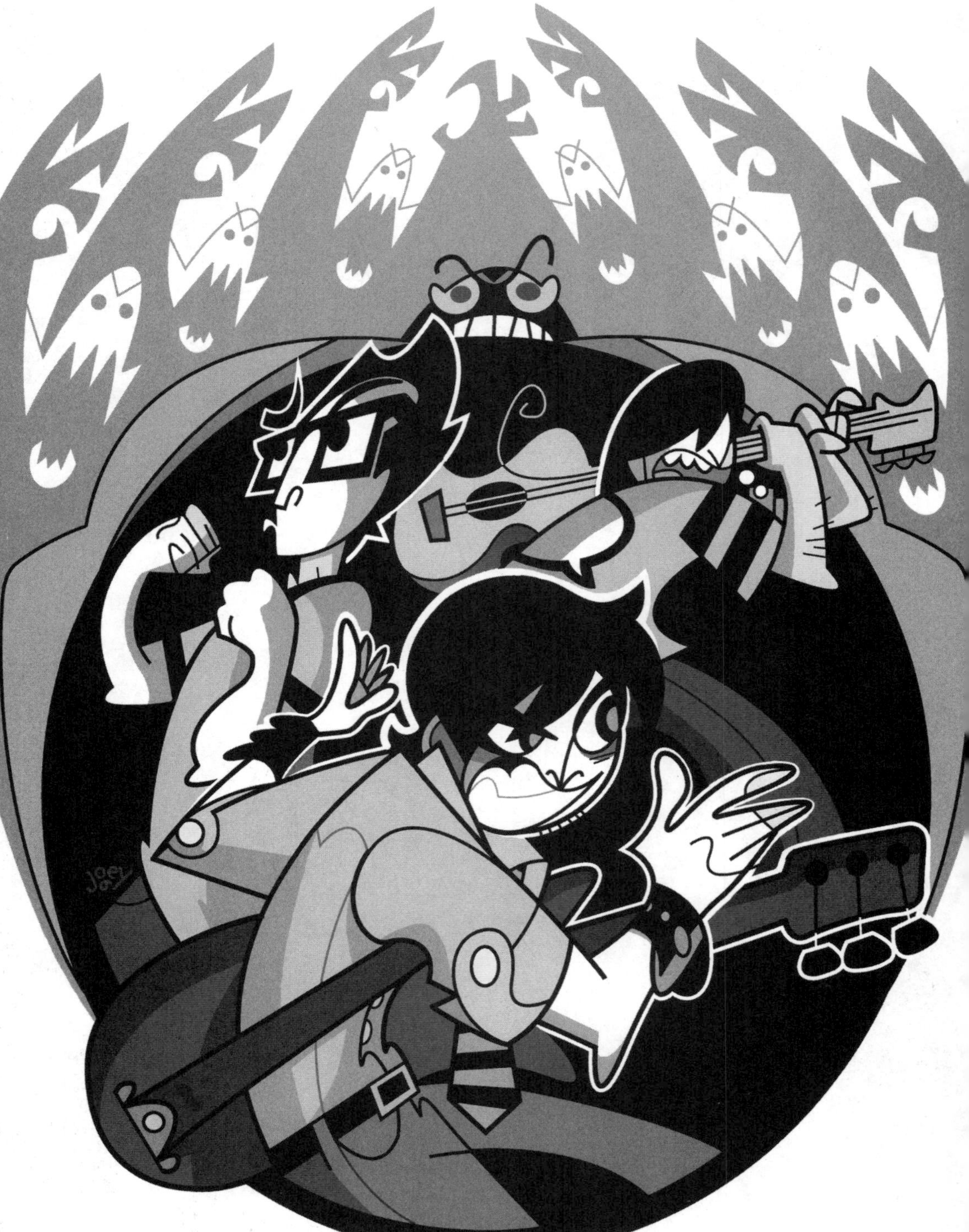

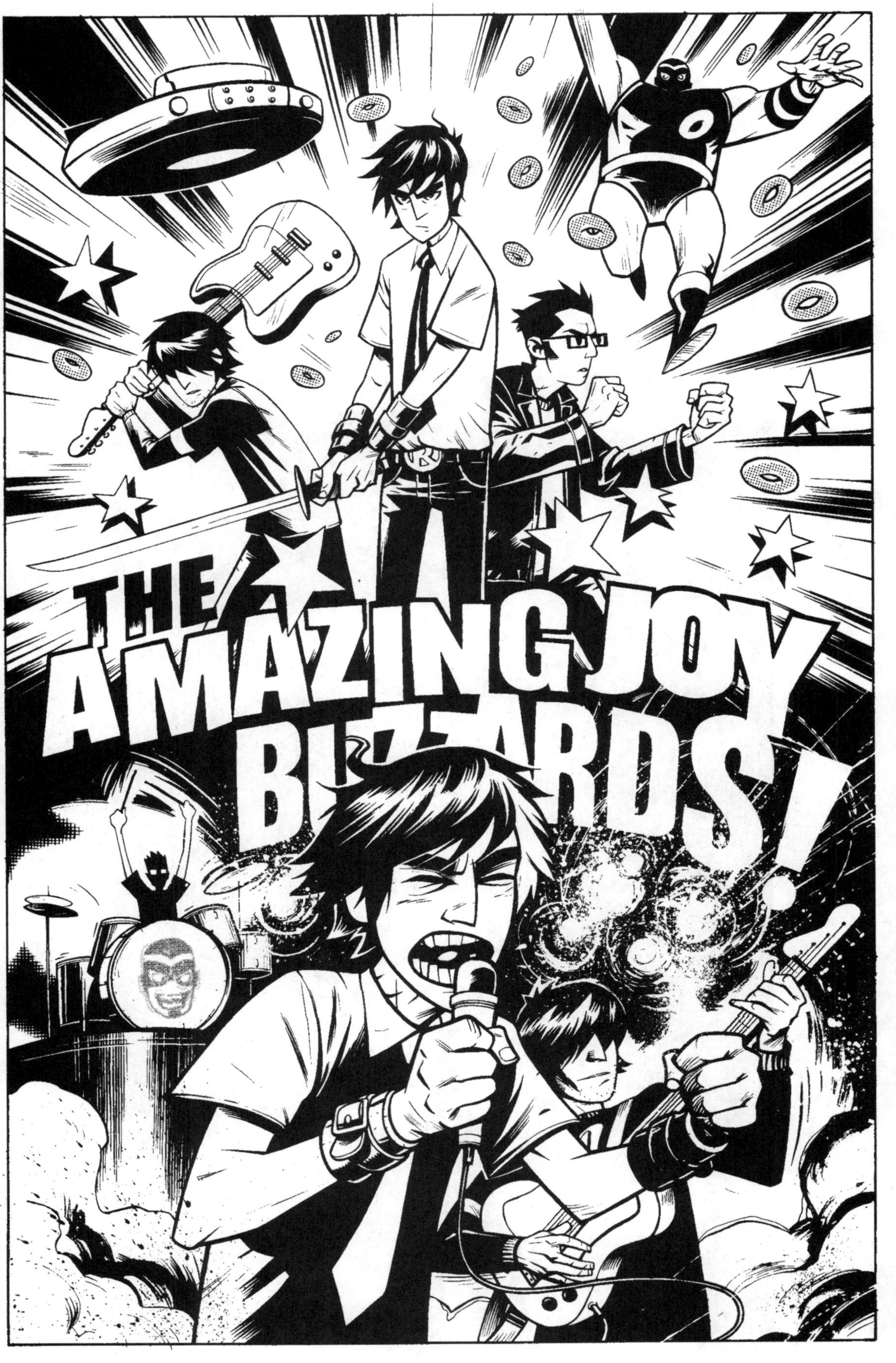
THE AMAZING JOY BUZZARDS!

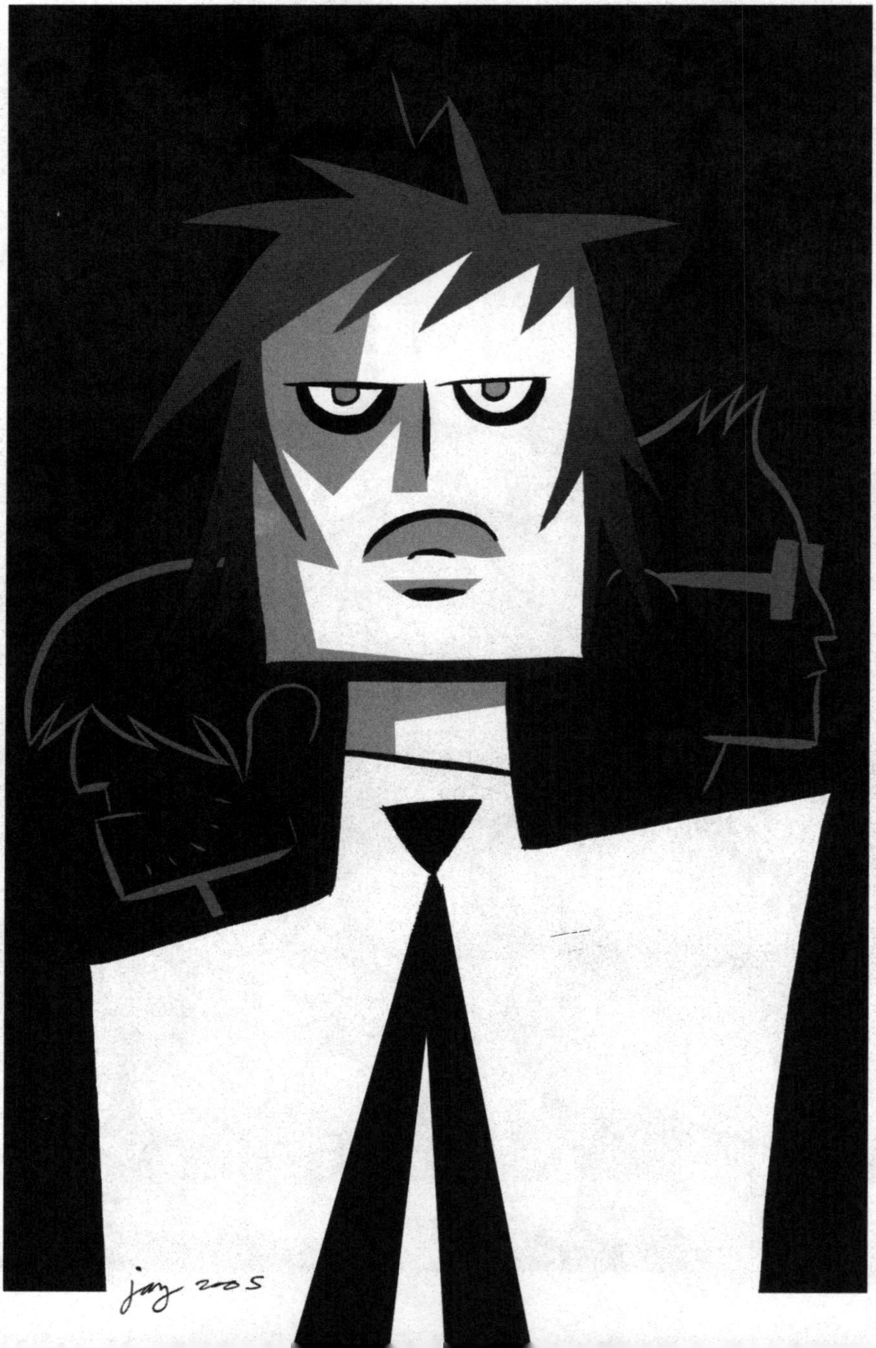
jay 2005

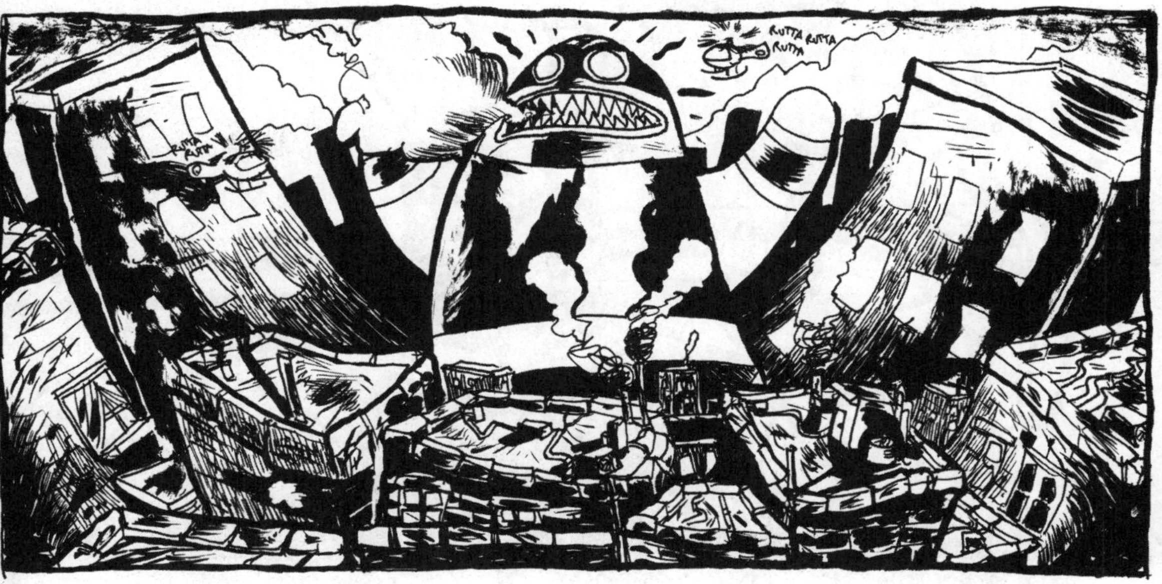
RUTTA RUTTA
RUTTA

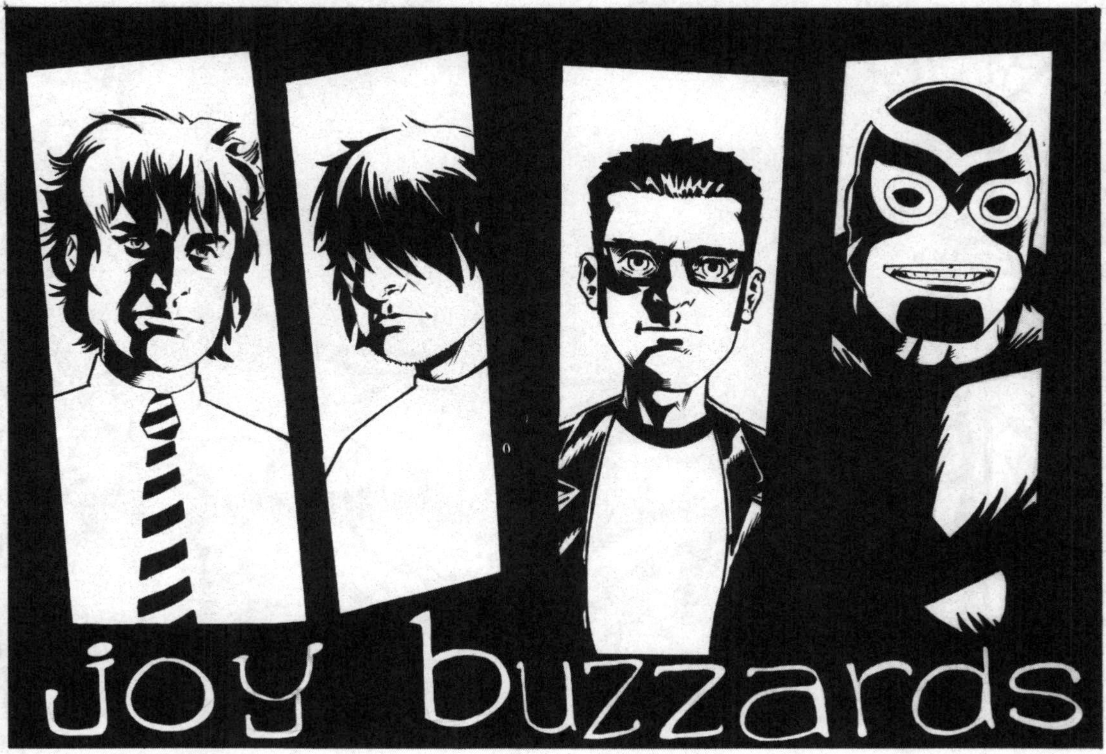
joy buzzards

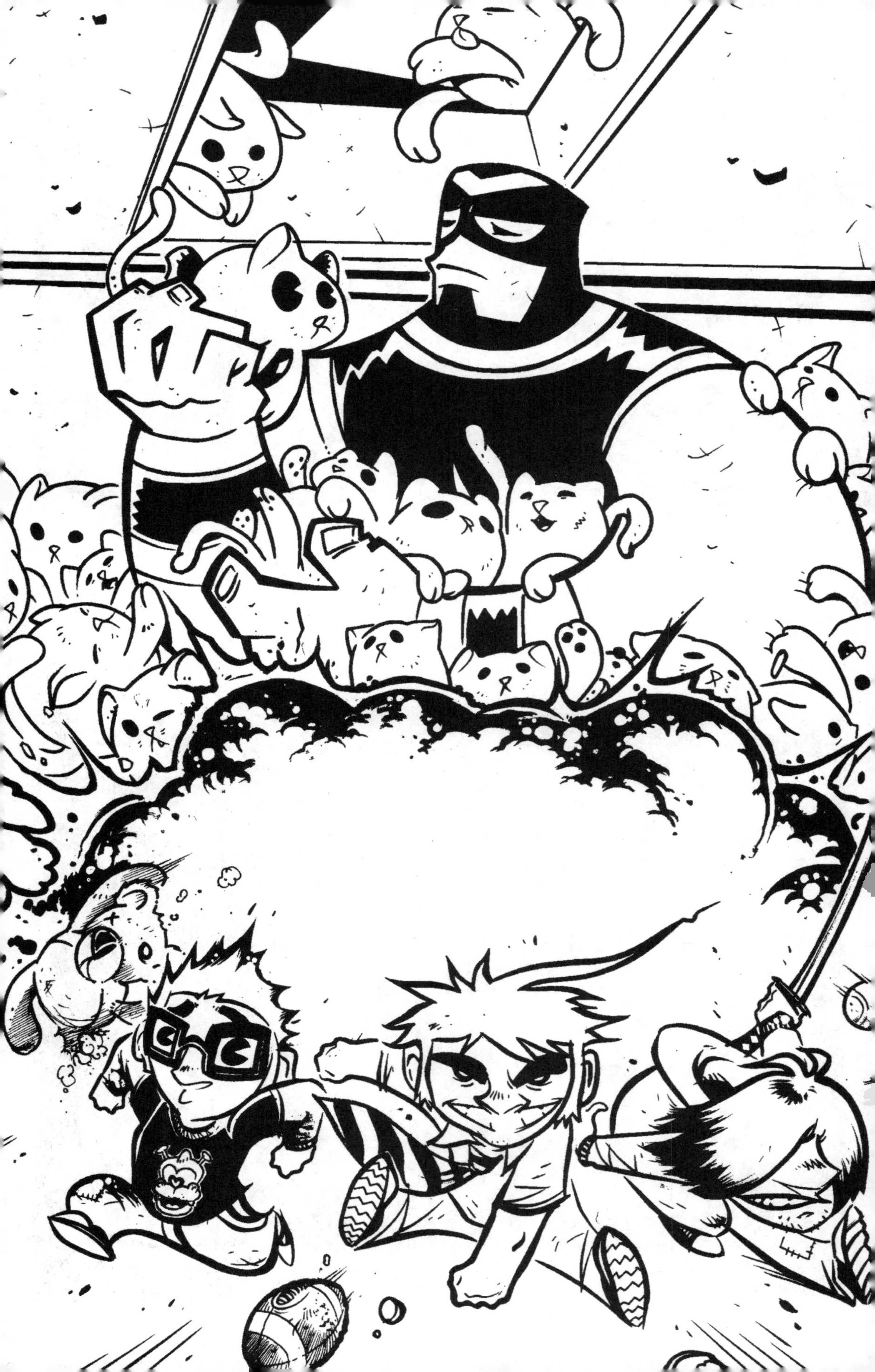

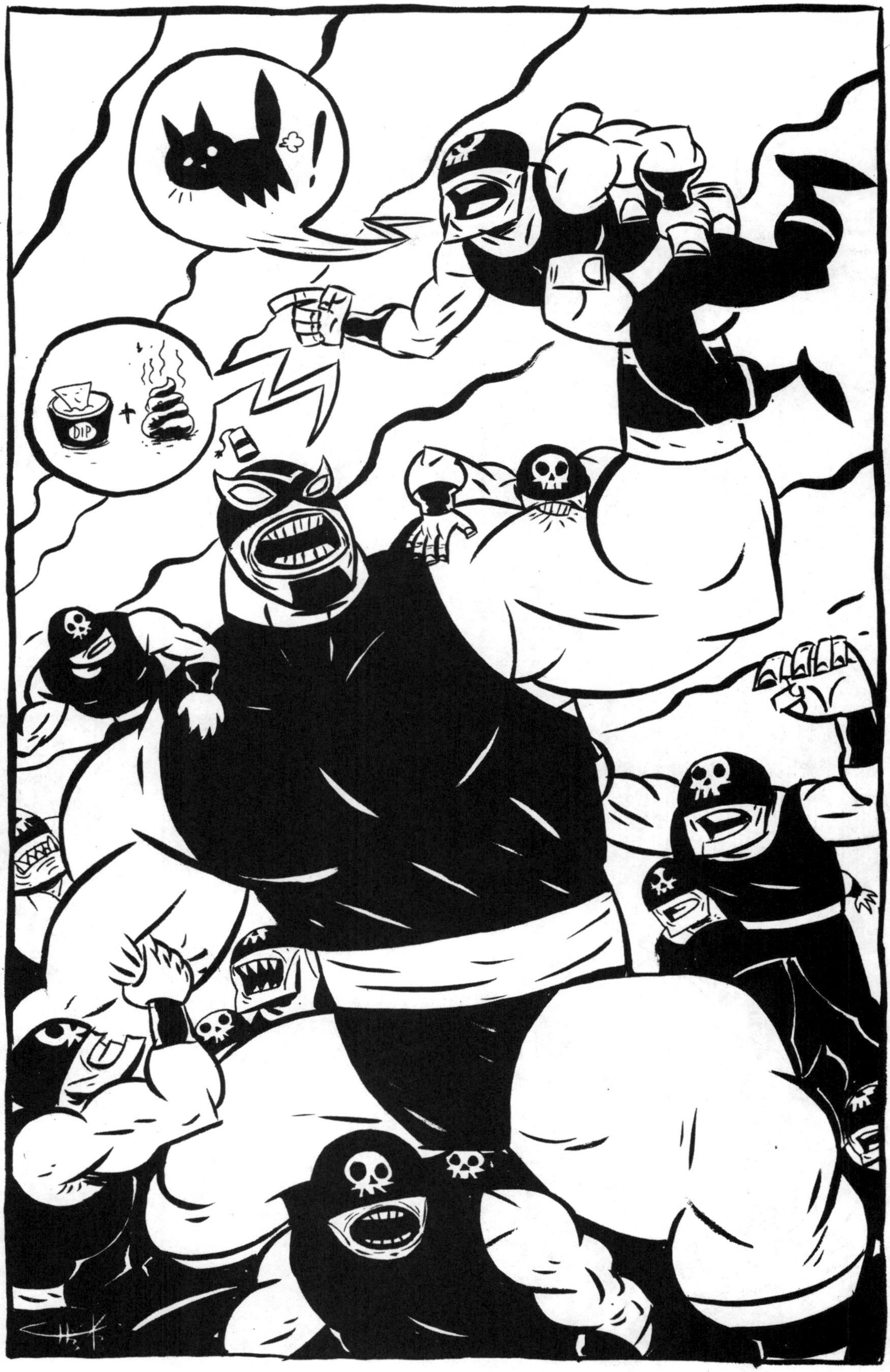
!
DIP

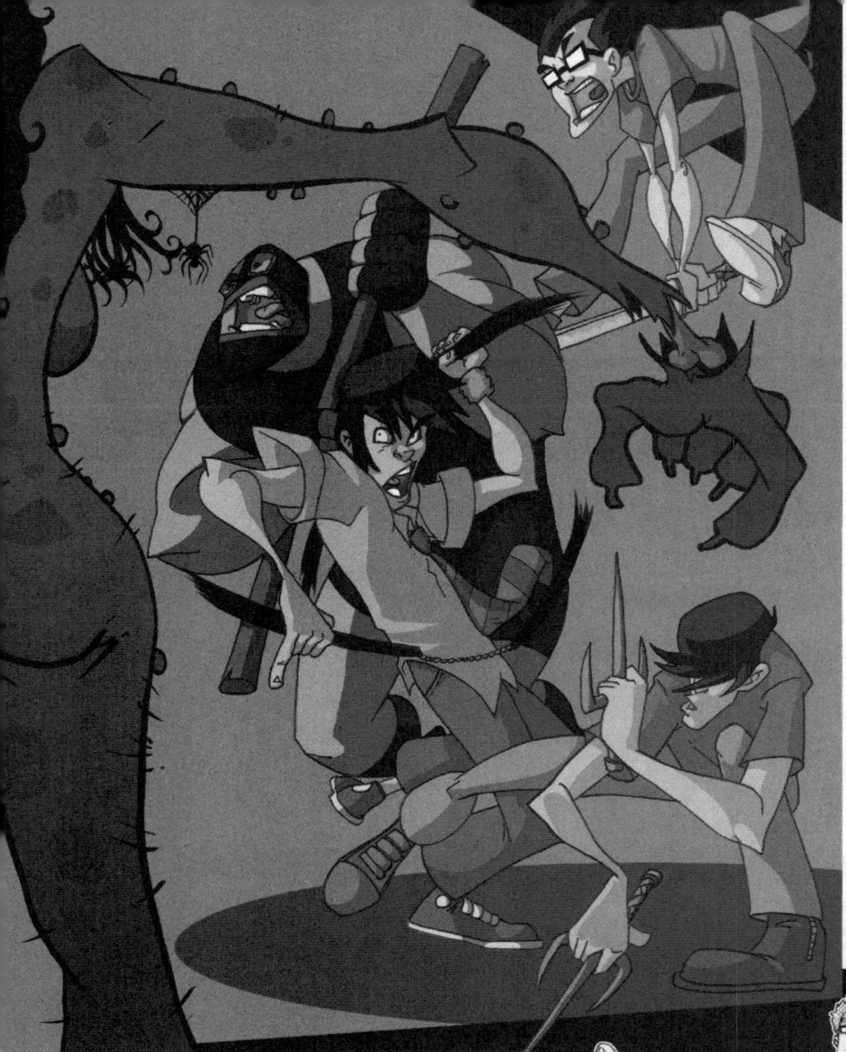

... *Matthew Humphreys*

James Stokoe
(FACING PAGE)

Zach Trover...
(BOTTOM LEFT)

Chamba...
(BOTTOM RIGHT)

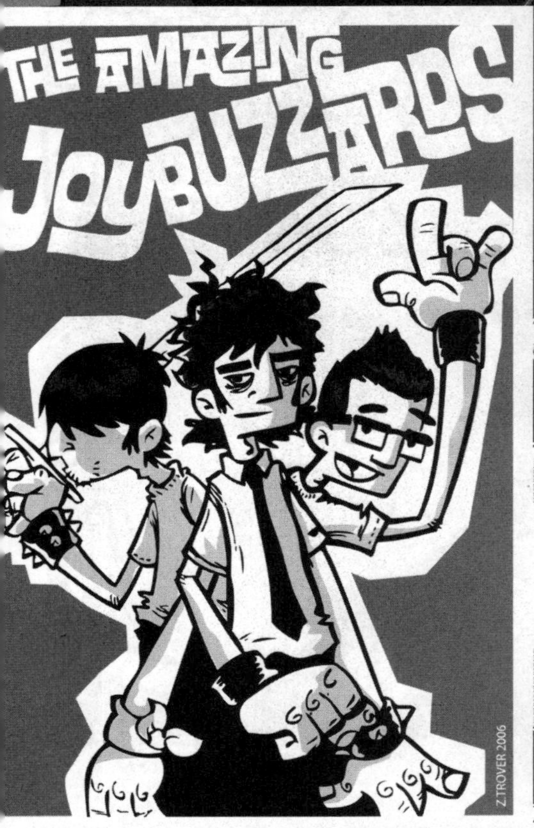
THE AMAZING
JOYBUZZARDS
Z.TROVER 2006

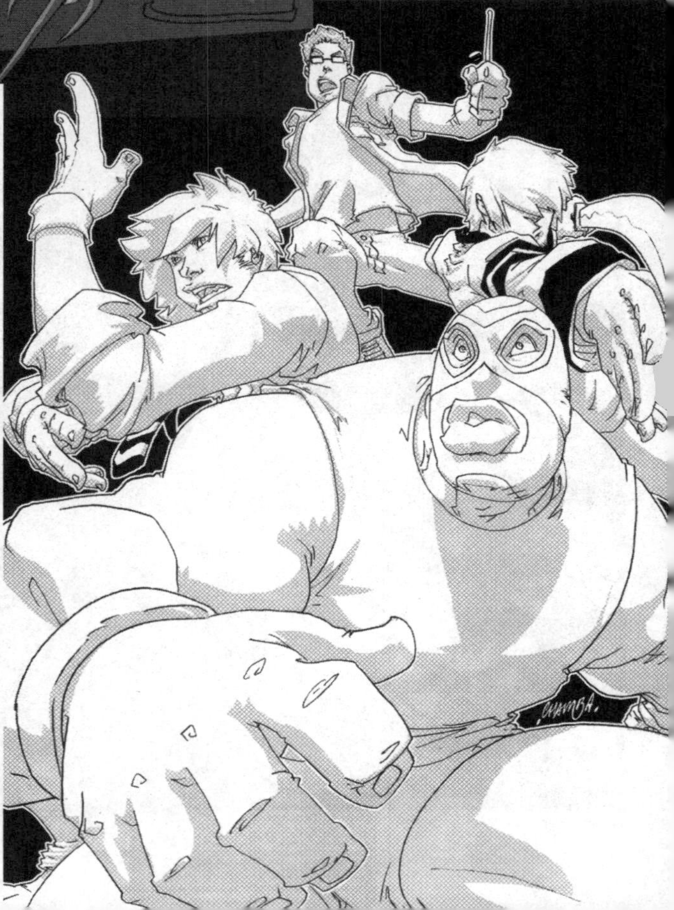
CHAMBA.

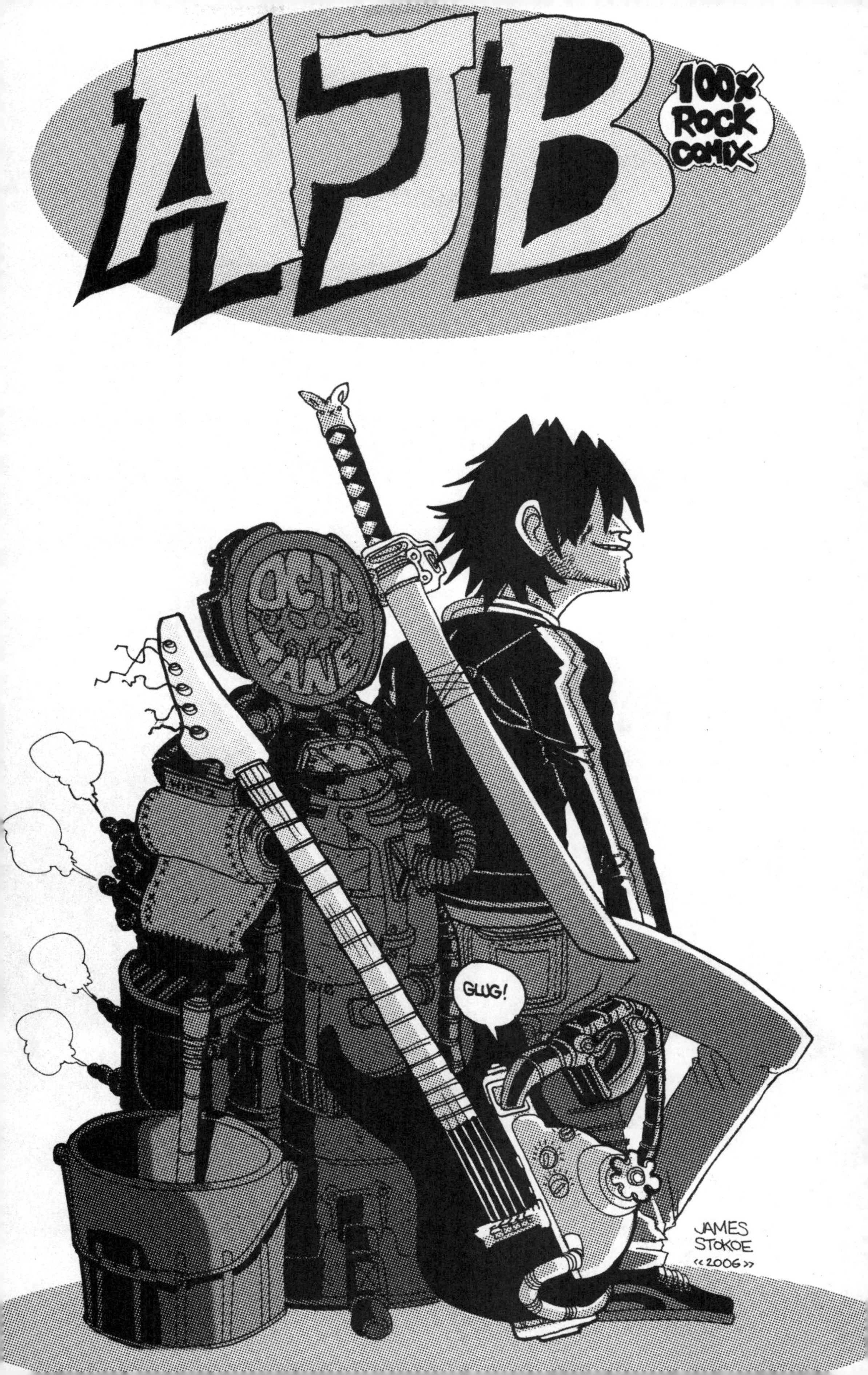

AJB
100% ROCK COMIX
GLUG!
JAMES STOKOE
<<2006>>

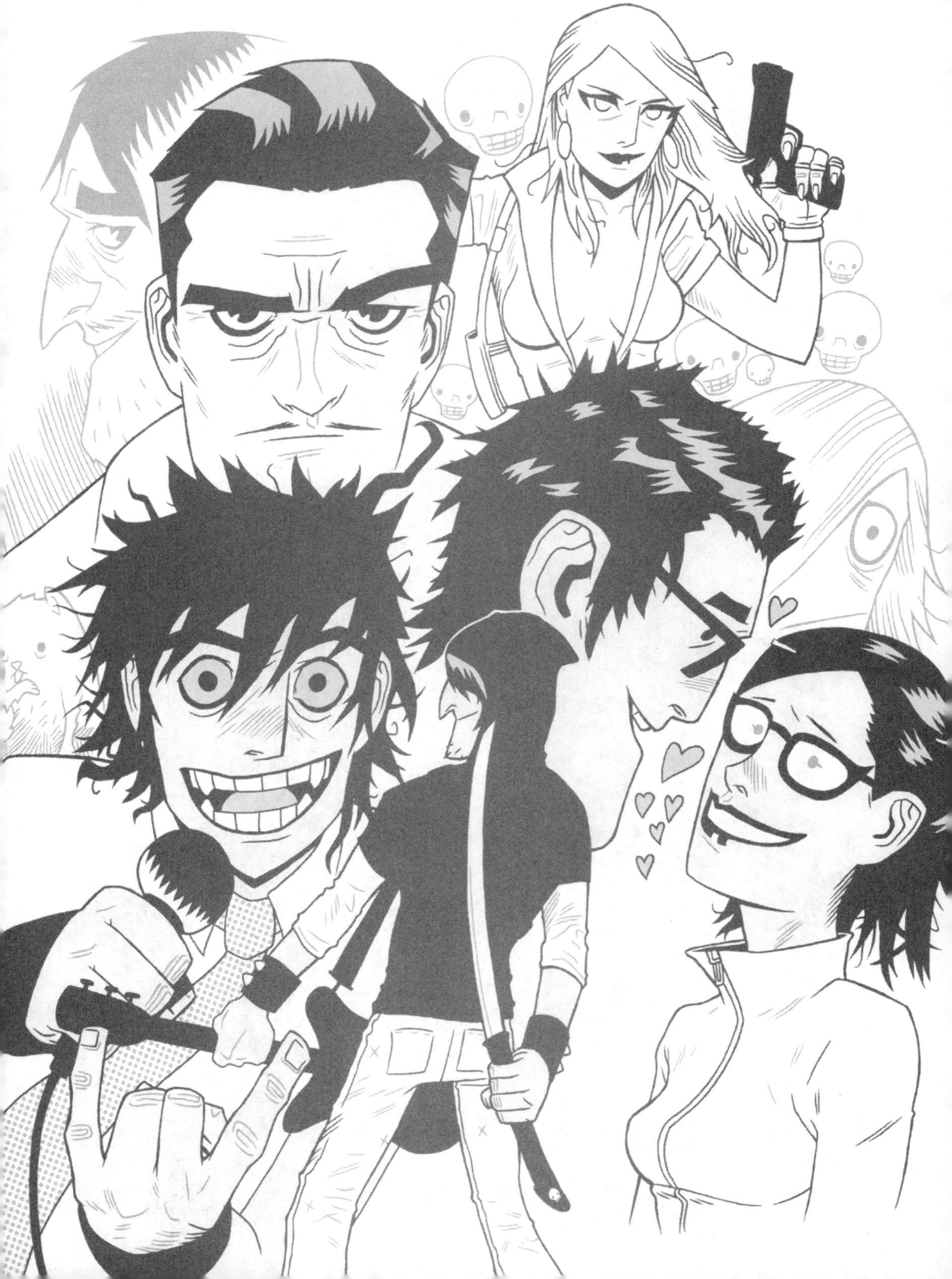

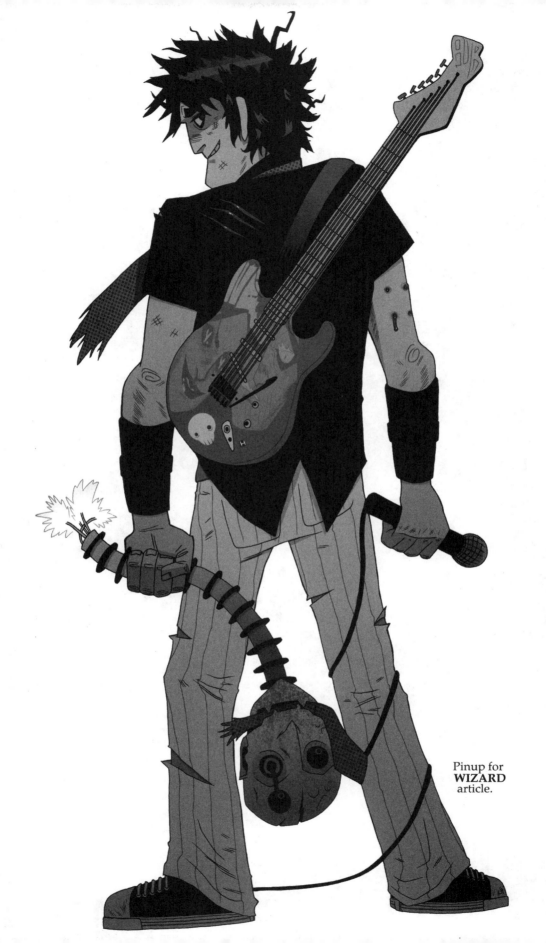

Pinup for
WIZARD
article.

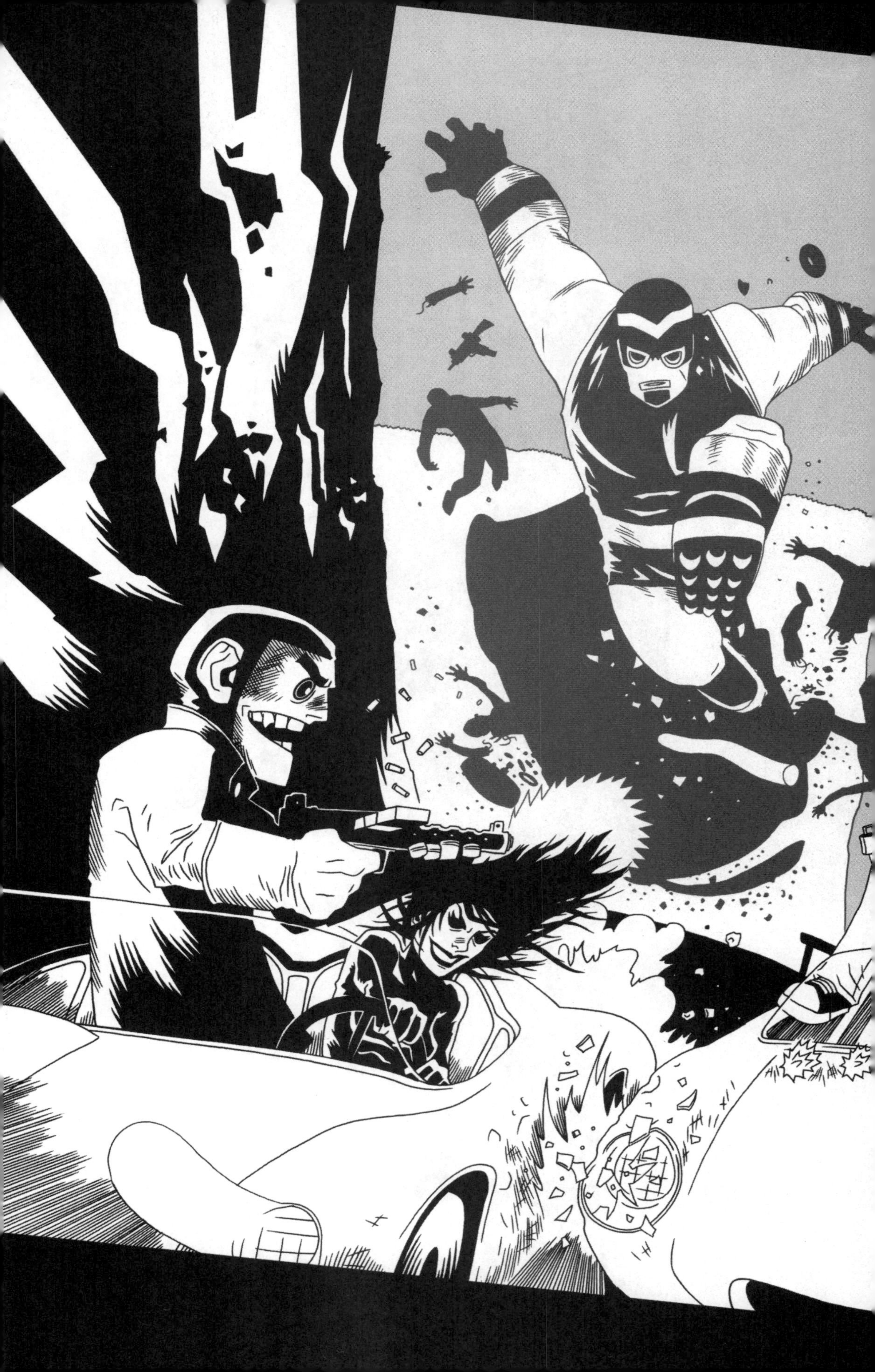

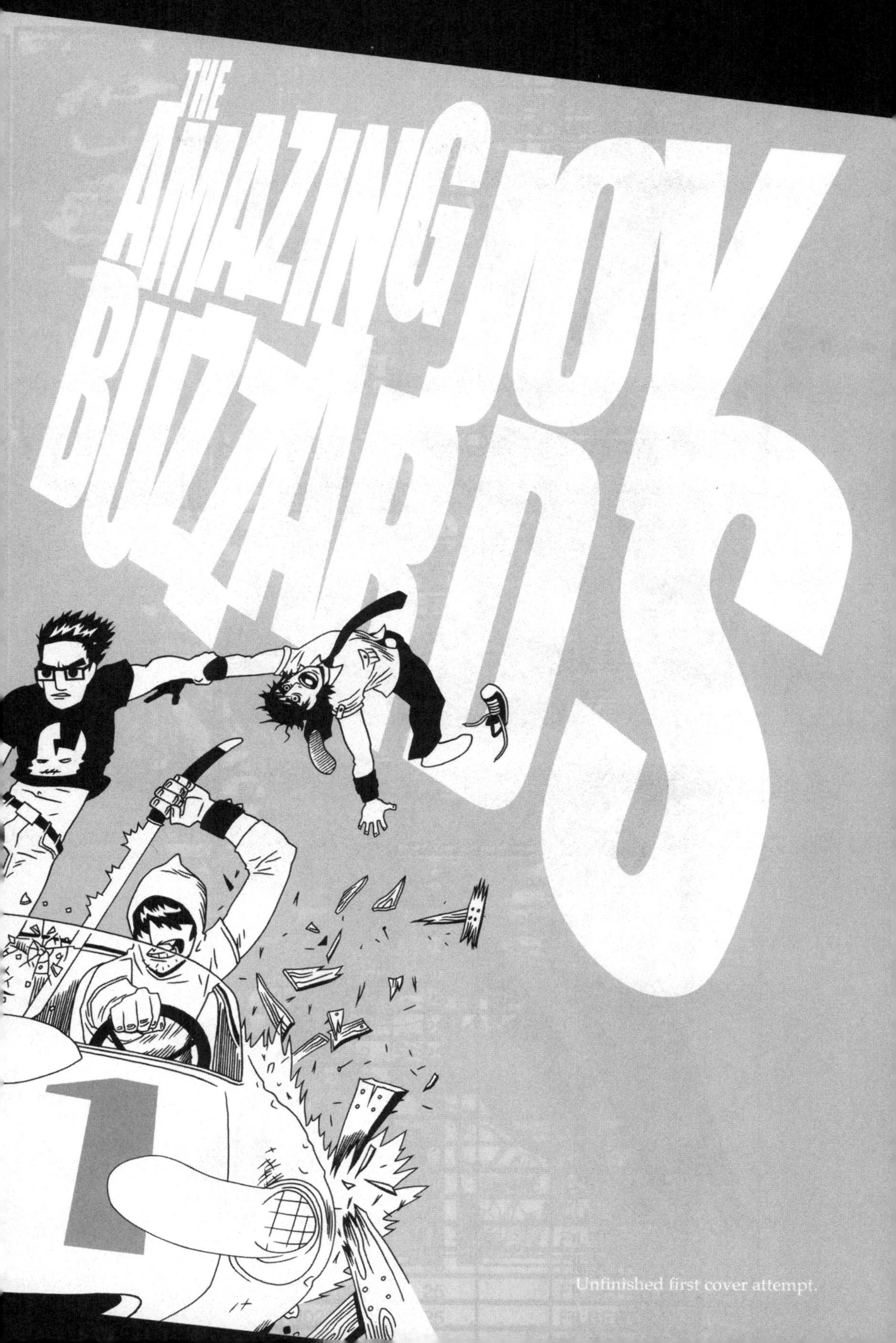
THE AMAZING JOY BUZZARDS
1

Unfinished first cover attempt.

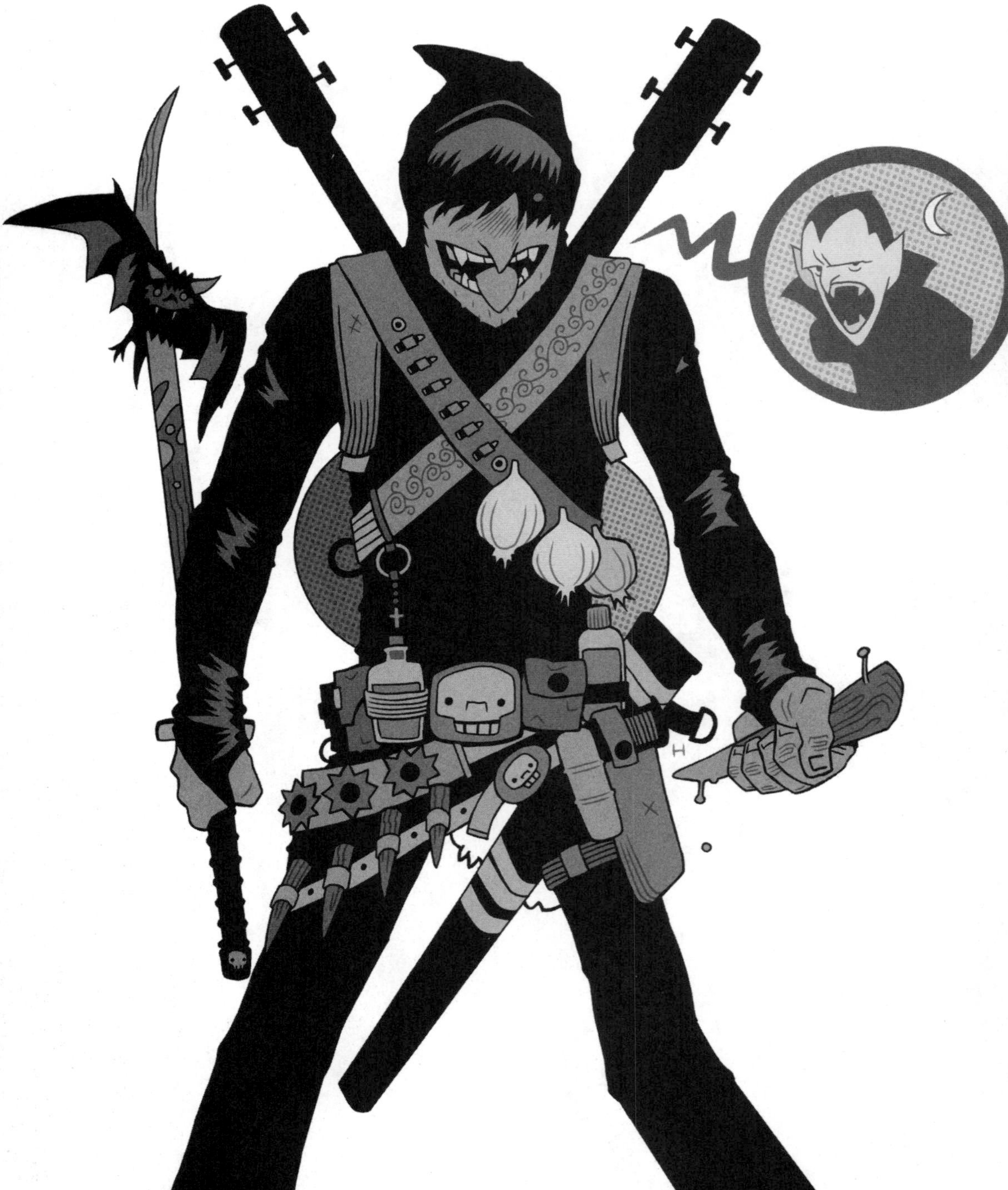

Cover to
THE FEARLESS
VAMPIRE HUNTERS.

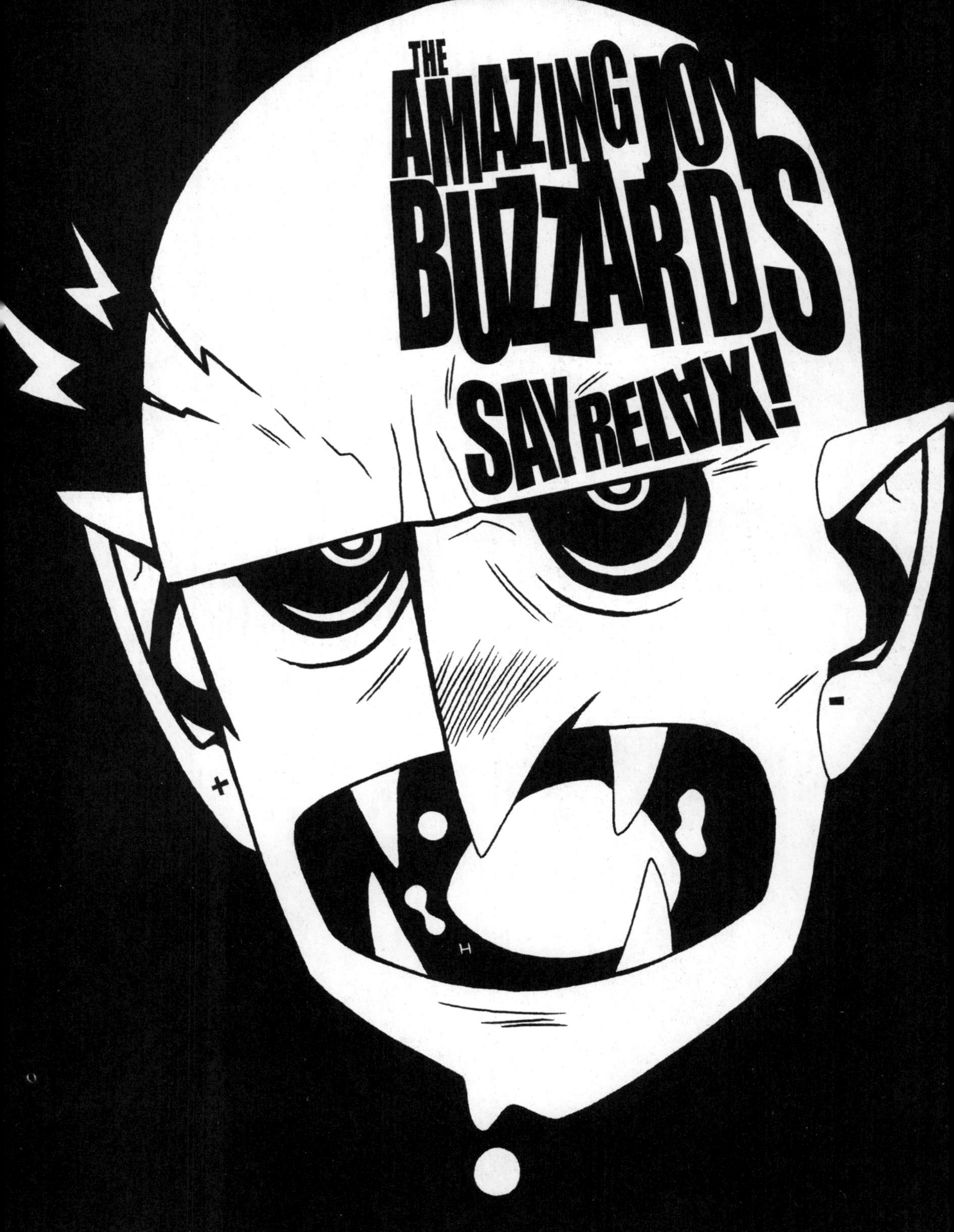
THE AMAZING JOY BUZZARDS
SAY RELAX!

AJB T-shirt design.

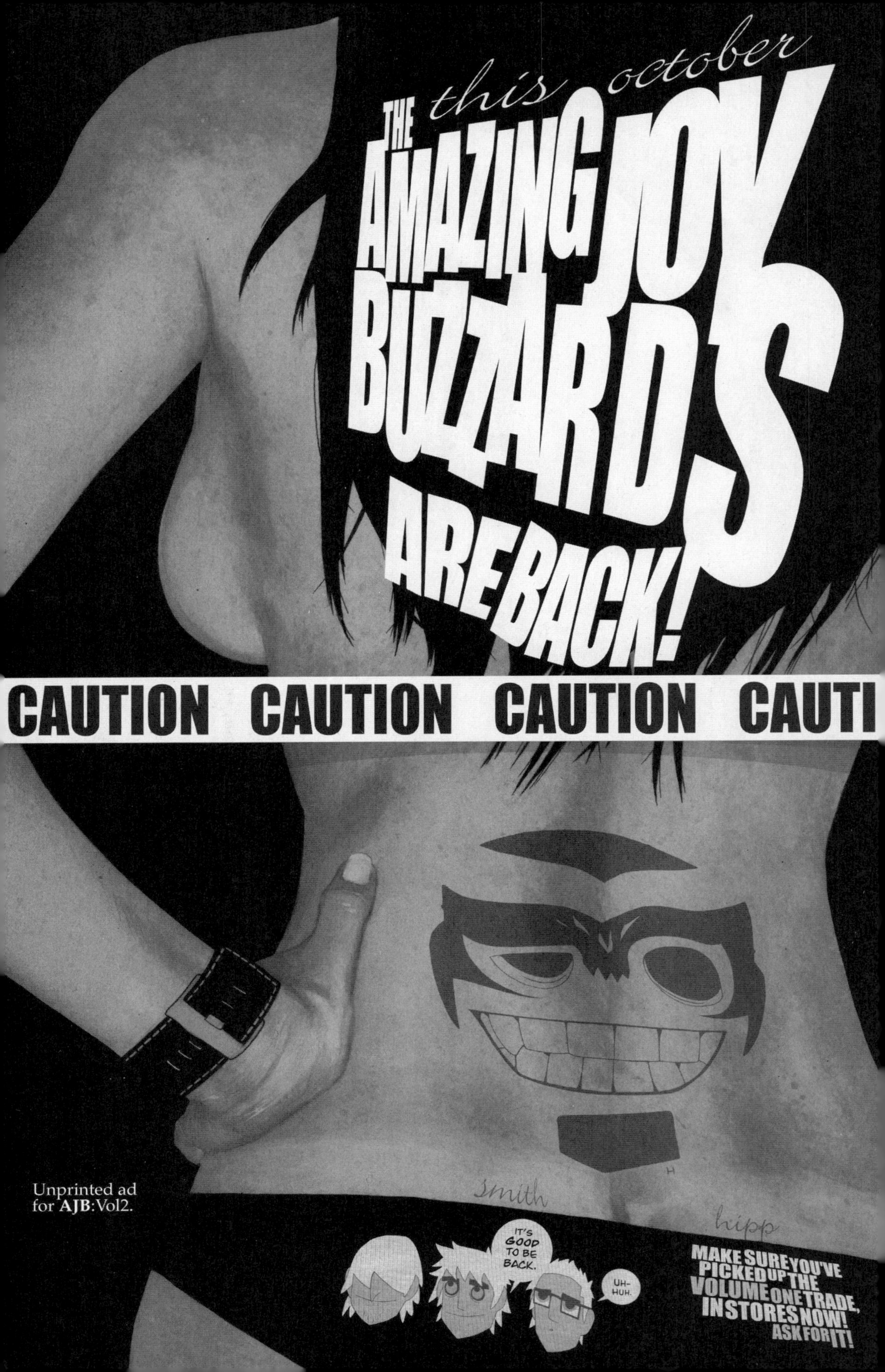
this october
THE AMAZING JOY BUZZARDS ARE BACK!
CAUTION CAUTION CAUTION CAUTI
H
smith
hipp
IT'S GOOD TO BE BACK.
UH-HUH.
MAKE SURE YOU'VE PICKED UP THE VOLUME ONE TRADE, IN STORES NOW! ASK FOR IT!

Unprinted ad for **AJB**:Vol2.

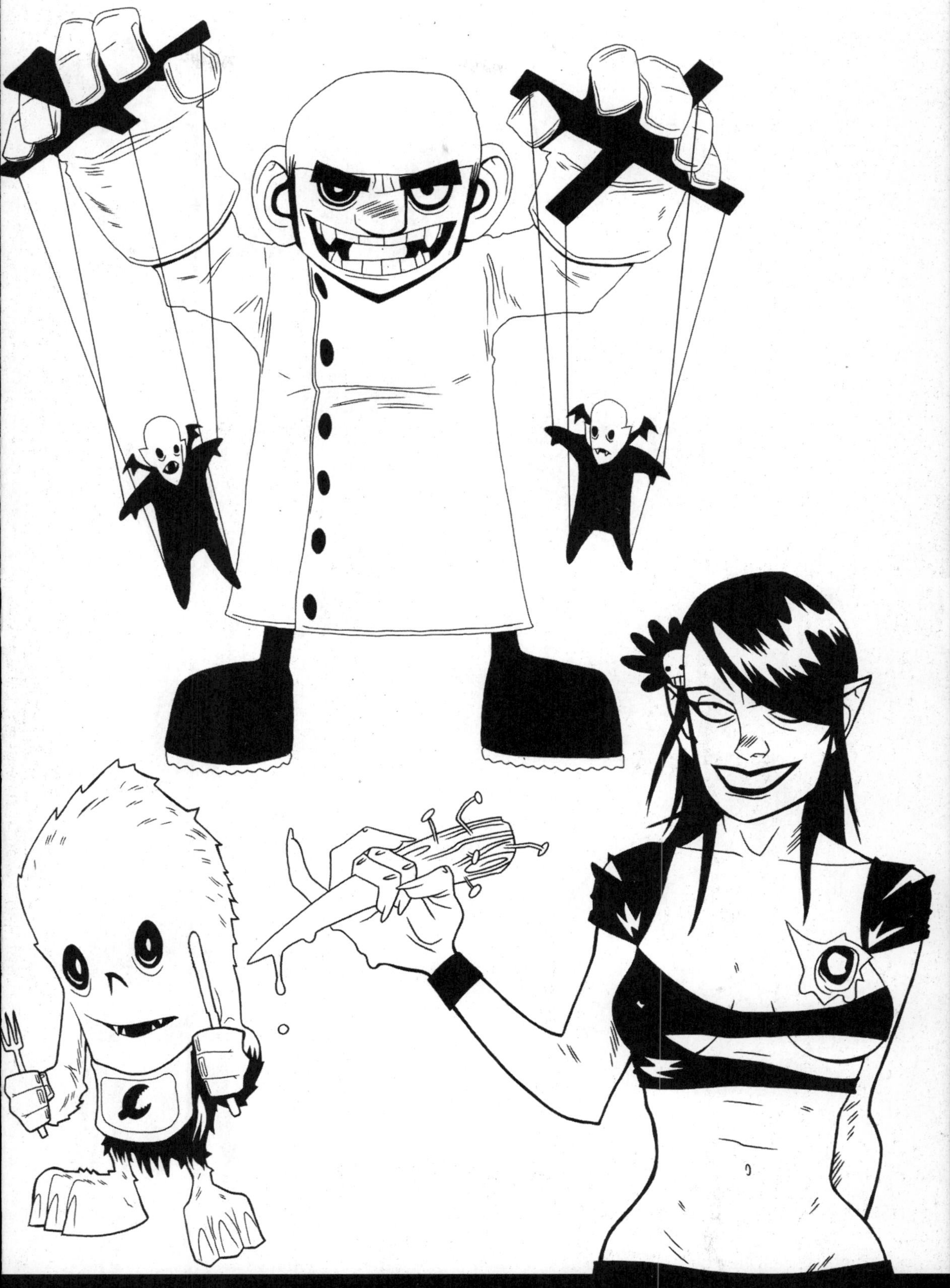

Hipp sketches. **The Puppeteer**, a **Wik-Wik** and some lady that's *not* **Ivep.**

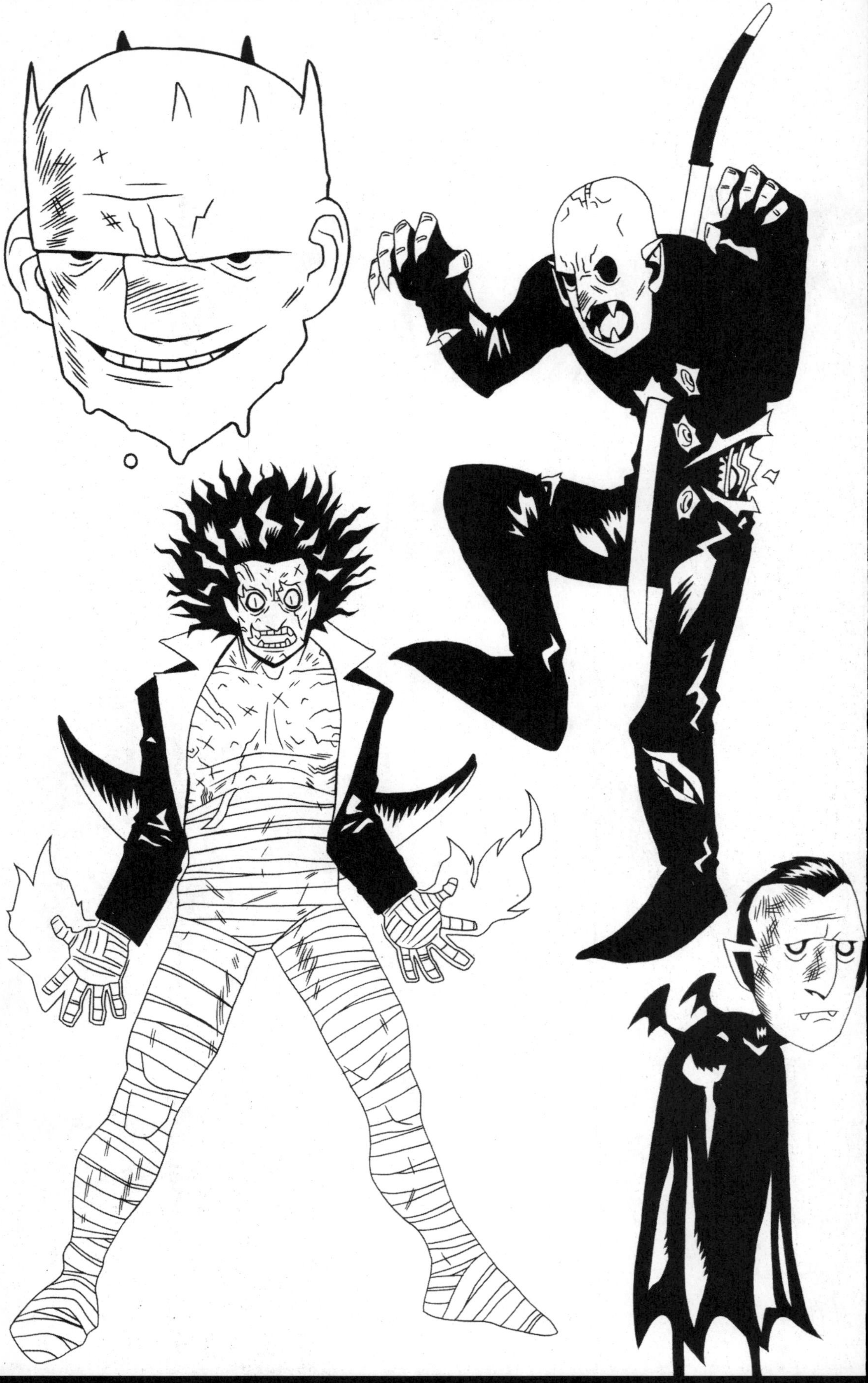

Galesh, your garden variety **Killer Vampire Robot**, the **Regurgitating Toilet Prince** and a Bat-fellow.

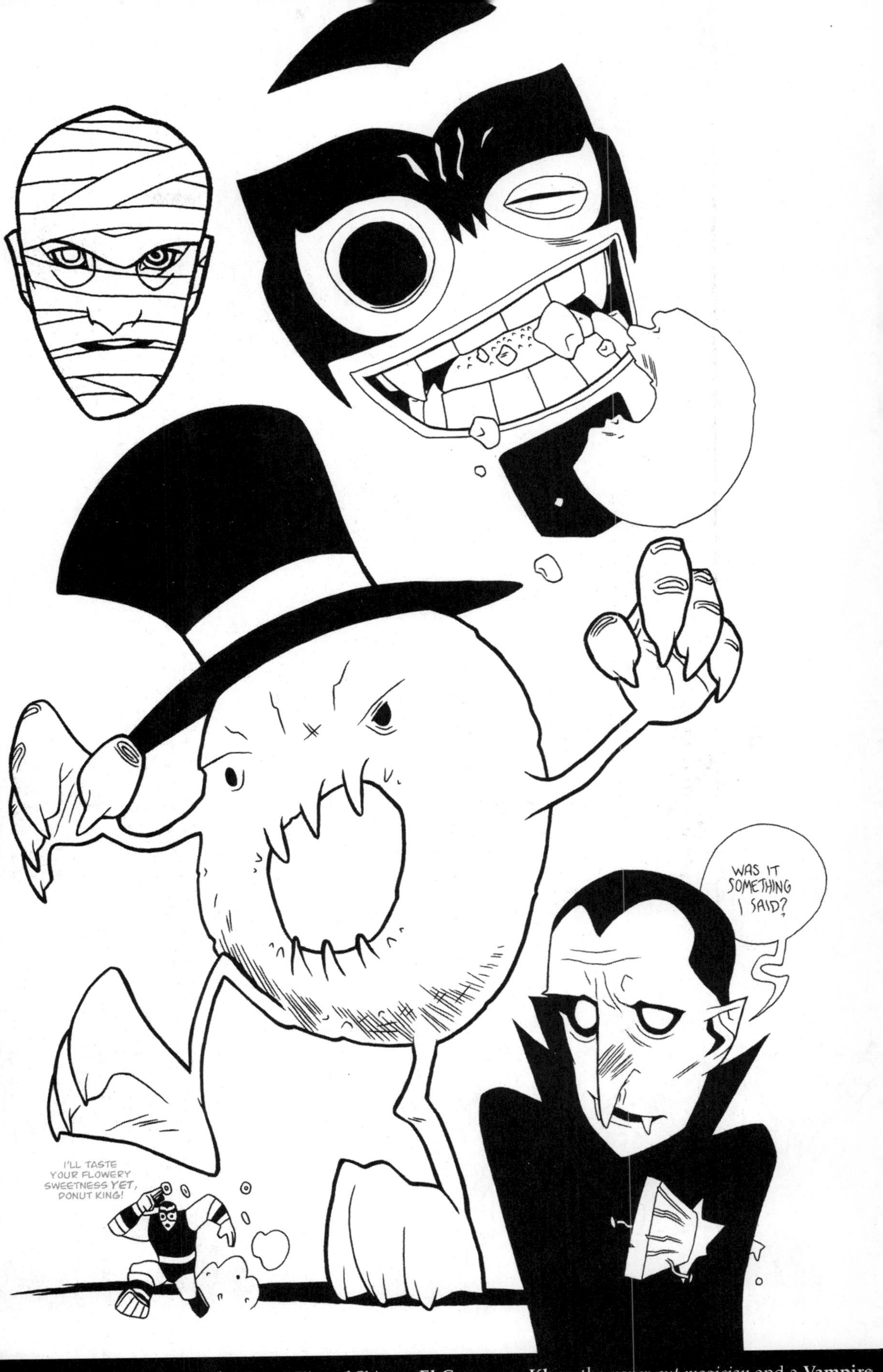
WAS IT SOMETHING I SAID?
I'LL TASTE YOUR FLOWERY SWEETNESS YET, DONUT KING!

Abe Doughman, the [illegible] **El Campeon**, **Klaus** the *paper-cut magician* and a **Vampire**

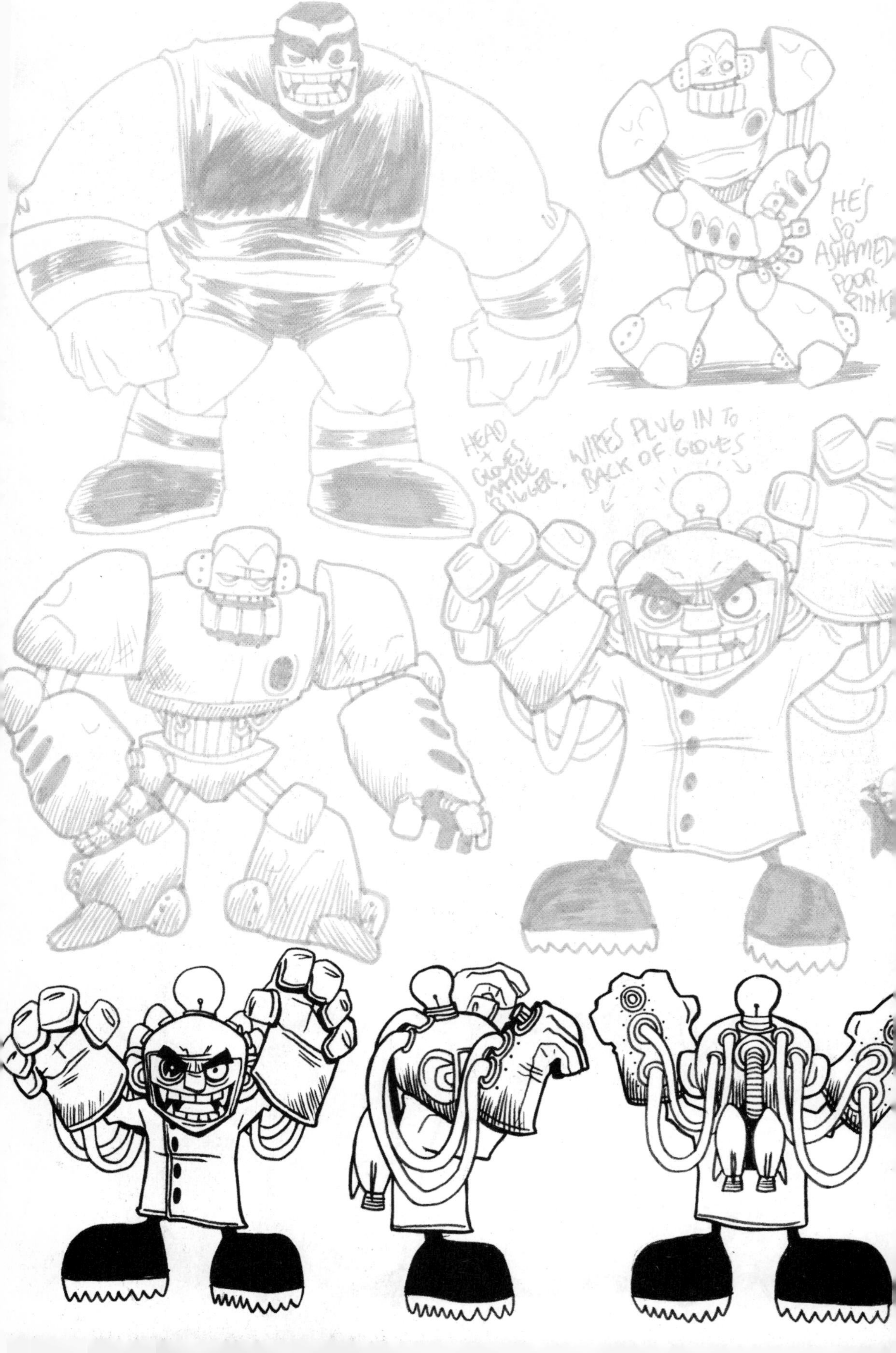
HE'S SO ASHAMED POOR RINK
HEAD + GLOVES MAYBE BIGGER.
WIRES PLUG IN TO BACK OF GLOVES